Aristotle and the Philosophy of Friendship

This is the first comprehensive study of the major philosophical works on friendship. The book gives central place to Aristotle's searching examination of friendship and self-love in the *Nicomachean Ethics*. Lorraine Smith Pangle argues that the difficulties in this discussion that have long puzzled scholars can be resolved once one understands the complexity of purpose of the *Ethics* as both a source of practical guidance for life and a profound, unsettling theoretical investigation into human nature.

The book also offers fresh interpretations of works on friendship by Plato, Cicero, Epicurus, Seneca, Montaigne, and Bacon. The author shows how each of these thinkers sheds light on central issues of moral philosophy: Is happiness to be found primarily in self-sufficiency, or in love and friendship with others? Is it possible to love another truly for the other's sake, or is all human affection rooted ultimately in self-interest?

Clearly and engagingly written, *Aristotle and the Philosophy of Friendship* provides a rich and thought-provoking examination into the nature of human selfishness, affection, and devotion.

Lorraine Smith Pangle teaches political philosophy at the University of Toronto. She is coauthor of *The Learning of Liberty: The Educational Ideas of the American Founders* and author of articles on Plato, Aristotle, the American Founders, and the philosophy of education.

D1564114

For Tom

Aristotle and the Philosophy of Friendship

LORRAINE SMITH PANGLE

University of Toronto

CAMBRIDGE
UNIVERSITY PRESS

CAMBRIDGE UNIVERSITY PRESS
Cambridge, New York, Melbourne, Madrid, Cape Town, Singapore, São Paulo

Cambridge University Press
The Edinburgh Building, Cambridge CB2 8RU, UK

Published in the United States of America by Cambridge University Press, New York

www.cambridge.org
Information on this title: www.cambridge.org/9780521817455

First published 2003
This digitally printed version 2008

A catalogue record for this publication is available from the British Library

Library of Congress Cataloguing in Publication data
Pangle, Lorraine Smith.
Aristotle and the philosophy of friendship / Lorraine Smith Pangle.
p.   cm.
Includes bibliographical references and index.
ISBN 0-521-81745-5 (hardback)
1. Aristotle. Nicomachean ethics. Book 8–9.   2. Friendship – History.   I. Title.
B430 .P25   2002
177'.62'092 – dc21
2002017407

ISBN 978-0-521-81745-5 hardback
ISBN 978-0-521-05267-2 paperback

Contents

Acknowledgments

This book began as a doctoral dissertation for the Committee on Social Thought at the University of Chicago. For their generous advice, support, and assistance, I thank Professors Leon Kass, Jonathan Lear, Robert Pippin, and Nathan Tarcov. For a lovely year of quiet study in Munich, during which much of the manuscript was completed, I thank Heinrich Meier and the Carl Friedrich von Siemens Stiftung. A slightly different version of Chapter 1 was published in *Ancient Philosophy* 21 (Fall 2001), and a condensed version of my analysis of *Nicomachean Ethics* Books 8 and 9 appeared as "Friendship and Self-Love in Aristotle's *Nichomachean Ethics*," in *Action and Contemplation: Studies in the Moral and Political Thought of Aristotle*, edited by Robert C. Bartlett and Susan D. Collins and published by SUNY Press, copyright 1999. I have benefited greatly from the thoughtful comments of friends and colleagues, including Robert Bartlett, David Bolotin, Timothy Burns, Susan Collins, Matthew Davis, David Leibowitz, Ronald Polansky, Linda Rabieh, and Devin Stauffer. For helpful readers' reports I would like to thank several anonymous referees and especially David Konstan and Michael Pakaluk. As for my indebtedness to Tom, as teacher, husband, critic, and friend, it is too long to recount and too great ever to repay. But justice requires some return, and friendship is generous in its reckoning, accepting what is possible, not what is due. And so I offer this book, in hopes that it may somehow discharge, for a little space of time, the simple interest on my debt.

Introduction

Friendship was a great subject of stories and of philosophical reflection in classical antiquity. Friendship was associated in the popular mind with courage, with republicanism, and with the spirited resistance to injustice and tyranny. The Greek poets celebrated the stories of such famous pairs of friends as Heracles and Iolaus, Theseus and Pirithous, and Orestes and Pylades. Festivals were held in honor of Harmodius and Aristogeiton, who were stubbornly credited in folklore with unseating the Athenian tyrant Peisistratus, despite the efforts of Herodotus, Thucydides, and Aristotle to prove that popular memory had gotten the story wrong.[1] Most famous of all friends were of course Achilles and Patroclus, but equally revealing is the story of Damon and Phintias, who were said to have lived under the Syracusan tyrant Dionysius. Phintias had been discovered plotting against the tyrant and was condemned to death. When he asked leave to return home first to set his affairs in order, Damon offered to stand as pledge for his safe return. Dionysius consented, though he marveled at Damon's simplicity. But when in fact Phintias returned on the appointed day to take his place on the scaffold and save his friend, so moved was the tyrant by the friends' mutual constancy that he commuted the sentence and begged to be accepted as a third in their friendship.[2] In the proud, unshakable loyalty and mutual trust of two men such as Damon and Phintias, we see classical virtue at its most impressive but also its most appealing, for it is the special charm and fascination of a great friendship that it seems at once so noble and so delightfully desirable.

The phenomenon of friendship, with its richness and complexity, its ability to support but also at times to undercut virtue, and the promise it holds out of bringing together in one happy union so much of what is highest and so much of what is sweetest in life, formed a fruitful topic of philosophic inquiry for the ancients. Plato and Cicero both wrote dialogues about friendship, and a number of others, including Plutarch and Theophrastus, wrote treatises on it, most of which have now been lost.[3] Epicurus devoted much

1

of his life to cultivating friendship and counted it as one of life's chief goods; he and Seneca both expounded their teachings on friendship in epistles to friends. But by far the fullest and most probing classical study of friendship is to be found in Aristotle's *Nicomachean Ethics,* which devotes more space to it than to any of the moral virtues and which presents friendship as a bridge between the moral virtues and the highest life of philosophy. The study of friendship in the classical authors is in many ways a study of human love altogether, and the Greek word φιλία can cover all bonds of affection, from the closest erotic and familial ties to political loyalties, humanitarian sympathies, business partnerships, and even love for inanimate things. But φιλία means first and foremost friendship, and it is the contention of Aristotle and all of the classical authors who follow him that precisely in the friendships of mature and virtuous individuals do we see human love not only at its most revealing but also at its richest and highest.[4]

With the coming of the Christian world, however, friendship fell into eclipse. One theologian, the twelfth-century Aelred of Rievaulx, did write a dialogue on friendship somewhat in the spirit of Cicero's; and Augustine, Thomas Aquinas, and others acknowledged a certain place for friendship as a special form of love in the Christian life. Yet Christianity's call to devote one's heart as completely as possible to God, and to regard all men as brothers, made the existence of private, exclusive, and passionate attachments to individual human beings seem inherently questionable.[5] Moreover, Christianity's emphasis on humility, chastity, and a childlike trust in God gave grounds for regarding with particular suspicion the fierce, proudly republican, and sometimes homosexual attachments that characterized the celebrated friendships of antiquity. It would be wrong to suggest, however, that the coming of Christianity resulted in a widespread weakening of particular human bonds and the replacing of them with the broadly diffused gentle glow of charity. Rather, the chief effect of Christianity upon personal relations was to elevate one particular human bond, that of family, which had received special sanction in the Scriptures. Along with the elevation of the family came the relative elevation of women, who enjoyed in Christian aristocratic Europe more liberty, education, and influence than they had had in Greece and Rome, and whose central concerns were not politics or friendship but love and family.

It is thus not surprising that with the Renaissance there was a certain revival of philosophic interest in friendship. In the sixteenth and early seventeenth centuries, Michel de Montaigne and Francis Bacon both wrote essays in a rather classical vein in praise of friendship, both arguing that not erotic or familial love (or, by silent implication, Christian charity) but, rather, friendship between mature, equal, and good men is the human bond par excellence. Montaigne portrays friendship as not merely the finest form of love but the finest thing in life altogether, answering the deepest longings of the soul and providing the noblest use of human capacities. Both writers maintain that, in contrast to friendship, every other human bond is more limited and more constrained, either by fortune or by low necessity, and hence is less reflective of and supportive of what is best in us.

In the four centuries since Bacon and Montaigne wrote, however, friendship has virtually disappeared as a theme of philosophical discourse. Kant treats it briefly as a matter of minor philosophic interest; Nietzsche mentions it as a potentially valuable but potentially enervating force, and likens the good friend to a good enemy; Emerson offers a hazily glowing tribute to friendship that scarcely rises to the level of philosophy; and Kierkegaard, with bold intransigence, rejects friendship as unchristian; but nowhere do we find another thinker who takes friendship as seriously or explores it as searchingly as do those of the classical tradition.[6] This devaluation of friendship is the result of a decisive new turn in philosophy that occurred in the years immediately after the publications of Montaigne's and Bacon's essays, the first editions of which appeared in 1580 and 1597, respectively. For it was early in the next century that Thomas Hobbes began to develop his powerful reinterpretation of human nature as directed neither to friendship nor to virtue, his argument that man is by nature solitary, and his analysis of our true condition as one of serious, always potentially deadly competition with other human beings for all that we most need and want.

Ever since the time of Hobbes, modern moral philosophy, even when it has not followed his teaching about the state of nature, has conceived of men's most important claims upon one another to lie outside the realm of friendship. Hobbes and Locke, understanding each individual's relations to his fellows to be rooted in self-interest, taught that these relations could be regulated by sensible laws and appeals to rational self-interest. Rousseau, fearing that the modern liberal project was resulting in the impoverishment and isolation of the individual soul, sought to counterbalance liberalism's spirit of cold calculation with a new emphasis on erotic love, now broadened to comprise a freely chosen friendship of two kindred spirits and pointed firmly toward the family as its natural fulfillment. Taking their lifeblood from this root, the great modern stories have almost invariably been love stories. The brittleness of the modern family may give us cause to suspect that Rousseau rested his own project too heavily on a slender and intractably wild reed in the human spirit. But the family's fragility has done little to discourage the ubiquitous hope of finding in one lifelong lover the chief companion of one's heart and mind.

When we move beyond the intimate ties of love and family, the most important claims upon us seem not to be those of friendship so much as broader and more abstract or universal claims, shaped, on the one hand, by a fundamentally Lockean understanding of human rights, and, on the other, by the belief in a duty to act unselfishly for the good of others that was given its clearest and most influential articulation by Kant. For Kant, there is of course nothing inherently wrong with acting out of affection for a friend, just as there is nothing wrong as such with acting out of self-interest, although both motives can lead us to be partial and unfair. But the only moral reason for an action is that it accords with a universalizable principle. Philosophy since Kant has largely followed him in understanding truly moral, praiseworthy human relations to be based on *altruism,* a wholly selfless benevolence toward others, guided either by absolute moral law or by a utilitarian pursuit of the greatest good for the greatest number. In comparison to the claims of friendship, the claims of universal human rights and of altruism directed to the good of humanity seem higher, more selfless, more rational, and more fair.

Yet increasingly, the ideas of rights and of altruism have both come under serious questioning. Do rights really exist? Is altruism really possible? If it is possible, how are our altruistic motives related to our self-interested motives? Is it possible to subordinate self-interest to altruism, such that all one's activities and associations are chosen only because they ultimately accrue to the good of humanity? Or if this is not possible – if we normally act with a view to our own good but sometimes choose actions that have nothing to do with our own good or even oppose it – is there any higher, unifying principle or faculty of the soul that decides between these contrary principles of action, judging them by a common standard? Or do we simply lurch inexplicably between unrelated, incommensurable principles of action? If, on the other hand, the idea of altruism is a chimerical one, are we indeed at root the solitary and selfish beings that Hobbes claimed we are? Or are there altogether different ways of understanding individuals' evident ability to transcend their narrowly selfish concerns? Perhaps this ability can be better understood in terms not of universal laws but of virtues that grow out of and give natural perfection to passions of the soul, and in terms not of egoism and altruism but of friendship, again rooted in the natural passion of human affection and so bridging the concern with self and the concern with others. It is considerations such as these that seem to have prompted a remarkable contemporary resurgence of philosophic interest in Aristotle's moral philosophy, and in particular, his treatment of friendship.

When we approach the classical studies of friendship with an eye to the modern reasons for rejecting it as a theme of central philosophic importance, we see that the classics and especially Aristotle address the concerns at the root of the modern demotion of friendship in the most direct and forthright way. Aristotle does not assume the natural sociability of man but searchingly questions it. In friendship, he and Plato both suggest, we can best see the true character and extent of our desire to live with others when that desire is shorn of all considerations of necessity and utility. Likewise, Aristotle assumes neither the possibility nor the impossibility of what we would call altruism, but instead offers a sustained and sympathetic exploration of what is really at work in the human heart when an individual seems to disregard his own good to pursue the good of others. Aristotle does not assume that the concern for a friend is necessarily tainted by partiality; he argues that friendship can be rooted in a true assessment of the friend's worth and, as such, can give the noblest expression to our sociability.

These three sets of issues, concerning the naturalness of friendship, the possibility of selflessness in friendship, and the relationship of friendship to justice, constitute indeed the central themes of all the major philosophical studies of friendship, and hence will form the main topics of inquiry for this book. What are the roots of friendship in human nature? How central to human happiness is loving and being loved? To what extent is the desire for affection and friendship reducible to other causes, to our defects and vulnerabilities and needs for things in themselves altogether extraneous to friendship, and to what extent is friendship itself a necessary or central component of the happiness of the healthiest human beings? How truly can and do human beings care for others for their own sakes and promote the good of others as an end in itself? Do they do this at all? Do they do it when the good of the other conflicts with their own deepest good? Or is every apparent selfless sacrifice in fact, in some complicated or disguised way, a pursuit of a greater good for oneself? To what extent can friendship answer the longing for a just community with others that political life invariably fails to answer perfectly? And what light does an examination of the problems of justice within friendship shed on the problem of justice as a whole?

This book is, then, an attempt to deepen our understanding of and engagement with the philosophical study of friendship, giving central place to Aristotle's treatment of the subject in Books 8 and 9 of his *Nicomachean Ethics,* a discussion which, for comprehensiveness, depth, and subtlety, has never been rivaled. In order to shed further light on the issues Aristotle explores and to see more clearly what is at stake in the positions he takes, I have interwoven the analysis of the *Ethics* with shorter expositions of the writings of Plato, Epicurus, Cicero, Seneca, Montaigne, and Bacon, as each of these authors develops in a fuller and more revealing way some aspect of Aristotle's thought, or carries some idea of his to a further extreme, thereby providing, in fact, a relevant and helpful contrast to Aristotle's position. These thinkers constitute a single tradition in the sense that they are engaged in a single conversation about the same problems in friendship and human nature. They all delve into these problems with utmost serious-ness and with evident confidence that through such a conversation in books across the centuries, we can make important discoveries about human nature and our own hearts in such a way as to live happier lives.

The book seeks to engage the arguments of each thinker on their own terms in just this spirit. It proceeds on the working hypothesis that the project of philosophy as these authors undertook it is indeed possible – that behind the different conventions and experiences and habits of mind of fourth-century Athenians, Renaissance Frenchmen, and modern men and women are permanent human problems that we can make progress in answering.

This admittedly controversial hypothesis is susceptible of only one test: We must read each work on its own terms, as carefully as possible and with as open a mind as possible, and see what light it sheds on life.

The Place of Friendship in the *Nicomachean Ethics*

Let us begin, then, by placing Aristotle's major discussion of friendship in the context that he himself chose to give it. Why does he include this study in a work on ethics, rather than letting it stand alone, and why does it come where it does in the *Nicomachean Ethics*? In raising the subject at the outset of Book 8, Aristotle says that friendship is either a virtue or involves virtue. For various reasons that will soon become clear, however, true friendship, in contrast to friendliness or social grace, turns out not to be a virtue at all; and the fact that it in some way involves virtue does not distinguish it from such subjects as rhetoric and politics, to which Aristotle devotes separate works. In some way, friendship seems to have an especially close connection with moral virtue, standing as a crucial link in a chain that the treatment of the separate virtues has not yet completed.

Now a central project of Aristotle's ethical writings, a project whose audacity we lose sight of only because it has become so familiar, is to demonstrate the unity of virtue and happiness, or as Aristotle says in the opening lines of the *Eudemian Ethics*, to refute the belief – which at some level or to some degree or at some moments *every* human being must hold – that what is really good for us is not what is most pleasant, and that what is right or noble is often neither good nor pleasant. Aristotle argues, to the contrary, that the activity of virtue is the very substance of human happiness. By the time the serious reader of the *Nicomachean Ethics* reaches the opening of Book 8, he or she will likely be impressed with the extent to which Aristotle has succeeded in making this case, with his rich portrayals of the virtues as perfections of the natural capacities of the soul. Yet the reader may well also be struck and troubled by certain problems that have emerged in the moral person's outlook and self-understanding. Virtuous action is presented as supremely choiceworthy in itself, yet at some level, the virtuous man expects to be honored or rewarded as a compensation or at least recognition for the noble sacrifice he has made of his own good. Virtue and happiness seem to fit roughly but not perfectly together.

The problematic fit between virtue and happiness appears most acutely at the two major peaks of moral virtue, greatness of soul and justice. The great-souled man has all the virtues in the highest degree, and he strives to be and to appear independent and complete in himself. Yet his life is less a flurry of joyful activity than a patient search for actions that are worthy of his dignity and that he is unlikely to find unless fortune favors him with rare opportunities; less a self-sufficient whole than a search for honors that he deserves and desires but that can only be provided by inferiors who are unworthy to judge him. Justice, also, "is more wonderful than the evening star and the morning star, and as the proverb says, 'in justice all virtue is gathered into one,'" yet justice is also thought with good reason to be "the good of another."[7] Can a life spent pursuing justice answer our longings for happiness, or is justice mainly good because it secures the peace and order that lay the groundwork for happy lives? The discussion of moral strength, moral weakness, and pleasure in Book 7 further underscores the question of whether the demands of duty are not, all too often, in conflict with the things that promise happiness. To the extent that they are, to the extent that our lower desires are at odds with what reason discovers to be noblest or most divine, then virtue will turn out to be less a harmonious wholeness than a stern subjection of inclination to judgment, less a fine-tuning of the strings to reach the perfect mean than a forcible straightening of warped timber.

In light of these problems, friendship now comes to sight as a third and perhaps highest summit of the moral life, on which virtue and happiness may finally be united. If the life of a great-souled man lacks clear content, if putting himself in the service of his inferiors seems slavish, and if actions aimed at winning honor from them seem undignified, the pursuit of serious friendship is a worthy outlet for his energies and talents (1124b24–25a1). Friendship likewise completes and goes beyond justice, or even renders justice unnecessary (1155a26–27). The goodness shown in noble friendship seems higher than justice, not only because its object is so worthy but because it is entirely dependent on one's own character and choice and is not defined and compelled by law (*Eudemian Ethics* 1235a3–4).[8] Paradoxically, acts of friendship seem both more truly generous and more conducive to one's own happiness than acts done strictly because they are moral. Acting for the sake of what is noble means having primary regard not for the beneficiary's good but for one's own virtue or the good of one's soul, whereas acting for a friend seems to be self-forgetting. And yet spontaneous acts of friendship tend to be more pleasant than impersonal acts of virtue for the doer as well as for the recipient. Aristotle's discussion of friendship, surrounded as it is by two discussions of pleasure, encourages the hope that in the realm of friendship, one may find all the nobility of virtuous action at its best without the ultimate sacrifice of happiness, and thus both a proof of his thesis on the unity of virtue and happiness and at least a partial answer to the question of what the substantive concerns and activities of the best life should be.

Almost immediately after concluding his discussion of friendship, how-ever, Aristotle moves into a discussion of the philosophic life. Here, in Book 10, he argues that the best life of all consists not in the active exercise of moral virtue but in the austere and almost solitary life of contempla-tion. Is this a conclusion for which we are prepared? In what way does it grow out of or even relate to Aristotle's treatment of friendship in Books 8 and 9?[9] This problem is but one aspect of the vexed question of the unity of the *Nicomachean Ethics* – the question whether the text as we have it really represents a single, coherent, carefully written and structured account of human virtue or something rather less.[10] J. L. Ackrill offers a penetrating analysis of the disunity that seems to lurk at the heart of the *Nicomachean Ethics*.[11] The central difficulty, as he sees it, is that Aristotle never really explains how the accounts of moral virtue in Books 2 to 5 and that of the philosophic life in Book 10 fit together into a single account of the happy life. Does the wise man have one overarching reason for all that he does? Is moral virtue ultimately in the service of contemplation? But moral action, like contemplation, comes to sight as an end in itself, and it loses its essential character if transformed into mere means to some further end.[12] On the other hand, Ackrill argues, if morality is not to be ultimately justified and made coherent by its subordination to philosophy, Aristotle does not provide any other, deeper explanation for the principles upon which the moral virtues rest, other than the fact that they are the sorts of things which well-bred people in fact approve. Ackrill thus argues that the teaching of the *Ethics* is in principle incapable of clear articulation, or "broken backed."[13]

The Character of the *Nicomachean Ethics*

The problem of disunity in the presentation of life's ends leads us to confront a further, equally vexed question in Aristotelian scholarship: Just what sort of a work is the *Nicomachean Ethics,* and for what purpose was it written? Is it merely a collection of course notes on more or less related subjects? This seems most doubtful. As Franz Susemihl and Richard Bodéüs persuasively argue, the assumption that the book consists merely of notes taken by students, or a revision of such notes made by a follower such as Aristotle's son Nicomachus, is unsustainable in light of the very great subtlety and carefulness of the writing that a close study reveals.[14] Is it an assembly of independent investigations into separate topics, not intended to be altogether systematic or to form part of a larger system of moral and political teachings? This view now enjoys some currency in Aristotelian scholarship,[15] but it fails to account for Aristotle's statements at the opening and closing of the *Nicomachean Ethics* about the architectonic nature of his project and its connection to the *Politics,* and likewise his statements at the opening and closing of his discussion of friendship in 8.1 and 9.12, marking it as an ordered part of a larger investigation, the subject of which he has identified as human happiness altogether. Or even if the order of topics is carefully arranged, may the *Nicomachean Ethics* be merely a handbook intended for a general audience of nonspecialists, on a matter about which precision is not possible? This latter view is certainly supported by Aristotle's own disclaimers in Book 1 regarding the limited precision that is possible in ethics, and also by Plutarch's comments on Aristotelian education in his *Life of Alexander,* as well as by the ancient collector of philosophical and philological trivia, Aulus Gellius.[16]

According to Gellius, Aristotle's works fell into two classes, the "exoteric" or public, and the "acroatic," which means "for hearing only." The exoteric teachings provided a training in rhetoric, logic, politics, and ethics, and they formed the subjects for Aristotle's "open admissions" evening lectures, attended by mature gentlemen and statesmen among others; the acroatic works dealt with the study of nature and dialectics, and they formed the subjects for Aristotle's restricted morning lectures. But although the *Nicomachean Ethics* is clearly addressed to a broader audience than are his logical and metaphysical writings, it would be incorrect to identify this work as merely popular, for Aristotle himself refers in it to his exoteric or popular writings as if they are other works with a different character, and scholars are now inclined to identify these works as Aristotle's lost literary works, especially his dialogues.[17]

On the other hand, if the *Nicomachean Ethics* is not among the works that Aristotle wrote in a popular, imprecise manner for a general audience, is it possible that it is intentionally obscure? This possibility, too, is suggested by Plutarch and Gellius in the discussions already cited. Plutarch, observing that Alexander not only had been a student of the popular lectures but also had been admitted to the acroatic teachings, says that Alexander,

when he had already crossed into Asia, and learned that certain discourses on these matters had been published in books by Aristotle, wrote him a letter in which he spoke up on behalf of philosophy. And this is a copy of it: "Alexander to Aristotle, prosperity. You have not acted rightly in publishing the acroatic speeches. For in what shall we surpass others, if the discourses in which we have been educated are to become common to all? But I would rather excel in my acquaintance with the best things than in power. Farewell." Aristotle, to soothe his love of honor, said in defense that those discourses were "both published and not published."[18]

Gellius reproduces the same letter by Alexander and also gives Aristotle's purported answer in full, for which he says his source is the philosopher Andronicus: "Aristotle to King Alexander, prosperity. You have written me about the acroatic discourses, thinking that they should be guarded in secrecy. Know, then, that they have been both published and not published. For they are intelligible only to those who have heard us" (20.5.12).

But such an idea of esotericism as is evidently implied in this letter is useless as an interpretive tool, for any interpretive aids that Aristotle may have given orally to his students are surely lost to us. Indeed, if his serious teachings are unintelligible without keys that he never committed to writing, then our plight as modern readers is grave indeed. But we have reason to hope that this letter, if not an outright forgery, is at least less than perfectly frank, and that as Plutarch hints, it is shaped by the wish to reassure Alexander that the rare knowledge upon which he prides himself has not become common currency. Would it not be very strange that a philosopher who found truths that he considered worth publishing should intentionally make them inaccessible and should be content for his own hard-won insights to die with his immediate circle? Is it not more likely that a wise man would have addressed himself to thoughtful readers in every time and place by writing books that, however difficult, are fully comprehensible on their own terms to all who have listened carefully and "heard" what is in the text?[19]

However, if the passages from Plutarch and Gellius fail to offer any useful explanation for Aristotle's obscurity, they do raise a crucial question: Who, precisely, was the intended audience of the *Nicomachean Ethics*? Aristotle himself takes up this question in Book 1, quoting verses from Hesiod:

> That man is best of all who thinks everything out himself....
> Good also is he who follows one who speaks well.
> But he who neither thinks for himself nor, listening to another,
> Stores it up in his heart, that man is utterly useless.
> (1095b10–13, quoting *Works and Days* 293, 295–7)

Presumably, then, it is the second group for whom Aristotle writes – neither the wise who need no instruction nor the obtuse who are deaf to reason and respond only to force, but an intermediate group who are capable of listening to and profiting from the words of the philosopher. Other comments about the intended effect of his book support the same conclusion: Ethics is a subordinate part of the science of politics, and the purpose of this study is not sterile knowledge but good action or praxis (1094a18–b11, 1103b26–30). Finally, we have Aristotle's direct account of what is needed in a good listener of his ethical discourse: He must be well brought up, already habituated in moral virtue, and sufficiently mature to have experience of the world and command over his own emotions (1094b27–95a13, 95b4–6).

Considerations such as these, together with the often neglected fact that the *Nicomachean Ethics* and the *Politics* are clearly intended to form two parts of a single whole, have led Richard Bodéüs to argue that the intended audience of the *Nicomachean Ethics* is current or future legislators.[20] As he sees it, the book's purpose is neither to offer a theoretical account of human psychology for the philosopher nor to provide a moral education to those who are not virtuous, but to assist those who are virtuous and who are entrusted with the moral education of others to see more clearly the end to which their actions should be directed and the principles that should guide them. They must, for example, understand the importance of early habituation, the ways in which education and laws must be adapted to fit the regime, and the dependence of moral virtue, even in most mature individuals, upon coercive legal sanctions.[21]

I believe that Bodéüs makes a major contribution in correctly identifying the primary audience of the *Nicomachean Ethics* and in describing much of what Aristotle hopes to accomplish in it. However, it seems to me that

Aristotle's project is both more complex and more ambitious than Bodéüs allows. In the first place, if this treatise were intended only for legislators, why would Aristotle have provided no parallel study of ethics and human nature for the student of philosophy? Bodéüs argues that the *Eudemian Ethics* is such a book, but it is very similar both in its starting points and in its way of proceeding, and as he himself notes, it does not derive ethical principles from more general principles of nature.[22] I am inclined, rather, to the view that the *Eudemian Ethics* is simply an earlier version of the same work; the differences between the two treatments of friendship in particular suggest that the *Nicomachean* represents a deeper and fuller rethinking of the same problems.[23] And what are we to make of the fact that the *Nicomachean Ethics* evidently developed as part of the curriculum for Aristotle's school? Although we do not know the extent to which Aristotle revised his course lectures in writing the book, the book does seem clearly to have grown out of some such course, whose audience would have included not merely the mature, well-bred citizens who Aristotle says are the right kind of listener for ethical discourses, but also the immature students of philosophy who attended both Aristotle's more public and his more restricted, advanced courses. Did Aristotle expect these theoretical-minded students to get no benefit from the course on ethics, or is there some particular benefit that they may have derived precisely from observing Aristotle addressing these most respectable citizens?

In this context, we should also consider Aristotle's remark at 1103b27–28 that "we are not investigating in order to know what virtue is, but in order that we may become good." Since Aristotle has said that the right kind of listener should already be habituated in virtue, and that those who lack such habituation cannot become virtuous through mere study (1103a14–18, 1105b9–18), this remark is puzzling; we would have expected him to say that we investigate ethics in order to become better legislators or teachers of virtue. But perhaps there is some sense in which even the mature, morally serious citizens whom Aristotle identifies as his primary audience do *not* fully understand what they are doing, and hence are not completely virtuous, or some way in which watching Aristotle's examination of their moral presuppositions can bring gifted youth to a virtue more complete than that of their less reflective elders.

In the second place, Bodéüs does not seem to give sufficient attention to the ways in which Aristotle not only clarifies the understanding of virtue current in fourth-century Greek society but also enters into critical, even transformative dialogue with it.[24] As Aristide Tessitore remarks, "Aristotle's appeal to the best sensibilities of morally serious persons is not merely a reflection or codification of the current social practice of notables."[25] Tessitore mentions Aristotle's criticism of the contentiousness and arrogance often displayed by men of high birth; also instructive is Aristotle's catalogue of the virtues and vices at 1107a28–1108b10, where he shows the extent of his innovation by repeatedly speaking of "nameless" virtues and vices, and by arguing against the common perception that each virtue is opposed to only one vice. Perhaps most important of all are Aristotle's omissions: his silent demotion of piety from the canon of the virtues and his explicit denial that modesty or shame, closely related to pious reverence, is a virtue in grown men (1128b10–25). Aristotle's presentation of all of the moral virtues as being substantially if not perfectly accessible to those in a private station; his portrayal of the man of greatness of soul as reluctant to wade into the political fray, except in a great cause; and his extensive discussions of friendship in the *Nicomachean Ethics* and of the life of cultivated leisure in the *Politics* all help to shape a moral ethos that is more rational, more independent, less turbulently political, and less dependent on the presence of a republican regime than was the ethos of the leading citizens in classical Greece.

In thus helping to foster a cultivated middle ground between the life of the simply political man and that of the philosopher, Aristotle performed a signal public service, both for his own countrymen and for citizens of the Roman Empire and of the Christian monarchies that succeeded it. This constructive engagement with conventional morality proves that the philosopher can indeed be the best of citizens. It allowed Aristotle to win for philosophy the trust and respect of his readers, and a certain toleration, at least, for his provocative claim in *Nicomachean Ethics* 10 that the philosophic life is the best and highest life for a human being.[26]

The great question is this. If, as Bodéüs observes in the pregnant final sentence of his book, the moral, civic life that hitherto seemed entirely an end in itself is really best understood as pointing beyond itself to philosophy, what does that imply about the philosopher's own relationship to the moral ethos he has encouraged and helped to shape? Does Aristotle, as Bodéüs suggests, simply have a clearer, more complete, more fully integrated version of the same outlook, and is his own most serious work that of educating legislators and teachers?[27] Or does he have a different perspective altogether? If it is the former, if there is a straight and direct ascent from the perspective of the morally serious citizen to that of the philosopher, it seems strange that Aristotle would not show more clearly how the two lives are related, and how the virtues and ends of the one develop and mature into the virtues and ends of the other. On the other hand, if the philosopher has a different understanding of human nature and human happiness, we might expect that, alongside his practical guides to ethics and politics, Aristotle would have written a separate, more rigorous study of human nature, beginning not from common opinion but from first principles.

But perhaps the truth is rather more complicated than either of these scenarios would imply. If, as Plato suggests with his metaphor of the cave, the path to philosophy is a twisting, difficult, even painful ascent, and especially if (to modify the metaphor) it is a path that must cross a chasm before one regains solid ground and finds new and stronger reasons for being good and a new core to one's happiness, then Aristotle's project becomes much more complex, and its puzzling character becomes easier to understand.[28] If, moreover, as the cave metaphor also suggests, the dialectical ascent to philosophy must begin from precisely the same ground upon which the moral if unreflective citizen stands, and must begin by following the same process of sympathetic clarification of moral opinion that Aristotle engages in with the most serious members of that citizenry, then it makes sense that there should be no essentially different ethics, no separate treatise on human nature, for the philosophic students.

As among Aristotle's broader audience, there would be among these students a range of different types, from quiet, thoughtful youths like Menexenus, to intensely political souls such as Alcibiades, to mathematically inclined students such as Theaetetus, who show little interest in politics and may already be too prone to dismiss the moral and political realm as merely conventional. But all who are to succeed in philosophy need to have had an education in virtue that has fostered in them a love of what is noble for its own sake, since such a love cannot be transmitted through logical proofs, and since without it, it is impossible to be serious about the most important human questions. At the same time, if the student is to progress in a solid ascent beyond a merely conventional outlook, he cannot simply replace assumptions of one sort with assumptions of another. He cannot, in particular, assume that any amount of knowledge of the nonhuman world can, by itself, reveal the most important truths about human life, or that any number of observable differences in the way human beings act, or even in the rules according to which they act, can exclude the possibility that human morality still has, beneath all its variety and all its hypocrisy, a universal, coherent, and natural core.

The serious student of philosophy must therefore become a serious student of ethics and must begin with a probing but respectful analysis of just those assumptions that the ordinary moral citizen holds. Only after drawing from the latter's necessarily uneven self-understanding the most coherent articulation of the principles implicit in his moral choices and aspirations is the student in a position to judge the ultimate adequacy of this outlook. If he can show that his own understanding of the phenomena provide the best answers to questions or problems implicit in those very opinions, then his philosophic undertaking will have the best possible grounding.

The *Nicomachean Ethics* therefore seems to have, as Tessitore argues, two groups of readers: the primary audience of morally serious citizens whom Aristotle wishes to help attain the most rational, happy version possible of the active civic life to which they are dedicated, and the student or potential student of philosophy.[29] Even the third class of human beings that Aristotle mentioned in his quotation from Hesiod, those incapable of following reason, are not forgotten: One function of the *Nicomachean Ethics* and especially of the *Politics* is to show how such people can be prevented, as far as possible, from harming themselves and others, and to teach the sober moderation of political hopes that such recalcitrance to reason makes necessary.[30] But Aristotle's dialogue with the active citizen who is not autonomous but who listens to reason takes precedence. It does so because this dialogue forms the foundation also for the more rigorous philosophic education, and because, as Hesiod's lines suggest, the most perfect student will need the fewest hints and profit the most from light but sharp spurs to the exercise of his own mind. But Aristotle's choice of emphasis is also a result of caution, of a keen appreciation of the inherent treacherousness of philosophic education.

This treacherousness has little to do with the conclusions to Aristotle's researches, about which he is quite frank: Such teachings as the superiority of the philosophic life, or the argument that true knowledge of the good is never contravened in action, or that the activity of true virtue, resting on knowledge, is the substance of happiness are clear for all to see. But Aristotle, who thought deeply about the requirements of good education, both moral and philosophical, was keenly aware of all the ways in which education could go wrong. He saw that even philosophic education was less simply rational and more dependent upon the proper shaping of the passions than is commonly thought. Inasmuch as it involves a turning of the soul to new tastes and judgments, it is not wholly unlike the habituation of children to virtue. In philosophic education, this turning involves the cultivation of certain austere and rarefied pleasures and the relinquishment of certain unfounded hopes. Although many of the truths of moral philosophy as Aristotle saw them are easy enough to recite, in the way that a drunken man may recite verses of Empedocles (1147b9–12), they are hard to accept into the depths of one's soul in such a way as to become truly sovereign there, and to purge the heart of bitter, unruly passions.

On the other hand, if the goodness of the philosophic life and the highest reasons for being virtuous are absorbed only slowly, the corrosive questions that philosophy is capable of unleashing against conventional morality are appallingly obvious: questions that expose the merely conventional basis and self-serving character of much of what passes for virtue; questions that, like Alcibiades' famous interrogation of Pericles, expose the dubiousness of unreflective reverence for law;[31] questions about the coherence of the reigning civic religion; questions such as Socrates' imprudent imitators pressed against the leading men of Athens, bringing the city's wrath down upon their teacher. Aristotle, like Plato and Socrates, was convinced of the innocence of the philosopher himself, and Aristotle went further than either of his predecessors in showing how helpful philosophy could be in guiding political life and legislation. But like his great predecessors, he also saw how destructive philosophic education could be when it failed, as it did with Alcibiades and Critias, with the Sophists who used philosophy recklessly for fame, and with the students of Sophists who in the worst cases treated it as a tool to be turned to whatever tyrannical use they desired. These are the ugly stepchildren of philosophy, who have lost the citizen's conventional reasons for being good without acquiring the philosopher's deeper reasons, who have retained the political man's ambition to rule over others without retaining the good purposes that are necessary if a ruler is to be a statesman and not a parasite upon the body politic.

Evidently with such educational failures in mind, Aristotle argues that it is naive to suppose that any argument that is rational is necessarily constructive, or that a teacher should adopt just any line of questioning that is pertinent to the subject, without thinking carefully about the pedagogical needs of the students and their stages of development. In the *Eudemian Ethics,* he explains his own reasons for writing carefully and always weighing his words not only by the truth but also by what is useful for the political communities to which he and his future students will belong:

For the statesman as well, it ought not to be considered superfluous to engage in a theoretical inquiry of such a sort as will make clear not only what a thing is, but on account of what it is; for such is the philosophic investigation about each thing. Yet this requires great caution. For there are some who, on the basis of the opinion that what characterizes a philosopher is saying nothing at random and speaking with reason, often without being detected make arguments that are extraneous to the subject and empty, doing this sometimes on account of ignorance, sometimes on account of boastfulness, with the result that even men of experience and capacity for action are taken in by these people, who neither possess nor are capable of either architectonic or practical intelligence. (1216b37–17a6)

It is therefore quite reasonable that Aristotle should have been rather clearer about his conclusions than about all the considerations that led him to these conclusions. In order to do right by the full spectrum of his readers, Aristotle aims to provide both the material needed for an ascent from common opinion to philosophic truth *and* the healthiest, most rational, most defensible stopping points along the way. Because the answers that one group of readers needs to hear and the questions that the other needs to ask are not always in harmony, it should not be surprising that the surface of the book sometimes seems puzzling and inconsistent, its order is often obscure, and the unity of its teaching is not always in evidence. If indeed some such dual purpose is at work in the *Nicomachean Ethics,* then all difficulties in the text – all inconsistencies, apparent repetitions, obvious exaggerations, unexplained shifts to important new themes – should be approached with this context in mind. Does a given difficulty, which may of course result from a mere lapse on Aristotle's part, or a defect in the transmission of his text, make sense in the light of the complexity of the book? Might the passage in question be designed to answer a problem not explicitly posed, or designed to give a provisional answer to a question, while at the same time providing the elements for a further exploration, leading to a different and more comprehensive understanding? Does the passage, so understood, help to provide additional support for conclusions that Aristotle states in a somewhat formulaic way?

In particular, I hope to show that Aristotle's extensive treatment of friendship in the penultimate books of the *Nicomachean Ethics,* standing between his full elaboration of the moral virtues and the discussion of the philosophic life, is an important and hitherto overlooked source of arguments, both explicit and implicit, for the life of philosophy, and that the movement to the philosophic life is part of the key to the order of arguments in these books. For while Books 8 and 9 have a surface order that is more systematic than is usually recognized – moving from the three kinds of friendship in 8.2–8.6 to the relationship of friendship to justice in 8.7–9.3 to the elements of friendship in 9.4–9.12 – these books also have an inner progression to a deeper understanding of the phenomena that is connected to the emergence of philosophy as a theme in Book 9.[32]

Aristotle's Introduction to the Theme of Friendship

In the light of the complexity of his overall project, it is not surprising that Aristotle should give a complicated account of the necessity of friendship in the good life. His justification of the turn to friendship in 8.1 stresses the ways in which friendship is regarded as both necessary and noble, and the ways in which the necessity and nobility of friendship are intertwined. He expands at much greater length on friendship's necessity than upon its nobility, suggesting that its most important grounds lie in individuals' needs or concerns with their own happiness and not in an overflow of generous benevolence or selfless sacrifice. Yet the necessity he describes is a rich and broad necessity, encompassing the needs not only for survival but also for natural fulfillment. "Without friends," Aristotle says, "no one would choose to live, though he possessed all the other goods" (1155a5–6). Friendship is an essential safeguard for the life, property, and political freedom or power that virtue requires as equipment for its full exercise, and it provides the worthiest objects of virtuous action (1155a6–10).[33] Moreover, it provides the guidance that young men need, the assistance that weak and elderly men need, and the clarity of insight that even the best men need in order to act and to think as well as possible (1155a11–16). In all of this, friendship appears less as an end in itself than as a crucial condition for the individual's welfare and virtuous activity.

But Aristotle also notes that friendship seems to be necessary in quite a different way that is rooted in our animal nature and that does not aim at virtue at all. Nature has implanted in many animals, and especially in human beings, a love of those who are kindred – of children and parents above all, but also of fellow tribesmen and even of the whole human race (1155a16–22).[34] Throughout most of Books 8 and 9 of the *Ethics,* Aristotle will push this natural root of friendship into the background, but here at the outset he gives it central place in his account of friendship's necessity.

Finally, friendship is indispensable to the political community: "Friendship also seems to hold the polis together, and lawgivers seem to be more seriously concerned with it than with justice. For concord seems to be something similar to friendship, and they strive most to attain concord and to drive out faction, its enemy" (1155a22–26). Without the concord that comes from a common purpose and the faith in a common good, without the sympathetic interest in one's fellows that makes one want to treat them equitably and to pursue their good along with one's own, no political community can exist in Aristotle's view; he considers it naive to think that a true community can ever be secured by a mere compact. Various combinations of self-interest and fear may hold alliances and empires together, but a political community that seeks to promote the good life for human beings requires something more.[35] Aristotle's stress on the need for friendship suggests that even good laws, even when supported by a dedication to justice among the citizenry, are not sufficient to maintain order and harmony. For, as he shows in his discussions of justice in the fifth book of the *Ethics* and the third book of the *Politics,* justice is not a single principle but, rather, a cluster of related but not wholly compatible principles, such that the claims of justice made by different citizens according to different principles or types of justice are bound to come into conflict. In particular, there is inevitable conflict between the claims of the few to honor and rule on the basis of excellence according to distributive justice, and the claims of the many to justice as simple equality, including their not simply unreasonable resistance to being ruled by anyone who is not of their own choosing and does not share their character and outlook. Since perfect justice is not attainable, patriotic affection of the citizens toward one another and toward the fatherland is essential for keeping competing claims from erupting into civil war. Finally, Aristotle argues, friendship not only underlies justice but also includes and goes beyond justice: "Where there is friendship there is no need of justice" (1155a26–27). Aristotle thereby implicitly raises the important question of the relation of friendship to justice. Do the best friendships simply incorporate justice, or do they in fact dispense with the need for justice, by creating either a perfect selflessness in each friend or a perfect unity of their interests and concerns?

Aristotle's account of friendship's necessity contains a mixture of his own observations and reports of common opinions, but when he turns to the nobility of friendship, he makes reference only to generally held opinions: "We praise those who love their friends, and having many friends seems to be something noble, and further, men suppose that good men and friends are the same" (1155a29–31).[36] These opinions provide useful starting points, but when examined in the light of Aristotle's whole treatment of friendship, they will prove to be in need of serious revision. Aristotle will argue that not every affection is praiseworthy but that we should love those who are good. He will contend that the best man will cultivate only one or a few friends. And surely it is an elementary error to identify those who are good friends to us with those who are good simply. Aristotle will actually suggest that this identification is less foolish than it seems, since only good men can be friends in the fullest sense. But his formulation prompts us to wonder and to doubt whether those whom most people consider the best friends really are the best people altogether, whether the virtues even of the truest friendship are the most important virtues, and whether the good man may not differ from the good friend, somewhat as he differs from the good citizen (see 1130b26–29). In all, the three opinions cited to support the nobility of friendship reflect less the perspective of the best individual as an individual than the perspective of the political man or partisan, a perspective which the lawgiver seeks to soften and to extend to the whole community, but not to transcend altogether.

By bringing out the rich variety of ways in which friendship is essential and is honored as noble, Aristotle shows that friendship is a growth with diverse and tangled roots, and that our natural sociability runs deep in us and yet is not altogether to be counted upon, since men consider it necessary to praise those who love their fellowmen and their friends. The complexity of friendship makes it a difficult phenomenon to analyze. Before we can determine whether friendship can ever live up to the hopes it evokes, we must understand better what lies at its core.

Aristotle, in this opening chapter, now proceeds to consider three different theories that seek to give a unifying explanation for the root causes of all friendships. The first two theories are indeed so sweeping that they attempt to account for all attractions, both animate and inanimate. First, there is the view, expressed in lines of Homer and Empedocles, that all friendship rests on a kind of similarity or kinship.[37] This theory is inadequate, Aristotle suggests, because it fails to account for the rivalries of "fellow potters" and others who pursue the same thing, so memorably characterized by Hesiod, and because it fails to take into account the power of complementarity in drawing people together (1155a32–b1).[38] Second, then, Aristotle brings up what he calls the "higher" or "more scientific" view expressed by Euripides and Heraclitus, who portray opposition and need as the root of all attractions (1155b1–6).[39] After briefly mentioning this view, Aristotle returns to the position of Empedocles, underscoring the suggestion that each position is weak in failing to account for the phenomena attested by the other. Most importantly, both seem inadequate in failing to give sufficient attention to what is specifically ethical and human in friendship (1155b8–10). For both leave out the evident human capacity to rise above need and above the simple animal inclination, seen even in cattle, to rub up against others of their own kind and, instead, to love others as ends in a generous or even selfless way. Aristotle therefore offers a third possibility of his own, which will become the theme of the next five chapters: the possibility that all true friendship rests on virtue.[40]

But why, after first reminding us of the "higher" or "more scientific" Heraclitean position, does Aristotle say that he will not investigate it, as being beyond the scope of his work (1155b8–9)? The superficial reason is, of course, that Heraclitus's thesis is in large part a theory about the nonhuman world, but why does Aristotle not follow Heraclitus's lead and openly explore the possibility that need is in fact *the* root of *all* human love?[41] The path of inquiry that Aristotle closes off here is precisely the one pursued in Plato's *Lysis,* and Aristotle's references at 1155a32–b8 to the sayings of Homer, Hesiod, Euripides, Heraclitus, and Empedocles are echoes of *Lysis* 213e3–16b9.[42] By making a point of his intention not to delve into this issue, Aristotle suggests that a comprehensive study of friendship would require precisely confronting and thinking through the possibility, explored in the *Lysis,* that even the noblest-seeming love is rooted wholly in need; and thus, Aristotle's discussion of friendship, read in isolation from the *Lysis,* would be incomplete or misleading.[43] For while he seems to take sharp issue with the *Lysis* in insisting on treating friendship as an expression of the uniquely human capacity and concern for nobility – and this appearance is by no means wholly deceptive – a careful reading of Aristotle's discussion, considered in the light of the *Lysis,* will show that indeed Aristotle does not fail to address the possibilities advanced there, that he concedes more to Socrates' argument than is at first glance apparent, and that, in fact, the question of the relation of friendship to need will be a major, though often submerged, subtext of Aristotle's entire discussion.

1

The Challenge of Plato's *Lysis*

In the *Lysis,* Socrates' dialogue with two young friends about friendship, Socrates pursues the unsettling idea that all friendship is rooted in human neediness and defectiveness and is treasured only because and only to the extent that we hope to get from others things that we are unable to provide for ourselves. "He who is good . . . be[ing] to that extent sufficient for himself . . . would be in want of nothing," Socrates argues, and hence would neither treasure nor love anything or anyone else.[1] The radical claim advanced in the central section of the dialogue is not merely that human love begins in need – this alone would be a rather unremarkable claim about human development – but that love begins and ends and is wholly driven by need. Moreover, the *Lysis* explores the possibility that the most important needs that cause us to love are not needs for the pleasures and activities of friendship as such, but are directed to other things that act as remedies for our defects in the way that medicine does for the defects of the body, and to which the human beings we call our friends are merely the means.

Is this claim about neediness the final teaching of the *Lysis,* and is it Plato's considered view of friendship and love, as, in different ways, Gregory Vlastos, Laszlo Versenyi, and David Bolotin argue? Or, as Hans-Georg Gadamer contends, does the *Lysis* teach precisely the contrary, that in true friendship we can and do love others for their own sakes in a way that is not driven by any need?[2] Or is it the case, as many other scholars have maintained, that this infamously aporetic dialogue teaches in the end nothing positive at all – that, as one of them has put it, the "shipwreck" of the *Lysis*'s arguments leaves only lumber for later dialogues?[3] Against this view, Gadamer and Bolotin both argue persuasively that a positive teaching can be found if one pays careful regard to the drama of the dialogue. "The confusion in which these half-children are left is not . . . negative per se," Gadamer suggests, but is a necessary confusion given their immaturity; the arguments of the dialogue do illuminate the nature of friendship when read in light of the boys' youth and character. Similarly, Versenyi argues that "although every account given of the nature of love is ostensibly rejected here, rightly understood just about every account is tenable and coherent with the rest. And although there is much in the dialogue that is playfully presented, hastily stated and incompletely developed, just about everything in it has serious import."[4] Hence Plato may provide the reader with the outlines of compelling arguments that, though facilely rejected, are not refuted. But which are his most serious arguments? Are they those that tend to show the selfish, utilitarian roots of friendly affection, or those that subsequently qualify the former?

The Problem of Reciprocity

Socrates paves the way for his argument about friendship and human neediness first by shaking Lysis's comfortable assumption that he is loved and lovable, especially in the eyes of his parents, simply for who he is, apart from any capacity he may have to assist those around him; and second by calling into question the assumption of Lysis and his friend Menexenus that the essence of friendship consists in two people's reciprocal liking for each other, which needs no particular justification and points to no particular end beyond itself. He begins to arouse the doubt and puzzlement that are the necessary prelude to any serious thought about friendship by asking Menexenus whether a friend is the one who loves, the one who is loved, or whether it makes no difference (212a8–b2).[5] Menexenus initially takes the view that it makes no difference: that two people will both be friends if either loves the other. This view is in keeping with the uncomplicated experience of young boys, for whom one's friends are one's playmates, and who are still untouched by, although not wholly unaware of, the anguish of unrequited love. Under questioning, Menexenus quickly retreats to the commonsensical position that neither of a pair is really a friend unless each loves the other (212c7–d1). But Socrates persuades him of the inadequacy of this definition also, partly by playing upon the ambiguity of the Greek word φίλος, which can be either a noun meaning "friend" or an adjective meaning "dear." Socrates reminds Menexenus that it is possible to *love* or be a friend to someone or something in a significant way without being loved in return, for we call people lovers or friends of horses, quails, dogs, wine, gymnastics, and wisdom. But to dislodge Menexenus from the view that the φίλος is simply anyone who loves, Socrates reminds him of the possibility that a person, such as a newborn infant, can be *dear* to another before he begins to feel love, or even when he feels hatred (212d8–13a5). It is easy to believe that this problem is just a linguistic or formal one, that as Aristotle suggests, quails, wisdom, and infants are all friends in at most a partial or analogous sense, and that a true friend is only one who loves and is loved in return.[6]

By puzzling for so long over the seemingly simple question of reciprocity, Socrates draws attention to the powerful element in human love that consists in the wish or demand to be loved in return. Yet he drives Menexenus away from the view that friendship is simple reciprocity, first by failing to offer this as an option (212a8–b2), and then by producing an array of apparent counterexamples (212d4–13a5). He thus forces us to wonder whether it really makes sense that something so fortuitous as the coincidence of similar feelings in two people should constitute the essence of being a friend, and whether its essence does not lie deeper, in the nature either of truly loving or of truly being loved. Socrates rejects as "impossible" the idea that being loved, however dearly, could by itself make one a friend – and being hated make one an enemy – since one who is loved but hates the one loving him would then be a friend to his enemy: "And yet it is very unreasonable, my dear companion – or rather, I suppose, it is even impossible – to be an enemy to one's friend or a friend to one's enemy" (213b2–4).[7] But Socrates does not categorically rule out the possibility that the essence of being a friend consists in a certain kind of loving, in an active affection and interest in what is beautiful or good, and as such not hostile, though it may well be indifferent to us. For the result that there may then turn out to be "a friend to a nonfriend" (213c1) is not so obviously irrational and is nowhere proved impossible.

By leaving unrefuted the idea that the root of friendship may be a love such as people also feel for horses, quails, dogs, wine, gymnastics, and especially wisdom, Socrates leaves open for the time being the possibility of an unselfish love for what is beautiful and good in itself. At the same time, however, he shows a willingness to contemplate the idea that the most important things we seek in friendship may in fact be available to us in solitude, and that the true core of friendship may be a love that is not directed toward other human beings as such, but only toward our own good.

Socrates' Thesis on Friendship

Having ostensibly failed to get at the essence of friendship with his question about reciprocity, Socrates turns to the question that we have seen Aristotle take up in his introduction to the theme of friendship in *Nicomachean Ethics* 8.1, the question of whether friendship is rooted in similarity, in difference, or in goodness. Socrates considers the notion that like is friend to like, rejecting it (and likewise the idea that friendships are rooted in mutual goodness) with the argument that bad people are incapable of friendship and good ones will not need it (214a1–15c2). He also rejects the idea that friendship is at root a union of opposites, each providing the other with what it needs. Without proving that no pair of opposites can become friends, Socrates at least shows that opposition as such is not sufficient to establish friendship, because the enemy is not a friend to the friend, nor are those who are just, moderate, and good friends to those who are unjust, undisciplined, and bad. But Socrates clearly considers the second view closer to the truth (or conducive to the discovery of the most powerful part of the truth), and he stays with the idea that some sort of difference and need lie at the root of friendship.[8]

Socrates' own hypothesis, developed at 216c1 ff., is that "whatever is neither bad nor good becomes a friend of the good because of the presence of an evil" (217b4–6). His model of friendship is the relationship between a patient or his body, itself neither good nor bad – being neither wholly healthy nor hopelessly ill – and the doctor or the medical art that he befriends because of the evil of illness from which he suffers (217a4–b4, 218e3–19a3). Now if all human attachments are like the sick man's love for the doctor, if we only love the good that we lack because of the evils that beset us, we will not love other human beings for their own goodness at all, whether we mean by this the ways in which they are good for themselves or their goodness in some more absolute sense. Aristotle will argue that we love them both for themselves and for the benefits we receive from them, but Socrates seems to say that we love other human beings only because they are good for us.

This account of friendship is, at least at first sight, both shocking and puzzling. All of us have acquaintances with whom we associate strictly because we need something from them – electricians, dental hygienists, and so forth – but we would not for a moment confuse these people with our friends. When we come to like or love a person, do we not move beyond simply appreciating what he does for us – whether that assistance remains on the level of practical services or extends to comfort, encouragement, and guidance in the most important matters? Does not friendship come into being only when one begins to love another for his or her own sake, as simply delightful and good?

Socrates concedes that there is force in this common view. Even as he posits that all friendship is based on utility, he accepts the premise that truly loving a person or object means loving it for itself and not as a means to something else that we want. Hence as soon as he offers his definition of friendship, he begins to qualify it (218c4 ff.). The real friend cannot be the being we love or seem to love because of the good it procures for us, he says, but instead, the true or "first friend" (219c5–d5) must be the good thing for whose sake we love its provider:

I suspect that all the other things which we say are friends for the sake of that – being some phantoms, as it were, of that – are deceiving us, and I suspect that it is that first thing which is truly a friend.... This, then, has been dismissed – the view that what is a friend is a friend for the sake of some friend. But then is that which is good a friend?" (219d2–5, 220b7)

Socrates continues quietly to suggest, however, that the ultimate good we love is only our own good. He thereby gently opens the question of whether all of our supposed friendships with other human beings are not confusions or boastful impostors, each seeming to be a love of the other for himself, and in fact not being a love of the other at all (since he is not "truly a friend"), but rather a love of the good we need for ourselves.[9]

Socrates then presses upon his interlocutors the further radical thought that all those good things that we seem to crave for themselves, or to which we imagine ourselves to be selflessly devoted, are also not intrinsically good or desirable, but are only sought as remedies for evil (220b8–d4):

> Then is what is good loved because of what is bad...? If what is bad should get out of the way and lay hold of neither any body, nor any soul, nor any of the other things which we assert to be, themselves in themselves, neither bad nor good, would what is good be in no way useful to us at that time, and would it have become useless? For if nothing were to harm us any longer, we would require no benefit at all, and thus it would become manifest then that we had been treasuring and loving what is good because of what is bad, as if that which is good were a drug for the bad, and that which is bad were a disease. And if there is no disease, then a drug is not required.

We love the doctor only for the sake of the medicine he provides, and medicine only for the health it restores, and even health we love only as a release from the evil of illness.

Not only does Socrates refuse to acknowledge a class of things that are good simply, as opposed to good *for someone,* but he also suggests that nothing is good even for us in and of itself, apart from the deficiencies it remedies or eradicates. Socrates' argument in the *Lysis,* which takes medicine as the key example of the good, and provides no account of a positive human happiness for the *sake* of which we wish to be healthy, suggests that evil, deprivation, and ignorance are the fundamental facts in our lives and that the good takes its meaning from them as something wholly derivative, as if life were nothing but a series of illnesses and recoveries.[10] David Bolotin, in his richly insightful and provocative book on the *Lysis,* argues that this is Socrates' most serious teaching, from which he pulls back only as a concession to the two unphilosophic boys.[11] Is he correct in this, or does Socrates exaggerate his insights about love and the human good in order to provoke thought, and does his subsequent retreat from this position bring him closer to the truth?

Problems with Socrates' Thesis

After laying out his thesis that all love is rooted in defectiveness, Socrates rather abruptly changes course at 220e6. Presenting a cryptic argument that there may be good without evil after all, he then considers a very different possible root of friendship, similarity or kinship. Instead of showing how his initial thesis needs to be modified to become completely adequate, or explaining how these two roots of friendship may coexist and be related to each other, however, Socrates will suggest that the arguments for each source of friendship refute the possibility of the other, and the dialogue collapses in apparent failure. But in the course of explicating his initial thesis, and especially in the examples and illustrations that he gives, Socrates does in fact hint at a number of limitations of the thesis and phenomena from which it abstracts. Not only do these hints point the way to a more comprehensive and adequate version of the thesis, but they also begin to show the connection between the love of the good we need for ourselves and the love of kindred souls introduced at 221e3. Let us, then, consider three problems of especial interest that emerge in Socrates' explication of his thesis.

First, Socrates seems to hint at a possible exaggeration in his thesis by spelling out its implications for the love of wisdom. If we love only what we need and do not have, it follows that "the ones who are already wise, whether these are gods or human beings, no longer love wisdom" (218a2–3). This conclusion follows directly from Socrates' radical characterization of love at 215a6–b2: He who is "good" and "sufficient for himself" not only would want or desire nothing but would not "treasure" or "love" anything either, including, evidently, what he already possesses. Wisdom would indeed not be treasured for itself were it merely a remedy for evils, but is there not a great deal of knowledge that would be good and delightful, even for beings that suffered no evils? If the wise man feels no love for his wisdom, then philosophy would seem to be not the happy life that Socrates presents it as being, and instead it is an endless search for something or a series of things that are never attained or that cease to be treasured as soon as they are each attained – or it is a prelude to some other goal altogether.

Perhaps wise men are so scarce that it is hard for us to say with any confidence what they would feel about their wisdom, but let us take another case that is more common. People who seek to acquire musical virtuosity do not, as they attain it, cease to treasure and love it, any more than a violinist who acquires a Stradivarius ceases to cherish it once it is his. To the contrary, they tend to love their virtuosity all the more because it is good and a source of joy to them, because they have labored to acquire it, and precisely because it is their own.[12] But the same considerations that allegedly make it impossible for the philosophic life of a wise man to be good and loved for itself would seem to make it impossible for any activity or accomplishment to be good and loved for itself. And if this is the case, would it not seem that life has no positive goal and is ultimately tragic or absurd?

The second hint as to a problem or abstraction in Socrates' thesis comes in his example of the father who is seeking a remedy for his poisoned son (219d5–20a1). Socrates is making the point that many of the things we care about and make much of are really important to us only for the sake of something else, and that what is truly dear to us is the final good for the sake of which we seek the instrumental good. Thus Socrates asks whether a father would not "make much of something else," such as the antidote for poison, "for the sake of [ἕνεκα] considering his son worth everything" (219d7–e2). This formulation is rather strange and unsettling, especially in the light of the careful distinction that Socrates has just been developing between what is done ἕνεκά του (for the sake of something) and διά τι (because of something) at 218d6–19b4. There he gives as his example of the difference the sick man who is "a friend of the doctor *because of* illness and *for the sake of* health" (218e4–5) and goes on to state the distinction in a general way: "That which is neither bad nor good, therefore, is a friend of the good because of what is bad and what is an enemy, and for the sake of the good and friend" (219a6–b2). But Socrates' formulation of the father's goal does make a certain sense in the context of his argument. If the only thing each man really loves as an end is the good for himself, then the true goal of the father's efforts is not the son as such but his own posture or activity of "considering the son worth everything," understood as part of the father's good and as a remedy for some evil the father suffers. But surely this is a distortion of the reality of parental love. With this example Socrates prompts us to consider a component of human love that is not reducible to seeking a remedial good for oneself, and not in any obvious way reducible to seeking the good at all. Parents love children not because they are good or good for them but because they are their own, and at the end of the dialogue Socrates will give the phenomenon of love based on kinship its due.[13]

Third and finally, Socrates gives an important clue as to the incompleteness of his account of the good in the conclusion to the whole argument at 220d8–e5:

Therefore, that friend to us, into which all the others were seen to terminate – for we asserted that those things were friends for the sake of another friend – has no resemblance to them. For they have been called friends for the sake of a friend, but what is really a friend comes to light as being of a nature entirely the opposite of this. For it has appeared plainly to be a friend to us for the sake of an enemy (ἐχθροῦ ἕνεκα), and if that which is an enemy would go away, it is no longer, as it seems, a friend to us.

Like the phrase "for the sake of considering the son worth everything" at 219d7–e1, the expression "for the sake of an enemy" here is very strange, as Bolotin points out.[14] We would have expected Socrates to say just the opposite, that the good we love instrumentally is loved for the sake of our own happiness or our own selves, whom we love most of all.[15] For the whole dialogue has stressed the self-interestedness of love. Is the ultimate end of needy love not clearly our own happiness, and would the "true" or "first" object of such love (219d4–5) not be ourselves?

Socrates is silent, however, about the possibility either of positive happiness or of self-love. Indeed, he discourages us from even considering the latter phenomenon by stressing the deficiency of anyone who loves and the goodness of what is loved. But Socrates alerts us to the incompleteness of his account of the good as merely remedial, stated most starkly at 220b8–d4, by the dubiousness of his claim that bodies and souls, "themselves in themselves," are "neither bad nor good" (220c4–5). While this claim echoes Socrates' statement at 217b2–3 that "a body, presumably – insofar as it is a body – is neither good nor bad," it disregards the subsequent development of this argument at 217b6–18b5, in which Socrates shows that bodies that are beset by evils in a serious way do eventually become bad themselves – not temporarily ill but permanently disabled. In a similar way, souls that neither have wisdom nor desire it are bad, and wise souls are good (218a2–b3). It thus seems more accurate to say that most bodies and souls are a mixture of bad and good, having elements that are healthy and others that are not. Do we not, at the very least, love for their goodness the aspects of ourselves that are good, and love for their potential goodness the aspects that are potentially good? Aristotle seems right when he argues, in contrast to Socrates, that good men naturally love themselves without qualification, and that inferior people love themselves also, if only to the extent that they consider themselves good (*NE* 1166a1–13).

But Socrates' most radical suggestion regarding self-love would seem to be that even when we love our own virtues, we are not truly loving them as good in themselves or loving ourselves as good in ourselves, but instead, we love our virtues only because they are useful, like medicine, for something further. What, then, is the ultimate object for the sake of which we love everything else, the object that Socrates calls an enemy? In his book on the *Lysis,* Bolotin suggests that this enemy is for each of us our own defective self, for whom we indeed feel a great attachment and concern, both deeper and less voluntary than the attachments to others that we ordinarily think of as love, but with whom we are in a kind of enmity because we are not yet good.[16] In a later reconsideration of the question, Bolotin concedes that to hate our bad condition, so long as we are not thoroughly bad, is not to hate ourselves, that we do indeed naturally love ourselves, and that our self-love may even be deepened by the presence of evils in our lives.[17]

All of these concessions are no doubt true. I think Bolotin's book is on the right track, however, in trying to see why Socrates might wish not only to refrain from identifying our ultimate concern as self-love but even to characterize the self that is our ultimate concern as somehow an *enemy* because of its defectiveness. Ordinary neediness and defectiveness are not enough to make one consider oneself an enemy. But the exaggerated defectiveness Socrates here attributes to human beings, in characterizing them as beings who love and seek nothing except cures for their ills and for whom life has no other positive content, would make the self who acts consider the needy, longing being for the sake of whom he acts to be nothing but an enemy. If all good is good only in the way that medicine is, as an escape from evil, if our needy self is like a chronically sick and petulant patient, for whom his caregiver can have no higher hope than that he might sleep peacefully, then we are indeed our own enemies, shackled by an inescapable self-concern to a neediness that plagues us.

Socrates' use of the word "enemy" to describe the ultimate object of our concern, and his silence on self-love, the most obvious and undeniable example of a love that is not utilitarian, not for the sake of anything else at all, are the strongest clues that Socrates' claims about love and utility are indeed an exaggeration.[18] For surely there is more wholeness and positive directedness in us and in our self-concern than this characterization allows. Healthy human beings seem to have within them a harmony of wants, resources, and virtues, which together are loved as the basis of a flourishing activity that perhaps is loved most of all. One may be, for example, curious about many things, and glad to be curious, because one has the intelligence to satisfy one's curiosity; what results is a learning, thinking, rational self that one is glad indeed to be. And if it is possible thus to love oneself, then it should be possible, by extension, to love one's own friends who are akin to us and whose virtues and happiness are like our own.[19] But Socrates' formulation that the good is loved for the sake of an enemy and Bolotin's gloss on this claim do, in their starkness, highlight the disturbing possibility that, much more than we would like to believe, our loves and friendships are, at root, a love of the remedies we need for evils within us. Socrates' thesis on friendship thus proves to be both powerful and in need of refinement, and we are now in a better position to see how his next argument, which seems at first sight simply to demolish the thesis, in fact indicates the needed corrective to it.

The Possibility of a Good Independent of Evil

Once Socrates has spelled out the full consequences of his suggestion about the good we love, he swears. "In the name of Zeus," he says, "if that which is bad ceases to be, will there no longer be hungering or thirsting, or any other such things?" (220e6–21a1). In the absence of evils, will we simply become like contented cows, or rather, like stones? Socrates' oath evokes the vehement, even indignant feeling we all have, in the face of arguments such as he has made, that life *must* have a positive goal, a happy activity or collection of activities toward which all our labors are directed, and which are good and satisfying in and of themselves, not in the way that water is satisfying to one (and only to one) who is parched, but in the way that dancing is intrinsically satisfying to one who is healthy and vigorous and graceful.

As much as we would like to think that there is, at least in principle, a human happiness wholly independent of and unshaped by evils, Socrates is cautious on this point. "Who knows," he says, what human life would be like if evils disappeared (221a5)? Perhaps human life is so thoroughly defined by deprivations and limits (above all, the limits imposed by death) that it is impossible really to understand what a divinely blessed life could be like. In particular, it is hard to know what it would mean to enjoy good things or pleasures or satisfactions that are not in any way an answer to our needs and desires, or what it would mean to have needs and desires which, taken in themselves apart from their fulfillments, are not at least in some degree painful and hence bad. To be sure, life holds unexpected pleasures, but may they not be unexpected simply because the lack that they answer is not present to consciousness at the moment it is met? Can we even imagine being alive and having no longings and no deficiencies? Does being alive not mean precisely being subject to changing feelings and wishes, to repeated cycles of want, longing, satisfying activity, satiety, fatigue, and new wants?

These reflections perhaps help us to see the serious thought behind Socrates' statement that a wise man would not love wisdom. If, as Aristotle says, happiness consists in activity, perhaps wisdom and all possessions and virtues are good only as means to activities such as contemplation. Perhaps we as human beings can experience contemplation as joyful and good only to the extent that it offers the possibility of change, of the fresh consideration of things that before were not conscious to our minds, even if at some level they were known. To regard everything all at once and never to change the focus of one's attention, but simply to find stillness in perfect knowledge, is *not* conceivable as human happiness.[20] If, then, the possession of wisdom is only a condition for the human good and not the human good itself, even for those who love above all to think, it will be loved much in the way that other conditions of happiness are loved. We surely do value the good conditions of our bodies and souls for their own sakes, and not merely for what results from them.[21] But in general, we seem to *cherish* the conditions for happiness only so long as they seem to us somehow fragile and uncertain. We do not normally feel much love for the daylight or the eyes by which we see, if we see well, or oxygen or our lungs, if we breathe well. If happiness consists above all in contemplation, then wisdom, providing both the capacity for and the objects of contemplation, would be more integral to happiness than all such bodily things, and (especially because wisdom is rare, like the prized Stradivarius) Socrates' claim that the wise man would not love wisdom at all therefore still seems an exaggeration. But the wise would love wisdom less than the delightful activity of thinking, and their love for thinking itself might well consist in a calm, quiet enjoyment, rather than in the fervent ardor that tends to characterize transient enthusiasms and loves for objects that one is uncertain of attaining or keeping. Intense love, then, may not be part of the happiest life.

Leaving aside the difficult but thought-provoking question of the dependence of all happiness upon *some* kind of evil, Socrates turns to a more limited and answerable question. Is it not possible for us even now to desire in ways that are beneficial, in ways that are harmful, and in ways that are neither (221a5–b3)? Even if some degree of pain and hence evil is an inseparable part of all desiring, there still seems to be a significant difference in this regard between types of desires. Some, like thirst, are good because meeting them provides a benefit that goes beyond the satisfaction of the desire, which may itself be only a relief from pain. Such desires are good to the extent that they remedy or prevent an evil, such as dehydration. Other desires, like the craving for heroin, are altogether bad, being both painful to experience and destructive to satisfy. But Socrates suggests that still other desires are neither. Among this neutral class of desires for things sought just for themselves and not as remedies would seem to be at least some of our desires to see, to know, to sing, to joke and laugh, and to enjoy the company of kindred souls. All of these things *can* be sought as relief from difficulties or sorrows, but they also seem choiceworthy for themselves, as an answer to no other evil than the desire for just these things or activities.

These things may not be "good absolutely," apart from being good *for* some particular being. We are tempted to think of such things as knowledge, beauty, and friendship as simply desirable and good, simply creating, by their very presence, an appreciation and hence a want for them, and hence we tend to think of them as having a goodness altogether different in kind from the goodness of remedies for evil. Socrates insists, however, that everything we desire is an answer to some want or incompleteness (221d6–e3), so that the discovery of the goodness of a thing is at once the discovery of an incompleteness or an as-yet-unrealized potential in us – an evil of sorts, at least if it goes unfilled – that the new thing satisfies. Yet these wants are not wants from which we would wish to be free, and this, I believe, makes their objects fundamentally different from the things that we find good instrumentally, as cures for evils we would wish never to have. In short, we experience these objects as being what we might call "good in themselves for us," or good for us as ends.

In particular, we are glad to have these wants, and not glad to have the needs that simply call for remedies, for three basic reasons. First, although being released from suffering is pleasant, its pleasure is no greater and is usually less than the suffering was painful, whereas the things I have called "good in themselves for us" are usually much more pleasant to enjoy than the want for them is painful. The want for them may indeed be felt only as an eager anticipation, itself more pleasant than painful; the satisfaction may be merely enjoyed, if minor, or truly loved, if it constitutes a significant part of our happiness. Second, remedies only remove impediments or lay the groundwork for our flourishing, bringing us only to a neutral state of readiness, whereas the activities we cherish for themselves constitute that flourishing itself. In a similar vein, Aristotle argues that there are pleasures that involve no replenishment of depletions or remedying of deficiencies, and that the activities of our unimpaired capacities are more truly and naturally pleasant than are the pleasures associated with these replenishments and remedies.[22] Third, and closely related to the second, the wants for things we consider good in themselves for us define what we are, so that a conceivable happiness that would not include these things would not be our happiness but that of a different being altogether.

Socrates exaggerates then, when he says to the two boys that the prior account of friendship as rooted in the love of needy beings for the good was wholly false, "some kind of idle talk, like a long poem strung together" (221d4–6). That account was not simply false but was incomplete, most seriously in failing to distinguish the need for remedies from other kinds of needs and wants, and in failing to take into account that aspect of human affection that is directed to what is one's own or akin to oneself. The final part of the dialogue provides the necessary supplement to what came before, and it helps us see the close connection between these two important omissions.

The Love of the Kindred and the Need for Companionship

Of the human desires that lead us into friendly intercourse with others, Socrates says that the desire for what is akin or one's own (οἰκεῖον) belongs to the class of desires that are neither beneficial nor harmful (221d1–e5). He emphasizes that the desire for companionship, like all human desires, springs from *some* sort of deprivation or want – in this case, the sense we all share that it is not good for us to be alone.[23] Yet unlike our need for assistance, this want is not clearly akin to ill health or something of which the healthy person would wish to be free. But why does Socrates simply equate the desire for companionship for its own sake with the desire for what is akin or one's own? Why does he not say that nonutilitarian affection can be for what is beautiful or good in itself, as well as for what is akin? His thought seems to be this: Being good in itself can really only mean being good for itself, and as much as we may admire an object as simply beautiful or good for itself, we only love in others what we desire or cherish as bringing us a needed wholeness or completion. We may admire the intricate mechanisms by which a spider entraps and subdues its prey, but that does not make us love the spider. A human being's excellence certainly does seem to inspire or heighten love, but Socrates is suggesting that this happens only in one of two fundamental ways. Either we love the virtuous person's virtue instrumentally, because we find it or hope it to be beneficial to us, or we love it as the flourishing of a kindred soul, whose company we crave because we feel incomplete without companionship, whose needs arouse our sympathetic concern, and whose excellence and happiness we enjoy vicariously, as in some way akin to our own excellence and happiness. Indeed, Socrates begins to suggest by 222b that a solid love for a kindred soul must also be a love of him for his goodness in important respects, or for the goodness which, being "akin" to him, is also "akin" to us (222c3–5). For simple resemblance, especially in trivial things, has been shown to be insufficient to bring friendship into being (222b3–8).[24] Conversely, two people who are good and thoroughly alike, neither of whom is so needy as to prefer any other, more useful companion, would seem almost certain to become friends whenever fortune brings them together. Here, perhaps, we finally find the basis for the true friendship the interlocutors have been seeking, which Menexenus divined ought to be somehow *essentially* reciprocal.

But Socrates' provocative questions have now driven us into a rather paradoxical position. We cannot conceive of a life that we would want that would be free of the desire for companionship, let alone free of desire altogether, yet we all sense somehow that perfection should mean self-sufficiency. The idea that the best human being would be in want of nothing and no one seems superficially logical yet unconvincing; yet the idea that he would be seriously needy does not seem right either. Perhaps we can resolve the paradox by saying that the best conceivable human being – the best that we could hope or wish to be, given all the limits and uncertainties of life as we know it – would be free of defects but not of desires.

What would this mean for friendship? There seem to be two plausible alternatives. The first is that the healthiest, strongest human being would be as self-sufficient as it is possible for an embodied being to be, able to create happiness out of his own resources anywhere, even on a desert island, and needing from fortune only the bare means to live. He would not be insensitive to the pleasures of the senses or to the enjoyment of good books and good conversation; but he could do without them, just as a man who loves good food might still get along perfectly well without lobster. The best man's self-sufficiency would be so great that the absence of friends and even of all human fellowship would not be a great loss to him. He would not, then, deeply cherish his friendships.

The other alternative, which seems at least more true to what we, as admittedly imperfect human beings, believe is essential to human nature, is that the very best human being *would* retain a significant desire or hunger for the company of kindred souls. This desire would indeed leave him more vulnerable than the first man we sketched; but as we have seen, not every want is to be wished away, and perhaps such happiness as is conceivable without any vulnerability to others is simply too cold, too narrow, too alien a happiness for us to wish for. Being deeply human, this second man would be happiest of all when he had one or more friends who were both very good and truly akin. But being strong, resilient, and largely self-sufficient, he would not feel an insatiable longing for a perfect soul mate, such as Socrates claims (rather humorously and with evident exaggeration) to have craved all his life (211d7–12a7), for then he would be almost surely disappointed. Instead, he would deeply desire only such a degree and kind of friendship as, in all normal circumstances, he is assured of being able to find and enjoy by virtue of his own capacity to love, to admire, to take delight in, and to win the love of others. If he found himself marooned in isolation, he would indeed be distressed, although not crushed; when his best friends died, he would indeed grieve. But the desire for friendship that would in the best case be met by a single bosom companion could be satisfied well enough in piecemeal fashion, by conversing with interesting souls of different sorts, by sharing at least the beginnings of his deepest interests with promising young people, by coming to know and cherish some splendid souls that he encounters only in books, and by the pleasure of offering the very best of himself, through his own writings, to true but unmet kindred souls in other times and places.[25] Thus, on balance, his wish for friends would bring him more pleasure than pain.

Nevertheless, if we concede that this best human being would be happiest of all in the possession of friends as splendid and extraordinary as himself, and that such friends are hard indeed to find, we must accept the consequence that our best conceivable man, if we leave him to take his chances with fortune, is likely to fall short of perfect happiness. This, I think, is not a result of a defect in him but a necessary part of what it means to be a limited, mortal being. The best man would, after all, also have a desire to be completely wise, a desire that is capable of significant but never perfect attainment. It seems, therefore, that one important quality of the best human being would be the capacity to accept limits and still to be very happy in the face of an imperfect attainment of all that he wishes for.[26]

Because Bolotin considers need to be the essential basis of any true and deep friendship, he is (at least initially) quite perplexed by Socrates' suggestion at 222d5–6 that the good can be friends of the good. He understands this formulation to refer primarily to the good man's friendship for himself and his own virtue, on the grounds that the good man needs virtue and virtue needs a needy being in order to come into its own. Bolotin ultimately acknowledges that good men might also be friends of one another, although he says that they would only be friends "in a limited sense" and that their friendship would lack depth.[27] He does argue convincingly that friendships of needy and defective people that are based solely on kinship and not on utility or mutual service, such as the friendships of childhood playmates, are indeed shallow: "Without the experience of those serious concerns in which one needs a friend, they would not treasure each other ... in a fully human way."[28] I believe, however, that there would be more depth and significance than Bolotin suggests to a friendship of two truly wise, mature, and good men – a friendship such as Plato must have had for Aristotle at the end – and by extension, that there is more depth and significance in those aspects of the friendships of other good men that rest on no other need but the friends' desire for company, and also on their admiration of one another, and that 222d5–6 shows Socrates' support for this possibility.

Nevertheless, although the friendship based on the highest form of kinship would seem, according to my argument, to be the friendship most truly good in itself, Socrates does not call either the desire for such friendship or its satisfaction good at all, as Bolotin justly points out. What are we

to make of this significant silence? Bolotin naturally takes it as evidence for
his thesis that there is nothing good as such considered apart from the evils
that put us in need of assistance. In the absence of such evils, or considered apart from such evils, according to Bolotin's reading, there may still be
desires and pleasures, such as those surrounding human companionship.
But these pleasures are so insignificant compared with the great goods we
need – above all, the knowledge of how we should live – that the former do
not rise to the level of deserving to be called good at all, and are indeed
"independent of our concern with, and thought about, the good."[29] Bolotin
takes as support for his view that there is a realm of desires independent of
good and evil, and that the desire for the kindred is such a desire, Socrates'
statement that "there will be, then, whatever desires are neither good nor
bad, even if the things which are bad cease to be" (221b5–6).

I believe that at this point Socrates is encouraging us momentarily to lose
sight of the fact that he has manifestly *not* established that there can be
desires apart from evil, if only the evil of potentially painful longing; he has
only shown that there are desires that are neither harmful nor beneficial.[30]
Socrates temporarily allows Menexenus to slip into the comfortable thought
that there can be elements of happiness totally unshaped by evil of any kind,
but by 221d6 he again gently reminds him that every desire is bound up with
a sense of deprivation and pain. If the pain of longing is, as such, bad, surely
the pleasure of satisfaction is, as such, good – and often far greater than any
pain that preceded it – and the satisfaction of our greatest and final wants
would seem to be the greatest good of all.

Hans von Arnim thus seems closer to the truth when he argues that
the things we desire directly for themselves and not to prevent or remedy
harm are the only true good.[31] Von Arnim certainly has Aristotle on his
side, for Aristotle argues vigorously in Book 1 of the *Nicomachean Ethics* that
there are or must be things that are good for human beings as ends and
not just as means or remedies. I suspect that this is really Socrates' view also.
But why, then, does Socrates cease to speak of the good when he begins to
discuss the desires and satisfactions that are neither harmful nor beneficial
as remedies?

I believe that Socrates' demotion of these desires and their satisfactions
is meant to make us reflect upon the very serious extent to which we, as
beings who are not yet wise, are all ill and in need of remedies. We cannot
successfully pursue the things that we consider to be the most good of all,
and in particular, true friendship, until we have come to terms with our deep
ignorance about ourselves and everything that matters to us. The desire for
the company of kindred souls, which Socrates calls neither good nor bad, is
especially problematic, even while it points us to enjoyments of a rich and
uniquely human sort. Human fellowship is sweet in itself, and no human life
can be wholly happy without it, however much Socrates' own life may attest
to the difficulty of its perfect attainment. Yet the joy that comes from the

company of kindred souls neither depends necessarily on the goodness of each friend nor pushes the friends to become better. The great comfort of feeling that one belongs to others, that they belong to oneself, and that one is loved for oneself just as one is tends rather to induce complacency. Pursuing the charms of such friendship can distract us from the task of thinking through what we need for true fulfillment, for these charms tend to mask altogether the neediness and the unhealthiness of our souls.[32]

If we saw our needs for what they were, we would perhaps bend our greatest efforts to becoming wise and would especially seek out companions who could help us in this search. This is why Socrates begins the dialogue by calling into question Lysis's comfortable confidence that the love of his parents is sufficient to make him happy, and he ends by encouraging in Lysis and especially Menexenus a new loyalty to himself, the philosopher, which threatens to supplant the boys' loyalty to their parents. Perhaps, then, even if a certain kind of friendship based on the kinship of good and wise souls is the only kind of friendship that is simply good in itself, Socrates refrains from calling friendships of kinship good because they are, at the outset, an obstacle to our highest good. For the pursuit of this highest good must begin precisely by *questioning* the goodness of what is one's own, the goodness of the reigning pieties of those among whom one is born, and the likelihood that simple fellowship with kindred souls can ever be the core of happiness, as bewitchingly desirable as it may seem.

By the end of the *Lysis,* then, Plato qualifies the argument of the earlier part of the dialogue, made most explicit at 215a6–c1, that the sole or at least an essential cause of all friendship is utility. So long as we remain needy and imperfect, the main root of any serious friendship for us will indeed be utility, as Bolotin argues, and this is more true the more we are aware of our mortality and ignorance. But the *Lysis* leaves room for two other types of friendships, based more on kinship than on utility.

The first is friendship based on kinship between ignorant and needy individuals who do not pursue the wisdom that they lack and do not acknowledge the significance of their neediness. In failing to face the truth of their condition, they imagine their love for one another to be wholly generous and unconditional. Yet almost invariably they still bring to friendship needs and expectations that are no less powerful for being poorly understood, and this state of affairs makes their friendship prone to misunderstandings and quarrels.[33]

The other alternative, which Socrates does not close off but does not investigate, would be a friendship based on kinship between those who have become relatively self-sufficient and wise, so that they could in a clear-sighted way cherish one another for what they are. What might the substance of such a friendship be? What role would love of the beautiful, about which the *Lysis* is so conspicuously silent, have in bringing and binding such friends together? And how, in terms of the analysis of the *Lysis,* are we to understand that form of the love of the beautiful that consists in a love of doing noble actions for the sake of friends? Plato leaves it to Aristotle to provide the most explicit discussion of these aspects of friendship, and to show what strength the mutual cherishing of two excellent souls might have, when shorn of the fervency that our defectiveness, acknowledged or unacknowledged, ordinarily brings to human love.

2

The Three Kinds of Friendship

When we return to Aristotle's discussion of friendship in Book 8 of the *Nicomachean Ethics* after examining the *Lysis*, we are able to see the ways in which Aristotle engages and responds to the arguments of the *Lysis*, at once silently conceding some of Socrates' central contentions and, at the same time, offering in Chapters 2 to 6 a sustained counterargument to Socrates' thesis about friendship and the good. Most prominent among Aristotle's tacit concessions is the fact that he nowhere attempts to argue that in friendship one can ever simply leave behind the concern with one's own good. To the contrary, Aristotle identifies the three sources of affection or types of objects that are loved or lovable (φιλητόν) as the good, the pleasant, and the useful, adding that the useful is loved only as a means to the good, and that the good that each man loves is not everything good but what is or what seems to him good for himself. Also striking is Aristotle's silence about the noble or beautiful as a fundamental and separate root of or inspiration for love.

Aristotle's account of the three objects of love differs in this important respect from his account of the three objects of choice in Book 2, which he lists as the noble, the beneficial, and the pleasant (1104b30–31). Is Aristotle here, in Book 8, subsuming both the noble and the beneficial under the good that we love, or is he identifying the good with the beneficial and suggesting that the noble as such is perhaps admirable and even choice-worthy but not truly lovable?[1] Aristotle underscores these doubts about the lovableness of the noble when he says at 1156b12–14 that the good are good for each other inasmuch as they are beneficial to each other. In analyzing friendships between good men, Aristotle will ultimately show that noble qualities do have a power to make the observer well disposed, but never will he attempt to argue that the noble alone is sufficient to bring love into being.

Indeed, his statement that the good we love is what appears to us good for ourselves would suggest that we love only what is beneficial; thus Aristotle

37

would seem to accept the Socratic thesis that love is rooted in need. But he introduces a potentially significant shade of difference in his analysis when he states that it is "the good" that is loved or lovable "simply," or without qualification, even if what each individual loves in fact is the good for himself (1155b23–25). This statement recalls Aristotle's analysis at 1113a25–33, in which he says that what is good simply is good for the good man, or judged good by him: Such a man is the standard of true virtue, true pleasantness, and so on.[2] Here also, at 1155b21–23, he suggests that what is simply pleasant is, like what is simply good, that which is perceived or experienced as such by a serious human being in a flourishing condition. This mention of the pleasant as a parallel case shows that Aristotle is not making any claim that the simply good is good in some absolute way, wholly apart from its being good or pleasant *for* something, if only for itself. For it would be absurd to speak of something as being intrinsically pleasant if it were not pleasant for anyone.[3]

Nevertheless, if a good man is the measure of goodness either as a beneficiary or as a judge of that goodness, this fact would seem to open the possibility of an objective appreciation of what is good, independent of its tendency to benefit oneself personally: The simply good would be that which a good man recognizes as good or potentially good *either* for himself or for another who is like himself. And if a man is most fully and truly lovable when he is both good for another and good and healthy in himself, may we not have here two reasons for love? Even if the first, the man's goodness for his friend, is necessary, it may not be exhaustive. The capacity to admire and delight in another's goodness for what it is may allow for a deeper and richer love than would otherwise exist. And if both causes can be at work simultaneously, then it is possible in some way and in some degree to have a true love of the other for his own sake, a love that is to that extent rooted not in weakness and deficiency but precisely in excellence and strength.

In pursuit of this possibility of loving another for his own sake, Aristotle continues in 8.2 to differentiate his position from that of Socrates. Refusing to become entangled in the bewildering web of paradoxes about reciprocity that Socrates throws about Menexenus, and refusing to follow the corrosive line of questioning that makes the real object of love something nonhuman, Aristotle insists firmly that friendship must be reciprocal. He thus remains true to our experience of friendly affection, which is never directed to an abstract good but always to another human being.

More importantly, in a passage that has distinct echoes of *Lysis* 212d5–8, Aristotle explicitly distinguishes friendship from other loves, especially loves for inanimate objects, with the argument that friendship must involve a wish for the good of the loved one as an end in itself: "It would be ridiculous, perhaps, to wish for the good of wine, but if one does at all, one wishes for it to be preserved, so that one may have it oneself. But it is said that one should wish for the good of a friend for his own sake" (1155b29–31).[4]

This unselfish disposition, for which the *Lysis* seems to leave no room, Aristotle terms goodwill. Here, then, is the paradox of friendship as Aristotle presents it: In seeking and choosing friends, we seek the good for ourselves, and apparently we only love another if and so long as he seems good for us; yet we are persuaded that we are not real friends unless we wish one another good apart from what is good for ourselves.

Aristotle concludes 8.2 with a preliminary definition. To be friends, men must feel reciprocal goodwill and wish the good for each other, with each other's knowledge, on the basis of one of the three lovable qualities he has enumerated (1156a3–5).[5] Now this definition contains within it several puzzles. First, how does the insistence on goodwill square with the insistence on reciprocity? In one sense it would seem obvious that friendship must be reciprocal, since we think of friendship as a sustained relationship between two people, but we also think that the essence of friendship is unselfish affection. Granted that such affection always involves a *desire* to be loved in return, why should it necessarily cease when it ceases to be returned? If genuine goodwill is possible at all, then it should be possible to befriend one who does not love us, or to remain a friend to one who has turned against us.

Second, how exactly is goodwill related to the affection that arises in response to the three lovable qualities? Does goodwill produce an attraction to and affection for another, or do desire and need for another produce goodwill? Or do both arise from something else? In particular, it is hard to see how the desires for pleasure and especially for what is useful for us can ever give rise to goodwill for others. Although all three types of love that Aristotle describes are grounded in a need or desire of the one who loves, only one – love based on the good – has the additional element of loving the other as good in himself, so that only here do we seem to have a clear basis for goodwill. Thus we must wonder in the third place whether we really have here three types of friendship based on three motives at all, or whether there is not just a single true type of friendship based on goodness and two shadows or impostors of it.[6]

Friendships of Utility

Indeed, as Aristotle proceeds in 8.3–8.6 to delineate the three forms of friendship based on utility, pleasure, and excellence, it becomes clear that he considers the first two to be friendship in only a truncated sense. That which rests on utility is clearly the furthest from perfect friendship. In such friendships, Aristotle says, each loves the other person only incidentally, or rather, he does not precisely love the other person at all but only his own good (1156a10–19, 1157a15–16; cf. 1159b19–21, 1167a15–21). But whereas Socrates treats this type of relation as paradigmatic of friendship and as most clearly revealing its deepest roots, Aristotle treats it as seriously defective and as friendship "only incidentally" and not in the fullest sense (1156a16–17).

Friendships of utility are commonly found between opposites, Aristotle says, such as the pairing of rich and poor, or ignorant and learned – or perhaps we should say rich ignorant and poor learned, since each must find in the other something that he needs (1159b12–24). They are also found between those who have similar things to offer at different times, as do guest and host in traditional Greek guest-friendships (1156a30–31),[7] and in general between allies. Aristotle suggests repeatedly that friendships of utility are most characteristic of old, crabbed men, who are incapable of giving anyone pleasure and narrowly intent on gain. The overwhelming impression he gives is that friendships of utility turn upon the desire for external goods or goods of fortune, but his mention of the learned and the ignorant at 1159b13–14 suggests that associations entered into for the sake of any benefit are properly classed as friendships of utility.[8]

Because such friends seek each other out for reasons only loosely related to their characters, because what each person will find useful varies at various times, and because one cannot count upon being able to be useful to another at the time when one needs something from him, friendships of utility are especially subject to disappointments, complaints, and ruptures. Even at their best they are attenuated, since there is no particular reason that those who find each other useful will also enjoy each other's company, whereas Aristotle will say that nothing characterizes friendship so much as spending one's days together (1157b19).

Friendships of Pleasure

Friendships of pleasure, by contrast, are much closer to the best form of friendship. Aristotle says that they are characteristic of the young, who live by their emotions and whose desires change rapidly. Like the desires that spawn them, such friendships are transient, but as long as they last they are warm and heartfelt, and the friends do cherish one another's company (1156a31–b6). In part simply because pleasures are increased while being shared, whereas useful goods are in general decreased, friendships of pleasure seem more generous and suited to free men than are friendships that consist in exchanges of goods and services (1158a18–21). More importantly, friendships of pleasure are sought for their own sakes. Every friendship of utility would become superfluous if the partners had direct access to the goods that they seek through it, but the sharing of pleasures gives life a sweetness that can be attained no other way. In enjoying one another's companionship for its own sake, then, friends of pleasure come closer than friends of utility to loving one another for their own sakes: The presence of the friend is cherished as an end in itself, even if the friend's complete good is not actively sought as an end in itself.[9]

Among friendships of pleasure, Aristotle classes attachments of erotic love. In keeping with his customary denigration of eros and his elevation of sober, gentlemanly virtue, Aristotle here portrays eros as based only on emotion and impulse and the pleasures of the senses, in contrast to the finest friendships, which rest on virtue and rational choice. He also criticizes love affairs on the grounds that they always consist somehow in the attraction of opposites, whereas he says the best friendships involve partners who are virtuous and equal and who give and receive from each other something identical or similar (1156b7–8, 33–35). Why is the friendship of opposites necessarily low, and why do the best friendships not rest on complementarity, rather than sameness? The problem seems to be that opposites tend to attract for reasons that are ephemeral, like the bloom of youth, or that are utilitarian, like the mutual usefulness of man and woman (cf. *EE* 1239b23–29). Aristotle does not present eros, as Aristophanes does in Plato's *Symposium,* as "finding one's missing half" – one who in a lasting way complements and completes what is lacking in one's soul. Virtuous people, he teaches, can be whole in themselves, and it is those who have such wholeness who can be the best friends. Therefore, he says, in the best case erotic love grows into a friendship between mature men who are similar and virtuous and love each other for their characters (1157a10–12).[10]

This analysis calls to mind another speech in the *Symposium,* Pausanias's encomium to eros, which turns out to be an attempt to defend his own pederasty. If, as Pausanias presents it, the erotic love of man for boy is nothing more than an exchange of pleasure for education, which in the best case ends in an equal friendship, it is indeed a somewhat sordid thing, especially on the man's side, and wholly inferior to the mature and essentially unerotic partnership it ends in. But in characterizing erotic love as such an exchange or as mutual indulgence in pleasure, Aristotle does insufficient justice to the uniquely human erotic longings of the soul that the speeches of Aristophanes and Socrates in Plato's *Symposium* both evoke so powerfully. Aristophanes portrays comically but vividly the longing for another who can be wholly and completely one's own and to whom one can belong without reservation, a longing that Aristotle recognizes but that he insists on subordinating to the nobler concern for virtue. Socrates and Diotima, on the other hand, give voice to the highest yearnings of the soul, the erotic yearning for great noble deeds and for an object worthy of devotion – yearnings that are rooted in our mortality and that can draw the soul upward to the purest love of wisdom.

Socrates' emphasis on the highest aspect of eros and Aristotle's apparent neglect of it may be traced to the differences in their purposes and primary audiences. Whereas Plato's *Symposium* may be characterized as addressed mainly to those, especially among the young, who may hope to find in a life of philosophy an answer to their deepest longings for happiness, Aristotle's

Nicomachean Ethics is explicitly addressed to the mature men who are the pillars of the community, including the fathers of youths who may be drawn to follow Socrates' lead, men who are not philosophic but whom Aristotle seeks to make well disposed to philosophy. For such men, friendship is indeed simply superior to erotic love.

After speaking slightingly of eros at 1156b1–3 and again at 1157a6–10, however, Aristotle introduces it a third time, and now instead of criticizing it, he brings out two crucial similarities between eros and the highest form of friendship: the importance for both of sharing one's days and one's pleasures with another, and the exclusivity of both (1158a10–15). This passage occurs in a chapter in which Aristotle elevates pleasure and shows it to be much more central to the best friendships than it at first appeared. If delight in the continual company of the other is of the essence of friendship, if the rareness of virtue and the limits of human time and energy make the friendships of the best men necessarily exclusive, and if our longing for friendship is indeed best satisfied not by many casual friendships but by a few or even one intimate one, then true friendship does bear an important resemblance to eros in its exclusivity.

Indeed, we may well wonder whether eros and friendship, in their best and fullest manifestations, might not converge, so that the strongest friendship would be confined to two and would even itself be erotic. If friendship at its deepest involves the fullest baring of one's soul and the greatest sharing of one's pleasures, it seems natural that such a friendship might well become erotic, as Montaigne's love for La Boétie perhaps became, and as many of the celebrated friendships of antiquity were thought to be.[11] Would it not even be felt to be a certain limitation upon the greatest friendships if any important longings for intimacy remained that could only be satisfied outside of them? Aristotle says that eros is like an extreme, suggesting that it involves extreme or excessive feelings of admiration, longing, devotion, and possessiveness.[12] But perhaps the very deepest form of erotic friendship, being friendship first and eros only secondarily, as Montaigne seems to present his friendship as being, might be an extreme not in the sense of an excess but in the sense of a peak or perfect completion, just as the virtues, though means in one sense, are extremes or peaks in another sense (1107a6–8, 1123b13–15).

But even if some of the greatest friendships have also been sexual, it is not clear that friendship at its deepest and most complete, and erotic love at its fullest and deepest, truly converge. It may be that the very best friendships are open to being erotic only in a limited sense, or even that the best friendships are only possible for those upon whom erotic longings have largely lost their maddening grip. The question of the relationship of friendship to eros is closely connected to the question of why and to what extent each is exclusive. Sexual love is of course exclusive in part simply because nature has made us pairing creatures. But even the most intense of heterosexual love affairs, such as that portrayed in Shakespeare's *Anthony and Cleopatra,* are exclusive for reasons other than biological ones. Eros perhaps inevitably involves extreme and hence irrational feelings both of admiration and of neediness. In intense love affairs there is a profound sense of vulnerability in the face of the other and incompleteness without the other that make the existence of all rivals intolerable. And as we have seen, Aristotle does not consider such neediness to be characteristic of the virtuous men who form the best friendships.

Even more importantly, eros involves intense devotion to the other person, and perfect devotion to more than one is unthinkable. The greatest love stories are stories in which this devotion is so complete that one or both lovers die for their beloveds, as Romeo and Juliet do. When in Book 9 Aristotle takes up the issue of devotion to and sacrifice for friends, he will show how much his own perspective differs from that of the heroic lover, and how much his conception of a truly wise and excellent friendship thus differs from full-blown erotic love. This analysis of devotion and sacrifice in friendship will pave the way for his final word on the right number of friends in 9.10, a statement that will indeed show a crucial difference between mature friendship and eros, precisely on this point of exclusivity.

Perfect Friendship

How precisely does friendship based on the good differ from the two defective forms that rest on utility and pleasure? If we take with utmost seriousness Aristotle's assertion that each person loves what is or seems best for himself, we will most likely understand friendships of pleasure to revolve around the pleasures of the body, friendships of utility to turn upon material advantage, and friendships of the good to provide the highest benefits to both partners, supporting them above all in moral virtue and in learning. This would mean, however, that friendships based on the good are essentially just friendships of utility with a higher good as the end.[13] If, on the other hand, we take with utmost seriousness Aristotle's statement that the perfect friend loves and seeks to benefit his friend for the friend's own sake, we should perhaps view friendships of pleasure and utility as including all those formed for the sake of all pleasures and benefits, high and low, and virtuous friendships as fundamentally different. And this difference is underscored by Aristotle's way of defining the higher class of friendship not by the good pursued but by the character of the friends. Thus we have friendship "for the sake of the useful," friendship "for the sake of pleasure," but friendship "of the good."[14] In this best form of friendship, Aristotle says that the partners love each other for themselves, cherishing each other for their characters and not for some incidental benefit that they provide each other.[15] Does such affection constitute an exception to Aristotle's assertion that men love what is good for themselves?

The picture is complicated by the fact that Aristotle asserts both that the good are good in themselves and also that they are good, pleasant, and useful to one another, and he never explicitly discusses the relation between these two sources of their friendship. The impression that he gives is that the friends' ability to benefit one another is a necessary aspect of their friendship and yet somehow is not at all the core of it. Of course, good men are quite likely to be good for one another. But what would happen if a man who was good in himself turned out *not* to be good for his friend? Would the friendship of two virtuous men persist if they were leaders of countries or parties that became enemies? Presumably not, even though their underlying goodwill for each other might remain. But then, is it not a little absurd to say that a good man loves his good friend truly for his own sake, for what he is in himself... and yet only if the friend also happens to be good for him?[16] Or is there such an intrinsic connection between the friend's being good in himself and his being good for his friend that somehow his very goodness (and not any separable benefit accruing from this goodness) *constitutes* his being good for his friend?

In 8.3 Aristotle develops the idea that partners in a perfect friendship, being good men, are naturally both beneficial and pleasant to each other (1156b13–17). Although he does not make clear how one's good character in and of itself can be beneficial to one's friend, he does explain why the goodness of each friend is naturally pleasant to the other. A strong and healthy soul takes a natural delight in contemplating other strong and healthy souls in action, both because they are beautiful and because they are akin. Perhaps, then, Aristotle is hinting at the intriguing possibility that it is through our openness to pleasure and not in our need for what is good that we come closest to cherishing another simply for what he is in himself. Or perhaps he means that the good are pleasant and good for one another in fundamentally the same way, insofar as what is good and what is pleasant should converge for the best human beings.[17] In particular, perhaps the contemplation of excellence is not merely pleasant but is an essential component of happiness. Could it be that this appreciation is the very core of good men's love for one another, and that the happiness it gives them is great enough to produce friendship wherever they meet, without the need for any further benefits to cement the friendship, so long as no serious conflict of interests arises to thwart it?[18]

In support of this possibility is Aristotle's discussion in 9.5, in which he suggests that the apprehension of excellence in another is not merely a source of pleasure but *the* root of goodwill. He describes goodwill as arising in response to virtue or excellence of various sorts, including beauty, generosity, and moral goodness altogether, and says that pleasure and utility are not sources of goodwill at all (1167a10–21). If we admire a being and consider it possible for that being to fare well or badly, it seems natural, even inevitable, that we should wish it well. Other factors, such as envy or a conflict of interest, may outweigh or obscure this goodwill, but to the extent that one admires a living being, it is impossible not to feel some degree of goodwill for it also.

But what is the precise relationship between goodwill and friendship? Aristotle stresses in 9.5 that goodwill does not alone constitute friendship but only creates a passive wish for another's welfare. It can emerge suddenly and wane just as quickly. Goodwill does not even constitute friendly affection, Aristotle says, since it lacks both intensity and desire (1166b30–34). But he does suggest in the same chapter that perhaps a goodwill that is grounded in a true apprehension of another's fine character needs only time and familiarity to blossom into heartfelt, active friendship. May it be that through man's natural sociability, a healthy, flourishing soul will come to cherish other good souls whenever it comes to know them well, and having once come to know them, will naturally feel a lively desire for their presence and concern for their welfare? May it be that delight in the goodness and presence of another excellent human being is the essence of genuine friendship, and that insofar as any friendship involves the pursuit of other pleasures and benefits, this pursuit is in fact self-regarding, neither arising from nor productive of goodwill, and as such wholly incidental and extraneous to the pure bond of true friendship?

Goodwill in the Lesser Friendships

If Aristotle's true teaching is that the two lesser forms of friendship resemble complete friendship only superficially and have no part in the goodwill that true friendship turns upon, it becomes puzzling why he continues to call the lesser forms friendships at all. He does speak at times as if friendships of utility, in particular, do not deserve the name of friendship. At 1157a14–16 he says that those whose friendship is based on utility do not love or are not the friends of one another, but only of their own advantage. But as soon as he has said this he in a sense takes it back, for he again calls associations of utility friendships at 1157a16–19. Aristotle finally resolves the matter by saying that friendships of pleasure and utility are friendships by analogy only (1157a25–32). Why does he waffle on this point and pull back from saying unambiguously that only a union of virtuous men who love one another for their characters is friendship at all?

One reason for Aristotle's continued inclusion of associations of pleasure and utility in the class of friendships is, as he says himself in this passage, his reluctance to break radically with common Greek usage and with the commonsense understanding of the phenomena (1157a26–32).[19] Behind this, perhaps, is a reluctance to be so harsh to the vast majority of mankind as to assert that they are simply incapable of friendship, since most people fall short of true virtue according to Aristotle, and most friendships are really only associations of utility (*EE* 1236a33–37). But this unwillingness to give offence cannot be the chief reason for Aristotle's classification. He does not scruple elsewhere to express contempt for the common run of people (e.g. 1095b19–22), and the morally serious readers to whom he addresses his book will at least believe their friendships to be of the finest type, even if they deceive themselves. Instead, it seems that, for a variety of reasons, friendships of pleasure and utility are to a much greater extent real friendships, and they are in much more important respects similar to the best friendships than the more noble-minded parts of Aristotle's presentation tend to suggest.[20]

Despite Aristotle's statement at 1167a10–14 that pleasure and utility are not sources of goodwill, Aristotle also says at 1156a7–10 that people in friendships of pleasure and utility do feel goodwill for one another "in respect of that for which they love" (ταύτῃ ᾗ φιλοῦσιν). John Burnet explains this obscure formulation as meaning that friends of pleasure wish one another to remain pleasant and friends of utility wish one another to retain their useful qualities, so that they may continue to enjoy what brought them together.[21] But surely this is not goodwill in any sense, any more than caring about the temperature of one's wine cellar is a reflection of goodwill toward one's wine. Aristotle's attribution of goodwill to these friends suggests something more, which accords with other passages in the *Ethics* and is confirmed by our own observations of the phenomena: Somehow there is an element of true goodwill in every friendship that turns upon pleasure, and even in the alliances and business partnerships that the Greeks would count as friendships but we would not.[22] Aristotle maintains, moreover, that there is in these relations a certain kind of affection. To be sure, he says that such friends love one another not for what they are in themselves but for the pleasure or good that arises from them (1156a8–19).[23] But at least in the case of pleasure-friendships, this is perhaps not quite the same as to say that they love *not* the other person but *only* their own pleasure, and regard the other person merely as a container or vehicle for it. In some way these friends do care for each other. As Aristotle stresses, however, the affection is based on an accident, resting on something that is incidental to their characters, and as such is shallow and transitory.[24]

The presence of some degree of genuine goodwill and affection is most evident, and most evidently necessary, in friendships of pleasure. The goodwill of pleasure-friends does not normally extend to wishing one another to become courageous, wise, or even rich, but they do genuinely like and wish to give pleasure to one another. After all, it is not possible for drinking buddies to have much fun together unless they like one another: Enjoying one another's wit, good spirits, whimsy, and so on is no small part of their fun. And when they do like one another, they endeavor to please and amuse one another partly out of affection and not simply as a means to their own enjoyment. The most pleasant companions are always warm as well as amusing; their affection is not for partying in the abstract but for the particular people they call their friends.

In friendships of utility the element of affection is much less important, though it is often present. Even colleagues and business associates who would never go out of their way to see each other usually feel, if they are working well together, a mutual friendly regard that goes beyond the selfish pleasure of knowing that the other is serving one's purposes. They are glad to see each other after a period of absence and glad to hear that the other is doing well, quite apart from anything they expect to gain. Their friendly regard does not in any sense drive the relationship, yet it is more than peripheral and often contributes enormously to its smooth functioning. And if a friendly sort of liking is common and helpful in associations of utility, Aristotle suggests that at least a minimal degree of goodwill is essential. Even the most perfunctory associations of buyers and sellers in the marketplace, which Aristotle classes as a type of friendship (1162b25–28), are impossible without a basis of trust that the goods sold and the money paid will be as they seem to be, not shams and counterfeits, and that each party will allow the other to enjoy what he has gotten in security and peace. The necessity of this foundation of trust is easy to lose sight of in a settled society, but we see it in the way aliens who have hitherto been hostile or unknown to one another must first persuade one another of their peacefulness of purpose and goodwill before they can become partners in trade. Perhaps the most transient associations of utility require only an absence of malice and not true goodwill, but the more extensive associations of fellow citizens, which Aristotle characterizes as predominantly utilitarian friendships (*EE* 1242a7–9, b22–27) do require goodwill: Aristotle indicates the importance of goodwill for utilitarian friendships when he says that "friendship seems to hold the polis together, and lawgivers give more serious attention to it than to justice" (*NE* 1155a22–24).[25]

But if we are right that Aristotle asserts the presence of genuine goodwill in friendships of pleasure and utility, it cannot be denied that he most conspicuously fails to account for it. No degree of desire for pleasure or assistance, and no degree of calculation about how one must behave in order to secure these things, can make one truly wish for the good of one's fellows in and of itself: Aristotle seems absolutely serious when he says that pleasure and utility are not the basis of goodwill (1167a10–14). Thus, in his definition of friendship as mutual goodwill, mutually known, there is a missing element that has yet to be supplied.

The Animating Concerns of Perfect Friendship

Leaving us for the time being with this unanswered puzzle, Aristotle begins at 1156b7 to flesh out his portrait of perfect friendship. As he does so, he reveals the driving concerns that fuel these friendships. Rather than beginning with such things as a patient's need for a doctor and asserting, in a way that carries little conviction to the heart, that this sort of need is the root of all friendship, Aristotle begins by taking the friendships of virtuous men on their own terms. It is precisely through seeing what virtuous men cherish in one another and in their friendships with one another that we begin to see why simple appreciation of the other for what he is is not the main substance of perfect friendship. In the process, we will understand better what the true common ground is between these friendships and the lesser types, and how this common ground explains the presence of goodwill in the latter.

As Aristotle describes the basis for the mutual goodwill and affection of good men and the superiority of their friendships to those of others, he introduces several new themes. He speaks repeatedly of the similarity that exists between good men, the durability of their friendships, the importance of trust, the time and familiarity that are needed to build this trust between them, and the steadfast refusal of both friends to listen to slander about the other once they have tested each other's characters for themselves (1156b7–32, 57a20–24). In particular, similarity between the friends now turns out to be not only characteristic of the best friendships, and most complete there, but in some way essential for every friendship:

Every friendship exists on the basis of the good or on the basis of pleasure, either simply or for the one who loves, and according to a certain similarity (ὁμοιότητα). For in this friendship will arise all of the above-mentioned things, and the friends will have them in themselves. For in this friendship the partners are similar (ὅμοιοι), and the other things – the simply good and the simply pleasant – are present, for these are what are most lovable. (1156b19–23; see also 1156b8, 14–17, 57b1–3)

Aristotle introduces this new criterion of friendship, similarity, so unobtrusively that some commentators bracket the lines in which it first appears as a criterion as mere repetitions.[26] Other editors and commentators, however, precisely because this new criterion seems to arise with so little warning out of nowhere, are troubled by its appearance and try to explain the words ὁμοιότητα in line 20 and ὅμοιοι in line 22 in other ways.[27] But if, as the *Lysis* seems to suggest and as Aristotle will show more fully, the attraction to those who are like us is a morally ambiguous basis of friendship, it makes rhetorical sense for Aristotle to minimize this element, suggesting with some exaggeration that virtue and virtue alone can provide the basis for satisfying friendships, and that similarity, insofar as it is important, works mainly to strengthen virtuous friendships and not the other kinds.[28] But if in fact every friendship rests much more fundamentally upon similarity than the surface of Aristotle's argument suggests, it follows that the higher and lower forms of friendship have more in common than they at first appear to have, and this is one important reason for Aristotle's refusal to exclude the lesser types from the category of friendship altogether.

But why is similarity so essential to friendship that Aristotle now says that every friendship depends upon it? I believe not only that a spontaneous liking for kindred souls is an essential ingredient in all human affection according to Aristotle, as these lines quietly indicate, but also that it provides the key to the unsolved puzzle of how goodwill comes to be present in friendships of pleasure and utility. In 9.5, as we have seen, Aristotle shows how the perception of excellence in another can produce goodwill, but he also points out how volatile and unreliable such goodwill can be, prompting us to reflect on what makes the difference between a momentary surge of goodwill and a steady concern for another's welfare. Time and familiarity, which he mentions there, are important, but they do not account for the whole difference between the transient goodwill one feels for another, such as an athlete, who seems in *some* way impressive, and the deep goodwill one feels for a close friend. In order to feel goodwill for a contestant at an athletic competition, a spectator not only must admire him but must sympathetically share his pleasure in the sport and his eagerness for victory. But in most such cases the concerns motivating the athlete are peripheral to the spectator, and hence the goodwill is very weak. When, on the other hand, one observes another who seems good and whose central concerns are just the same as one's own, the possibility of a powerful and sustained feeling of goodwill is much greater. These elements of resemblance and shared goals are indeed the themes of the chapter immediately before 9.5 and evidently are intended to provide a crucial supplement to what Aristotle says there about goodwill. Thus Aristotle would seem to agree with Socrates that the affection that is not directed beyond another human being to something else necessarily involves the recognition of the other as in some way a kindred soul.

At the same time, Aristotle's insistence on the connection between virtue and goodwill suggests that, if affection and goodwill for those who are good depend on some degree of similarity, affection and goodwill for those who are similar may also depend, in some minimal sense, on the attribution of goodness to them. When one has goodwill for lost strangers, babies, or kittens, one does not attribute moral virtue or any sort of excellence to them, but one does view them as beings that are at least innocent or not deserving of evil; one views them as ordered beings, with natural and healthy desires for good things, capable of a happiness that need harm no one. In contrast, a being with an existence we cannot think of as good, be it a virus, a cancer, or a brutal tyrant, cannot possibly evoke goodwill.[29]

In 9.6, Aristotle will shed further light on the way in which sympathetic goodwill can arise between people. There, he discusses concord, the friendly harmony of goals and efforts that exist when people agree about what is good and work together to attain it. Concord is important as a bridge between passive goodwill and active friendship, inasmuch as shared efforts can strengthen people's concern for each other. This sympathetic concern, which depends in only the most minimal way on the attribution of goodness to the other, is the true root of goodwill in friendships of pleasure and utility, and because it is critical to the goodwill of virtuous friendships as well, both similarity and goodwill arising from similarity turn out to be significant shared roots of all three types of friendship.

However, the goodwill that arises in such friendships, if true and generous, is also weak and unreliable, and not in itself a sufficient motive for continued exertions on the other's behalf when the benefits for which the friendship was formed cease to flow. The shallowness of this goodwill is a result of the shallowness of the virtue of the two friends. Each meets the other with only a small part of his soul, or with a part that other parts cannot help despising; each finds in the other little that he can truly cherish, and few deep, abiding concerns into which he can enter sympathetically.[30] When his wishes change, as wishes are bound to do that are not grounded in a deep knowledge of oneself and an appreciation for what is naturally, permanently good and pleasant, his friendships change also. Therefore, there is nearly always some degree of confusion or mutual self-deception in friendships of pleasure and utility. Each partner acts generously and believes his and his friend's generosity to be based on goodwill, yet in fact each troubles himself about the other only so long as the time he invests brings a good return in pleasure or other benefits.

Still, if we may for a moment be irreverent toward friendships of virtue, we may ask whether even they are so abiding primarily because each man's goodwill is so strong or, rather, because each is able to please and benefit the other in abiding ways. Is goodwill the engine that propels friendships of virtue, or are they, like other friendships, fundamentally driven by pleasures and benefits, and are ruptures and disappointments less common in them mainly because each man's need for the other is less changeable? Aristotle, of course, does not directly answer this question. But his very stress on permanence and trust as elements that distinguish virtuous friendship must give us pause: Why is it, we may ask, that virtuous men care so deeply about having friends who will stand loyally beside them and turn a deaf ear to slander (1156b11–12, 25–29, 1157a20–24)? With the introduction in 8.4 of the concerns for durability, trust, and similarity in the best friendships, Aristotle indicates some of the reasons why simple delight in the goodness of another person, however important it may be, is never enough by itself to establish a full-fledged friendship. If it were, we would expect good men to have little concern with reciprocity, to cherish most the best people they know of, whether alive or dead, and to enjoy friends much as a connoisseur enjoys good paintings or concertos, returning to the best ones again and again, but fundamentally promiscuous in the search for excellence. The desire everyone has to find in another a kindred spirit and a steadfast, loyal partner suggests that the real heart of friendship lies less in contemplation or admiration than in an active exchange of pleasures and benefits, in an intimate sharing of activities, and in the perhaps vague confidence that the other will somehow always be there for one when one needs him.

By continuing to treat friendships of pleasure and utility as real friendships, Aristotle highlights the importance of pleasure and utility in all friendships, including the very highest.

The Utility of Perfect Friendship: Aristotle and Bacon

Although Aristotle says that the best friends are useful to one another both as benefactors and as allies in good deeds, he is relatively silent on the specific benefits they bring one another. Thus it may be helpful at this point to turn briefly to another author, Francis Bacon, who makes a strong case for the centrality of utility or (what is not quite the same thing) of mutual benefits in all serious friendships. In his charming essay "Of Friendship," Bacon describes three great benefits or "fruits" of friendship, which go far beyond the low-level utility of friendships of profit or convenience. First, friends are necessary to the health of the soul. In opening one's heart to a friend, one finds an alleviation of sorrows and a magnification of joys. Second, friends help one to judge and act wisely. In conversation with a friend, one can sort out one's own thoughts better than one can in solitude, and one can receive the good counsel of another who combines the perspective of an outsider with the goodwill and tact of a friend. And third, friends can act on one another's behalves in ways that they cannot act for themselves, bringing one another honor, pleading one another's causes, and bringing to completion projects and purposes that are cut short by death.[31]

In all of these ways we may say that friends are useful to each other, and yet their capacity to benefit each other depends on their being more than friends of utility or convenience. Even a friendship whose only goal is profit requires a minimal amount of goodwill and fairness to function, but the richer benefits Bacon speaks of require genuine affection. Opening one's heart to another can lighten sorrows and magnify joys only if the other is a friend who fully shares them. Only the counsel of a true friend is trustworthy: "It is a rare thing, except it be from a perfect and entire friend, to have counsel given, but such as shall be bowed and crooked to some ends which he hath that giveth it."[32] No rebukes are more bearable and more likely to be heeded than those that are prompted by love. And nothing but confidence in a friend's selfless goodwill would give hope of his faithfulness after death. But Bacon indicates a still deeper respect in which friendship is beneficial: "A crowd is not company; and faces are but a gallery of pictures; and talk but a tinkling cymbal," he says, "where there is no love."[33] Friendship is beneficial because no one who is truly human wishes to live life alone, and because the only companionship that satisfies the heart is the companionship of love. Even if the benefits of friendship could somehow come to us from a stranger or a machine, they would not be as desirable, because we cherish the affection behind the benefits as well as, perhaps as much as, the benefits themselves.[34]

There is, however, a darker side to Bacon's presentation of friendship.[35] The need people have for companions to whom they can unburden their hearts is so strong, Bacon says, that it causes many to trust others to their own detriment. He gives examples of rulers, even shrewd and ruthless ones, who have brought danger or ruin upon themselves by trusting friends. His essay gives eloquent testimony to the human need to have a friend, but it does not explain what, in human nature, disposes one to be a friend. Whereas, in the essay "Of Friendship," Bacon suggests without explanation that selfless devotion is possible, in the short essay "Of Followers and Friends," he denies that any friendship is possible that does not rest on self-interest: "There is little friendship in the world, and least of all between equals, which was wont to be magnified. That that is, is between superior and inferior, whose fortunes may comprehend the one the other."[36] Thus Bacon suggests that the human soul, far from pointing to a natural, happy ordering of activities and ends, is fundamentally incoherent in its impulses and longings, chaotic in its sociability, and ill suited to find happiness in friendship. If Bacon's view is not ultimately tragic, it is because he sees such sufficient flexibility in human nature that it is possible to attain a substantial degree of happiness by turning one's attention in different, more acquisitive, or otherwise self-interested directions. Yet still he hints that a longing for friendship may remain in our hearts that simply cannot be met in the way that we would wish.

Aristotle presents no such disproportion in the elements of our souls. Does he think that human beings are truly more selfless or more deeply social in a way that does not amount to selflessness? Does his more sanguine portrayal of the possibility of friendship between virtuous equals ultimately depend on the much greater weight that he gives to contemplation as a focus of excellence and a truly shareable source of happiness? Or does Aristotle believe that the healthiest human beings have no such great need for friendship as Bacon claims? All of this remains to be seen.

Pleasure in Perfect Friendship

Aristotle's presentation of friendships of utility as base and vulgar and his reticence in discussing the role of utility in perfect friendship are traceable, in large part, to his rhetorical strategy of distancing himself from the *Lysis*'s teaching that deficiency is the chief root of friendship and its goodness, and of emphasizing instead the ways in which friendship can grow out of virtue and strength. But this denigration of utility is more than rhetoric. Aristotle's deeper point is that however much mutual assistance may support and intensify friendship, friendship's core cannot lie here, but must lie instead in an uncalculating sociability and desire for companionship, without which no friendship could exist. And to the extent that friendship grows out of a desire for companionship as such, it is essential that it be pleasant companionship. In 8.5 and 8.6, Aristotle proceeds to show just how central pleasure is to friendship in general and to the noblest friendships in particular, thus providing a further reason for his refusal to reject the lesser forms of friendship as spurious.[37]

Aristotle describes friendships of pleasure as characteristic especially of the young, whereas old people are inclined mostly to those of utility or are not given to friendship at all (1156a24–27, 31–33, 57b13–16). These comments recall his suggestion at 1155a12–15 that the concerns that bring old people to friendship are chiefly the desires for care and help, whereas those in their prime seek allies and companions in noble actions. Taken together, however, Aristotle's association of the different types of friendship with different stages of life casts a certain shadow over friendships of virtue. Why would a virtuous man not continue throughout his life to cherish other virtuous men more than anyone else, maintaining friendships with those he has known and forming new friendships with those whom he meets? Does a virtuous character decay together with the vigor and strength that give it success in great enterprises?[38] Why should a man who is capable of rising above the selfish concern with money, security, and life itself in his prime become preoccupied with these things in old age? To the extent that this happens, and the interest in virtue and in virtuous friendship wanes, we must suspect that there was something defective in the man's dedication to virtue all along, and that it always rested on a false sense of invulnerability and a self-deception about the depth of one's desire for security. But if much of the apparent virtue and many of the apparently virtuous friendships that we see around us are vulnerable in this way to the harsh, clear light of old age, surely true virtue is not so vulnerable but rests on a deep self-understanding that cannot be shaken.

Nonetheless, Aristotle suggests strongly that even the most virtuous men tend to lose their capacity for friendship in old age because of the simple decline in their capacity to give and enjoy pleasure (1157b13–16, 58a1–6).[39] Aristotle now gives a powerful statement of the importance of pleasure and ties it to what is fundamental in our nature: "Most of all nature appears to flee what is painful and to aim at what is pleasant." No one can pass his days with someone who is unpleasant to him, but "nothing characterizes friends so much as living together" (1157b16–17 and 19).[40] When he returns to the theme of pleasure in friendship at 1158a23–25, he makes this point even more forcefully: "No one could continually endure the good itself, if that were painful to him." But having opened up a potentially critical gap between virtue and pleasure, Aristotle hastens to close it at 1157b25–28, reminding us that the simply good is also supposed to be simply pleasant, or naturally and invariably pleasant for a good man, so that presumably everyone who is good will also be pleasant to everyone else who is good. Perhaps a person of absolutely perfect virtue (if such a man has ever existed) would necessarily be pleasant to other virtuous men, but Aristotle's repeated references to the old remind us that even unusually virtuous men can still be prickly, vain, cranky, and infirm in all sorts of ways that make their company unpleasant and keep them apart. The problem is that even if the good as such is always pleasant, it is not necessarily pleasant in proportion to its goodness. The pinnacles of moral virtue are justice and greatness of soul, the latter of which involves a kind of austere pride and self-sufficiency, but it is the lower virtues of generosity, sociability, and wit that most conduce to one's being a delightful friend.[41]

Aristotle's discussion of friendship in the *Rhetoric* brings out this problem even more vividly. The people we find it most pleasant to spend our days with, he says there, are those who are good-tempered and accommodating and who tell good jokes. Moreover, they make us feel good about ourselves by laughing at our jokes, refraining from criticizing our faults, praising our virtues, especially the ones we are afraid we lack, and in general knowing "good things, not bad things, about their neighbors and about ourselves." They are also the ones who put us at ease by admitting their own faults and by not appearing to us too formidable (*Rhetoric* 1380b35–81b37). All of these pleasant traits reflect a certain virtue but also a certain willingness not to be overly exacting about virtue.

As a result, we see that friendship, even at its very best and purest, rests only partly on virtue, and also – perhaps equally, or perhaps even more – on pleasure and on a *pathos* of spontaneous affection that is only loosely connected to virtue. For this reason, we are not surprised when Aristotle acknowledges at 1157b5–7, almost in passing, that friendship is not one of the virtues. It is, to be sure, more than a transitory desire or enjoyment; it involves the choice and the settled disposition to do good to another and is fully realized only in active intercourse and benevolence (1157b5–12, 17–19): In these ways it is like a virtue.[42] Friendship also resembles the virtues inasmuch as they, too, involve pleasure and the emotions: A virtuous man is one who has been trained to take pleasure in the right things in the right way. But pleasure is far more central to friendship. Acts of virtue are chosen because they are noble, and we are always glad when we have done them, but friendship is not friendship unless we enjoy the prospect of the next meeting as much as the memory of the last and cherish our time together, whether it seems to us noble or not. Since friendship does not depend simply upon our good character and upon things we have in our power to choose, it cannot be commanded, in Aristotle's understanding.[43] According to Aristotle, we can expect a virtuous man to display the social virtue of *philia* toward all his associates, steering clear of both grouchiness and obsequiousness, and gracefully accommodating himself to the reasonable requests and wishes of others, but this virtue does not involve affection, which is the very soul of friendship (see *NE* 4.6).[44]

We are now in a position to see the ultimate inadequacy of Aristotle's first definition of friendship as mutual goodwill that is mutually known and that rests on one of the three lovable qualities. The main problem is not, as it seemed at first, that the lesser forms contained no basis for goodwill, but rather that, once we see the centrality of the desire for companionship and shared activity with a kindred soul that is the chief pleasure of friendship, it becomes evident that goodwill is only the beginning. It is the sharing of activities and indeed one's whole life that matters. In the absence of shared activity, goodwill tends to be passive and ineffective, but the more one shares and enjoys sharing one's life with another, the more the other then becomes one's own, and his good becomes a part of one's own good, in a generous and expansive and not a narrow, instrumental way (1157b31–36). It is then that passive goodwill blossoms into deep, habitual, and active affection. If we are right about the presence of goodwill in friendships of utility, then their decisive defect lies not in a lack of goodwill but in the limited capacity of the partners to take pleasure in each other. This conclusion is supported by Aristotle's characterization of the old men who seek what is useful as being unsuited to true friendship, not through a lack of goodwill but through an incapacity to enjoy spending their days together (1158a4–10).

Thus Aristotle shows that pleasure is not a bonus that comes incidentally out of the friendships of virtue but, instead, is absolutely fundamental to complete friendship. This being the case, it would be irrational to say that ordinary pleasure-friendships are only shadow-friendships, aiming at something that only resembles the goal of true friendship. Both friendships of pleasure and those of virtue truly aim at pleasure and truly achieve it, although the perfect friendship does this in a more stable and reliable way and brings other benefits in addition. But to the extent that the friends are or imagine themselves to be happy and fortunate, they will have no concern with any of the benefits that consist in useful services. Thus, Aristotle says, "those who are blessed (μακάριοι) have no need of useful people, but they do need pleasant ones" (1158a22). Aristotle criticizes these people who are blessed by good fortune with the remark that "they should perhaps seek friends who are good as well as pleasant, and also good for themselves" (1158a26).[45] But if they could only count upon their good fortune and their friendships to last, they might well find nothing missing in these friendships, and Aristotle would have little grounds on which to persuade them that theirs are inferior to the best kind. It is the durability of virtuous friendship that proves most decisively its superiority, in the eyes of ordinary people and even in the eyes of the virtuous, and this is the point that Aristotle emphasizes when he concludes his discussion of the three types of friendship at 1158b1–11.

In sum, Aristotle's analysis of complete or perfect friendship shows that it flourishes not chiefly in the admiration of virtue but in the sharing of activity, and that it expresses a powerful desire to share one's life with others and to make others one's own. It remains to be seen in what activities such companionship can flower most fully. More importantly, it remains to be seen whether, in our desire for satisfying shared activity, the most powerful desire is for the sharing as such or for the activity as such. In the next chapter, we will explore the possibility that the deepest longing of the human heart is for the simple communion of souls that occurs in true friendship, and that this communion can be so satisfying, so perfect, so noble and selfless, that it solves all the problems of the moral life and heals the divide between virtue and happiness.

3

Aristotle and Montaigne on Friendship as the Greatest Good

Aristotle's discussion of the different types of friendship has so far been confined to friendships between equals, and his analysis has shown many reasons why equality is important in friendship. To the extent that the friendship turns upon utility, it is of course essential that the friends have something of more or less equal value to offer. To the extent that it turns upon pleasure, they must have similar capacities to please, and since the greatest pleasure in friendship is the pleasure of companionship and shared activity with a kindred spirit who has similar aims and feelings and desires, equality and similarity contribute enormously to the pleasantness of friendships. And Aristotle has stressed repeatedly that the perfect friendship of virtue will be a friendship of equals, each fully worthy of the other's confidence, trust, and generous support.

In 8.7, Aristotle turns to friendships between unequals, such as father and son, elder and youth, husband and wife, or ruler and subject. Not only do these unequal friendships differ as a class from those discussed previously, but each of them also has its own peculiar character and problems, and indeed each contains within it, as it were, two different friendships. For Aristotle says the superior and inferior have different virtues and functions and different grounds for their affection (1158b17–19). Thus, he explains, the partners do not receive the same thing from each other and should not expect to receive it. But somehow the friendship must be made equal if it is to remain desirable on both sides, and the necessary "equalization" is achieved when the better and more useful partner receives more affection than he gives, in proportion to his superiority. This proportional affection is apparently like the honor a country owes it outstanding citizens and benefactors: Honor does not truly repay heroes for their sacrifices, but it is the best a country can give, and hence public benefactors must content themselves with it. Likewise, greater affection from the inferior friend "in a sense" equalizes the friendship, without really making his contribution to the friendship equal. No amount of affection can really repay one's parents for giving one life, but if they receive and content themselves with filial respect and devotion, the friendship will be lasting and equitable in a sense.

Because affection cannot truly make up for great disparities in wisdom, talent, or virtue, these unequal friendships are fundamentally distinct from other friendships in which things different in kind are exchanged. When a poor but charming and convivial man goes to dinner with his rich friend, and in exchange for an evening of engaging stories gets a free meal, there is no lingering sense of indebtedness on either side, although perhaps there is also no stable and solid friendship unless each perceives that, in ways deeper than stories and money, they are fundamentally equal and alike. But when one is continually falling into the debt of another in ways that he cannot repay except by fervent affection and gratitude, it becomes a question whether the superior will continue indefinitely to value the friendship enough to maintain it. Therefore, Aristotle says, although proportional equality or some sort of compensation according to merit can rectify an unequal relationship up to a point, in cases of great disparity the inferior cannot expect the superior to become or to remain his friend. This point is reached when the difference between two people becomes so great that their most important feelings and wishes and interests are no longer shareable.

Thus the greatest obstacle to friendship seems to be not so much inequality in the degree of benefits given, since a good parent gives benefits that can never be repaid, but a permanent inequality in the attributes of two people in any respect that the superior puts great store by, whether it be wealth, power, virtue, or anything else. The equalization effected by giving greater affection in response to greater merit can at best work only at the margins, to correct relatively small differences in merit between friends. As Aristotle says, whereas the proportional equality of rewards according to merit is the most important form of equality for justice, it is of less importance for friendship than is "arithmetic equality," or simple equality in the worth or position or acquirements of two individuals (1158b29–33). In a political community, even a democracy, people do not really expect their fellow citizens, much less their leaders, to be their equals in every important respect. The most important political task of the community is not to establish numerical equality among the people but, as Thomas Jefferson said, to ensure that those whom nature has endowed with virtue or talent can be drawn most effectively into positions of responsibility.[1]

Now if great differences in fortune or quality can prevent or destroy a friendship, this problem puts to the test the degree to which human beings can wish one another's good for one another's sake. A perfectly selfless love would wish that our friend might become immortal, all wise, and deficient in nothing, even though this change would spell the end of the friendship, but no one wishes that, Aristotle says (1159a5–12).[2] We want good for our friends as the beings that they are, which is to say, as human beings who are our friends and hence a good to us. And even then, Aristotle says, we do not wish them all the greatest goods, "for each man wishes for his own good most of all" (1159a12).[3]

With these bold statements about the primacy of our concern for our own good, Aristotle reveals his judgment as to the relative importance or rank of our friends' good, of our own good, and of that part of our own good that is friendship itself among the ends that human beings seek. Not only does he state plainly that we care for our own good more than for the good of our friends, but he also clearly implies that even our desire to possess friendships, understood as a good for us, is not our deepest concern. If it were, we would presumably cherish most the people most capable of love and never relinquish a friend, no matter how much inequality arose between us, whereas Aristotle says that when great disparities arise between people, "they are no longer friends, or even expect to be friends" (1158b33–35).

Now all of these conclusions, however boldly Aristotle has drawn them, can so far only be considered provisional. To substantiate his claim about the primacy of our concern with our own good, Aristotle will have to account for the examples of people who do make sacrifices for their friends, who no doubt wish that their friends' good and their own might converge, but who would be willing to set their friends on paths that would carry them out of their lives, if that were clearly best for the friends. To substantiate his implicit claim about the rank of friendship among the goods that human beings seek, Aristotle will also have to give an account of those cases in which superiors do show great dedication to those under their protection, without seeming to receive any equivalent return. Further support for these contentions will be very important to find, because there is something in virtually everyone – something serious and good – that resists Aristotle's suggestions that we all care most about our own good, and that love or friendship is not the most precious thing in life. Aristotle is aware of and acknowledges the force of this contrary position, and in the next chapter (8.8) he turns to the theme of the intrinsic goodness of affection, which in some way everyone recognizes. Aristotle thus questions the contention of the *Lysis* that affection is mainly a product of need and not one of life's great goods. Yet even as he does so, he indicates his agreement with Socrates that what we imagine to be a seriousness about friendship for its own sake is in large part fueled by desires for other things.

Most people prefer receiving affection to giving it, Aristotle says, because they love honor, and affection is similar to honor. Honor, in turn, is something people love not for itself but for other reasons. Thus most people desire especially to be honored by anyone in power (including the ruling majority, in a democracy) because this raises their hopes that they will get whatever they need. Such people would then prefer to receive than give affection because they hope for benefits from their friends. These are the common run of people, whose chief concern is neither excellence nor cultivating the most excellent form of friendship. A less vulgar form of the love of honor seeks honor not just from anyone or from the powerful, but from those who are good and wise and therefore qualified judges of merit: This nobler love of honor is driven not by a hope for favors but by the wish to possess virtue and have this possession confirmed. Perhaps noblest of all would be a sense of honor whose chief concern is not the approval of others at all but, rather, the good witness of one's own sovereign judgment. To the extent that high-minded men seek honor from others, Aristotle suggests that they love it because their own judgments of themselves are in need of support, not because they love it for its own sake.[4]

This analysis of the love of honor stands in striking and sobering contrast to Aristotle's statements about honor elsewhere in the *Ethics*. At the very outset he said that the common run of people aim only at pleasure and that it is only cultivated people who seek honor (1095b19–23; but cf. 95a20–24). Now, however, it seems that ordinary people love honor, too – especially from the powerful, to be sure, out of a hope for benefits, but also from anyone at all – for Aristotle says that ordinary people love flatterers, who are or pretend to be their inferiors and who often have nothing to offer but their feigned admiration and affection. Thus ordinary people, too, have some concern with excellence, but they are indiscriminate in their willingness to take confirmation of if from anyone at all. And just as the love of honor turns out not to be the exclusive preserve of cultivated gentlemen, so even a gentleman's concern with honor turns out to be no certain proof of a deeper concern with virtue, contrary to the suggestion of Book 1 (1095b26–30), since those most ambitious for honor may, in fact, only seek honor and power as means to wealth and pleasure. Even the great-souled man, who despises the opinion of the masses but does want honor from good men and indeed is "primarily concerned with honor and dishonor" (1124a4–11), now appears defective in lacking perfect self-confidence and self-knowledge. Indeed, we may question whether even the great-souled man's love of honor is as pure as Aristotle suggests, or whether Aristotle's account does not to some extent flatter him. If he only wants honor to be certain of his virtue, why is he persuaded that honor is his "due" (1124a7)? The fact that he considers himself entitled to it and takes it so seriously as to make it his primary concern, even though he also knows that honor is "nothing great," suggests that he is not quite sure that his own life of virtuous action makes sense on its own terms, and that it needs some further reward in order to be fully satisfactory to him.

The discussion of honor and affection in 8.8 thus amounts to a dramatic demotion of the love of honor. This presentation is an important prelude to Aristotle's discussion of politics and political friendship in the following chapters and will serve to heighten the puzzlement he will provoke there as to why rulers and other superiors love their inferiors, a question that will be fully answered only in Book 9.[5] We may well wonder, however, whether Aristotle's characterization of honor as utterly lacking inherent worth or desirability is not an exaggeration, perhaps made with a view to throwing the question of political men's motives into sharper relief. Is there not, after all, *something* inherently desirable about honor, even if in the end it is much less desirable than true affection or friendship, and certainly less desirable than the good things one is honored for?[6] Is it not perfectly natural for a beautiful person to enjoy the admiring eyes of people he or she will never meet again, for an athlete to enjoy not only victory (the surest proof of excellence) but the cheers of the crowd, and even for the very wisest men to write books that begin with such words as "Thucydides the Athenian wrote this," seeking to ensure not only that posterity would profit from his wisdom but also that future generations would never forget whose wisdom it was? Indeed, isn't it simply human to enjoy not only honor but even merely being seen when one is performing splendidly, just as it is displeasing to be seen in weakness, ugliness, and ineptitude? For the eyes of others seem to magnify our successes and failures, making them more real, and making us more real; this phenomenon is part of what it means to be social beings. Perhaps, indeed, the excellence of living beings altogether carries with it a directedness to being observed. For if excellence comprises what is beautiful as well as beneficial, then just as the beneficial comes into its own only when it benefits someone, so also perhaps nobility or beauty comes fully into its own only when it is admired.

Even if honor has some intrinsic worth for us, however, Aristotle certainly seems right to argue that affection is more truly desirable for its own sake, and thus affection promises to be a more eligible compensating factor in balancing unequal friendships than honor would be. If affection arises naturally as a response to what is useful and pleasant and especially what is good, this suggests that affection naturally will be greater on the side of the inferior or the greater beneficiary. If affection is good in itself to receive, then it may plausibly close the gap in unequal friendships and make them equally valuable to both parties. However, Aristotle's argument that it is the love of honor that makes men prefer receiving affection to giving it implies that the most clear-sighted person will not share this preference. In other words, if in a particular friendship he finds himself loved more than he loves, he will not count that as a point in favor of this friendship, or as an advantage that makes up for the fact that he gives more than he receives in other respects, or finds in this friend a less-than-perfect soul mate. A superior who was entirely satisfied with the equalization Aristotle has described would seem to show poor judgment.

Aristotle does not account for the motives of the inferior partner in an unequal friendship, but his comment that people like honor from those in power because it raises their hopes surely points to the most usual reason why people seek friendships with their superiors. Thus a friendship that was satisfactorily equalized in the way that Aristotle describes would be a defective one on both sides, uniting two people who are drawn together by the desire to be the passive recipient of good things, the superior hungry for honor or outright flattery and the inferior seeking assistance or power or gain.[7] Moreover, to the extent that the inferior is drawn to the superior out of a hope for benefits, his affection will be mercenary, if not altogether feigned. Thus we must wonder whether even the problematic equalization that Aristotle describes really works in practice.

In the best case, of course, the inferior will love the superior at least partly for his virtue, and the superior, without imagining that this affection truly balances the friendship, will simply accept it as the best that the inferior has to give. But why, precisely, is affection owed on the one side, and what is the motive for the superior partner's love on the other? Do we owe and give affection to virtuous people simply for their virtue? No one feels obligated to a stranger for his virtue. If someone we admire takes notice of us, we may feel grateful simply for that, and if he shows affection, we will certainly feel inclined to return the affection. But normally, people feel obligated only to those who benefit them, and perhaps then only to those who do so in a certain spirit, free of ostentatious display and mercenary calculation. A just person will try to return every favor if he can, but only favors prompted by goodwill and affection produce heartfelt affection and gratitude in return. But in these cases, the superiors are preeminent in precisely the active affection that is the mark and virtue of friendship. If the inferior party manages to equalize this friendship at all, it will be by repaying an active, effective love with a greater degree of passive or ineffective love. But we may well wonder whether, in the paradigmatic and most revealing example of unequal friendship, that of parent and child, the parents do not in fact care more as well as do more for their children, and this is precisely what Aristotle indicates at 1159a27–33 and even more explicitly at 1161b21–22. In the archetypical unequal friendship, then, there is no equalization.[8]

Perhaps in some unequal friendships, however, the superior party does not have the intense love of a parent and rather casually dispenses benefits that cost him little to give, while winning intense devotion from his beneficiary. This sort of friendship arises most often between an older and a younger person. When the mature Goethe befriended the young Eckermann, he provided him with valuable advice and introductions, but it was Eckermann who spent his days thinking of Goethe and writing down every word he could remember of their conversations. No doubt there have been at least a few marriages that fit this description – the traditional image of a marriage – in which the husband is both intrinsically superior and the greater benefactor, and the wife repays him with devotion and endless attention to his comfort. And in politics, we can at least imagine a leader ruling in the same spirit as Goethe entered into his friendship with Eckermann, with love for his country but no great need of it or of high office.

But what would give such a leader the motive to take the tremendous pains needed to rule well? Perhaps it would be a spirit of noblesse oblige and a desire to exercise and hone his own capacities by taking on fascinating challenges, rather as Robert Bork wished to serve on the Supreme Court because he thought it would be an "intellectual feast." But the Robert Borks of the world (at least if they are so frank) do not endear themselves to their countrymen. Leaders who are beloved give the impression of loving their country wholeheartedly and thinking ceaselessly of its welfare, with the fatherly affection of Washington or the warm compassion of Franklin D. Roosevelt, whereas those who are ruled usually devote less attention to the happiness of their rulers.[9] On the whole, then, we may doubt whether most unequal friendships are ever equalized by the greater devotion of the inferior party. Why these friendships are pursued by the superior remains for the time being a mystery.

The obvious answer to this question, which seems by now to be almost begging to be stated, is that it is rewarding to be a benefactor, and that loving is simply better than being loved, and hence it is fitting that the superior should love more. Aristotle comes close to saying as much when he shows that most people prefer being loved to loving only on questionable grounds. He does indeed say that affection is the proper virtue of a friend and is praiseworthy, but we have seen that for Aristotle, the virtues of friendship as such are not the highest virtues. Giving more affection does not make one worthy of friendship with a person who surpasses one in virtue as a whole; Aristotle portrays as ridiculous the lover who loves another more virtuous than himself and imagines that his great devotion makes him worthy of an equal return (1159b16–19). Instead, Aristotle continues to maintain, it is virtue that makes one worthy of affection and more. By continuing to suggest that affection is at heart a response to virtue or some other good, and by arguing that in an unequal friendship in which proportional equality is properly established it is the inferior who will love more, Aristotle upholds the impression that affection, the virtue of a friend, is more properly the virtue of the inferior than of the superior.

If loving as an inferior means being, like Eckermann, only a faint glimmer in the constellation of a great man's friendships, or worse yet, being loved only as a flatterer, or not being loved at all; if being the superior in an unequal friendship means pursuing low motives or acting without any clear motives, then it is abundantly clear that the great happiness of friendship is to be found only in equal friendships, and it is to these that Aristotle now returns. Once again he stresses that equal friendships are truly satisfactory only when based on virtue, and again he notes that friendships of opposites tend to be friendships of utility or convenience (1159b12–24). But the examples he gives of opposites who become friends – rich and poor, ignorant and learned, lover and beloved, ugly and beautiful – are again examples of superior and inferior, and they serve yet again to highlight the unanswered question of why it is that superiors love their inferiors. Aristotle's return to the theme of equal friendships at the end of 8.8 thus seems both to arise from and, in its details, to reinforce a perception that his first attempt to account for unequal friendships and their dynamics has been incomplete, accounting only for some such friendships, and those only in part, and leaving quite unexplained those that are perhaps the most important and interesting.

Yet this provisional account in 8.7–8.8 is extremely helpful in bringing out the most important phenomena and problems that still need to be considered in the remainder of Books 8 and 9. In particular, at the very outset of an extended discussion of friendship and justice, which stretches from 8.7 to 9.3, Aristotle brings into sharp focus the massive fact that everyone feels that friendships should be fair, and that, however seldom this may actually be accomplished, people ought to be loved and rewarded in proportion to the good they have bestowed. At the same time, with his mention of mothers, he reminds us of the great love often felt by benefactors, and our sense that being a benefactor is or should be rewarding in itself. By stating so boldly that we love our own good most of all, by suggesting that friendship is one of life's lesser goods and that affection, its characteristic virtue (1159a33–35), is one of the lesser virtues, and properly only a response to virtue or benefit, and at the same time by reminding us of mothers' love and acknowledging the common perception that such love is noble, Aristotle evokes in us and incites us to begin examining the deep-rooted inclination to believe just the opposite of what he has been suggesting: the inclination to believe that love is the very core of what is precious in life, that loyal devotion, even to one who fails to return one's love, is not foolish or ridiculous but is supremely noble, and that loving and being loved in return is the greatest blessing we can have as human beings. Before proceeding with an examination of Aristotle's account of friendship, it will perhaps be helpful to look at one of the most powerful cases ever made for this view, which is found in Montaigne's essay "Of Friendship."

Montaigne's Praise of Friendship

Montaigne brings before us in sparkling colors the bright promise of friendship, with all the moral nobility and sweet satisfaction that we imagine might accompany its perfect realization. True friendship, Montaigne says, is not, indeed, within the grasp of most people: He claims that a friendship such as his with La Boétie is a thing "so entire and so perfect that certainly you will hardly read of the like. . . . So many coincidences are needed to build up such a friendship that it is a lot if fortune can do it once in three centuries."[10] It is different not just in degree but in kind from ordinary friendships, he says, resting on different principles and following different rules. Yet the rhetorical success of Montaigne's essay is such that even as he shows contempt for the loves and friendships of all the rest of us, even as he asserts that the entire female sex and most of the male is incapable of true friendship, he nonetheless charms us with his portrait of it and paints this friendship in such a way that we feel that we, too, have had at least a glimmering of such a thing, and that to realize it perfectly would indeed be happiness. How, then, can we as ordinary human beings judge the merit of Montaigne's claims? We cannot expect that his account be true to our experience; we can only demand that it make sense on its own terms.

Montaigne's account of friendship is so interesting because he shows what one would have to maintain to argue that friendship is simply the peak of human life. Like Aristotle, he says that virtue in both parties is a prerequisite of perfect friendship. For such a friendship, "in which we act from the very bottom of our hearts, which holds nothing back, truly it is necessary that all the springs of action be perfectly clean and true" (142). But Montaigne seems to suggest that virtue is only a condition of perfect friendship and not the whole, perhaps not even the chief reason for the friends' love.

Aristotle, in contrast, says that virtuous friends love one another for their goodness. But to love for a reason is not to love for the sake of loving; it is to take the other's virtue or capacity to benefit us as a standard by which we determine whether a friendship is worth pursuing and worth maintaining. Does it follow that for Aristotle, what we really love in loving a friend for his virtue is virtue itself and the friend only incidentally, just as what we really love in loving a friend for his usefulness is our own good? Do we, whenever we love for a reason, love something else more and more truly than we love the other person? Socrates, in Plato's *Symposium,* argues provocatively that it is really only the pure essence or form of virtue that we love, and that we love individuals only incidentally, as imperfect vehicles or instantiations of virtue. But Aristotle never goes so far. In his account, we love virtue because we love fine, flourishing human beings: We love to contemplate them and to live with them. Nevertheless, Aristotle makes clear that the noblest thing, and the thing that is most important for the man who judges correctly, is not friendship but virtue, for friendships are and should be dropped, he says, when one falls far behind the other in virtue.

One alternative, which comes closer to Montaigne's position, would be to say that it is friendship that matters most, and that one chooses a virtuous man for a friend only because such a man has the greatest capacity for faithfulness, honesty, generosity, and so on, and because our own capacity to love is heightened by our ability to admire our friend. But then, are we saying that friendship is just a good experience that we want for ourselves, and that we choose a friend as the most promising occasion for this experience, the way we would choose a suitable hall for a wedding banquet? Surely not. It is the friend that we love; Montaigne is unambiguous about that, and he has the profound insight that to give any reason at all for the love is to point beyond and away from the friend to something else as our highest concern.[11] Therefore, Montaigne refuses to say that he chose La Boétie for any quality or combination of qualities. His friendship, he says, rests on "not one special consideration, nor two, nor three, nor four, nor a thousand" (139).

We learn from Montaigne's and La Boétie's other writings that they shared deep common interests, as Renaissance humanists and lovers of classical antiquity who favored republican Rome over monarchic France, and as thinkers who viewed Christianity with deep skepticism.[12] They must indeed have been delighted to discover all that they had in common, but Montaigne scorns to say that any such mundane thing as "shared interests and opinions" can explain or go to the bottom of his love: "If you press me to tell why I loved him, I feel that this cannot be expressed, except by answering: Because it was he, because it was I" (139). Montaigne therefore places great importance upon the freedom with which true friends choose one another, the freedom of each to stay or go, and the freely chosen submission of each to the will of the other. The friends do not choose one another for their qualities, and the friendship is not in the service of anything else. It is, in itself, the highest good.[13]

The question is whether Montaigne can be consistent in maintaining this bold position. He certainly does not flinch from confronting its corollary: that the truest friend would do anything for his friend, and would even commit an act of impiety or sedition if the friend commanded it. Montaigne retells the story of Gaius Blossius's confrontation with Gaius Laelius, which he finds in Cicero's dialogue *Laelius On Friendship*. The year was 133 B.C., and the Roman consuls had just condemned Tiberius Gracchus for attempting to stir up revolution against the Republic. Laelius, an adviser to the consuls, was questioning Blossius as one of the chief confidants of Gracchus. When Blossius said that he considered himself duty-bound to do anything Gracchus demanded, Laelius asked, "Even if he had requested you to set fire to the Capitol?" "He never would have requested me to do that, of course ... but if he had, I should have obeyed," answered Blossius.[14] (Montaigne quotes these words verbatim from Cicero with the single change of "Capitol" to "temples.")

Laelius and Montaigne both criticize this answer, but on very different grounds – Laelius for its impious and seditious tendency, and Montaigne only for its imprudence. Since Blossius was confident of the virtue of Gracchus, Montaigne says, Blossius should have contented himself with insisting on that virtue, rather than revealing so frankly that all his deepest loyalties were on the side of his friendship and not his country or its gods. Yet Montaigne does not hesitate to suggest publicly that all true friends have the same ordering of priorities:

Those who charge that this answer is seditious do not fully understand this mystery, and fail to assume first what is true, that he had Gracchus' will up his sleeve, both by power over him and by knowledge of him. They were friends more than citizens, friends more than friends or enemies of their country or friends of ambition and disturbance. Having committed themselves absolutely to each other, they held absolutely the reins of each other's inclination, and if you assume that this team was guided by the strength and leadership of reason, as indeed it is quite impossible to harness it without that, Blossius' answer is as it should have been. If their actions went astray, they were by my measure neither friends to each other, nor friends to themselves.

For that matter, this answer has no better ring than would mine if someone questioned me in this fashion: "If your will commanded you to kill your daughter, would you kill her?" and I said yes. For that does not bear witness to any consent to do so, because I have no doubt at all about my will, and just as little about that of such a friend. It is not in the power of all the arguments in the world to dislodge me from the certainty I have of the intentions and judgments of my friend. Not one of his actions could be presented to me, whatever appearance it might have, that I could not immediately find out the motive for it. Our souls pulled together in such unison, they regarded each other with such ardent affection, and with a like affection revealed themselves to each other to the very depths of our hearts, that not only did I know his soul as well as mine, but I should certainly have trusted myself to him more readily than to myself. (140)

What a tangle of arguments is here to be unraveled!

In his discussion of this essay, Allan Bloom emphasizes the philosophic roots of Montaigne's and La Boétie's friendship. He points out that such friendships have always been looked upon with suspicion from at least the time of Socrates, because of the inevitable tension between the traditions, regimes, and religions that demand men's loyalty and the philosophy that insists on questioning all received opinion. Montaigne attempts to reassure his audience about the potentially seditious and impious character of a great friendship by insisting that true friendships are always governed by virtue and reason and that, therefore, true friends would never burn temples. But as Bloom points out, the virtues of philosophy and friendship are different from the virtues of conventional piety and patriotism and in fact do not rule out such actions.[15]

The one silent change that Montaigne makes in the passage, replacing "Capitol" with "temples," indicates that he sees wise friends' greatest potential opponent to be not political authority as such, but revealed religion as such. As Bloom also points out, it was the Renaissance humanists who rediscovered and reanimated the profound contest or quarrel between classical antiquity and the Bible,[16] but what is most intriguing about this passage from Montaigne is that it seems to attempt a new synthesis uniting what is most impressive in the spirit of antiquity with what is most moving in the spirit of the Bible. Montaigne wants to say that in this best and noblest of friendships, one can be as deeply, lovingly, trustingly devoted to a friend as Abraham was to God, as fully prepared to follow him anywhere and to make for him even the sacrifice of his most beloved child, and yet one can be absolutely certain (as, it seems, one can never be with an inscrutable God) that the friend will never command anything evil.[17] Thus one's devotion to reason and virtue can stand uncompromised without qualifying one's perfect devotion to another living being. A perfect friendship, Montaigne suggests, is the answer to the problem posed by both the essay "On Voluntary Servitude" and the sonnets of La Boétie's to which, in different editions, it stood as the preface: the problem that, in devotion to God as in erotic love, one part of the soul willingly and even eagerly surrenders the liberty, the autonomy of judgment and action, that another part prizes most highly.[18] Can friendship heal this rift in us? Or is this attempted synthesis between the principle of autonomous reason and the principle of loving obedience in fact a most elaborate and ingenious evasion of life's most important problem?

Montaigne can say that he would kill his daughter if his will commanded it and simultaneously insist that he would never kill his daughter, because in fact the first statement concedes nothing. Everyone does what his will commands in everything, and no one is free to do otherwise. But one can also know one's heart well enough to know – at least with almost perfect certainty – that certain things one would never do. Montaigne insists that he is as sure of his friend as he is of his own will because he knows his friend through and through. But what if his friend, whose judgment had always before seemed as clear and solid as a diamond, suddenly demanded something inexplicable?

Montaigne's answer seems evident from his approval of that of Blossius: He would obey his friend – at least in anything up to and including the burning of temples, and perhaps in anything at all – in perfect confidence that his friend can do no wrong. Can he justify such deference to his friend as being ultimately in the service of virtue because he trusts his friend's character and good judgment better than his own? Let us concede that one may trust another more than oneself in a certain way: One may discover, through experience, that a friend's heart is more generous, his vulnerability to temptation less, his good judgment swifter and more certain than one's own. Still, one can only be certain of another's virtue insofar as one possesses an independent knowledge of virtue itself. In doubtful cases one may well give a proven friend the benefit of the doubt, but the possibility can never be absolutely ruled out that one may someday face a choice between following the friend and following what one's own judgment clearly and distinctly determines to be right. But to Montaigne, the contemplation of such a choice is anathema. In ordinary friendships, indeed, Montaigne says,

you must walk . . . bridle in hand, with prudence and precaution; the knot is not so well tied that there is no cause to mistrust it. "Love him," Chilo used to say, "as if you are to hate him some day; hate him as if you are to love him." This precept, which is so abominable in this sovereign and masterful friendship, is healthy in the practice of ordinary and customary friendships. (140)[19]

Kant says that even the best friends must approach each other with caution,[20] but Aristotle agrees with Montaigne that tried and true friends need have no such mistrust: Each can open his heart to the other without fear and without reserve. Nevertheless, for Aristotle, one must never lose sight of the fact that one's highest loyalty is to reason and to what reason shows to be right. One must never abdicate one's judgment, and one must part ways with a friend who goes wrong if that friend cannot be set back on the proper course again (1165b13–22). Montaigne, in contrast, considers the loyalty of true friends to be the very highest loyalty. A perfect friendship is the noblest thing in life, and in such a friendship, losing their very wills in one another, he and La Boétie reserved for themselves nothing that was their own, neither their independent powers of judgment nor any other duties, for "a single dominant friendship dissolves all other obligations" (141, 142).

Why, we might ask, is Montaigne driven to go so far as to wish to dissolve his autonomous self, with his autonomous, reasoned judgment, into the being of another? The answer seems to be, in part, that the very logic of noble devotion demands it. To be devoted to another is, after all, to be devoted to the good, the benefit, the utility of the other. But if each friend, being noble-minded as well as devoted (as Montaigne insists great friends must be), deeply desires to be a generous benefactor to the other, then being such a benefactor is in fact a greater good in the benefactor's eyes than is the low-level good he gives away when, for example, he pays a friend's debts. The result is a certain strange inversion of priorities:

If, in the friendship I speak of, one could give to the other, it would be the one who received the benefit who would oblige his friend. For, each of them seeking above all things to benefit the other, the one who provides the matter and the occasion is the liberal one, giving his friend the satisfaction of doing for him what he most wants to do. (141)

To illustrate such noble generosity, Montaigne tells the story of Eudamidas and his friends Charixenus and Aretheus, to whom he bequeathed in his will not money, for he was poor and had no money to give, but the nobler opportunity of looking after his elderly mother and his unmarried daughter, and Montaigne tells us that both friends were well satisfied with the gift.

But there is a problem and indeed an absurdity in the friendship in which two people make it their highest aim to be the other's benefactor, an absurdity that we all fall into when we quarrel over a restaurant bill that we and a friend both wish generously to pay. The most noble-minded person, with the greater sense of delicacy, will in fact relinquish the bill, thinking to himself, "I will be noblest of all and will selflessly give away the pleasure of being generous." But what if both simultaneously decide to make this sacrifice? The result will be endless standoffs or ridiculous infinite regresses. The absurdity consists, at bottom, in a certain confusion or self-deception within each friend: Each is competing for the position he covets – that of selfless benefactor – but neither is willing to face squarely the fact that in doing so, he is seeking what he considers the greatest good for himself, and that this is a good he cannot share with the one he seeks to benefit. Montaigne's solution is apparently to transcend the whole perplexing dynamic by seeking a union so perfect that no vexing trace of "mine" and "thine" remains:

In this noble relationship, services and benefits, on which other friendships feed, do not deserve even to be taken into account; the reason for this is the complete fusion of our wills. For just as the friendship I feel for myself receives no increase from the help I give myself in time of need, whatever the Stoics say, and as I feel no gratitude to myself for the service I do myself; so the union of such friends, being truly perfect, makes them lose the sense of such duties. (140–41)

Let us assume for the sake of argument that some such merging is somehow possible; is it, as Montaigne insists, noble? Is there merit in looking after what is, after all, only oneself, and is serving the interests of a double-size self really any more noble or impressive than looking after one's single self? If two people could merge into a seamless whole, all ideas of devotion as well as generosity and justice would become inappropriate in describing that whole's relation to itself. Thus, while Montaigne describes his friendship as being splendid and rare precisely in attaining perfect communion, he must use stories of other friendships to persuade his readers that perfect friendship is supremely noble. Even in praising his own friendship and his own friend La Boétie, he cannot help falling back into the language of justice and separateness and obligation. "We went halves in everything," he says, and "as he surpassed me infinitely in every other ability and virtue, so he did in the duty of friendship" (143). We are tempted to suspect that Montaigne and La Boétie simply could not bear to abandon the belief that their friendship is supremely noble. Refusing to pride themselves on being each other's benefactors, they perhaps still had a noble sense of self-overcoming precisely in their refusal to take any credit for self-overcoming, precisely in the vehemence with which they used to "hate and banish from between them these words of separation and distinction: benefit, obligation, gratitude, request, thanks, and the like" (141). But if in this friendship devotion is so perfect that it dissolves independent judgment and trumps all other duties, and the union of the two is, in turn, so perfect that it dissolves even the possibility of devotion and service between the friends, it becomes hard to say on what grounds the friendship can still be called noble.

Nor is it clear how friendship could be counted as the very best thing in life, if in its perfection the friends are truly like "one soul in two bodies," as Montaigne says (141).[21] How could they ever assist each other in their neediness, comfort each other in their sorrows, or teach each other anything new, however long they conversed together? But perhaps the very core of friendship's goodness has nothing to do with comfort and assistance, and lies in the simple, irreducible sweetness of intimacy itself, to which Montaigne directs our attention and which Aristotle also acknowledges. This sweetness is the sweetness of expanded aliveness, an expanded sense of being, that comes with knowing and cherishing, with being known and cherished, with the vicarious but vivid experience of another's being and the enhanced awareness of one's own. Such intimacy, in its peak moments, is always in some degree physical – for it always involves the contact of eyes, if not also of skin – and is always riveted in the present moment. Past, future, and all distractions melt away; one is simply there, with one's whole being, with another, with his whole being. One welcomes anything and everything from the other and feels a complete freedom to voice one's own deepest feelings, one's most whimsical playfulness, or nothing at all; speech and silence are equally welcome and equally delightful. We need not insist upon the fact that such intimacy requires that there remain two souls and not just one; may Montaigne not still be right to consider the sweetness of such moments of near-perfect union the very best thing in life?

Yes, and yes, and no. Such sweetness is precious indeed, but fleeting; it arises obliquely, out of shared activities of a wholly different sort, and begins to slip away the moment one tries to hold and keep it. Like the sweetness of basking in a hard-won victory or a tropical sun, the pleasure of basking in affection is precious in moments of cessation from the intense activity of conversation and thought, or hard work, or pleasure seeking; but the substance of life lies not in basking but in full activity. Such moments have an intensity of their own, but also a deep stillness that would turn to flatness (or restlessness) if one did not, after a little while, turn one's focus to other things – although, of course, one may do so together with one's friend and remain in satisfying contact. Such moments may indeed be the sweetest moments in life, but they are not the best thing in life, if life is good.

If even these peak moments of friendship depend on a friend's being another and not merely more of oneself, the goodness that we attribute to friendship as a whole depends greatly upon two friends' being both other and different in ways that allow them to assist each other, as benefactors or as partners, in things that are valued apart from the friendship. It is nothing other than the conviction of love's nobility that allows us to consider the loyal, generous, devoted service that friends give one another to be higher and more important than the good results actually secured by such friendly service. Montaigne, by insisting on the nobility of his friendship with La Boétie, confirms the powerful truth that only when friendship is understood as the noblest and highest thing in life can it be convincingly portrayed as the very best thing in life.

"Of Friendship" in the Context of Montaigne's Other Essays

If, however, the internal difficulties that we have seen in Montaigne's "Of Friendship" lead us to doubt the validity of the ranking of friendship among life's goods that he presents there, the rest of his essays force us to question whether the position he seems to take in this essay really is his final position on the subject at all. For in his other essays Montaigne rarely mentions the joys of intimate friendship, let alone the nobility of perfect devotion. Instead, he expands upon the importance of knowing oneself, moderating one's passions, disentangling oneself from all the charming snares of the world, and learning to depend for one's happiness on oneself alone and on the natural pleasures that fortune places within easy reach. If in "Of Friendship" Montaigne extols the overcoming of a narrow concern for self, in his other essays he reveals, gently but relentlessly, the deep delusions and dangers that continually, perhaps invariably, bedevil human attempts at noble self-overcoming.

Montaigne is a champion of virtue, but his is virtue of a new kind, which he expounds throughout the *Essays* in a sustained, critical engagement with the ancient Epicureans and Stoics. He agrees with the Epicureans that nature has given us reason so that we may each pursue our own good, and even boldly asserts that "all the opinions in the world agree . . . that pleasure is our goal" (37, 56). Self-knowledge is all-important, but chiefly, it seems, as a means to living well or pleasantly. Coming to terms with our mortality is crucial, but not, as the Stoics tend to think, in order to die well and nobly (795). Any death is really good enough; it will soon be over and it will not matter how it transpired, but the best one is the one least felt (55, 252). Trying to steel oneself against all the evils that may befall one is foolish because most will never come, and because in trying to prepare for an unknown future, we neglect the present that is the only thing we really have (803–5). The thorough acceptance of death is necessary not in order that we may live and die heroically but so that we may fully enjoy life's pleasures: "Among the principle benefits of virtue is disdain for death, a means that furnishes our life with a soft tranquillity and gives us a pure and pleasant enjoyment of it, without which all other pleasures are extinguished" (57). Once a man has come to terms with death, no one can have any power over him, and no fear can gain a foothold in him (60, 63); only then can life's true sweetness reveal itself for what it is. The greatest virtue, then, is the moderation born of reason and self-knowledge that allows one to enjoy life's pleasures to the fullest, precisely because one does so within reasonable bounds and without unreasonable demands or fantastic hopes or fears (120). And a large part of living moderately and pleasantly is learning to detach oneself from the empty pursuit of honors, offices, and the favor of the great – pursuits which, together with unseasonable hopes and fears, cause us to be "never at home" (8). Montaigne holds up his own retirement as a worthy example, and his own soul as one that has found a home in itself. Without becoming an utter recluse, he says, it is wise to cultivate a taste for solitude (175–78, 629).

Courage is important as well as moderation, but the courage that Montaigne admires most is that which breeds a calm independence; he is suspicious of the courage that manifests itself as an eagerness to sacrifice oneself for one's country or cause. He perceives at the root of the impulse to self-sacrifice a deep and unnatural cruelty toward oneself, which produces, in turn, a deplorable cruelty to others. Thinking that we need to suffer in order to become good, we end by "thinking that we gratify heaven and nature by committing massacre and homicide, a belief universally embraced in all religions" (148–49). Montaigne therefore argues that there ought to be moderation in virtue as in everything else, for excessive virtue is strangely "savage" and harsh to those we ought most to love (146).

In his essay "Of Cruelty," Montaigne develops a fascinating hierarchy of levels of goodness or virtue that shows the problem with virtue understood as self-overcoming or sacrifice. He begins with the innate goodness of "souls naturally regulated and well-born," which happily and peacefully follow the lead of reason, and argues that true virtue must be something higher and more impressive, involving the overcoming of contrary inclinations (306–7). But then Montaigne observes that it is a problem with virtue if it needs a "rough and thorny road," and depends upon the presence of vice in oneself to contend with and to conquer. Better, then, is the cheerful harmony of a soul that has no disorderly passions to overcome, and that actually rejoices most when it can enjoy itself in the face of "shame, fevers, poverty, death, and tortures" (308).

As his example of this higher virtue he brings forth Cato the Younger, whose life he elsewhere calls the "noblest" (777):

When I see him dying and tearing out his entrails, I cannot be content to believe simply that he then had his soul totally free from disturbance and fright; I cannot believe that he merely maintained himself in the attitude that the rules of the Stoic sect ordained for him, sedate, without emotion, and impassible; there was, it seems to me, in that man's virtue too much lustiness and verdancy to stop there. I believe without any doubt that he felt pleasure and bliss in so noble an action, and that he enjoyed himself more in it than in any other action of his life. . . .

I go so far in that belief that I begin to doubt whether he would have wanted to be deprived of the occasion for so fine an exploit. And if his goodness, which made him embrace the public advantage more than his own, did not hold me in check, I should easily fall into this opinion, that he was grateful to fortune for having put his virtue to so beautiful a test and for having favored that brigand in treading underfoot the ancient liberty of his country. (308–9)

Here, as repeatedly throughout the *Essays*, Montaigne tries valiantly to defend Cato against the charge, which no one forces him to introduce, that Cato's brilliant deeds had a darker motive. He presents it as a fault of his own corrupt age that every seeming virtue now has "profit, glory, fear, or habit" as its motive (170); he shares Plutarch's annoyance at the coarse souls who attribute Cato's death to fear of Caesar, and heaps scorn on an anonymous, hypothetical charge that Cato's death was due to ambition (170–71), but he does not quite manage to extricate Cato from the charge that he ought to have bent the laws and his own pride a little to save Rome's freedom (89), or that he was strangely indifferent to her ruin when it came (777). Montaigne portrays as a mad, "runaway courage" that proud defiance that leads some Stoics and even Epicureans to welcome pain and to taunt their tormentors to inflict even more of it so that they may prove their mettle; yet it turns out that *all* courage, when viewed as a noble self-overcoming, is in fact "greedy of danger" and eager to find occasions to put itself to the proof (250–51, 38, 308). Montaigne's last words on Cato indicate that his virtue was a little too "strained," that he was too often "mounted upon his high horse," that perhaps he is not necessary as a model after all, and perhaps he was most exemplary, in the end, when he submitted most meekly and naturally to the needs and the pleasures of nature (793, 851).

If Cato, who seemed to stand at the peak of Montaigne's moral hierarchy, ends up crumbling upon his pedestal, Socrates, the other paragon set up in "Of Cruelty," remains standing at the end of the *Essays,* an almost superhuman model of inner harmony and constancy, who, however, died not tearing out his entrails in defiance of a tyrant, but quietly, in a painless death, perhaps deliberately brought upon himself because he was old and knew it was the best time to go (620). The self-sacrificing Cato is associated with the spirit of poetry, which induces a "frenzy" and transports the poet "out of himself," whereas the memory of Socrates, the calm sage who knows and secures his own good, is preserved for us by "the most clear-sighted men who have ever lived" (171, 793). But in the end, Montaigne gives us neither of these but, rather, his own portrait of his own lazy, healthy, charming self, who seemed at first to stand on the lowest rung of the moral hierarchy, as the most attractive and credible model for our own reformation. It is Montaigne, the man who so unabashedly lives with and for himself, who turns out to be most capable of a gentle, genuine, truly useful philanthropy, based not on a thirst for glory or power or superhuman virtue but on natural human compassion and goodwill. Not by sacrificing himself for the public good, but by lending himself to it, occasionally and circumspectly, does he present himself as being able to accomplish the most.

In the same spirit, Montaigne presents himself in his mature retirement as only lending himself to his friends but belonging to himself. He strives to be beholden to no one, the favorite of no great man, up to the ears in no one else's troubles (114, 618, 766–84). He enjoys the company of others for what it is worth, but remembers that he must be his own best friend:

> Certainly a man of understanding has lost nothing, if he has himself....
> We should have wife, children, goods, and above all health, if we can; but we must not bind ourselves to them so strongly that our happiness depends on them. We must reserve a back shop all our own, entirely free, in which to establish our real liberty and our principal retreat and solitude. (177)

For true friendship, although sweet, is "annoying by its rarity," or even nonexistent (628, 799).[22]

Viewed in the light of the teaching of the whole book, and taken together with La Boétie's essay "On Voluntary Servitude,"[23] to which it was ostensibly designed as an introduction, Montaigne's essay "Of Friendship" can perhaps best be understood as serving a special pedagogical purpose. La Boétie's youthful essay is on the surface a manifesto against human tyrants, a call to liberty, and an attempt to explain the strange forces that keep men, naturally born for freedom, in voluntary thralldom to tyrants and kings. Many of the essay's arguments, however, could apply as well or better to men's willing but abject surrender to a god who does not exist or to the church and priests that tyrannize over their minds. There is something in the human soul, La Boétie and Montaigne both perceive, that strangely longs for a perfect, self-denying, somehow ennobling devotion to something outside of and higher than oneself. Both men are at pains to point out the foolishness and ugliness of this longing in most of its fanatical manifestations, as men surrender their liberty to vicious kings and attempt to placate inscrutable gods by obeying the irrational commandments that they imagine them to give. Yet somehow both men have felt the power of this longing for devotion within their own hearts.

"Of Friendship," while adding much to the charm of Montaigne's book for the casual reader, is perhaps designed to focus and answer the most thoughtful reader's lingering objections to his largely pleasing portrayal of a happy, rational, autonomous, moderate life lived according to the clear light of nature. If we do still wish for a perfect devotion, the essay implicitly asks, what would it have to be like so as to be marred neither by a craven surrender of reason, nor by a senseless self-destruction, nor by a surreptitious competition for the moral high ground with the object of our devotion? If we do still wish to find an object truly worthy of devotion, what would the character of that object have to be?

"Of Friendship" indicates that it is of the essence of loving devotion, understood as the highest and best thing in life, that it must seek a perfect union with the loved one. For if separate selves remain, the interests and happiness of the two will be distinct, and invariably there will be conflicts as the two seek either to secure good things for themselves or nobly to give them away. If devotion is to be perfect, there can be no higher standard by which to judge the friend and friendship, no reservation of separate judgments that can open the door to ruptures. Yet if such a union is not to be base, it must be the union of two souls equally perfect in virtue and in wise self-knowledge. Each must find in it neither devotion to an unworthy inferior nor surrender to an inscrutable superior, nor a marriage with one who is opposite and, to that extent, unlikely to concur in one's judgments, but a friendship and merging with a perfect other self. If and only if the two could become truly one soul, the subjection of each to the other would be no more irrational than the subjection of each to the reason he finds within him. Having brought us this far, Montaigne leaves it to us to see that the love of this merged soul for itself (a love that real friendship can only approach) would really be no different from the love that a good man can have, far more easily and reliably, with his own self. When read in this way, "Of Friendship" is the linchpin of the *Essays'* argument that it is indeed folly to look outside of ourselves for a fragile happiness that at best only approximates a healthy self-love, rather than seeking our happiness within.

If this was Montaigne's argument, it seems elegant; but was it, in the final analysis, wholly persuasive even to Montaigne himself? Was Montaigne's friendship with La Boétie just a moment of rare sweetness in life, which Montaigne wished to share with his readers but which he was far too wise to languish in mourning the loss of?[24] Or did this brief friendship have such a hold upon him that even decades after he lost it, even in the face of his most resolute cheerfulness and determination to enjoy life for what it offered, he still spoke from the depths of his heart when he wrote that in friendship, "the facts surpass even the precepts of philosophy," and that the rest of his life, by comparison, was "nothing but dark and dreary night" (143)?

A number of other passages suggest that perhaps these lines are indeed in good earnest. In "Of Diversion," Montaigne speaks of his "overpowering grief" as a thing only pushed aside and never left behind, and he observes that the memory of a true friend is as fresh and vivid after a quarter century as it was the day that he died (634–35). In "Of Three Kinds of Association," he confesses that he cannot quite shake off "a fantastic desire for something I cannot recapture" (622). He sees well the merit of being able to adjust oneself to such human beings as fortune actually brings one, but he cannot quite do it (623). He speaks of a youthful need to oppose and moderate his erotic passions, and a continued need to do so with other, unnamed inclinations – such as, we must suspect, the longing for friendship (776). He tries to train himself "to stick to myself and break away from outside things," but confesses that he keeps slipping his own leash (800).

All of these comments, too, might be made for our edification, as exaggerations of nothing more than the occasional wistful mood, offered in order to make us smile at Montaigne's charming failings and resolve to learn his lessons in self-sufficiency better than he himself did. But it may be that these twinges of melancholic longing that Montaigne allows to show are in fact indicative of an important difference between him and Aristotle, turning on the different degrees to which the two thinkers found a fundamentally self-sufficient, moderate, rational life in accordance with nature to be truly satisfying. Aristotle argues in Book 10 of the *Nicomachean Ethics* that a self-sufficient happiness is attainable in the philosophic life. Montaigne is, at the least, more cautious on the question. He remains somewhat vague as to just what the natural pleasures are that can make life truly full and satisfying, and suggests at certain points that life holds no positive, substantial good (364, 701–2, 849). Perhaps Montaigne did find in philosophy a solid happiness, and did, behind a politic veil of skepticism, truly solve to his own satisfaction the most important questions concerning God and the nature of being, and in his little study tower spent his happiest hours reflecting and building upon some such solid understanding of nature as Aristotle claims to have. But perhaps he was in earnest with his skepticism and his remarks that most of human philosophizing, most subjects of study, are vain and worthless, a mere hunt for what can never be captured (117–18, 370, 378, 794). Perhaps he thought it ultimately impossible for man truly to know anything beyond his own human heart and mind.[25]

Montaigne might well have reasoned, as he suggests in the "Apology for Raymond Sebond," that *if* the world is a rational place, then there can be no such angry God and no such afterlife as Christians imagine, and we can hope to attain a solid knowledge of nature; yet he may never have been able to dispose of the doubt that perhaps the ultimate reality is irrational (389), and a cruel tyrant does await us after death. In this case, we may well imagine that the philosophic life seemed for Montaigne less than fully and endlessly engrossing, and at the same time, that philosophy's injunction to come to terms with death may have seemed especially burdensome. It is hard enough to reconcile oneself to what one understands to be certain annihilation, but it would be far harder to accept the probability that death means annihilation, the possibility that it is the prologue to unknown torments, and the certainty that one can never settle the question in this lifetime.[26]

If philosophy truly seemed to Montaigne to provide practical guidance but no sustaining food for the soul, if its chief lessons are that we must accept our own insuperable ignorance and a death of probable but not certain annihilation, then Socrates' ability to die with such a calm cheerfulness must have seemed superhuman to Montaigne. And the charm of escaping himself and the knowledge of his own frailty and mortality by plunging and losing himself in an all-engrossing, loving devotion to another must have been potent indeed. It is perhaps not insignificant that Montaigne, usually so fluently eloquent, found his words failing him when he tried to capture the ineffable sublimity both of Socrates' calm death and of friendship.[27]

But we must leave Montaigne with these speculations. A more definitive reading of his essay on friendship must await a fuller study of his complex and elusive teachings on both the theoretical life and the theological problem, so as to determine the extent to which Montaigne saw, in a life of self-sufficiency, the basis for a solid happiness. But if this question must remain open in Montaigne, there is no such ambiguity in Aristotle. Indeed, Aristotle implicitly offers a bracing challenge to Montaigne and to all skepticism: the challenge that if we truly think through everything that is implicit in our human longing to give ourselves in a noble devotion to something beyond ourselves, if we think it through all the way to the bottom, then we can solve the most important and urgent questions, and can find a life of happy tranquillity and satisfying activity that leaves no gnawing fears and no aching hungers. To begin to do so, we must probe the strange and manifold connections between our desire to be nobly devoted to others and our stubbornly persistent desire to secure justice for ourselves.

4

Friendships in Politics and the Family

In opening his thematic discussion of the relationship of justice to friendship, Aristotle says, "It seems, then, just as we said at the beginning, that friendship and the just deal with the same things and involve the same persons" (1159b25–26). In fact, what Aristotle said at the beginning of his treatment of friendship was somewhat different: "When men are friends they have no need of justice, but when they are just they need friendship in addition, and justice in the highest sense seems to involve an element of friendship" (1155a26–28). The first clause of this earlier statement is ambiguous, for although it might be taken merely to mean that successful friendship must include justice, it encourages the more pleasing thought that friendship dispenses with the need for justice altogether, or at least that it automatically produces justice without effort. Aristotle's new formulation of the relation of justice to friendship suggests that these more hopeful readings would be unjustified. Friendship would automatically include justice if mere goodwill were enough to secure justice, but Aristotle has shown that even the most ardent goodwill is not enough to equalize benefits where capacities are highly unequal, and that goodwill alone is often too thin a reed to rely upon. Friendship would dispense with the need for justice if true friends entered into such a seamless union that they lost all sense of "mine" and "thine," so that the very idea of justice between them ceased to make sense, or if friends ceased to care about justice because each was as happy to give as to receive, and so could not be bothered with keeping accounts. Aristotle clearly considers the idea of a seamless union chimerical, and we have seen Montaigne's difficulty in maintaining it with any consistency. As for the possibility of becoming indifferent to justice, Aristotle acknowledges that friends often talk as if they have banished the concern for it, and that friendship is indeed characterized by an unwillingness to keep strict accounts. But he will go on to raise sustained questions as to whether this phenomenon is what it appears to be.

Aristotle cites with approval the oft-quoted proverb that "the belongings of friends are in common" (1159b31), but the context suggests that he attaches a rather different meaning to this saying than the usual one.[1] For the context is Aristotle's examination not precisely of the extent of friends' willingness to share with one another but of the extent of friends' *claims* upon one another's willingness to share, claims that are always understood as being grounded in justice. "To the same extent that community exists, friendship also exists, and likewise justice," he says, and "the just naturally grows greater with greater friendship, since it pertains to the same people and reaches to the same extent" (1159b29–31 and 1160a7–8).[2] Friends do indeed lose track of the small change that passes between them and may even share all that they have, but in doing so, they do not forget about justice or cease to care which one of them benefits from their possessions. Close friends give freely to one another both because they wish to and because they are glad to acknowledge and repay their friends' generosity. When all is going well, the claims of justice are so overlaid with generosity that no one seems to be thinking about justice at all. It is when difficulties and conflicts arise that we feel the force of our friends' claims upon us, and it is when they let us down that we realize we have all along been assuming ourselves to have claims upon them, claims of justice that are not less but greater the stronger the love between us has been, and the more selflessly we have given in the past. Thus, Aristotle says, it is more terrible and shocking, because a greater injustice, "to defraud a companion of money than a fellow citizen, or to fail to help a brother than a stranger, or to strike a father than anyone else" (1160a3–7). Perhaps it is only the small change that is ever really forgotten, and perhaps even then, the fact that it was forgotten is not forgotten and can generate claims of its own.

In the same way that justice is necessary to friendship, so some degree of friendship is a necessary concomitant or precondition to justice, according to Aristotle (1159b29–31, 1160a7–8). That is to say, at least the rudimentary elements of friendship, beginning with a recognized common interest, are essential for the establishment of justice. Aristotle says not merely that justice cannot be enforced where no bonds of community exist, but that obligations of justice do not in the full sense even exist there (1134a24–30). To modern eyes, this understanding of justice looks quite restrictive. We tend to think that other human beings have some just claims upon our time and resources, even where no ties of friendship, common citizenship, or even treaty obligations bind us to them.[3] This more expansive sense of obligation rests in no small part on the sense that fortune is capriciously unjust in its distribution of everything good, and that it is incumbent on us to try to rectify this injustice. Aristotle, while perfectly cognizant of fortune's capriciousness, nevertheless applies the ideas of justice and injustice only to human beings capable of partaking in reason, and he insists that true justice must include not only fairness in the commonly recognized sense of equality in exchange but also fairness in the equally widely recognized sense of establishing or preserving the common good of a community.

Thus, while Aristotle is aware of the limited or provincial character of Greek notions of justice, especially the prephilosophic idea that justice consists in helping friends and harming enemies, he ultimately endorses the Greek idea that the claims of justice are essentially coextensive with those of friendship and the political community, and that in the best case, that political community is quite small. Aristotle evidently determined that only a sense of justice grounded in a powerfully felt sense of community is likely to take deep root in the human heart, deep enough to support virtue and a lasting dedication to a greater good that transcends men's narrowest and most immediate concerns.[4] By contrast, our modern sense of obligation stretches to include people we will never meet and for whom we care little if at all, but it is consequently thin and fragile even with regard to our nearest neighbors.

Now if the association that provides in the most complete way for the good of its members has the first and most compelling claim upon them, this fact sets the stage for a great rivalry, for (even setting aside the claims of piety) both the political community and the family claim this distinction. Thus the ties of family and of political community enter Aristotle's discussion in 8.9–8.10 in a contentious spirit: Somehow, the most salient fact about these relationships is the comprehensive, extreme, and hence controversial nature of the claims they assert. Although Aristotle has stressed that the best friendships are equal friendships, it is in the mostly unequal ties of family and political life that we see much of the greatest intensity and devotion that are to be found in human relations, as well as great possessiveness and great demands. Aristotle's discussion of the dynamics of unequal friendships up to this point has left the particular character and intensity of these relationships unaccounted for, and especially the devotion of parents to children and of rulers to those under their care. In 8.9–8.12 he will examine in detail each of these types of association and the claims made on its behalf in the light of the other, and also in the light of men's relationships with the gods, who are, with parents and fatherland, considered to be the source of the greatest benefits to human beings, and the object of their deepest obligations.

These rival associations are of course in many ways very different. Indeed, the ties of family, politics, and piety differ so much in point of equality that, although Aristotle always calls the parent–child bond a friendship and leaves it ambiguous whether the relationship of ruler to ruled can properly be called a friendship or not, he is quite clear that between men and gods true friendship is impossible.[5] Yet here in the case of the greatest benefactions and obligations, just as earlier in the case of the most defective friendships of pleasure and utility, the associations that in critical ways fall short of complete friendship turn out to be most revealing about the nature of friendship. Through a sustained, searching, but also gingerly exploration of the motives and expectations at work in all of these unequal relationships, Aristotle reveals dynamics that are characteristic of every friendship, including the best and most equal. In particular, he explores the ways in which all friendships are shaped by the deep-rooted and well-nigh-ineradicable human concern for justice. At the same time, he sheds further light on the question of how important friendship is among the ends that people pursue and ought to pursue, and he offers reflections on how well the various types of family and political relationships are able to fulfill the promise of friendships to provide the sphere of the most noble and satisfying action.

Aristotle begins in 8.9 with the political community, which makes the best prima facie claim to provide in a comprehensive and sovereign way for the good of its members. "All other communities aim at some partial advantage," Aristotle says, citing as examples the associations of fellow sailors, soldiers, members of a deme (or section of a city), and tribesmen, whereas the political community includes and governs all of these more limited and partial associations (1160a14–18). As Aristotle first puts forward the claims of the political community in 8.9, he presents the polis as having arisen in the most natural and organic way out of smaller tribes that coalesced for the sake of their common good. The picture he evokes is one of a simple people, close to the earth, fraternal in spirit if not united by actual ties of kinship, working hard for their sustenance, and coming together in moments of relaxation to enjoy harvest festivals and the like. The benefits of such a community are undeniably common and enjoyed by everyone. There is here no slavery and no rich, idle ruling class, and indeed, Aristotle heightens the impression of harmony by refraining from making any mention of inequality or rule at all. At the same time, the overall tone of the society seems low; in describing it, Aristotle also makes no mention of nobility, heroism, wisdom, education, or human excellence in general, while speaking repeatedly of utility. He says that it is the aim of the lawgiver to seek the common advantage; he does not present the lawgiver's aim as cultivating virtuous citizens capable of judging and ruling well.[6]

However, it would be misleading to say that the community depicted in 8.9 is nothing but an extended friendship of utility. For right at the heart of this simplest, most unambitious and uncorrupted community, the community most clearly and consistently directed to meeting life's basic needs for all of its members, we see a directedness to something completely different from the collective self-interest that seemed to unite and define it: a concern with worshiping and sacrificing to the gods. The political community, claiming authority over all lesser associations, necessarily asserts its sovereignty over the religious associations as well, and in turn is given new meaning by them. To be sure, Aristotle introduces the theme of piety with a rather odd choice of emphasis:

Some of the associations seem to come into being for the sake of pleasure, such as religious associations and guilds, which exist for the sake of sacrificing and fellowship – for all of these seem to come under the political one, and the political community aims not at the advantage of the present moment, but at that of the whole of life – [their members] sacrificing and coming together for this purpose, giving honor to the gods, and providing themselves with recreation and pleasure. For the ancient sacrifices and festive gatherings appear to have arisen after the harvest as a kind of offering of firstfruits, since it was at this time that people had the most leisure. (1160a19–28)

Why does Aristotle bring pleasure, recreation, and leisure so prominently to the fore? Is this the emphasis that the low, utilitarian city gives to piety? That seems unlikely, for there is nothing utilitarian about pleasure. To understand piety in utilitarian terms would mean viewing it not as celebration and thanksgiving but as a calculated effort to secure divine favor for the sake of good harvests and victory in war, or it would mean viewing piety, as certain modern philosophers do, as just a support to the morality that civic order and justice require. Aristotle's sketch suggests that utility is not the engine that drives piety, even the civic piety of very utilitarian communities but, rather, that it springs up in spite of our utilitarian concerns, taking sustenance from the sense that meeting the needs of survival and security can never be enough, if only because life, however secure, must inevitably end. The contrast Aristotle draws between the "advantage of the present moment" and the somehow more dignified good of the whole of life evokes the longing we feel, in the face of life's brevity and its tendency to be consumed in the ultimately futile task of prolonging itself, to find something greater or more splendid to lift it out of its petty, mundane course. Franz Susemihl's and Ingram Bywater's suggested emendation of the evidently defective text of this passage, which would have the effect of introducing the theme of piety with the contrast between the advantage of the moment and the complete good of the whole of life, would strengthen the suggestion that it is life's brevity that leads us to look for something higher as an object of devotion.[7] But perhaps Aristotle also means to suggest that even endless utility and security would not satisfy the human heart either, because human beings are naturally directed to seek not merely utility but also joy, and a pleasant activity that gives one a window on the whole of which man is a part.

At the same time, Aristotle's emphasis on the pleasure and recreation provided by religious festivals serves to illuminate this paradox: Even at the moments at which human beings are most clearly seeking to lose themselves or transcend or sacrifice their self-interest in devotion to something higher, they are also pursuing their own good by ennobling or sanctifying their lives, if not also through the pleasures of good fellowship. With this pregnant image of a simple people sacrificing to the gods and enjoying themselves in the process, Aristotle introduces the theme of sacrifice into his discussion of friendship. How can we best make sense of the desire to dedicate one's life and sacrifice one's interest to the good of others, which is seen most vividly in man's worship of the gods, but which finds perhaps its most revealing expression in the attempt to rule and benefit other human beings in a magnificent way, like a divine guardian or shepherd? In approaching this question through the route that he does, Aristotle indicates that political hierarchy is not a violation of man's natural wholeness, but is itself a natural expression and development of a powerful, original impetus to transcend utility and strive for something noble, an impetus that is seen right at the heart of the simplest and most fraternal societies. Through the desire to make of one's life something splendid, men are impelled into the competition to rule and to test and prove their merit through ruling.

Aristotle now proceeds, in 8.10–8.11, to provide a new account of the political community, an account in which the concerns with virtue, excellence, and ruling become prominent themes. But if the political community as initially described in 8.9 seemed successfully to secure the common good while deemphasizing virtue, in the new account, in which virtue comes to the fore, the issue of the common good becomes much more problematic and perplexing. This is partly because the political realm in which the concern for virtue tends to be played out is a realm of intense competition for scarce honors and offices, but also partly because ruling well is thought to be pursuing the good of others and not of oneself.

Aristotle provides an account of the various regimes that are so many ways of resolving or managing this competition to rule. He sketches his classic division of regimes into three good and three corrupt types. Here as in *Politics* 4.2, he says that the best of all regimes is the rule of a single, virtuous king. A true king, in contrast to a tyrant, rules with a view not to his own advantage but the advantage of his subjects. He can do this because he himself is in every way superior, self-sufficient, and in need of nothing. Second best is aristocracy, which Aristotle defined implicitly by describing the failings of oligarchy, its corruption. Oligarchy is bad because in it the things of the city are not distributed according to merit, the oligarchs take all or most of the good things for themselves, the offices are always in the same hands, and the oligarchs care above all about money. In a true aristocracy, it would seem, the greatest share of honors, offices, and wealth would go to those who are best; yet the best men, being in office, would *not* take the lion's share of good things for themselves, but would rule like a good king for the benefit of the ruled; nor would they stay indefinitely in office, but power would be rotated between different men, and those in power would care most about virtue, not money.

With this implicit definition of aristocracy, Aristotle points delicately to a fundamental tension in political life and in virtually everyone's understanding of politics, a tension that gets worse the more serious a community becomes about promoting and rewarding merit. Ruling is considered an intrinsically good thing that only the best deserve, but ruling well is also considered a noble thing, good *not* for the ruler but for the ruled. These two opposing views become oddly conflated in the opinion that public-spirited men should serve selflessly in, but not monopolize, the highest offices. We believe that the best men should be rewarded with offices (considered as something good), but that being noble people, they should not keep them. We believe moreover that good men, when they fulfill the duties of their offices, are devoting themselves to the good of others, and that they should be rewarded for this self-denying service by being given pay or some other good thing, and nevertheless that they ought *not* to profit from their offices but should serve nobly. The uneasy accommodation that is usually reached between these views is to say that good rulers should not profit materially from office but instead should be rewarded with honor, which people both believe and do not believe to be finer and better than money. Aristotle, however, has said that honor is not loved for its own sake and is not craved by the best and most self-sufficient men. He thus leaves it a grave question how the friendship between the best men and those they rule and benefit can ever be equalized or maintained.

Continuing with his sixfold classification, Aristotle says that the third best regime is timocracy, the rule of all who meet a property qualification, and the third worst is its corruption, democracy. The perverted forms become less bad according to the number of people who partake in them, because, although virtue is not the criterion of rule, they aim at the advantage of successively greater numbers of people. Thus democracy is better than oligarchy, and both are better than tyranny. With timocracy Aristotle does not claim, as he does with aristocracy and monarchy, that the rulers rule for the sake of the ruled, but timocracy is still relatively good because its rulers and primary beneficiaries, who set the tone for the whole community, are a large and fairly decent segment of the population. Timocracy thus combines the advantage of a broad franchise with the insistence on a certain respectability and the moderation and responsibility that come with having an economic stake in the community. Before discussing in detail the possibilities for friendship in each of these regimes, however, Aristotle turns to the community that is found in the family.

Friendship within the Family

Although the political community seeks to provide in the most comprehensive and sovereign way for the good of its members, its very comprehensiveness creates a certain problem. The extensiveness of the community that is needed to sustain sovereign rule, and the inclusion of such different aims and different types of human beings under its auspices, means that the simple wholeness and fraternity that men wish to find in it will always be somewhat elusive. Many members will be tied to the community only by utility and will be kept from injustice only by force. A good lawgiver seeks to cultivate fraternity among a people, and good kings are said to love their peoples as fathers do, yet citizens are never as close as brothers, and a king can never know or love or benefit his people as does a parent, who gives life itself, as well as nurture and education (1161a10–17, 62a4–7). Thus the family enters the discussion of political friendship as a rival claimant to provide in the most comprehensive way for the good of its members. It is parents whom Aristotle calls the greatest benefactors, and clearly the family that has the first and deepest claim upon our hearts. Not only does it provide for what is good in an unparalleled way but it also "has a greater degree of what is useful and pleasant than do friendships with those outside the family, inasmuch as members of a family share more of their life in common" (1162a7–9). In comparison with the political community, the family is more unquestionably natural, "for man is by nature more a coupling than a political being, inasmuch as the household is prior and more necessary than the polis, and procreation is more widely shared with the animals" (1162a17–19).

In the *Politics,* where Aristotle makes the case for the political community, he claims not only that man is naturally political but that the polis is "prior" to the household, since the polis is the completed and self-sufficient whole of which the household is only a part, and the polis provides for or points us toward our natural and highest fulfillment in a way that the family does not (*Politics* 1252b27–53a25). From the perspective of the polis, members of a household are no more than "peers of the manger," united for the sake of the lowest needs, whereas the polis provides not only for living but also for living well (*Politics* 1252b12–15 and 27–30). From this point of view, if the family can be said to be prior, it is only in the sense of having come first in time.[8] But as Wayne Ambler has ably argued, the polis's own claims to naturalness are not unproblematic. On close reading, the *Politics* shows that the polis not just accidentally but unavoidably must distort and violate true standards of nature, even as it attempts to fulfill human nature.[9] For this reason, we find in every political community elements of arbitrariness, violence, and mere convention, which in the happiest families, following simple inclination and enjoying a sweeter harmony, are much less in evidence; at the very least we can say that such families are held together by bonds of affection more powerful and natural than the bonds that unite fellow citizens. Therefore, from the family's perspective, all other connections, including those of citizenship, are more limited and conditional: "Political friendships and those of fellow tribesmen, fellow sailors, and others such as these seem to have more of the nature of a partnership, and appear to exist by virtue of a certain agreement" (*NE* 1161b13–15).

What is most impressive about the family is the unconditional nature of its bonds, which Aristotle emphasizes. On the one side, he says, the child, owing everything to his father, can never discharge his debt, and hence can never rightly disown him (1163b18–21). On the other side, parents, whose love is far deeper than most of the love that arises in response to what is pleasant, useful, or even good, are almost never inclined to disown a child. Parents love children "as their own," and even "as themselves" (1161b18, 28), and this love of one's own is so deep and unqualified that, at its purest, it does not depend upon the child's returning the love or even knowing the parent at all: Some mothers "give their own to be raised by others, and love them and know them, but do not seek to be loved in return, if both are not possible, but it seems to be enough for them to see their children faring well and to love them, even if the children give them nothing of what is due to a mother, because they do not know her" (1159a28–33).[10]

It is striking that love comes closest to being perfectly selfless when the object of the love is most fully and indisputably one's own, both similar to oneself and formed by oneself. Here, in the discussion of parents' love for their children, Aristotle first uses the famous formulation of the friend or loved one as "another self" (1161b28–29). With the possible exception of the love of husband and wife, all the bonds of affection within the family are more or less strong to the extent that each person is certain that the other is his or her own, and to the extent that each sees in the other another self:[11]

Parents know better that their children are their own than children know that they come from their parents, and the bond that ties begetter to offspring is closer than that tying offspring to its source. For that which comes from something belongs to it, such as a tooth, a hair, and the like, but to that which has come from it the source does not belong, or does so to a lesser extent. And there is a difference in terms of time: The parents love children as soon as they are born, but they only come to love the parents with the passage of time, as they acquire understanding or perception. (1161b19–26)

Because the certainty that the child is one's own is never quite so absolute in the case of the father as in the case of the mother, and perhaps also because a father only fully recognizes a kindred soul when the child becomes capable of speech, whereas the mother feels a more primal bond of unity and kinship from the outset, the love of mothers is deeper and more unqualified. In the same way, brothers, the paradigmatic case of intimate companions, are close to the extent that they are similar and feel one another to be their own, and cousins and others relations have the same bond in a more diluted form (1161b27–62a4).

In this chapter Aristotle brings together a constellation of closely related ideas that all point back to the insight at the end of the *Lysis*: that not need as such but belonging as such is the truly irreducible root of human affection. Just as Socrates speaks of the kindred (οἰκεῖον) as a source of friendship but seems to have in mind the kinship of spirit more than of blood (*Lysis* 221e3–22a7), so Aristotle, in discussing precisely the power of common descent, shows that what is akin (συγγενής) is loved for its similarity (ὁμοιότης) to us, and for the sense that it is our own, and most of all when we are its source.

The idea of the "other self" that first appears here in its biological sense will reemerge in Book 9 to characterize true friendship between kindred spirits, who can enhance for one another the very best activities in life and whose similarity and mutual belonging run even deeper than blood. But no doubt literal kinship defines most people's closest ties, and here in Book 8, Aristotle does full justice to the sweet, uncalculating, naturally rooted closeness of family bonds.

Yet such closeness in the family is only half of the story. The traditional family is also the locus of extreme inequalities and extraordinary claims, not only of parents upon children but of husbands upon wives and ancestors upon descendants. Aristotle seems to regard all of this as perfectly natural and perfectly reasonable. He presents the rule of men over their wives and children as only what is due to men by virtue of their superiority, and the claims of parents and ancestors to honor and deference as no more than what is just in light of their unanswerable claim to be their offspring's greatest benefactors (1161a15–21, 62a4–7). But is the picture Aristotle paints quite so simple? At the very least, we may say that the claims of justice he depicts parents as making, however natural these claims may be, cast a certain shadow over his simultaneous portrayal of the family as natural in the sense of being naturally sweet and fulfilling and rooted in inclinations that are universal among the higher forms of life. Mother birds would never dream of demanding honor from their grown nestlings, or reminding them of all they have done on their behalf; the animals simply care for their offspring as a matter of course. The human family, however, presents two conflicting pictures of itself, and the pictures clash especially on the question of justice.

According to one picture, the child is so completely the parent's own and loved so naturally and so deeply that no question of justice can arise between them. Aristotle gives this argument in Book 5: "There is no injustice in the unqualified sense toward what is one's own, toward one's property or one's child, until he reaches a certain age and becomes separate; they are like part of oneself, and no one would choose to harm himself" (1134b9–12). This is what the family says, in effect, to anyone who is inclined to interfere between parent and child, and it is why political communities have traditionally not allowed children to bring lawsuits against their parents: The authority of parents can be assumed to be benevolent and should be left intact. This is what parents say to outsiders, but to ungrateful children the message is different: "We have done everything for you, given you everything, sacrificed everything for your welfare, and nothing you could possibly do could repay this debt." No one expects any credit or reward for taking good care of his own roof or his own feet. Children are more precious than either of these, but they are also, especially in the long run, more separate, and the extent to which parents do expect credit and honor and recompense from their children and even their distant descendants reflects the extent to which the efforts of child rearing are not so unambiguously rewarding as is taking care of what is unambiguously one's own.

Perhaps what is true of family love is to some extent true of all friendship. One loves the other as another *self*, and to that extent truly seeks the other's good for his own sake, but one also loves him as *another* self, and one is not content endlessly to promote another's good and get nothing in return. Even or especially in the family, where the natural desire to benefit is at its strongest, the claims for just recompense are revealingly great.

Marriage and Justice

Aristotle uses the political relations of kingship and aristocracy as a model for the relationships of parenthood and marriage, just as he uses family relations as a standard of comparison that sheds light on political ones. Like kings, parents and especially fathers claim obedience and honor on the grounds of their superiority in conferring benefits:

> The friendship of a king for those he rules depends on his superiority in doing good: for he does good to those he rules, if indeed he is good and takes care of them so that they may fare well, just as a shepherd does his sheep. Thus Homer called Agamemnon "shepherd of the people." That of a father is of the same kind, but it differs in the magnitude of the benefits; for he is the cause of their being, which is regarded as the greatest of goods, and of their rearing and education. And the same things are attributed to ancestors. By nature a father rules over his sons and ancestors over descendants and a king over those he rules. These friendships turn upon superiority, and that is why children honor their parents. (1161a11–22)

In marriage, likewise, husbands claim to rule over their wives on the basis of superiority, but it is less clear whether this is a superiority in conferring benefits or of some other kind:

> The association of husband and wife appears to be aristocratic. The man rules by virtue of his merit, and with regard to those things that are proper for a man. What is suitable for a woman he turns over to her. When a man takes charge of everything, he transforms the association into an oligarchy, for he does this against the principle of merit, and not by virtue of his superiority. Sometimes women rule because they are heiresses. But this rule is based not on merit but on wealth and power, just as in oligarchies. (1160b32–61a3)

This analogy between aristocracy and traditional marriage, which John Stewart criticizes as "more ingenious than useful," is indeed rather strange and fraught with ambiguities.[12] As in other discussions of rule according to merit, Aristotle gives a certain defense of a traditionally common ruling arrangement, a defense that in fact holds up a standard by which many or most actual instances of that rule may be measured and found wanting.

The Greeks tended to justify slavery (when they tried to justify it at all) with the argument that it is right for the stronger and better to rule the inferior

(*Politics* 1255a12–21), and that a victorious warrior's manly strength and courage entitle him to possess and rule the cowards who have surrendered to him, especially when these are barbarians. War and politics were the honorable pursuits of men in ancient Greece, and the courage or manliness (ἀνδρεία) by which they won victories and defended their freedom tended to be the most celebrated virtue.[13] Those who were deficient in courage were seen as fit for servitude, and manual labor was seen as fit for slaves. Aristotle, however, ranks justice and especially wisdom more highly than courage.[14] He points out that chance and injustice often cause better men to fall into the hands of worse, and he accepts slavery as truly just only in those rather rare cases in which one man rules another for the good of both, and being ruled well is beneficial for the slave because "he participates in reason only to the extent of perceiving it, but does not have it" (*Politics* 1255a21–29; 1254b16–23).[15]

Apparently for the same reason that he implicitly denies the justice of despotic rule over intelligent men, Aristotle denies the justice of such rule over wives: This practice he condemns as barbaric. He thereby gives the impression that marriage as practiced by the Greeks was generally just, and reinforces this impression with his suggestion, in the *Nicomachean Ethics,* that marriage as practiced in Greece is analogous to aristocracy. But what does he mean by this analogy? Does he mean that husband and wife in a just marriage truly share authority in the household, each being sovereign over children and servants, but in different ways? Or does he mean that a husband's rule over a wife is aristocratic inasmuch as he is superior, so that he properly has ultimate authority over everything, although he should leave the execution of certain tasks up to her?[16]

The difficulty in assessing Aristotle's true opinion on the just division or balance of authority in marriage is that he has so little to say about women, and he never gives a full account of how he considers men and women to differ in the virtues relevant to rule, and especially in prudence or wisdom. In the *Ethics,* his only explicit statement about the differences in virtue between men and women is that women are more given to unrestrained mourning (1171b10–11). In both the *Politics* and the *Rhetoric,* he characterizes women as less courageous than men (*Politics* 1277b20–22, *Rhetoric* 1360b39–61a7). In the *Politics,* he calls men "more given to commanding" (ἡγεμονικώτερον) than women (1259b2), but does this mean that they are more capable of ruling, or merely more likely to take charge? And if the former, is it because they are wiser, or merely more able to secure obedience? On the crucial virtue of wisdom, he makes only the cryptic remark that while a woman possesses the deliberative element, "it lacks authority" (*Politics* 1260a13). This could mean, and it certainly seems to mean, that women are capable of reasoning correctly but are prone to impulsiveness or moral weakness.[17] But in fact, Aristotle never says that moral weakness is a particularly feminine failing. And his comment on the deliberative element is open to a different reading, suggested by the difference he mentions a page before: Perhaps a woman's reason is sovereign over her to the same extent that a man's is over him, but her judgments carry less authority with *others,* and especially with men. Our suspicions about this statement are reinforced by yet another statement, fraught with precisely the same ambiguity, just a few lines later. In illustrating the idea that the virtues are different in man and woman, Aristotle quotes the saying of "the poet" that "to a woman silence is an ornament" (*Politics* 1260a30). The line is a verse from Sophocles' *Ajax* (line 293) where it is, in fact, spoken by a madman.[18] An examination of this great play, which turns out to be all about manly anger and womanly weeping and quiet wisdom, leads us to wonder whether Aristotle's allusion to it is not a signal that we should look here for a fuller consideration of themes that he himself touches upon with only the lightest of brushstrokes.[19]

In Sophocles' play, the hero Ajax, second in prowess only to Achilles among the Greeks at Troy, has just lost to Odysseus in the contest for Achilles' armor, and has vowed bloody revenge upon Agamemnon, Menelaus, and his nemesis Odysseus. In his physical strength, his apparent self-reliance, and his fierce pride and thirst for honor, Ajax is the epitome of heroic manliness. But Athena has turned his wits, causing him in his rage to fall upon the army's herds in the belief that they are its captains. As he is leaving the tent at midnight upon this brutal errand, his wife Tecmessa asks him where he is going and urges him to go back to sleep, but when he dismisses her with the line Aristotle quotes, she gives up. Ajax then proceeds to butcher and torture the animals, a deed that plunges him into such shame when he recovers his senses the next day that he commits suicide. The ineffectualness of Tecmessa's objection shows how a woman's reason may be sound yet lack authority: It lacks it because she is unwilling or unable to fight to carry her point, and because manliness as such, embodied in the proud warrior for whom courage is the paramount virtue and honor the only possession that matters, has little respect for reason as such.[20] Silence, from this point of view, seems a most dubious virtue in women.

In comparison with the raging Ajax, the unheroic, sober, and patient Tecmessa is a sympathetic figure. Ajax has been a great man, but in Sophocles' play we see mainly the horrible limitations of his greatness. To be sure, his insanity has been inflicted by the goddess Athena, but it is a peculiar insanity that changes nothing in his soul and merely distorts his perception of physical objects. His unwillingness to bow to force or necessity is somehow impressive but not admirable; his towering indignation is awe inspiring but not wise; his incapacity to live without the honor he thinks is his due bespeaks a greatness but also a rigidity that finally proves brittle as he breaks into the tears he thought he would never shed. Tecmessa, a captive princess given to Ajax as booty, has learned well the virtues of bowing to necessity and has come to love her husband and find joy with him and their small son. Hers is the wisdom of gentleness, of remembering kindness more than insults, of adaptability, of knowledge of her own limitations. But Tecmessa's limitations, especially in this warrior society, are serious ones. She cannot fend for herself or her child and is devastated by the loss of her lord and protector.

In contrast to Tecmessa's realistic yet vulnerable sense of connection, Ajax yearns and strives for perfect autonomy. He refuses to acknowledge his need for anyone, including the gods. Yet his life and actions have meaning only in the heroic context of helping his friends, punishing his enemies, and following laws and standards of behavior that he did not himself create. His refusal to bow to anyone leads him to break trust with those who need him, denying the very nexus of mutual obligation that gives his life meaning, and so revealing an intractable tension in the heroic striving for self-sufficiency. This tension would seem to be solved if Ajax could achieve godlike invulnerability. Yet the gods in Sophocles' play show a problem of their own. Their involvement with human beings seems premised upon a craving for honor from them and a desire to punish those who dishonor them. But why should truly self-sufficient beings need applause from and enjoy triumphing over such weak subordinates?

Odysseus, the third major figure in the play, combines all of Tecmessa's wisdom with all of Ajax's manliness to produce a steely strength.[21] He has a flexible willingness to adapt his loves and hates to necessity that looks downright unmanly, but he alone has the courage to face squarely the hard truths of the human condition without raging and without weeping.[22] Odysseus has, like Tecmessa, a propensity to remember the good in others, to forgive their faults, and to find common ground with them. Recognition of a common fate and shared vulnerability gives him a gentle, diffused sense of humanity, even as recognition of the harshness of life, and the ultimate necessity of looking out for oneself, place chilling qualifications upon his loyalties.

If human wisdom has elements characteristic of women as well as elements characteristic of men, and if the wise Odysseus reveres above all divinities the female goddess of wisdom Athena, still it may be no accident that the character who successfully combines these qualities into a humane whole that is stronger than mere manliness is portrayed as both human and male. Indeed, being otherwise human and yet invulnerable as Athena is might well make it harder rather than easier to be wise. Odysseus has learned that exultation over the defeats of others is never sensible for human beings, whose happiness is subject to such sudden reversal. But perhaps this is only a special case of the general truth that for all such beings as we are and observe and can even coherently conceive of, happiness or well-being is, if not precarious, at least fundamentally conditioned by a nature that one does not control, an insight which ought to produce a great sense of moderation and little desire to gloat. At the same time, to the extent that the ultimate truths of our human condition are harsh ones, wisdom will require a rare degree of courage, such as we see in the heroic Odysseus and not Tecmessa. For wisdom requires mastering the temptation to dissolve into tears in desperate moments, tears that always show an incapacity completely to accept hard necessity, and a furtive hope that one's suffering will somehow move the pity of the universe and make it relent. Ajax exclaims upon this susceptibility of women to weeping, and it seems likely that here, if anywhere, is the serious kernel of truth to his bombastic claim that silence in women is an ornament.

Because honor and vengeance do not as often lie within their grasp, women are less prone to the madness of seeking to force all the world to honor them, and to wreak fabulous punishments on others for putting themselves first. The sobriety that comes with this necessary moderation makes it likely that ordinary women will in judgment be the equals of such ordinary men as they find themselves married to, even if they lack the strength and determination to win the authority that their judgment deserves, and even if their lack of boldness and toughness may handicap them in reaching the greatest heights of human wisdom. Some such conclusion is suggested by Sophocles' *Ajax* and at least contradicts nothing in Aristotle: We may guess that it is perhaps what Aristotle might have said, had he chosen to say more about women's true capacities. But for reasons that are not yet altogether clear, even if Aristotle was not wholly serious in his suggestion that silence in women is a virtue, silence about women seems to have been regarded as a virtue by this philosopher.[23]

Our examination of the *Ajax* suggests that if it is just for authority to be allocated strictly on the basis of wisdom (the standard that, in Plato's *Republic*, gives the philosopher title to rule), then marriages should generally give something close to equal authority to husband and wife. At the same time, the play shows why such a standard will never be met in any society that has not undergone a radical reevaluation of the virtues of courage and manliness. The image of marriage as a truly harmonious sharing of deliberation and rule, involving mutual respect, mutual support, and mutual exhortations to virtue, was not without charm even for the Greeks, and it is one theme of the pseudo-Aristotelian *Oeconomica* (3.4). But a look at other parts of this work that portray the husband as ruler, and especially at Xenophon's *Oeconomicus,* the fullest portrayal we have of marriage in classical Athens, will show just how far such a genuine partnership is from the reality Aristotle had before him, or even from relatively enlightened Greek opinion.[24]

In Xenophon's depiction of Socrates' conversation with the improvident gentleman Critoboulus, Socrates easily guesses and wins Critoboulus's admission that there is no one to whom he turns over more things of importance than to his wife, and almost no one with whom he converses less (3.12). The wife was typically not the husband's partner in deliberation or his friend, but simply the chief steward of the household. In contrast, the thoughtful and noble-minded Ischomachus, whom Socrates holds up as a model for Critoboulus, takes unusual care to educate his wife, and is shown consulting with her in the governance of the servants and promising to do so in the rearing of any children they may have (7.12, 7.30, 9.11–13). Yet he reserves to himself the prerogative of assigning her duties to her, confining her to the house, and determining how she will dress and occupy herself; he takes pride in the alacrity with which she grasps and obeys his orders (7.10–43, 9.16–17, 10.1–13).

However, rather than criticizing such male rule as Ischomachus exemplifies, let alone calling for the equality of women as Socrates does in Plato's *Republic,* Aristotle seems to endorse male rule with his suggestion that not merely shared rule but the husband's rule *over* the wife is consistent with the requirements of aristocracy. Yet Aristotle does hint, however quietly, at problems with husbands' claim to rule. His comment on heiresses is one indication of a doubt. If the occasional woman with a substantial inheritance of her own sometimes rules because of this inheritance, how often may it be the case that the men who, because of convention, normally bring most of the money to marriages, rule by virtue of this money, or by virtue of some other form of power, and not their greater merit? Aristotle does not say, but he prompts us to wonder. His comment on benefits is a further indication of a problem. Aristotle says that husbands, being superior, get the larger share of benefits (*NE* 1161a24);[25] he does not and perhaps could not plausibly say of husbands, as he says of true aristocrats, that in ruling they put the good of the ruled above their own (1160b12–14). Everyone recognizes self-rule to be a good thing, and the capacity to exercise it well is perhaps a good parent's greatest gift. But when men who are equal to or only moderately more capable of ruling than their wives insist on commanding them, as well as the children and servants, they unjustly deprive the women of the opportunity to develop their own virtues.[26] In marriage, as in politics, we see the tension between the justice of concentrating authority in the best hands and the justice of dispersing it, the tension between the justice of giving the greatest benefits to the best and the justice of demanding that rulers rule for the benefit of the ruled, and the elusiveness, even in the most intimate relations, of a perfect common good.

But Aristotle indicates perhaps the most serious difficulty in the idea of marriage as an aristocracy when he combines his description of paternal rule as analogous to monarchy and his account of marriage as analogous to aristocracy. If the father rules the children as king, and merely delegates to his wife the tasks for which she is suited, such as weaving, then it is no aristocracy at all but a monarchy or tyranny. For the rule of a single person over others in all matters that they are not competent to manage by themselves is not aristocracy but monarchy, and the rule of one person over others in all respects, without regard to merit, is not oligarchy but tyranny. What fundamentally distinguishes an aristocracy from a monarchy is, of course, the number of those who rule, and it is on this question of how many rulers and benefactors a family has that Aristotle hedges and indeed contradicts himself.

If husband and wife are truly functioning as an aristocracy, then authority is truly shared, even if unequally. This is what traditional husbands like Ischomachus, when they are genteel, say to wives: "We are managing this family and household together, each taking charge of the things we do best, and consulting together about everything concerning the welfare of our children." But to the children, especially when they have been disobedient or ungrateful, fathers say something different: "I am in charge of you and know what is good for you, and you must obey me as your king; I have given you life, and nurture, and education; to me you owe everything that you are, and for that you must forever honor and defer to me, and teach your own children to do likewise." When Aristotle compares a father to a king, he lets the father make such a claim to be the sole source of everything good for his children (1161a15–17).[27] But when he is discussing the family as a whole and focusing on the closeness of the bonds within it, especially the extraordinary love of mothers for children, he changes the formulation, using the same terms to describe the benefits that parents, in the plural, give to their children (1162a4–7).

Thus Aristotle shows that fathers, much more than mothers, are inclined to hyperbole in the claims they make to deserve to rule the family and to be honored by it. This difference is tied not only to the fact that men love rule and honor more, but also to the fact that women love their children more and find this love more satisfying in and of itself: They do not feel such a need for compensation. In this common project of raising children, in the wife's devotion to the children's welfare, and in the value she places on the husband's irreplaceable assistance in securing their welfare, we find perhaps the strongest reason for wives' willingness to acquiesce in husbands' demands for the lion's share of authority and honor in the family.

Aristotle brings out the same difficulty at *Politics* 1259a37–b10 when he says that the relationship of husband to wife is an instance of political rule – this being the alternation of ruling and being ruled in turn, in accordance with law, of citizens who are more or less equal – but with the one modification that in marriage, it always somehow turns out to be the husband's turn at the helm. Does this change leave "political" rule in any way intact, or have we simply returned to tyranny or despotism? Not simply, at least not usually; the family, especially when there are children, provides scope for more of a true common good, more affection, and more consultation and genuine consent than can exist in a whole political community. At the least, marriage tends to be a softened despotism. In the better cases, where at some level husband and wife both recognize a rough equality of good sense between them, the husband's rule will be somewhat ceremonial and known to be such, like the prerogatives that members of a polity insist on when it is their turn to preside.[28]

Thus it is not hard to envision a best practical regime in the family, as in politics: a mixed regime of sorts that would provide a compromise between the dictates of strict justice and the necessity of recognizing and accommodating the claims of overwhelming strength. Such a regime, in the family, would involve a mixture of paternal monarchy with parental aristocracy, with more honors and prerogatives for the man, a division of spheres of responsibility with significant freedom allowed to each in the management of his or her sphere, but also mutual advice and consultation on all important decisions. For such an enhanced role, women would need a serious training in virtue so as to be models for all of their children, male and female, the knowledge and confidence and hardiness that would come from a less cloistered life, and more respect from husbands if they were truly to share authority over the children.

Such a reform of Greek practice was neither impracticable nor unthinkable, as Plato's *Republic* shows, but was Aristotle advocating it? This is far from evident, for his critique of current practice in the *Ethics* is so subtle as to be nearly imperceptible. And unlike Locke and Rousseau, who offer clear practical programs for the reform of society and marriage that involve careful attention to the education of both boys and girls, Aristotle's detailed discussion of education in Books 7 and 8 of the *Politics* makes no mention of educating girls. He does indeed censure the Greek polities for failing to attend adequately to the education and regulation of women, but rather than proposing specific reforms, he contents himself with pointing out, in a general way, the need for legislators to ensure that women's lives are regulated so as to support, rather than (as at Sparta) to undermine, the goals of the regime.

Aristotle's discussion of marriage in the *Nicomachean Ethics* seems even less designed to reform actual practice; its chief purpose seems to be to deepen the thoughtfulness of his predominantly male readers on the question of their own beliefs about the family and marriage as these shed light on more fundamental questions.[29] The most thoughtful reader of these chapters, as of Xenophon's *Oeconomicus,* may begin to wonder why it is that gentlemen have such difficulty talking about marriage and the family without contradicting themselves. Why do they at one moment speak and think as though they, being superior, deserve the lion's share of everything good, especially rule and honor, while at other moments saying and even believing that they are selflessly sacrificing their good for the good of those under their care, and at still other times persuading themselves that their marriage is a true partnership of equals in the service of a common good? These issues are part of the broader probing into questions of justice and the common good in 8.9–8.12, and especially into the question of why it is that ruling over others appears so attractive and so noble.

Parental Rule

In comparison with the problematic claims of husbands, a much less problematic claim to rule on the basis of superior merit is clearly the one made by parents, especially when their children are small. It is not superiority alone, however, but only superiority combined with a steadfast love and devotion to the child's welfare that gives the parents a credible claim to deserve to govern their children. Rule over children for the parents' own sake is tyranny. Hence parents' claims to honor and obedience, when they are just, rest not upon their superiority as such but upon their superiority as benefactors. Aristotle endorses these claims, observing more than once that fathers or parents are the greatest benefactors. Yet even here, there may be some exaggeration, both in the duration of the deference demanded and in the extent of the benefits claimed. For how is it that "by nature" ancestors rule over their descendants? Certainly Aristotle does not regard the past as simply superior to the present, or ancestors as simply wiser than descendants. By highlighting the claims of ancestors, Aristotle gives another indication that the life of caring for the good of others is, especially in the light of one's own mortality, not simply satisfying or satisfactory, and seems to be in need of a great compensation.

Of the three benefits that parents take credit for – those of life, nurture, and education – the one that can only be given by parents, life itself, is given at no cost at all to the father and usually only a moderate cost to the mother. Does one really owe one's father anything for this? The furnishing of life's necessities is indeed costly and indispensable and is indeed usually done by the parents alone; their claims on this basis are the strongest. But the provision of what is most precious, a good moral and intellectual education, is always shared with others: the political community and its laws, the religious teachers and priests, and often other teachers as well. If it is true, as Aristotle acknowledges, that the family is the first and often chief provider of moral and intellectual education, he also gives increasing indications, as the discussion proceeds, that the family as such has an ambiguous relationship to both virtue and wisdom.[30]

In his interwoven discussions of politics and the family in 8.9–8.12, Aristotle suggests at first that fatherhood and marriage rest, like true monarchy and aristocracy, on the superior virtue and wisdom of those who rule, but as the discussion proceeds, it becomes increasingly clear that these political analogies force the family into a mold that does not completely fit. The family is truly shaped and defined not so much by conventional and questionable claims to rule according to merit as it is by the natural inclination of men and women to unite in couples, the shared love of children whom both parents cherish as their own, and the shared project of raising them: Aristotle says that man is more naturally a coupling than a political being (1162a17–18). It is these elements of pleasure, utility, and above all the love of one's own that Aristotle comes to focus upon as the discussion proceeds in 8.12, finally concluding that "children seem to be the bond that holds marriage together . . . for children are a common good for both partners" (1162a27–29). This is, significantly, Aristotle's only use of the expression "common good" in the whole of the *Nicomachean Ethics*. To the extent that children are the focus of marriage, to the extent that women do take a meaningful part not only in their nurture but also in their moral education – as, to some extent, they have of course always done – marriage does turn out to provide a true and even uniquely powerful community of interests and purpose.

But what precisely is the "common good" that is children? Children are good as new beginnings and fresh promises, as beings uniquely suited to elicit tenderness and hopes, as beings naturally directed toward, and not yet corrupted away from, complete human perfection. Children also provide an especially appropriate and pleasing object and opportunity for their parents' own activity of generous benefaction, an activity that expands the life and being of those engaged in it, as Aristotle will show in detail in 9.7. And yet, according to Aristotle, children as immature beings can be said to be good only in a qualified way, as beings whose "nature" it is to strive for perfect goodness, and yet whose attainment of their natural end is anything but assured. In the end as in the beginning, parents love their children whether their potential goodness is realized or not. They love them more, perhaps, when they turn out to be virtuous, but above all simply because they are their own.

In much the same way, other friendships within the family may respond to and be strengthened by the virtue of their members. As Aristotle says, the friendship of husband and wife "may even be a friendship of virtue, if they are good, for there is a virtue appropriate to each, and they can rejoice in this" (1162a25–27). The friendship of siblings is likewise strengthened by virtue, and children usually find it easier to love and honor parents when they are virtuous, although the goodness that children most love them for is their goodness to themselves, and they may even come to hate the virtues of their parents that take them away from them. Virtue, when it is present, is a supplement to family love, but the true bedrock of the family is the uncalculating, unwavering love of one's own. It is both the great strength and the great limitation of the traditional family that its bonds are, or are meant to be, unconditional. The traditional family demands one's first and last loyalties, to itself and to the gods and beliefs and way of life it represents. And if its relationship to virtue is ambiguous, its relationship to philosophy – which arises out of and never leaves off the rigorous, uncompromising questioning of gods, customs, traditions, and family – is deeply, inherently hostile. As we see in the dramatic encounter with Cephalus at the beginning of Plato's *Republic,* Socrates must remove the fathers before he can talk freely with the sons, and the conflict between the claims of fathers and the claims of wise teachers will become an explicit theme in 9.1–9.3.

Friendship in Political Life

If the family is not by its nature directed to virtue and provides opportunities for virtuous friendship only occasionally and fortuitously, what are the possibilities for virtuous and serious friendships in political life, which gives scope for the greatest exercise of moral virtue? In democracy and timocracy, the possibilities for uncomplicated, fraternal friendships seem to be the greatest.[31] Aristotle likens timocracy to the association of brothers, and democracy to the equal relations of people in a household that has no master, where each can do as he pleases (1161a3–9). The different stations and different interests of ruler and ruled do not, as elsewhere, present a barrier to friendship, yet the tone of the society, being lax with respect to virtue, will not tend to foster the most virtuous or noble-minded political friendships. In the more seriously corrupt regimes, the prospects for virtuous political friendships are of course even worse. Oligarchs, ruling unjustly, have little basis for friendship with their subjects and no good reason to trust or treasure one another; and tyrants have the fewest opportunities for friendship and the most reasons to suspect the friendship of those around them.[32]

For honorable, legitimate monarchs, the prospects for friendship would seem to be much better, yet Aristotle indicates that the best friendships are largely outside their aim or beyond their reach as well:

Those in power seem to have separate groups of friends: Some are useful to them and others pleasant, but the same men are seldom both. For they seek neither those who are pleasant and virtuous, nor those who are useful for noble ends, but when they want pleasure they seek witty people, and otherwise ones who are clever at doing what they are ordered to do, and these qualities seldom are found in the same person. As has been said, it is the serious man who is at once pleasant and useful. But such a man will not become a friend to a superior, unless he is also superior in virtue. Otherwise, he will not be able to establish proportional equality as an inferior. But such men are seldom found. (1158a27–36)

These monarchs who keep their friends in separate compartments are not very serious about virtue, and Aristotle's description suggests that they may tend to be kept from a concern with virtue by the pressures of urgent and sometimes unsavory business, the desire for relaxation and escape from these pressures, and the consequent lack of serious leisure, as well as by the difficulty good men have in being their friends.

Interestingly enough, whereas Aristotle stresses rulers' tendency to compartmentalize friendships, and presumably, in doing so, to keep everyone at arm's length, Bacon emphasizes the opposite tendency of rulers to seek out people to whom they can open and unburden their hearts, even at great risk to themselves, citing such examples as Sylla and Pompey the Great, and Julius Caesar and Brutus.[33] The example of Caesar and Brutus, and the famous English friendships between Henry II and Becket and Henry VIII and Thomas More, are examples of deep friendships that have arisen between truly virtuous men and rulers, but the fact that each of these friendships ended in the death of one friend at the hands of the other illustrates Aristotle's point that the proper balance is very hard to establish and maintain.

The problem is not, as Martin Ostwald and H. Rackham suppose, that good men are unwilling to pay kings the greater affection they owe in return for the greater benefits they receive and cannot otherwise repay.[34] The problem is rather that rulers, in bestowing their friendship, imagine themselves to be bestowing an incomparable benefit, and therefore make extravagant demands upon the loyalty and deference of their subject-friends, whereas the latter, knowing themselves to be good men, and in the most important respects by no means their rulers' inferiors, believe that they are perfectly capable of repaying their honor and favors with good counsel and assistance in all just and noble undertakings; they believe themselves to owe no more affection than they receive. The rulers sooner or later demand that they place loyalty and gratitude before integrity and justice, but this good men are unwilling to do, and so the friendships founder.

What, then, of the rare ruler of complete virtue and wisdom, who never would make unjust demands upon his subordinates? Aristotle gives no example of such a man, and we can find no perfect example either: He is a limit case, a theoretical construct intended to shed light on the issues and problems of political rule and not to describe any actual rulers. When we imagine the friendship of such a ruler for his people as a whole, and the particular friendships he might form with his most excellent subjects, the problem that arises is how any of these friendships can attain the balance that friendship needs. What is the motive for a truly virtuous man to love and benefit his fellows, insofar as he is not deficient or needy and hence not driven by the hope for any benefits from them in return?

Aristotle discusses the true king's friendship for his subjects in terms of two or perhaps three pregnant analogies, comparing a king's rule to that of a father over his sons and that of a shepherd over his sheep, and hinting likewise at a comparison with the rule of gods over men. Aristotle's frequently reiterated analogy between the good king and the father is rhetorically effective, lending an aura of dignity to the claims of fathers and an aura of naturalness and affection to the claims of kings, but at a deeper level, it also calls the claims of both into question. As we have seen, the assertion of fathers that they are all as far superior to their families, including their grown or nearly grown sons, as a wise and virtuous king is to his subjects is doubtful. On the other hand, the king's claim – even or especially the best king's claim – to love his people as a father loves his own children is even more doubtful. For Aristotle has shown paternal love to be rooted in a conviction that the child is profoundly one's own, depending for his being upon oneself, akin by nature, and shaped by one's own care and educative efforts. No king can have any such sense of kinship with the people he rules, whose lives are so different from his, and whose relations with him are so distant and formal, and all the less so to the extent that he is truly a king in the Aristotelian sense of being superior in every way to his subjects.

Perhaps, then, the better analogy is with the shepherd's rule over his sheep, which like a father's care involves real solicitude, but which also involves a difference in kind between ruler and ruled (1161a10–15). But this analogy, however rich its resonances for Greeks, let alone for Jews and Christians, has problems, too. If we are seeking a basis for true affection and friendship between ruler and ruled, we will not find it here. A shepherd may indeed love his sheep, but only as Midas loved his gold or Imelda Marcos her shoes; a shepherd tends his sheep only so that he may have more of them to shear and eat. That Aristotle did not mean for such thoughts to be far from our minds is confirmed on the next page, where he says:

Where there is nothing in common between a ruler and ruled, there is no friendship, and no justice: for example, between craftsman and tool, soul and body, or master and slave. All of these are, to be sure, benefited by the one who uses them, but there is no friendship or justice toward inanimate objects, nor toward a horse or ox, nor toward a slave as a slave ... although there may be insofar as he is a man. (1161a32–b8)

If there is no more room for friendship and justice between a master and his horse or ox than there is between a master and slave, how much less is there between shepherd and sheep? For even an ox may be his master's partner in work, to the small extent that he pulls hard when pulling hard is required, and a horse may be a partner and "friend" to a much greater extent, just as slaves sometimes are when they come to care about the welfare of their masters. But with dumb sheep no partnership of any sort is possible.

One may, of course, object that the image of the king as shepherd is only an imperfect analogy, and that while shepherds are poor and in need of food and clothing, a true king is different in being "self-sufficient and superior in all good things" (1160b3–4). The good king, then, is really more like a god in doing good without needing anything in return. But Aristotle is, at best, ambiguous as to whether it really makes sense to think of the gods as doing this. He refers to Homer's appellation of Zeus as "father," but his own less anthropomorphic presentation of god or the gods suggests that they are beings wholly different in kind, who have no bodies and no part in procreation, and who share with men only the capacity for contemplation. Men consider the gods as their benefactors, to be sure, and in trying to repay them with honor, imagine themselves to be in some degree equalizing an unequal friendship or satisfying the requirements of justice (1163b15–17, 1164b3–6). But Aristotle never says that the gods themselves recognize any friendship or ties of justice as subsisting between themselves and the men who seek to honor them. To the contrary, he says that friendship between gods and men is impossible (1159a3–5), that the gods do not partake in moral virtue (1145a25–26, but cf. 1134b28–29), that honor, which is all men have to offer the gods, is of no intrinsic worth (1159a17–18), that it is absurd to think of the gods as taking part in moral action, including acts of generosity (1178b8ff.), that the gods, being simple and whole, must have only one unvarying pleasure (1154b25–26), and that their only activity is contemplation (1178b8ff.).[35]

In sum, Aristotle's analysis of tyranny and kingship suggests that the possibility of friendship between ruler and subject faces grave problems on both sides. To the extent that the ruler is similar to the general run of people and shares their outlook, believing that wealth, pleasure, honor, and the freedom to pursue one's desires with impunity are the most desirable things, he will serve his own good and not theirs, but to the extent that his concerns are of a different order, and especially to the extent that he is self-sufficient, he has no clear reason for devoting himself to solving the people's problems.

Now, while these difficulties for political friendship in monarchy are indeed significant, it is also fair to say that Aristotle's account in 8.10–8.11 has the effect of exaggerating them, and leaving the careful reader quite at a loss as to why, in Aristotle's understanding, a good man would ever wish to rule or care for his countrymen's welfare. There are at least five possible answers to this question that Aristotle's account up through 8.11 either explicitly rules out or implicitly obscures. First, it may be that honor or glory is in some way intrinsically good, and that Aristotle has deliberately understated its value. Second, by stressing the king's self-sufficiency, Aristotle draws attention away from the fact that even the wisest and best human beings, if only because they have bodies, are vulnerable, and share the need we all have for a society that provides peace, security, and good laws. Third, to the extent that the best man shares needs with others, he will feel at least some kinship and sympathy with them; he will wish for peace, security, and good laws for his fellows' sakes, as well as his own. Fourth, the difference between him and his inferiors will be one of varying degrees; they will in that crucial sense not be like a flock of sheep. Even if his deepest concerns are not shared by the mass of his fellows, they will be shared by a few, and he may well feel a special kinship with and desire to be in a position to benefit those few. Fifth and most importantly, the man who cares for virtue will want that virtue to have a suitably serious and extensive field of action. This fact alone does not explain why one would feel affection for the beneficiaries of one's virtuous action, but in 9.7 Aristotle will show how the activity of being a benefactor does generate a certain affection for and grounds for friendship with the beneficiary. By postponing that important discussion, and by framing the discussion of 8.9–8.11 as he does, Aristotle leaves us with the troubling impression that of the superiors who exercise rule, only parents have a solid basis for affection and friendship with those they rule, and that even the family bond is not so inherently satisfying as to keep parents from making extravagant claims to honor as a return for all that they do.

Thus Aristotle sharpens in our minds the question of whether and how there can ever be truly selfless benefaction. In this way, he prepares the ground for the pinnacle of his discussion of friendship and equality in 8.12–8.13, where he will show just how deep-rooted our demands or expectations for an equal return in friendship and in virtuous action are, how keen our sense of entitlement becomes when we perceive a friendship to be unequal, and how incoherent and confused we become in expecting a reward for good deeds precisely to the extent that they were done without expectation of reward. This analysis, in turn, will pave the way for a new beginning in Book 9, in which Aristotle will discuss the very deepest roots of friendship, and in which philosophy will become an explicit theme.

However, before turning to those chapters, we must complete our discussion of friendship in political life. Even if Aristotle's account of monarchy has understated the possibility for such friendships, it certainly seems correct to say that perfect monarchic rule and perfect friendship do not go together, for the essence of friendship lies in partnership, reciprocity, equality, and freedom in the choice and continuation of the association. Thus we should expect to find the most complete, serious, and rewarding political friendships not here but in aristocracy or among the fellow leaders of a healthy timocracy or democracy who share a serious dedication to virtue. To the extent that political men are serious about politics, they will always find themselves in competition for rule, but to the extent that they are serious about virtue, they will also find a true kinship with one another, and a common purpose in carrying out just and patriotic projects. Is it not possible that among such men, as partners in the exercise of moral virtue on the grandest and noblest scale, we will find the very best friendships? Is it not also possible that the great pleasure of such friendships may complement the more difficult and austere pleasures of virtue to such an extent as to make these lives perfectly happy and complete, and so vindicate the moral life? In other words, may not the sweetness of a partnership in justice make up for the fact that justice itself is the good of another, and may not the efforts to help a worthy friend realize his potential give the finest and most satisfying outlet to the talents of a great-souled man?

Aristotle, however, says nothing about friendships in aristocracies, apart from his comparison of these friendships to those of husband and wife. This discussion, and the implicit treatment of the questions we have just raised, is offered in full and fascinating detail, and in a thoroughly Aristotelian spirit, by Cicero.

5

Cicero's *Laelius*: Political Friendship at Its Best

In his dialogue *Laelius On Friendship,* which explores the friendship and the self-understanding of two noble Roman statesmen, Cicero expounds a more promising variant of Montaigne's view of friendship as both noble and unsurpassably good. Cicero has chosen Gaius Laelius, a respected leader and devoted friend to his colleague Publius Scipio Africanus the Younger, as the aptest vehicle to set forth a rich and pleasing but also revealing praise of friendship. The dialogue was written in 44 B.C., after the Republic had fallen and Cicero had been driven into retirement, in a world in which great friendships among eminent leaders of a thriving political life had become impossible. It is set in 129 B.C., when the Republic was still vibrant and full of brilliant leaders, if not wholly healthy: The troubles that were eventually to bring it down were already in evidence, as Cicero reminds us with hints throughout the dialogue, and especially with the story of Tiberius Gracchus.

This is the same Gracchus whose loyal friend Gaius Blossius is praised with such unreserve by Montaigne. Montaigne's source for the story is Cicero's dialogue, although what Montaigne does not report is that Laelius himself bitterly condemns Gracchus for his sedition and Blossius for his loyalty.[1] Montaigne's and Laelius's different judgments reflect their different priorities, for Laelius makes it clear that friendship must give way to the demands of virtue, including the duty to one's fatherland, and thus he stops short of making the problematic claim that Montaigne makes that friendship is the most noble thing in life. At the same time, these two very different assessments force us to wonder whether Gracchus was as thoroughly bad as Laelius claims, or whether the latter was not something of a partisan in his condemnation. And indeed, the case of Gracchus was complicated. If he was from one point of view a conspirator against the Republic, he was from another point of view an agrarian reformer responding to the desperate troubles of the Roman poor; and if indeed his response to these troubles was a program that loosened the aristocratic Senate's secure hold on power, helping ultimately to pave the way for the rise of Caesar, it may be that some such shift of power was sooner or later inevitable. Be this as it may, the friends Laelius and Scipio represent the old Roman patrician class at its most impressive: Both are urbane, proud, highly educated gentlemen, courageous military commanders, gifted orators, and public-spirited statesmen, dedicated to preserving in their country the rule of the best, soberest, and wisest, over against the caprices and violence of the mob.[2]

After the death of Scipio, Laelius converses and reminisces with his two young sons-in-law about his great friend and about friendship. Since his interlocutors have little to say beyond the politest of questions and encouragements, the dialogue is essentially Laelius's encomium on friendship.[3] Like Montaigne, Laelius maintains that happiness requires both virtue and friendship, that there is no true friendship without virtue, and yet that friendship is somehow the thing we want most of all. With the single crucial qualification that friendship must be ruled and limited by the demands of virtue, Laelius's praise of friendship could scarcely be more glowing. Laelius indicates but does not deign to dwell upon all the ways in which friendship is useful for life's lesser purposes and for attaining and preserving virtue;[4] his chief claim is that friendship is simply and wonderfully good in itself (31). He urges his young companions to "put friendship before all things human," arguing that life would not be worth living without it (17, 22). Just as Montaigne places the chief joy of his life in his friendship with La Boétie, so Laelius counts his own friendship with Scipio as unquestionably the best "of all the blessings that fortune or nature has bestowed on me," and in short, he says, "my life has been happy because it was spent with Scipio" (103, 15).

Laelius gives an account of the origins of friendship that accords with his claim that friendship is an end in itself and the keystone of our happiness. The true source of friendship, he argues, is a natural sociability that we share with many of the lower animals but that attains a much higher and nobler form in human beings (27, 50, 80). Cicero expands upon this theme in *On Duties,* where he speaks of the bonds that unite us not just to kin and countrymen but to all humanity.[5] As if in direct reply to Plato's *Lysis,* Laelius insists on the existence of a powerful natural attraction of like for like, and above all of virtuous men for one another (*Laelius,* 50). As if in direct response to Plato's *Symposium,* Laelius insists that genuine love "is not the daughter of poverty and want," but has a nobler lineage, springing up spontaneously and even inevitably in response to the excellence of a virtuous soul (26–31). Even virtue in an enemy can arouse the first stirrings of love, and virtue combined with kindness toward oneself and frequent intercourse creates "a marvelous glow and greatness of goodwill" (29). If friendship's roots were in neediness, he continues, we should expect the neediest men to be the ones best suited to friendship, whereas, in fact, it is the most resourceful men who are most desirous and capable of friendship (30, 51).

Laelius's praise of friendship is charming because he expresses what most people want to believe about friendship – that it is at heart natural and generous, a testimony to the inherent goodness and not the poverty of the human soul, and that devoting one's life to promoting the happiness of others in the end can bring the very greatest happiness to oneself. Cicero encourages us to join Laelius in these assessments. Yet the dialogue, in its drama as well as its substance, also casts a palpable shadow over the bright glow of friendship. The central conversation between Laelius and his two sons-in-law, Quintus Mucius Scaevola and Gaius Fannius, is occasioned by the sudden and suspicious death of Scipio in 129 B.C., in the midst of continued efforts to uphold the power of the Senate; and the framing story, in which Scaevola retells the dialogue to Cicero, is occasioned by the rupture of a long, intimate, and celebrated friendship between Publius Sulpicius, then tribune of the plebeians, and Quintus Pompeius, then consul, in 88 B.C.[6]

Friendship, Cicero reminds us, is not simply to be counted upon. Virtue requires us to be prepared for the possibility that fortune may at any time deprive us of friends such as Scipio through death and, hence, requires us to avoid letting them become so important to us that we become unstrung at their deaths and neglect our duties (8). Although the virtue of two friends ought to be a guarantee against the more bitter loss of a friendship to a deadly quarrel, the case of Sulpicius and Pompeius suggests that the virtue of a friend is perhaps never an absolutely sure thing, that virtue requires one to dissolve the friendship when the other has fallen into serious wrongdoing, and that the degree of virtue and wisdom possessed by even exceptionally good men is not sufficient to preclude bitter disagreements about what is right. But an even darker shadow may fall across political friendship when we consider the deep fractures in Roman society that underlay Sulpicius's and Pompeius's rupture and probably also Scipio's death. Perhaps great political friendship necessarily involves alliances and enmities against others who are not simply in the wrong.

Do these shadows Cicero casts over Laelius's bright praise of friendship hint at a serious disagreement with Laelius's position, or do they simply stand as a reminder that life's most precious gifts are also fragile? In order to understand Cicero's own judgment of Laelius's opinions about friendship, we need to examine how Cicero intends us to evaluate the man himself. Certainly the fact that Cicero chose for his spokesman a historical figure of sterling character is important; equally significant is what Cicero shows us of his character in the dialogue itself.[7] Here, too, we find evidence that Laelius is an unusually generous and noble-hearted man. Laelius's noble spirit is seen in the trust he places in the gods, in his refusal to blame them for the untimely and undeserved death of Scipio, and in his declaration that it would be shameful to let his grief over his friend's death keep him from performing his duty as an augur (8). His comments on political affairs and his sons-in-law's observations are direct reminders that Laelius has also been an honorable citizen and has acquitted himself well in offices of great responsibility, both in the military and in political life. Above all, he shows his noble spirit in friendship itself, in his refusal to let personal ambitions get in the way of his friendship, in the pleasure he has taken in assisting Scipio while he lived, and in his eagerness to secure Scipio's glorious memory now that he is dead. He is sufficiently warmhearted and free of vanity that he gladly gives the highest praise to Scipio, who was by far the greater general, orator, and statesman, while speaking modestly about himself. He is content if posterity remembers him chiefly as a great friend to Scipio (15).

Now of course, if we may for a moment be irreverent toward Laelius, we may observe that to the extent that the inequality in this friendship was mutually recognized, it is natural that the noble-minded Laelius not only would have shown greater devotion but also would be inclined to magnify the value of devotion and friendship, thereby lessening the sense of inequality. On the other hand, to the extent that the best friendship is an equal partnership in great enterprises, equality of merit is really crucial, and Laelius will want to understand his friendship as fundamentally equal. And indeed, the question of equality is a delicate one for this friendship.

The fact that Laelius is not wholly free of vanity or sensitivity about his true standing vis-à-vis Scipio is seen in Cicero's *Republic* (1.18), where Cicero tells us that Scipio used to give Laelius the place of honor at home, "for there was a kind of rule in their friendship, according to which Laelius honored Scipio like a god in the field, on account of his unexcelled glory in war, while at home Scipio in his turn revered Laelius like a father, on account of his greater age." Now sincerely honoring another like a father means, of course, honoring him not for his accumulation of years but for his past benefactions and for the attainment of the wisdom that is presumed to come with years. But Cicero does not present Laelius as Scipio's teacher or benefactor, and despite frequent references to Laelius's *reputation* for wisdom in the *Laelius,* Cicero conspicuously fails either to say in his own name or to credit Scipio with the opinion that Laelius is in fact wise.[8] Cicero gives a poignant hint as to the delicacy of Laelius's situation when he has Laelius himself report Scipio's ironic condescension in the *Laelius,* but here Laelius says that it is to Scipio's elder brother and not to himself that Scipio used to give such tactful, undeserved deference (69).[9] It is understandable that Laelius, who treasures nothing more than Scipio's friendship, cannot acknowledge to himself that his friend's respect for him is partially feigned. Nonetheless, avoiding the truth about a matter of such central importance to oneself must necessarily cast a shadow over one's claim to wisdom.

How, then, does Laelius himself understand the balance in this friendship? He clearly is willing to acknowledge to all the world that Scipio is the greater general, but if he considers Scipio's deference at home to be sincere and deserved, it can only be because he counts himself as in some respect wiser than Scipio. True, Laelius is modest in his claims to wisdom, but his modesty has a ring of irony. He denies having the ability that he ascribes to certain Greeks to speak extemporaneously on any subject that may be proposed, but this is scarcely a skill he considers it worthwhile to cultivate (17; cf. 45). Laelius is interested in theoretical questions as a gentleman of leisure should be, but he shares the usual gentlemanly contempt for those who lose themselves in contemplation of the heavens and miss what lies at their feet. He values the practical branches of philosophy for the guidance they can provide for action and the speculative branches mainly for training young minds.[10] He counts moral virtue as the sole test of true wisdom and ranks Cato as wiser than Socrates, "for the former is praised for his deeds, the latter for his words" (9–10). Perhaps most striking of all is his judgment that contemplation taken strictly in itself is not even desirable: "If a man should ascend alone into heaven and behold clearly the structure of the universe and the beauty of the stars, there would be no pleasure for him in the awe-inspiring sight, which would have filled him with delight if he had had someone to whom he could describe what he had seen" (88). By contrast, Scipio recounts at the end of Cicero's *Republic* a dream in which he has such a vision of the universe, which fills him with contempt for the pettiness of Rome and all earthly glory, and which he presents not as grist for friendship's mill, but as a sublimely delightful reward for having fulfilled one's duties among men (6.9–6.29).

Laelius is far more serious about politics than about philosophy, although here, too, he has the detachment of a great-souled man who does not need to rule in order to respect himself. In his dramatic presentation of Laelius, then, Cicero makes the intriguing suggestion that the type of man who will be most devoted to friendship is a man of an intermediate sort, at home in both the intellectual world and the public realm, but not completely devoted to either. He will, indeed, be a man very much like Montaigne, with an unusually noble spirit and a great breadth of interests, talented and serious enough about public service to be an able partner in great enterprises, but not single-mindedly ambitious; thoughtful enough to be a good partner in conversation, but perhaps not himself a philosopher of the first rank.

The real wisdom that Laelius cherishes is what he has learned from the Stoics: the insight that virtue is really all that counts and that being virtuous and happy is entirely up to us. Laelius's son-in-law Fannius praises him for just the sort of wisdom he esteems highly when he tells him that "your wisdom, in public estimation, consists in this: you consider all your possessions to be within yourself and believe human fortune of less account than virtue" (7). Laelius charmingly protests that Fannius's praise is too kind, but silently he concurs in it, for later he, too, will implicitly claim that all his goods are within himself (9, 30). But is this true? If life's brightest joys are in friendship, is Laelius's happiness not more vulnerable to fortune – and is he not therefore less wise – than he imagines?[11]

Laelius addresses this question directly. He concedes that his concerns make him less perfectly self-sufficient than a solitary thinker, but for all that, he does not concede that his life is defective. He argues that the need for friendship is a healthy need, inasmuch as friendship has an intrinsic goodness, and that the cold, narrow self-sufficiency that would wall the heart off from all of the vulnerabilities that come with friendship is not a self-sufficiency worth having. Laelius criticizes both the Epicureans and the Stoics for carrying their pursuit of self-sufficiency to such an extreme that both friendship and human happiness are blighted. A brief look at Laelius's encounter with these two schools reveals the relative strength of Laelius's understanding of friendship and the great difficulty of maintaining that human happiness can be found in perfect self-sufficiency.

Laelius and Epicureanism

Laelius reserves his harshest criticism for the Epicureans. He scorns as both base and foolish the petty-minded caution of certain subtle Greeks, who, he says,

teach that too much intimacy in friendships should be avoided, lest it be necessary for one man to be full of anxiety for many; that each one of us has business of his own, enough and to spare; that it is annoying to be too much involved in the affairs of other people; that it is best to hold the reins of friendship as loosely as possible, so that we may either draw them up or slacken them at will; for, they say, an essential of a happy life is freedom from care, and this the soul cannot enjoy if one man is, as it were, in travail for many. (45)[12]

Laelius goes on to condemn the fundamental Epicurean tenet that the chief good in life is freedom from pain and care. If this were one's standard, he argues, one would never pursue great projects with steadiness and would have to abandon virtue altogether (47).

The extant remains of Epicurus's own writings and Cicero's lengthy discussion of Epicureanism in Books 1 and 2 of *On the Ends of Good and Bad Things* both suggest, however, that Epicurus and his followers were in fact more serious about friendship than Laelius here assumes. To be sure, a great deal of what Epicurus says would seem to imply that friendship is either a matter of indifference to the wisest man or is good only instrumentally. Epicurus argues that pleasure is the sole good in life and pain and fear of pain the sole evils, and that every action aims to secure pleasure and avoid pain. The real goal of a wise life is indeed simply to avoid pain, for Epicurus teaches that the state of freedom from pain turns out to be the greatest pleasure. This pleasure can be varied but not increased by any of the specific activities that we think of as pleasant.[13] We are fortunate that the real needs of nature are simple and easily met. Once we have dispelled the bodily pains of hunger, thirst, and cold, and the mental pains of superstitious fear and unnatural desires for superfluous things, we find ourselves as happy as it is possible to be. In particular, the alluring life of public affairs and politics is nothing but a "prison."[14] Hence a wise man sees that the only things worth seeking are the health of the body and the calm of the soul, or "a stable condition of bodily well-being and assurance of its continuance." All pleasures are either physical or based on physical pleasures, and Epicurus defines mental rejoicing as simply the expectation that our nature will continue to enjoy the pleasures of the senses while avoiding pain.[15]

According to this line of reasoning, virtue, philosophy, and friendship are all good only instrumentally: virtue to avoid punishment and the fear of punishment, wisdom to dispel superstitious fear and teach us our true needs, and friendship to provide a bulwark against violence and deprivation.[16] Epicurus frankly acknowledges at least once that not only the need for assistance from one's neighbors but also goodwill and concern for others altogether are simply an outgrowth of deficiency and imperfect self-sufficiency:

We must not suppose of the heavenly bodies that their motions, turnings, eclipses, risings, settings, and related actions are the result of some being who arranges and ordains or has ordained them and at the same time enjoys complete blessedness along with immortality. For troubles and cares, anger and kindness do not accord with blessedness, but rather these arise in weakness, fear, and need for one's neighbors.[17]

Against Epicurus, both Cicero and the Roman Stoic philosopher Seneca argue that if friendship is simply utilitarian, and if it is openly regarded as such, it cannot be relied upon to fulfill even the narrow function assigned to it. One who begins a friendship only for the sake of advantage will abandon it precisely when he is needed, they say, because at that moment the friend will become disadvantageous to him.[18] If the only goods worth caring about are health, security of life and limb, freedom from want and injustice, and perhaps the liberty to pursue life's lesser pleasures in peace, then the best security for these goods would be not friendship at all but a strong state, such as the Roman Empire when it was at peace and left private citizens relatively free and secure, or better yet, the modern liberal state.

There is force in these criticisms, to be sure, but Epicurus might well have much to say in reply. If our natural needs are extremely limited, then our demands upon our friends even in times of crisis are likely to be similarly limited; if we are content with a place to sleep and a bowl of soup, and our friends are similarly austere in their requirements, then it is likely that at least some of them will have this much and more to spare. There is pleasure, as well, in helping another, especially when one has plenty: As Epicurus says, "it is more pleasant to confer a benefit than to receive one."[19] And good Epicureans, being free of both greed and ambition, are especially unlikely to get into the sorts of scrapes from which people typically need friends to extricate them.[20] These considerations help Epicurus's argument for the instrumental value of hedonistic friendship without saving it completely;

when disasters are serious and widespread, or one's own troubles are serious and chronic, it is not clear why Epicurean friends would not melt away.

In fact, however, it is evident from accounts we have of Epicurus's life and fragments of his letters that he himself treasured philosophy and especially friendship (though not moral virtue) as truly good in themselves, and not merely hedges against misfortune. Philosophy and friendship, he says, are the chief concerns of the noble man, and they are beyond a doubt the chief concerns of his own life as well. Although, indeed, Epicurus usually presents reason as merely a tool for banishing foolish fear and vain desire, he does also speak of it as a "blessedness" that seems most choiceworthy for its own sake, not as the means to but as the goal or reward for such self-mastery.[21] He describes philosophy as intrinsically pleasant and even exalted: "Remember that you are mortal by nature, and that, although having but a limited span of life, you have entered into discussions about nature for an eternity and forever, and seen 'things that are and will be and were before.'"[22]

His praise of the inherent goodness of friendship is even stronger. "Of the things that wisdom provides for the blessedness of one's whole life, by far the greatest is the possession of friendship," he writes. "Friendship dances around the world exhorting all of us to wake up to blessedness." Diogenes Laertius says of Epicurus that "his friends were so numerous that they could not be counted by entire cities," that he traveled widely and repeatedly to see friends, and that friends came to him from all over and lived with him in the little community he established in his famous garden.[23] On the day of his death, although in great pain, he still was made happy by the presence and the memory of good friends. In short, Epicurus clearly found friendship to be one of life's greatest pleasures, and he even castigates as "savage" and "mad" the Stoics who seek such extreme self-sufficiency that they are insensitive to the joys of friendship and the pain of losing friends. In order to secure the joys of friendship, Epicurus says, one should be ready to run risks, endure great pains, "never give up a friend," and even on occasion face death.[24]

Phillip Mitsis has made a strong case that because the need for friendship entails such vulnerability to pain and disappointment, Epicurus fails to reconcile his belief in friendship's intrinsic goodness with his goal of tranquil self-sufficiency.[25] In turn, David O'Connor has responded with an interesting attempt to defend Epicurus's consistency, arguing that Epicurus had a unique conception of friendship that does fit within the confines of rigorous hedonism. Not only will good Epicureans' freedom from greed and ambition make them less needy and burdensome to one another, but it will remove the most serious causes of discord among friends.[26] O'Connor rightly emphasizes that the chief benefits of Epicurean friendship – those of studying together and supporting one another in the adherence to Epicurean principles – are shared benefits that as such require little risk or sacrifice.[27] And as for the risk of suffering at the death of a friend, O'Connor points out that Epicurean friendship consisted more in a diffused good fellowship than in exclusive attachments to single soul mates.[28] For this reason, and because Epicureans were persuaded that death, and hence the death of a friend, was not really an evil, they would be far less vulnerable to the pain of a friend's death.

All of these considerations are most helpful, but how are we to explain, in hedonistic terms, Epicurus's concessions that friends do and should take real risks and make real sacrifices for one another? How are we to explain the considerable risk Epicurus ran when he was shipwrecked and almost drowned in a voyage to visit friends?[29] Can such a thing be explained simply as an effort to cultivate many possible refuges in case of persecution? But why court present danger to avoid a danger wholly speculative? This story lends weight to the idea that friendship was indeed an irreplaceable good in its own right for Epicurus, but how can we reconcile this fact with his other principles? At the very least, Epicurus's regard for friendship contradicts his physical hedonism, or his claim that all that matters to happiness is the possession and confident hope of physical pleasure. It seems also to contradict his claim that freedom from pain is the greatest pleasure, since he says that both giving and receiving affection bring a positive, active enjoyment that is different from mere repose.[30]

But it is even a question whether Epicurus's regard for friendship can be adequately explained in hedonistic terms at all. Epicurus's statement that "friendship is choiceworthy for its own sake"[31] need not imply that one regards friends and their good as a separate end beyond one's own pleasure; it may merely mean that friendship is a great pleasure for oneself.[32] Could the willingness to face death for a friend be explained in terms of a calculus of pleasures, life without friends being more miserable than death?[33] But why not turn one's back on the one friend and find others? When Epicurus says that "the wise man suffers no more pain by being tortured himself than by seeing a friend being tortured,"[34] does he see this sensitivity to the friend's pain as merely a cost that one occasionally has to pay for the pleasure of friendship? But why should a clever hedonist pay such a cost, rather than withdraw from the friendship (just as he comes indoors when a beautiful day turns rainy) and remind himself that it is not he who suffers?[35] Epicurus seems to be describing a feeling that arises not from calculation of pleasure but from genuine concern for the other for his own sake.

In Cicero's *On the Ends of the Good and Bad Thing*, the Epicurean spokesman Torquatus explains that the followers of Epicurus are, in fact, divided on the subject of whether friendship can be wholly explained in terms of hedonistic calculation (1.66–70). Some Epicureans maintain that the wise man loves his friends as much as himself, either spontaneously or by a kind of compact, because it is necessary to do so in order to "secure uninterrupted gratification in life" (1.67). Torquatus approves of this line of reasoning, seeming not to see that it is impossible to love as much as oneself what one only loves for the sake of oneself, and indeed, that such instrumental love is not friendship at all, if friendship includes goodwill. Love that is given only because one can get one's pleasure no other way is not real love any more than virtuous action that is done for a reward is true virtue.[36] And what is the great pleasure of friendship, after all, if one knows one is not loved for oneself? Thus another group of Epicureans argues that friendship has only its *beginnings* in calculations of pleasure, but that intimacy engenders affection strong enough to persist when no practical advantage is to be expected from the friend.[37] Although Torquatus thinks this last group is making unnecessary concessions, it seems that they alone do justice to the joys and the generosity of friendship as Epicurus presents them. Cicero, therefore, argues that in being a devotee of friendship, Epicurus betrays or transcends his own hedonistic principles.[38] He is a better man than he professes to be, and in his inconsistency, he bears striking witness to the truth of Laelius's claims for the power and preciousness of friendship.

Laelius and Stoicism

Just as Laelius shows his depth of feeling and nobility by refusing to accept the Epicurean teaching that freedom from pain and trouble is the only proper goal of life, so he shows his humanity by rejecting the Stoic teaching that virtue is the only thing that matters (46–48). Laelius has far more respect for the Stoics than for the Epicureans. The historical Laelius was himself a student of Diogenes the Stoic and Panaetius, and in Cicero's dialogue, Laelius reserves his highest praise for the Stoic Cato for bearing the death of his son with equanimity (9). Laelius is impressed by such strength yet is not ashamed of his own sorrow at the loss of a friend he knows is irreplaceable (10), and later he gently takes the Stoics to task for the "hard" and "unyielding" quality of their virtue. He argues that virtue should properly be more elastic in response to the fortunes of one's friends (48). What he seems to mean is that virtue's other demands should properly relax to allow one to attend to suffering friends, to weep with them, plead for them, and make allowances for them.[39] The Stoic insistence on strict justice and strict indifference to fortune seems to Laelius to leave too little room for friendship. In fact, the Stoics have as much difficulty holding consistently to the principle that nothing matters except virtue as the Epicureans have in holding to the simplest version of hedonism. For both schools, it is the undeniable goodness of friendship that presents the most obvious challenge to their ideals of self-sufficiency.

What room, then, does remain for friendship in a strictly Stoic life? The Stoic writer who gave the most attention to the theme of friendship was the Roman statesman, orator, and author Seneca, born a century after Cicero, whose sententious epistles to his friend Lucilius challenge the reader with bracingly clear moral exhortations and a characteristic murkiness on the deeper questions.[40] Seneca, like Laelius, struggles to maintain that the wise man is perfectly self-sufficient and yet cherishes and even craves friendship for its own sake. When Seneca is insisting most rigorously that virtue is the only choiceworthy end in life, and that the wise man, being perfectly virtuous, is perfectly self-sufficient, he reduces friendship to an opportunity for virtuous action. Friendship, in this understanding, is fundamentally an internal good: Insofar as it consists in the benevolent exercise of virtue, it depends only upon oneself. The wise man thus wishes to have friends but can endure their loss with equanimity: "Just as Phidias, if he lose a statue, can straightway carve another, even so our master in the art of making friendships can fill the place of a friend he has lost."[41] He can win another friend simply by being a friend. In the best case, then, it would seem that the wise man would be equally a friend to all mankind, or at least to all who give promise of benefiting from his greatest gift, his moral teachings. Considering friendship in this light, it is indeed absurd to grieve over the death of a friend, for potential objects of assistance are everywhere and can even be found among foreigners and those not yet born, if one is a writer.

To seek from friendship more than an object of beneficence is to begin relying for one's happiness on what fortune can take away, and the Stoics, seeking to build out of virtue alone an impregnable happiness, teach their followers to cultivate a ruthless indifference to the goods of fortune. Wealth is not to be sought but is to be avoided like an illness that possesses and tyrannizes us much more than we possess it. Comforts and luxuries, offices and honors, are so many sources of trouble and distraction. Life itself we are not to regard as good, but only as the stage upon which good and evil take place. A long life is no better than a short life; all that matters for happiness is the quality we give to life with our own virtue. Rather than dwelling on hopes, anxieties, and plans for the uncertain future, we should learn to content ourselves with the present and with pleasant memories of the past, which are secure. So far does Seneca go in seeking to flee fortune's power that he says we should learn to welcome death:

Dying well means dying gladly. See to it that you never do anything unwillingly. That which is bound to be a necessity to you if you rebel, is not a necessity if you desire it. This is what I mean: he who takes his orders gladly, escapes the bitterest part of slavery, – doing what one does not want to do." (epistle 61.2–61.3)

The question to be asked in all of this is whether, in refusing to treasure what fortune can take away, Seneca is not making himself even more of a slave to fortune than otherwise, for now he allows fortune to determine what he will hold important.

To be sure, when Seneca comes to discuss that blow of fortune that warmhearted men consider the most grievous of all, the death of a loved one, his tone is slightly different. Precisely the same sense of nobility that finds it so impressive to scoff at riches, honors, and life itself cannot quite reconcile itself to scoffing at the lives of friends. These, Seneca says, one must cherish, and yet be prepared to let go when their time has come:

You may judge it the most grievous of ills to lose any of those you love; while all the same this would be no less foolish than weeping because the trees which charm your eye and adorn your home lose their foliage. Regard everything that pleases you as if it were a flourishing plant; make the most of it while it is in leaf. . . . But just as the loss of leaves is a light thing, because they are born afresh, so it is with the loss of those whom you love and regard as the delight of your life; for they can be replaced even though they cannot be born afresh. (epistle 104.11)

Because it seems noble to love one's friends, it is on the front of friendship that Seneca's Stoicism is least guarded. If Seneca were perfectly consistent, he would content himself with exercising his own virtue as well and as benef- icently as possible. He would enjoy equally the contemplation of good men everywhere, whether they were physically present to him or present only in his memory or in the writings of others.[42] He would remind himself that it is not in his power actually to secure the lives, the happiness, the presence, or the affection of those who please him; he would count all of these things as goods of fortune that must be held as lightly as possible. But such an attitude perhaps makes distinctions in theory that cannot be made in practice. As a man who longs to be virtuous, he longs to accomplish good, and he cannot help caring greatly about the success of his efforts to reform his friends and entertaining high hopes for the enduring influence of his own writings.[43] But Seneca hopes for more: He hopes that the friends he makes will love him and prove helpful to him in turn (epistle 35.1).

Indeed, so great is Seneca's desire for friendship and desire to believe friendship is a great good that he seriously qualifies his claim of self- sufficiency for the wise man in order to make room for the fullest, richest friendship in the best life.[44] If the friendship that consists in bestowing ben- efits is desirable, how much more desirable, how much fuller and richer and sweeter, is the friendship in which one can both help and be helped? Thus he presents even the very wisest men as needing spurs to action, friendly rivals to keep them in practice, and help in deliberation: "Even one who is running well is helped by one who cheers him on" (epistle 109.6).[45]

But if friendship in the best case involves not just active benefaction but mutual love, assistance, and worthiness (cf. epistles 3, 7.8–7.12), a good friend turns out, after all, to be rare and hard to replace. Thus it comes as no surprise that Seneca, though he praises the self-sufficiency that allows one to face a loved one's death without tears, cannot meet this standard himself: "He who writes these words" against mourning, Seneca confesses, "is no other than I, who wept so excessively for my dear friend Annaeus Serenus" (epistle 63.14). Seneca's ideal of self-sufficiency simply breaks down in the face of his deep need for friendship, which he has not fully accepted or understood. He is, by his own admission, not wholly wise.

It is to Laelius's credit that his ideal and his practice are less seriously at odds: He never goes as far as Seneca does in trying to scoff at everything fate or the gods hold in their power. He more freely admits that much of what is precious to him – friends, political liberty, success in the world – is fragile and uncertain. He never claims that friendship is merely an opportunity to exercise virtue, or that a good friendship is simply replaceable. He seems nobler than Seneca in remaining true to what his heart tells him is important, even if it costs him great pain. But can he simply face down the fate that threatens him, or does his more humane and seemingly more honest acceptance of his own natural concerns lead him into evasions and self-deceptions of equal seriousness?

The Fissures in Laelius's Self-Understanding

One telling sign that Laelius does not fully understand his own heart is the fact that he contradicts himself on the relationship of friendship to human neediness. As we have seen, he wants to maintain that although human beings need friendship, friendship does not grow out of any other, more fundamental needs but is, to the contrary, a reflection of the abundance of one's virtues and resources. He sees true friendship as a kind of overflow on the part of strong souls. At moments, Laelius denies that friendship has anything to do with need at all:

To the extent that a man relies upon himself and is so fortified by virtue and wisdom that he is dependent on no one and considers all his possessions to be within himself, in that degree is he most conspicuous for seeking out and cherishing friendships. Now what need did [Scipio] Africanus have of me? By Hercules! None at all. And I, assuredly, had no need of him either, but I loved him because of a certain admiration for his virtue, and he, in turn, loved me, because, it may be, of the fairly good opinion which he had of my character; and close association added to our mutual affection. Although many and great advantages did ensue from our friendship, still the beginnings of our love did not spring from the hope of gain. For as men of our class are generous and liberal, not for the purpose of demanding repayment – for we do not put our favors out at interest, but are by nature given to acts of kindness – so we believe that friendship is desirable, not because we are influenced by hope of gain, but because its entire profit is in the love itself. (30–31)[46]

Yet Laelius cannot quite rest content with this position. He knows that the substance and delight of friendship somehow lies in activity, and that if friendship is a noble and serious thing, it must be connected to the noblest and most serious activities.[47] Since contemplation and sharing in contemplation are not really central to Laelius's life, the activity of his serious friendships can only come in performing acts of kindness and in assisting his friends in great enterprises. Thus Laelius feels compelled ultimately to contradict or seriously qualify his statement that he and Scipio had no need of each other. He then moves to the position that Seneca takes in epistle 9, acknowledging that friendship does somehow rest on need, if only the need for *occasions* to render one another services:

Indeed, I should be inclined to think that it is not well for friends never to need anything at all. Wherein, for example, would my zeal have displayed itself if Scipio had never been in need of my advice or assistance either at home or abroad? It is not the case, therefore, that friendship attends upon advantage, but, on the contrary, that advantage attends upon friendship. (51)

When, in his less Stoical moments, Seneca concedes that everyone needs to be befriended as well as to befriend, he attributes this need to human imperfections, but Laelius tries to maintain that even the perfect life would involve some need, for the sake of friendship.

How coherent is this position? Can a degree of neediness really be thought good because it gives scope for friendship to blossom? In some way it is good that we enjoy such things as back rubs and dinner parties, and even that we feel cravings for back rubs and dinner parties, because they are pleasant to receive from loved ones and pleasant to give to those who enjoy them. Being open to pleasure and capable of delighting in many things is good because it conduces to friendship; we may also say it is simply good in itself. But is this the sort of thing Laelius has in mind when he speaks of the advice and assistance he gave to Scipio? Surely Laelius is thinking of more serious assistance, worthy of a more serious friendship, of times when Scipio was truly discouraged or faced with a dangerous predicament. In such cases Laelius was glad to be of help, glad even to be needed, but was Scipio likewise glad to be discouraged or perplexed so that Laelius might help him? Would not everyone prefer to be always confident and always surefooted, rather than needing a friend to lean upon? But if so, is Laelius not concealing from himself the fact that his wish for his friend's happiness and his wish to be a cause of that happiness are in some tension? Laelius's waffling on the importance of need in friendship makes us wonder whether friendship does not appear at its noblest, most intense, and most important when it involves serious needs and problems from which every sensible man would in fact prefer to be free. To the extent that friendship depends for its lifeblood upon such difficulties, its goodness is qualified, and it appears less as an end in itself than as a means to something beyond itself.

Indeed, the most telling sign that Laelius does not fully understand his own heart is the fact that he fails to give a clear and consistent account of how his central concerns for virtue and friendship fit together. Throughout the dialogue, Laelius betrays his ambivalence as to whether the friendship that virtue makes possible, or the virtue that friendship expresses and sustains, is really the ultimate end in human life. Laelius urges his listeners to "put friendship before all things human" (17), and he praises virtue largely because it provides the essential foundation for friendship (20), suggesting that only in friendship does virtue come fully into its own. On the other hand, Laelius calls friendship the "handmaid" of virtue, and a "comradeship along the road to the highest good" (83), as if the highest good were something altogether different. In keeping with this ambivalence as to whether friendship points beyond itself or is itself the peak, Laelius sometimes identifies the sweetest, brightest part of friendship as reverence for the friend's virtue, and sometimes as simple affection (82, 51). In the same way, he sometimes identifies the gods' greatest gift to men as friendship, and sometimes as wisdom, which he prizes as a foundation for virtue (47, 20).[48]

Closely connected to the question of the chief end in life is the slightly different question of what the core of happiness consists in. Laelius clearly thinks our highest loyalty must be to virtue, but should we and can we honestly count ourselves happy as long as we are virtuous, and treat friendship as a somewhat unreliable bonus? Or does virtue's chief contribution to happiness consist in the fact that it lays the groundwork for good friendships? This question would be somewhat academic if virtue invariably produced the best friendships and true friendship invariably supported virtue. Laelius sees and acknowledges, however, that this is not the case. Private friendships are the spawning ground of conspiracies against the common good, and they lead men such as Blossius into evil acts that they might never otherwise have contemplated (36–43). Even among honorable men, the desire not to be separated from one's friends can stand in the way of serious endeavors that one ought to undertake (75).

For the most part, Laelius rejects the idea that one ought to make any compromise with strict virtue for a friend's sake, or indulge or defend any vice in a friend, but he is less than perfectly consistent. He grants that the demands of propriety can sometimes be set aside for friendship: We can entreat favors for a friend from an unworthy man, for example, or lose control of our anger in attacking one who has treated our friend unjustly, and these lapses of dignity and self-control will escape blame because one's motives are generous (57).[49] Likewise, friendship requires certain limitations upon, if not deviations from, strict truthfulness, since too much frankness often destroys friendship (69, 89). Laelius even wavers on the question of whether friendship does not sometimes justify the actual indulgence of vice: "Even if by some chance the wishes of a friend are not altogether honorable and require to be forwarded in matters which involve his life or reputation, we should turn aside from the straight path, provided, however, that utter disgrace does not follow" (61).[50] Now Laelius himself is such a man of honor and piety that he would probably never be drawn into wrongdoing for the sake of friendship or for any other reason. Virtue is his polestar, but he cannot bear to treat friendship as merely subordinate and ancillary. Hence, he ultimately comes down on the somewhat unstable but humanly understandable position that friendship is the sweetest thing in life and the core of our happiness, even while virtue is life's highest end.

Yet even here Laelius cannot quite rest content. He reveals an awareness that friendship is in fact not unambiguously sweet, and this awareness comes out in his discussions of the rareness of great friendships. Laelius wants to argue that the charms of friendship are obvious to absolutely everyone, and that as much as human beings may disagree about the value of other good things, "all, to a man . . . believe that without friendship life is no life at all" (86). Yet he also concedes that despite all the promptings nature gives men to treasure friendship, "we somehow grow deaf and do not hearken to her voice" (88). In fact, Laelius complains that men are more painstaking in all other things than in friendship, that many care more for riches than for their friends, and that even "if any shall be found who think it base to prefer money to friendship, where shall we find those who do not put office, civil and military rank, high place and power, above friendship?" (63)[51] Thus, he acknowledges, friendship is extremely difficult to maintain not only through the changes of youth and the infirmities of old age but through the countervailing temptations of men's best years as well. Although Laelius often speaks as if friendship is naturally so good as to constitute a happiness that needs no reward, he also seems to believe that true friendship is something rare and heroic, even divine, that makes the friends worthy of eternal fame (15, 24).

These observations prompt us to wonder what the deepest reasons really are for Laelius's taking friendship so seriously. Does he love the life of virtuous friendship as much as he does because of its sweetness, or does his love for this life draw much of its power from a hidden source – from the fact that friendship seems to promise something further? I believe Cicero quietly indicates that much of Laelius's attachment to friendship is fueled by the promise friendship seems to hold of providing a bulwark against misfortune and death, and that the most important way friendship does this is quite subtle and indirect: Friendship, by both supporting and giving occasion for noble acts of selfless devotion, seems to make one deserving of, and hence seems to promise, the support of a benevolent divine providence.

To be sure, Laelius believes that he is all but immune to the blows of fortune. Yet he is deeply concerned with honor. He can accept death, but he cannot accept oblivion, either for himself or for his friends. He is not certain whether Scipio's soul is immortal, although he hopes that it is, but at the very least, he clings to the comforting thought that Scipio "lives" in his own memory and will always live in the memories of good men (102).[52] He, too, hopes for a glorious memory, if only as the devoted friend of a great man (15); it is important to Laelius to believe that the honor in which men hold departed friends is so great that "though dead," they are "yet alive" in some meaningful way, and that *everyone* honors a great friend (23, 24). It seems to be Laelius's faith in the justice of the gods and of human honor that allows him to accept fortune's blows calmly and to maintain his integrity unwaveringly. Might this faith not be the glue that holds together his complicated and potentially fractious view of virtue and friendship as life's dual ends? The external supports of eternal glory and some kind of divine favor are evidently so important to Laelius because neither simple affection nor the austere life of virtue answers all of what he hopes for from life, or seems quite a sufficient reward for all that he must endure. Having failed to clarify to himself the true relationship between his central concerns, he thus continually shifts his ground, now seeming to place his happiness in affection, now in virtue, and now in his expectations of honor and his rather vague hopes for divine protection.

It is less than clear to the onlooker, however, that Laelius's faith in honor and in the gods is well grounded. If we have no firm reason to expect an afterlife, we can rely for our happiness neither on compensation there nor on honor from future generations of men when we will no longer exist to enjoy it. More seriously, there is an incoherence in Laelius's claim to deserve honor or other protection as a result of his great friendship for Scipio: the incoherence of claiming at once that such friendships are life's sweetest gift *and* that they entail heroic steadfastness and sacrifice. By revealing this confusion in the mind of his spokesman for friendship, Cicero raises the question of whether the disposition to cherish friendship more than anything else in life is not necessarily connected to the confusion of believing it to be at once heroically deserving and unsurpassably sweet.

As a result of these problems with Laelius's self-understanding, his relative lack of interest in philosophy appears increasingly to show not just a difference of taste with Scipio but a serious inferiority to him. Laelius's interest in philosophy is limited by a complacent belief that he already knows what knowledge is worth pursuing and what is not. Rather than seeking to discover all the secrets of the cosmos, in its origins and ruling principles, in the relationship of mind to matter, and of virtue to necessity, Laelius rests content with a faith he does not question. In his relationships with the gods, with Scipio, and even with himself, Laelius prefers a noble-minded trust to penetrating questioning. He therefore has an opinion of his own self-sufficiency that is inadequately grounded, an opinion that he has not fully squared either with his faith in providence or with his devotion to friendship.

In contrast, Scipio appears more consistent in his self-understanding, and less in need of doubtful external supports to make his life seem worthwhile. In the *Republic,* Cicero shows him not only to have a more penetrating intellect than Laelius, but also to make a more convincing claim to possess the self-sufficiency that Laelius agrees is the test of wisdom. In contrast to Laelius, Scipio shows delight in contemplating all manner of things, especially what is eternal and divine and hence precisely *not* of practical use. He says that his studies have convinced him that human glory is ultimately petty and ephemeral, and that the business of defeating enemies and solving the public's problems is properly to be classed among "things necessary rather than things desirable." He cites with approval the saying of his grandfather,

Scipio Africanus the elder, that "he was never doing more than when he was doing nothing, and never less alone than when alone" (*Republic* 1.27). For Scipio, as for Laelius, philosophy provides an occasion for delightful conversations and friendships, but he finds friendship less essential, and is more inclined to stress the pleasures of communing with himself or taking part in "a gathering of most learned men" by studying the writings of those who have come before (*Republic* 1.28).

As in our study of Montaigne, we are again led to wonder whether friendship, while indeed valued by everyone sensible, is perhaps only treasured as the highest and best thing by those who regard it as supremely noble and deserving of honor. In the last chapters of Book 8 of the *Nicomachean Ethics,* Aristotle examines the sense of entitlement and desert that characteristically accompanies a seemingly selfless devotion to friends, and begins to reveal the deep confusions that lurk at the heart of virtually every friendship, and the more so the more noble-minded it is.

6

Quarrels, Conflicting Claims, and Dissolutions

In *Nicomachean Ethics* 8.13–8.14, Aristotle returns from a discussion of friendship in politics and the family to his broader theme of friendship and equality. Here, in the course of examining the reproaches and quarrels that arise in certain confused or deceptive forms of utilitarian friendship, he in fact offers his most profound reflections on the critical question of the relation of friendship to justice.[1] Aristotle opens 8.13 with an explicit return to his threefold classification of friendships as based on utility, pleasure, and virtue. The sympathetic concern that grows out of kinship or similarity, which had come to appear as a fourth and crucial root of friendship, and which figured prominently in the previous chapters, now recedes again from the picture. Instead, Aristotle focuses attention on the difficulties of establishing and maintaining equality between friends, especially when their capacities differ greatly, reminding us of the unsolved questions of what motivates benefactors to act as they do, and how most unequal friendships can ever really be balanced to everyone's satisfaction.

Quarrels

"Complaints and reproaches arise solely or chiefly in friendships of utility, and with good reason," Aristotle says (1162b5–6). But the reasons he goes on to give to explain why complaints and reproaches do not arise in friendships of virtue and pleasure in fact indicate just how unusual these friendships would have to be to be perfectly free of grievances:

Those who are friends on the basis of virtue are eager to do good to one another, for this belongs to virtue as well as to friendship, and for those who vie with one another in this way, there are no complaints or quarrels. No one is annoyed with one who loves and benefits him, but if he is cultivated, he retaliates by doing good in return. The one who surpasses the other, achieving what he aims at, will have no complaint against his friend. For each desires the good. (1162b6–13)[2]

This language of competition and retaliation shows the problem, and the problem arises because good men's kindnesses to one another have a dual motivation. They seek to benefit one another both out of friendship and out of a desire to be and to prove themselves virtuous. When people vie to do good, it is this last motive that predominates, for goodwill and affection are not contentious. If two people loved each other just as they loved themselves, and acted only out of love, they would work in harmony to secure the good of both. But when one perceives that another is trying to put him in his debt and monopolize the position of benefactor and superior, he resists. To be sure, the would-be benefactor does seek to give his friend something good, but he seeks to take something even better, the noble, for himself. Even or precisely when men are most concerned to act nobly, then, they in fact engage in a subtle attempt to get the better of one another.

Can this problem be solved by recognizing the ultimate selfishness and unseemliness of such contests, and taking nobility a step further by allowing one's friend to pay for dinner, do one a favor, or run a greater risk? This is something of a solution, and surely the most cultivated friends will not be ostentatious and quarrelsome in their attempts to do good. But on some level the competition must necessarily remain, if only in the form of an infinite regress of noble self-denials. Nor is it clear, apart from the absurdity of an infinite regress, that this sort of self-denial is congenial to noble souls. Passive acquiescence in the benefaction of others seems unlikely ever to satisfy their longing to cultivate excellence and do good in a splendid way. And on the other hand, being a benefactor to another who is graciously allowing one to do so in order to please oneself would be utterly unsatisfying to anyone who saw it clearly. In one way, then, the competition at the heart of the noblest friendship is more intractable even than that at the heart of a vulgar utilitarian friendship, for partners in utility can arrange their relations so that they both profit equally, whereas the nobility that virtuous friends seek to exercise toward one another can in a certain sense come only at one another's expense.[3] The friendship that was utterly free of friction and grievances would have to be quite different, turning not upon the giving and receiving of benefits but upon some other activity that can be truly shared.

"Nor do complaints arise very much in friendships of pleasure," Aristotle continues. "For both simultaneously get what they seek, if they enjoy spending time together. And a person would appear ridiculous if he complained that he did not enjoy his friend, for he is free not to pass his days with him" (1162b13–16). There is an immediacy and a transparency to pleasure friendships that minimizes quarrels: While people may promise to be useful and break their promises, or seem to be good when they are not, it is perhaps impossible, as John Cooper points out, for anyone to appear pleasant and not be so.[4] But this explanation, too, exaggerates the absence of friction by focusing on the unproblematic side. It would indeed be ridiculous to reproach one's friends for not being amusing, but as Aristotle says a bit later, people do feel hurt and reproach friends who once seemed to love them and now neglect them (1165b2–6). The friendships of pleasure-seekers are rarely so casual as an amusement park, where each wanders on whenever he grows bored, with no attachments and no expectations of return. Most such friends, like the lovers Aristotle characterizes as pleasure-seekers, desire affection as well; as he observes, lovers wish to be loved for themselves and complain when their love is not reciprocated, even when there is nothing lovable about them (1164a2–4). In presenting friendships of pleasure as free from reproaches, Aristotle is once again abstracting from the irreducible, ubiquitous human desire for affection, companionship, and a sense of belonging. A pleasure-friendship that was perfectly immune to complaints and reproaches would have to be a friendship of rare frankness, not to say ruthless coldness, in which each knew that he was loved only for his pleasantness and sought no lasting love or security. But Aristotle is surely right that even ordinary pleasure-friendships are relatively free of reproaches, because, as he has said, the pleasure sought is truly common, and because, as he will show, these friendships are less subject than others to confusion and self-deception.

Friendships of utility are the ones that are especially ἐγκληματική, or "prone to complaints," according to Aristotle. At the outset and on the surface, he seems to say that complaints arise only in friendships of utility because in these friendships people are out for their own good, whereas in virtuous friendships they seek one another's good, and in pleasure-friendships a common good. The narrowness of utilitarian friends' focus, the scarcity of the goods that they seek, and the tendency of people's judgments to be biased in their own favor are all factors that contribute to quarrels. It will become increasingly clear, however, that the most important reason for reproaches in friendships has less to do with the type of good being pursued than with confusions and deceptions surrounding that pursuit, and that these confusions and deceptions can arise in all sorts of friendship.

The most straightforward form of utilitarian friendship, a simple commercial exchange, is in fact not particularly subject to complaints, especially in its most frankly self-regarding form, hand-to-hand cash transactions. Commercial exchanges that allow time for payment are more problematic, because the creditor's friendly trust sometimes turns out to be misplaced, but if the goods are not defective, there can never be any real dispute about what is owed. All such transactions on fixed terms Aristotle classes together as "legal" types of utilitarian friendship, which he compares to the explicit written law, contrasting them with another type of utilitarian friendship that he calls "ethical," which he compares in turn to the unwritten part of justice (1162b21–63a9). "Ethical" friendships, unlike those of buyers and sellers, do not rest on fixed terms, but instead, their premises are slippery and submerged. One begins by giving a gift or favor "as if to a friend" (1162b31), and one ends by expecting an equal or greater return, and complaining if one does not receive it.[5]

Here again we see an ambiguity as to whether utilitarian friendship is friendship at all. Aristotle goes on to say that one who accepts what appears to be a free gift, only to discover afterward that an equal return is expected, should realize that he went wrong in accepting a good deed from the wrong person, because the benefactor "was not a friend," and the favor was not done out of friendship (1162b31–63a6). If ethical friendship only pretends to be friendship, the other type of utilitarian friendship, that based on fixed terms, does not even make a pretense of being generous. And yet Aristotle does continue to treat these as forms of friendship that require equalization, just as other forms do. Although utilitarian friendships are seriously defective in comparison with perfect friendship, they are an essential part of the discussion of friendship because they reveal most clearly certain dynamics that operate more covertly in all friendships.

In particular, ethical friendship reveals a characteristic mixture of conflicting intentions. Such friendships are ethical inasmuch as they involve a concern both to act generously and to secure justice, but these two moral concerns are at odds. The reason for the slippage in ethical friendships, Aristotle says, is that "all or most men wish for what is noble, but choose what is beneficial" (1162b35–36). A weak attempt to be noble soon collapses and the friendship shifts grounds, because one or both of the friends lack self-knowledge and clear-sightedness. They can wish for one thing and choose another because they actually wish for the second thing even more, but without fully acknowledging it to themselves. Aristotle leaves it ambiguous whether this contradiction characterizes everyone or just most human beings. At any rate, he indicates that the treachery of ethical friendship, which at first seemed to belong only to the lowest type of friendship, utilitarian friendship, is in fact likely to play some part in virtually all friendships.

Aristotle gives sound advice as to what one should do when inexplicit expectations erupt into open complaints: return the favor, if you can, as if it were not a gift but a loan, and measure what is owed by the benefit gained and not by the effort that it cost to provide it. For in a friendship of utility, what matters is the benefit each derives. In a friendship based on virtue, by contrast, the return that is owed should be measured by the virtuous choice or intention of the giver, since choice is the decisive factor for virtue and character. It follows that in these cases, one will normally owe more than the cash value of the gift or favor one receives, because the benefit was given in a generous spirit, and generosity calls for both a return and gratitude. Aristotle reiterates that in such friendships people do not complain when their good deeds go unreturned; they are too cultivated for that. But, especially since Aristotle himself says that not only an equal return but gratitude is "owed," we may wonder whether virtue or good breeding ever stops people from silently registering debts in the back of their minds and being disappointed when they meet with ingratitude.

Thus vulgar ethical friendships shade over into more refined ethical friendships, and these in turn give way gradually to friendships of virtue, in a single continuum. In the low form of ethical friendship, one only pretends to give as a friend and then demands a return. In the more high-minded form, the giver genuinely believes himself to be a friend and to be acting generously, but then he demands an equal or greater return, equal if he now decides the gift was really a loan, greater if he still considers himself to have been nobly generous and to deserve a reward as well as a return. In contrast to both of these types, the virtuous friend will never demand a return, but he may still have a sense of entitlement, and precisely because he never claims the return and the gratitude to which he feels entitled, perhaps all the greater a sense of entitlement.

Of these three types, the first is deceitful but not confused, and the second is clearly confused as to whether he is engaged in a profitable partnership or an act of noble generosity. People in friendships of virtue do not suffer from this confusion; they do not see themselves as engaged in a profitable partnership. But are they wholly free of confusion? The fundamental confusion in ethical friendships turns on the question of whether a good deed is choiceworthy for its own sake or whether it needs to be rewarded. If an unsolicited good deed is done *for the sake* of a reward, it seems that no reward or even return is really owed, although as Aristotle says, a decent man will make some return. People who clean windshields uninvited and then hold out their hands for change are called hustlers and have no just claim on the drivers, although many people will pay them anyway, wishing to be kind. High-minded ethical friends are not like squeegee pests; they are not acting only for a reward, but in some sense, they see a fine act as good in itself, and they may be prompted by affection as well. But to the extent that they feel betrayed when their good deeds meet with no return or acknowledgment of indebtedness, they reveal that they have in fact acted *in expectation* of a reward. Shutting one's eyes to one's expectations at the time of acting does not make the act disinterested, but only confused.

Here, then, is a great paradox of the noble: It is only when one can be indifferent to any reward that one seems to deserve it. Now there seem to be two possible ways to choose a virtuous action without confused expectations of a reward. One would be to choose it in the recognition that it is a sacrifice, bad for oneself and one's own happiness, but noble and therefore intrinsically choiceworthy apart from any reward. We may wonder, however, whether such a disposition toward virtue and one's own happiness is humanly possible. Can love make it possible? If one has a great enough love, can one sacrifice one's own good for the sake of another, without thinking that this sacrifice is itself somehow best for oneself, and without expecting anything back? To be certain that such a person is not secretly motivated by the hope for a reward, we would have to see his response if his sacrifices were met with ingratitude and cold indifference. Could he be content never to be acknowledged, and accept ingratitude without anger and with no more disappointment than one would feel at not winning a lottery?

The second way to escape confusion in the performance of noble actions is to choose them as both noble and good for oneself, and this seems in fact to be the outlook of all those who are most serious about virtue. All such people seem to say, "I am not in the final analysis depriving myself of what matters most; a pure soul is worth more than diamonds." But is anyone so perfectly pure in motive? Clearly, many think that they are, that not only have they not acted for the sake of a reward, but also that their happiness does not require that they be paid off after the fact, and the universe is not evil or tragic if they are not. But may there not be a lingering but powerful hope even here, a hope that precisely their willingness to forgo a reward makes them especially worthy of reward, and that somehow the world will come through for them? Could they bear it if noble people routinely fared worse than evil people and routinely were laughed at? Could they say that this adversity is trivial compared with the great good of having a noble soul, and the laughter is the laughter of fools?

But perhaps these questions imply too strict a standard for perfect virtue. After all, it is not only heroes but all decent observers who wish for virtue to be rewarded, and who believe that the virtuous man's beneficiaries are indebted to him. Is it not, as Aristotle himself treats it in 8.13–8.14, a simple requirement of justice that virtuous benefaction be rewarded? Thus the question arises whether a virtuous man could not choose virtue for itself and yet still be consistent and unconfused in maintaining that generosity ought to be returned and virtue rewarded, as a matter of justice. Does this belief create a subterranean sense of entitlement and expectation that necessarily contaminates the purity of his motive? Or may he consistently say that while his beneficiary is indeed indebted to him, he himself does not need any reward, although he welcomes it as a kind of icing on the cake?

The question to be asked here is this: Why is any debt incurred at all, if indeed the act is good for the virtuous man and he is made happier by performing it? Does every freely given benefit require a return, or only those that involve sacrifice? A camper who runs out in a midnight thunderstorm to bring in everyone's clothes from the clothesline puts his friends in his debt, because it is better to have dry clothes without getting a midnight soaking than with one, but the camper who entertains his friends around the campfire with lovely music does not make them feel indebted in the same way, because creating beautiful music is even more pleasant than merely hearing it. If his friends "owe" him anything, it is only thanks, and only owed in the sense that a good person will want to express his pleasure and warm regards to one who has delighted him. Such thanks, for the musician who plays for the love of it, will indeed be no more than icing on the cake.

On the other hand, if his friends are indifferent to a performance that the musician knows was good, he will be disappointed by what this shows him about them, but not bitter or aggrieved.

But is most noble action so unambiguously good as making beautiful music? When we believe the beneficiaries of virtuous action owe a substantive return, it is because we perceive the benefactor to have made a sacrifice that needs a reward. But this judgment suggests that we are unsure of whether virtuous action truly is good in itself, or we consider it good to do it, but not as good as benefiting from it. This is perhaps the secret view of virtually everyone regarding generosity: It is indeed good to give, but even better to receive. But if this is the outlook of virtuous men, can they choose virtue for its own sake? Can they be content endlessly to accept the lesser of two goods, endlessly to be on the less advantageous side of all their transactions with others, without reward? If not, they are to some extent, out of the corner of their eyes, acting with a view to a reward, and to that extent they are confused.

In 8.14, Aristotle examines more closely the balance sheets of unequal friendships and sheds more light on the question of just what is required to make one satisfied with a friendship. He says that the one in a friendship who is the greater benefactor thinks that his superiority entitles him to more, and that a friendship ceases to be a friendship at all and becomes a λειτουργία, a public service or charity, if a man does not get out of it any fair return. It is not immediately evident what would constitute the desired fair return. Aristotle has often stated that some kind of proportional return is what is needed to balance unequal friendships, but he has spoken of proportional equality in two different senses. In one sense, justice is served when the honor paid to each is in proportion to what he has done: The winner of a race should get the biggest trophy, the one who finishes second should get the second biggest, and so on. There is in such matters no effort to say – indeed it would be distasteful to say – that trophies and other honors are the pay meant to equal the years of hard work and sacrifice that an athlete or a hero makes. These things are offered merely as tokens of recognition.

But in other contexts, Aristotle has spoken as if proportional equality is only secured when the return is equal to the contribution: If a builder's house is worth five times as much as a carpenter's bed, then proportional equality requires that he receive five beds as the recompense for one house (1133b18–28). Aristotle indicates now that friendship is really only satisfactory when proportional equality in the latter sense is established, so that each gets a return of equal value to his original contribution, although it may be in goods that differ in kind. Superiors and benefactors "suppose that, just as those in a business partnership who contribute more also take more of the proceeds, so it should be in friendship" (1163a30–32). Now if one partner contributes more than another to a venture that fails, it is only fair that the former should take a proportionally greater share of whatever capital remains. This is fair, but it is not enough to make the partnership satisfactory or worth continuing, for what each seeks in every business dealing is to receive goods that provide an equal return for the time and resources he has invested. This, then, seems to be the type of return to which benefactors privately feel themselves entitled.

The more high-minded way of looking at what is appropriate for a man of superior merit is expressed in the rejoinder Aristotle has the *inferior* friend make: It is the mark of a superior man and a good friend to come to the aid of the needy, he says, voicing a noble idea for obviously self-interested reasons (1163a32–34). The generous superior with his covert sense of entitlement is simply the mercenary inferior turned on his head: Both, operating in the world of practical affairs, take with utmost seriousness the common goals of providing for life, security, liberty, wealth, and comfort. The one imagines himself to be nobly rising above concerns that preoccupy the other, but in taking the provision of these things for someone as his goal, and in taking so seriously his own risk or sacrifice of them, he shows his position to be very close to that of the other. If he truly saw the best of all things as acting nobly, he would welcome happily every opportunity to perform a public service, and would seek out decent and needy men to be his friends so that he could benefit them. But instead, like the mercenary inferior friend, the superior sees generosity as noble, but benefiting from generosity as most advantageous, and so his need for a reward is ineradicable. Therefore, Aristotle says that in friendship as in political life, the superior party who performs great services must be given honor, since "no one can put up with the smaller share in everything" (1163b1–9). The competition to be the greater benefactor is evidently one that loses its savor if one finds oneself invariably winning it, unless one can reap honor in the process and find this honor satisfying.

It is striking that Aristotle now presents honor and not affection as the appropriate medium for equalizing unequal friendships, although he has previously argued that honor is without intrinsic worth (1159a17–18). This choice seems to be dictated by the fact that, as Aristotle now stresses, "friendship seeks what is possible, not what is deserved. For that is not possible in every case, as with the honor given to the gods and to parents" (1163b15–17). For reasons that Aristotle has begun to adumbrate and that will become even clearer in 9.7, it is hard for beneficiaries to love their benefactors more than they are loved, but it is quite possible for them to honor them more. But if ruling means service to others, if no one can put up with the smaller share in everything, and if honor (or money) is really all the political community has to give its outstanding benefactors, we can never expect a king who is genuinely self-sufficient to wish to rule, nor can we expect anyone who is wise to the paltriness of honor to be satisfied with this as the return for endless public service. Thus, the best will be disinclined to serve, and the most ambitious will not be the best.

If such is the case among human beings, what about the gods, whom Aristotle mentions again as examples of those to whom we owe an unrepayable debt, and whom we should hence honor as much as we can? If the gods need human honor, there is something wrong with them, but if they are indifferent to it, then not only a full recompense but even the barest beginning of a recompense is impossible. Like Aristotle, Socrates in Xenophon's *Memorabilia* says that the gods *must* be satisfied with each sacrificing to them according to his ability, for "life would not be worth living for human beings if what came from the wicked were more gratifying to the gods than what came from the good" (1.3.3). But if honor as such is at all pleasing to the gods, the volume of smoke and praise accorded them must make some difference and have some power to secure their favor. If the divinity, then, is not an intolerable tyranny, it must, at the very most, care about human virtue and give no independent weight to honor and worship.

The other unrepayable debt that Aristotle mentions again here, the debt to parents, is capable of a much more solid return, for children can do parents real services, especially when they grow old. Therefore, Aristotle says, while children can never discharge their debt to their parents and hence can never justly disown them, a father is unlikely ever to disown his son, for "apart from the friendship that is natural, it is only human not to reject his assistance" (1163b23–25). This statement throws the unqualified love of parents into a new shadow. Aristotle reminds us that even good parents, the most generous human benefactors we know of, are subject to the self-contradictions of ethical utilitarian friends, pursuing their own good even as they seem or claim to act only for the good of others, expecting a reward precisely to the extent that they have acted without thought of a reward, and prone to bitterness when no such reward or even gratitude is forthcoming.

In the last two chapters of Book 8, while appearing to examine minor, rather casuistic questions regarding the assessment of the precise return that is owed to different people under different circumstances, Aristotle in fact opens up troubling incoherences at the roots of all ordinary friendships and ordinary noble-minded activity. To think these incoherences through to their twisting, subterranean, far-reaching ends is to cease to be the same person one was before one started: It is to begin becoming philosophic. But Aristotle contents himself with quietly indicating the issues that need pondering. To criticize more explicitly the defects of ordinary noble-minded friendships would only be to risk breeding cynicism among readers too eager to debunk noble-mindedness and too little inclined to make the difficult effort necessary to attain a virtue free of self-contradiction.

Book 8 leaves us with the unanswered question of what will remain of human attachments once the confusions that accompany them are excised. To a greater or lesser extent, we may expect that the simple affection for one's own or for kindred spirits will remain, for at heart this inclination seems to be natural and irreducible and, hence, necessarily unconfused. Aristotle has in these chapters abstracted from love of the kindred and from the sympathetic goodwill that it entails, an abstraction that he signals not only by his return to the threefold classification of friendships at the beginning of 8.13, but also by his repeated comparison of friendship to a contract that is fulfilled or ended when its terms are met (1162b33–34, 63a3–6 and 25–26).[6] This abstraction has allowed him to bring our confusions about friendship and justice into sharp focus, but perhaps it has also made the prospects for unconflicted friendship look darker than they really are.

Likewise, by framing his whole discussion in 8.13–8.14 on the premise that virtue needs a reward, Aristotle makes simple generosity look all but impossible. Is the desire to be a benefactor necessarily prone to the confusions he portrays here? Or is there a solid, unconfused source of this desire that does not involve one in absurd competitions to get more of the noble for oneself and that does not include covert expectations of reward? Is true virtue not, after all, supposed to be thoroughly satisfying in itself, so that those who practice it without any remuneration should not by any means feel that they have gotten the short end of the stick? If there still is, as Aristotle has led us to hope, a form of virtue that is perfectly clear-sighted and complete in itself, needing no payoff to make one happy, then the lovers of this virtue must take a view of noble action rather different from the common view, which honors dying for a cause as the peak of virtue. To these most clear-sighted of noble men, virtue at its best and fullest would have to be something less stern and resigned, and altogether more joyful and satisfying than our customary conception of it.[7] Although such virtue might be found in full bloom in public life at rare and auspicious moments, its chief expression would more likely be not in sorting out other people's troubles, but in the happy pursuits of private life. But what its precise nature would be, and how it would be related to friendship, remain to be seen.

The Emergence of Philosophy as a Theme

With a perfunctory "so much for this subject," Aristotle closes Book 8, but the opening chapters of Book 9 do not turn out in any obvious way to take up a new theme.[8] In 9.1 Aristotle resumes a superficially uninteresting discussion of how to assess just how much is owed when an unsolicited gift has been given, reiterating his assertion that in friendships of virtue no complaints arise, and that where repayment is expected, the true benefit to the recipient should be the measure of the debt.[9] Aristotle himself underscores the fact that from every ordinary point of view, the first three chapters of Book 9 are simply the continuation of a single section on quarrels, conflicts, and dissolutions of friendships that began at 8.13, for at 1165b6 he uses the expression "as we said at the beginning" to refer to the argument of 8.13.[10] But suddenly and repeatedly, among Aristotle's illustrations and examples, philosophy appears as a new theme, which has been absent from Book 8 and which will become increasingly prominent in the remainder of the *Nicomachean Ethics*. The appearance of philosophy marks, in fact, a crucial new beginning. In Book 9, Aristotle will provide not only a deeper examination of friendship that lays bare its ultimate roots, but also a revisiting of certain earlier themes to show how a philosophic soul who has worked through one's own confusions about virtue, selflessness, and desert may come to regard one's friendships and the place of friendship in one's own life.

Philosophy first comes to sight in a discussion of how to repay benefactors, and in contrast with sophistry. Aristotle's theme is the proper assessment of a return in friendships in which two people seek things different in kind. He first mentions a musician who performs for a tyrant for money, not for the love of music. Then he brings up Protagoras, who taught for pay but rather grandly left it up to his students to assess what his instruction was worth to them and to pay that amount. As Stewart aptly observes, "perhaps the pressure exercised by means of this method was more considerable than Protagoras wished it to be thought."[11] This device, although apparently gracious, seems in fact to have been well designed to enhance both Protagoras's earnings and his fame. Next, Aristotle speaks of the other Sophists, clearly Protagoras's inferiors, who also taught for pay and who also exercised a kind of pretense, albeit of a less refined sort. Claiming to teach knowledge that, Aristotle says, was in fact worthless, they had to collect fees for their instruction in advance. The relationship of true philosopher and student stands in contrast to all of these, as a friendship based on excellence in which the greatest benefits are freely given for the sake of the friend (1164a33–b6).

What is the significance of this progression? Aristotle has said in the previous chapter, 8.14, that no one is willing to serve the political community without any return, but all seek either profit or honor. It is inconceivable that anyone could choose to spend his life doing such things as reforming the tax code with complete anonymity and utterly without pay. Music is more intrinsically pleasant than are most of the tasks of governing; music would surely remain, even if all the problems that necessitate government were to disappear. But perhaps, if the musician can be indifferent to money, he cannot be indifferent to every return, including honor: It is of the essence of all the arts that they seek to please and be honored by an audience. Perhaps music is also in some way too partial or incomplete an activity of the soul to constitute the most independent happiness. Certainly it does nothing to remove, and (by its tendency to encourage a romantic mood) may even reinforce, certain moral confusions that undermine the artist's independence. Those who study the cosmos and the human soul engage in a more comprehensive activity that can be inherently most rewarding and that promises to clear away delusions and self-misunderstandings. Yet the temptation has always been great to use knowledge for honor and gain, as the Sophists did.

The true philosopher, in contrast, is more austere in his outward life, even as he is more intently and happily absorbed in his inner life. He has little hunger for the things for whose sake people crave money, and surely no delusions about the value of honor. Yet the striking thing is that he is willing to be a benefactor to those who are seriously his inferiors; he is even, Aristotle suggests, the benefactor par excellence, and the philosophic friendship that Aristotle presents as paradigmatic of virtuous friendship is not that between two mature philosophers but that between a philosopher and his student. Nor is Aristotle idiosyncratic in this choice: Both Plato and Xenophon portray Socrates as the friend of his students, but they do not present him as the close friend of other philosophers, and are reticent even about depicting conversations between Socrates and those students such as Plato who were most nearly his equals. It would be surprising if mature philosophers who knew and respected one another did not develop some sort of a friendship based on mutual admiration, a sense of kinship, and shared benefits from discussions. But evidently, the greater degree of activity and warmth, and surely the more decisive benefits, would be found in a teacher–student friendship.

Protagoras was not a true philosopher because he used knowledge in the service of gain, and he was not a true friend because he accepted only students who could pay and gave them only what they paid for. A true teacher like Aristotle's teacher Plato, in contrast, must have real affection for and interest in his students. Though not his equals, they must be sufficiently promising and sufficiently akin to him that he can take pleasure in their company and find the activity of teaching them inherently rewarding. Aristotle does not explain just how teaching may be helpful for the philosopher, but Plato's own portrait of Socrates suggests that even more important than the value of being pressed to get one's own thoughts in the clearest possible form may be the value of watching what happens to others' souls as they confront certain arguments. And in the case of Socrates, whatever profit he gained from these discussions seems to have been supplemented by the enormous pleasure he took in the simple act of conversing with the promising young.

But why, then, does Aristotle suggest that any return is owed to the philosophic teacher? Is it simply to underscore the magnitude of the benefits conferred? One certainly will not owe a debt to him as one does to a banker, or to a house painter who has trusted one to pay when the job is done. The philosopher has not acted for a reward and does not need one. While the gratitude and affection of a good student will surely please him, they are not critical to him, and being wise, he can have little concern for honor. Perhaps the strongest sense in which gratitude and affection are fitting is that these are the natural response of a good man to someone who has helped him, and indeed, one betrays an impoverished soul if one does not respond in this way. If honoring the philosopher is fitting, the chief reason must be that it is good for us, or good for others who may take notice, to recognize excellence.

Conflicting Claims

Aristotle's introduction of philosophy into the discussion of friendship leads directly into the question of how to assess conflicting claims upon one's loyalty.[12] Having brought up the great benefits for which philosophic students are indebted to their teachers, and the honor that seems to be due to those teachers, Aristotle is now forced, as it were, to address the counterclaims of the fathers who are those teachers' most serious rivals. The traditional father par excellence is one who demands unqualified deference to his judgment and loyalty to the ancestral ways he represents. His claim, resting on the wisdom that is supposed to accompany age and ancestral traditions, naturally comes into conflict with other claims to wisdom and expertise. "Should a person assign all prerogatives to his father and obey him in everything, or should he trust a doctor when he is sick and vote for a military expert as general?" Aristotle asks (1164b22–25). There can be only one answer, but Aristotle states it as gently as possible: If he denies the justice of fathers' demands for the ultimate honor of obedience to all their counsels and commands, he does stress the duty to take care of them in every extremity. Yet the rational grounds even for this claim are not perfectly clear.

Indeed, Aristotle is at pains to emphasize the difficulty of making all such assessments. The rival claims of fathers, teachers, experts, benefactors, men of outstanding virtue, and bosom companions are difficult to weigh because they differ not only in degree but in kind. The qualities of the present, the benefits of the past, and the promise of the future all seem to have different claims upon us. An expert such as a doctor "ought" to be listened to not because one owes him a debt but because it is prudent to take expert advice. A good military man has a similar claim upon the office of general, as well as a claim according to distributive justice: Men of moral excellence and great capacity seem to deserve the highest offices, inasmuch as we and they tend to think of these offices as something good. The duty to repay our benefactors and creditors seems to be a fundamental duty, based on commutative justice, but it sometimes seems nobler to make a magnificent gift than to repay a debt.[13] And when one wishes to show great generosity, it is a question whether it is nobler to display it toward close companions, whom one wishes to benefit out of simple affection, or toward men of outstanding virtue, who may be less close but who seem to deserve help the most, as they promise to make the best use of it.

As a general rule, Aristotle says that benefits conferred should be repaid before one gives gifts or favors to friends. But this rule admits of exceptions, and some of these exceptions, if taken seriously, are potentially far-reaching. As an example of such an exception, Aristotle says that one should ransom one's father before repaying a debt, and indeed, even before ransoming oneself. But as Michael Pakaluk observes, this is not really an exception, if one's greatest debt is to one's parents.[14] So perhaps, then, it is sometimes an exception, and, for a reason not wholly explained, one ought to put one's father first even if he is not the one to whom one owes the most. Twice in this chapter Aristotle expresses with approval the most extreme claim of the family, the claim that filial duty requires one to put loyalty and honor to one's parents ahead of one's own liberty and even survival. On the other hand, Aristotle says, if giving a gift is nobler or more necessary than repaying a debt, one should give the gift. What would be an example of such a noble gift that is not a repayment? Perhaps just this gift to one's father, or perhaps a gift to a very good and wise man. Such a gift is not owed as the repayment of a loan is owed, but it may be appropriate in the deepest sense, inasmuch as everything beneficial is most beneficial of all for the one who is able to put it to the best use.

Aristotle gently pushes this thought further. There is even something unfair, he says, in an exchange in which a bad man does a favor for a good one, and the latter repays him with an equal favor (1165a5–7). Aristotle diverts our attention from the radical implications of this statement by turning immediately to the related case of a good man who is reluctant to make a loan to a bad man who has previously made a loan to him. His reluctance is reasonable because the second loan is unlikely ever to be repaid. But this, Aristotle has said, is a different case from the first; evidently it is not altogether just to expect a good man to help a bad man in building his wall even if the latter has previously helped the good man to build his. In the deepest sense, a good man seems to owe his greatest assistance and efforts to others, family or strangers, neighbors or foreigners, who are good, and who will make the very most of his assistance. Aristotle sketches these exceptions quickly and lightly, but they suggest that there is something questionable or incomplete or abstract about commutative justice altogether, and that what is in the deepest sense just or fitting is for each to have what he can use best, or that all goods and honors should be distributed according to merit.[15]

Instead of carrying out an explicit and radical critique of conventional notions of justice regarding the possession and exchange of property, Aristotle reiterates the necessary imprecision of all discussions of passions and actions (1165a12–14). But why are these matters not subject to perfectly precise statements of principle, even if the principles can only be applied to the diverse and complex particular cases in equally diverse ways? The imprecision of Aristotle's account is at root a result of his rhetorical intent, for it would serve no constructive purpose to undermine even faulty notions of justice if one cannot reasonably expect to replace them with better ones. Instead of stating bluntly everything that is wrong with ordinary notions of morality and justice, Aristotle undertakes to clarify them and make them more rational insofar as this is possible. At the same time, he reproduces certain fundamental confusions or contradictions so as to make them more visible to those who have eyes to see them, while pointing the way toward resolutions that cannot take place in the practical political world, but only on a plane that transcends the moral perspective of the serious citizen.

For those who have gained the most from philosophic instruction, the demands of family and the deepest loyalties and affections of the heart are especially likely to be at odds. One will pay to one's wisest benefactors the honor of seeking and respecting their opinions; one will give them the affection that grows from admiration and gratitude, which are "owed" not as a repayment but as a natural and healthy response to virtue and to assistance; one will feel toward them and their circle a deeper sense of kinship even than that which binds families together. Aristotle portrays the attentions owed to family with deliberate imprecision, but with hints that they are for the most part formal and rudimentary. To family as family – say, to one's great-aunt – one owes an invitation to one's wedding and an appearance at her funeral; to parents who have fed us when we were small and helpless we owe sustenance in return when they are old and needy, and certainly honor as well. But what honor? This Aristotle does not directly say, but it is not the deference to wisdom that one owes a doctor, general, or philosopher, nor is it the truthfulness one owes a close companion or brother, but something else, perhaps more a matter of courtesy and outward deference than anything else. In all of this Aristotle shows by example how fathers should be treated: One should bow to their most extreme claims, treat them respectfully even while honoring other claims upon oneself of a very different sort, and leave the precise truth of one's relative loyalties decorously veiled.

Dissolutions of Friendships

The problem of conflicting loyalties, especially those involving family on the one side and philosophic friendships on the other, leads into a discussion in 9.3 of the dissolution of friendships. In keeping with the delicacy of the preceding chapter, Aristotle is silent about the family in this chapter. He begins by observing how natural and unremarkable it is for friendships of pleasure and utility to dissolve when they no longer serve their purposes, but he also indicates how natural it is for people even in these friendships to expect otherwise, to expect to be loved for themselves and with an abiding loyalty, for such love is the natural completion and perfection of friendship. But if Aristotle agrees that the best friends should be steadfast, what is one to do when one's friend ceases to be good, or never grows into the good man that his early promise led one to expect? What if loyalty bids one stay and one's love of virtue makes an old friend now repugnant to one? Aristotle answers that steadfastness in the deepest sense, as an abiding love for another

and joy in his company, is not really at our command. For it has become
increasingly clear that love is not possible where likeness does not exist.
When a friend becomes wicked, Aristotle says, it is in fact wrong to go on
loving him, for "what is evil neither is nor should be an object of affection"
(1165b15).[16]

Now there is, of course, something of a contradiction here: What is wrong
cannot be strictly impossible. Aristotle asserts that only the good is lovable,
even while he also concedes that what is similar, even if it is evil, can be
lovable, too. The possibility that kinship even among the bad may be a
source of friendship is one that Aristotle has consistently kept out of view, in
support of virtuous friendship, but he allows traces of it to show: "One should
not be a lover of evil, or come to resemble what is base, and as has been
said, like is friend to like" (1165b16–17).[17] Aristotle thus suggests that if a
person's resemblance to oneself, good or bad, can lead one to love him, one's
love for another can also bring one to resemble him, and that friendships
with those who are similar but growing worse are especially dangerous: He
advises breaking with such friends. The imperative to do so, if moral, is
clearly self-interested, in the sense that it is one's own virtue one has in view.
Aristotle balances the coldness of his advice not to love a friend who has
gone bad with the more generous, if not perfectly compatible injunction
to stand by such a friend as long as there is hope of curing him. Putting
the two together, we may say that if there is hope of restoring him to virtue
and to equality with oneself, *and* if one can continue to associate with him
without danger to one's own morals, one should stand by him. At the very
least, Aristotle says, one should be more serious about saving his character
than about saving or repairing his fortunes.

It certainly does happen that friends who are quite good go into serious
decline, but this is not common: As Aristotle has argued, complete virtue
is by nature a stable thing, resting not only on deeply ingrained habits but
also on clear and unshakable insights. The more usual experience is that
friends simply find themselves drifting apart, because the interests that once
united them were ephemeral, or more seriously, because of the gulfs that
arise especially in friendships that begin in childhood, "when one remains
a child in understanding and the other becomes a man in the best sense of
the word" (1165b25–29). Thus Aristotle suggests that the most decisive gulf
will be one of understanding, which of course would be troubling not only
when it separates one from childhood playmates but also when it creates a
rift with those who were dearest of all in childhood, one's own family. In no
such case should one treat the other as a stranger: Some special regard is
due to all with whom one has once been intimate, for the sake of the former
friendship.[18] But unlike in the rarer case of a friend who was once wise
and good and has begun to slip, there is little hope here of reestablishing
equality and intimacy between the friends. True friendship in these cases
becomes impossible, Aristotle says, for the two people will not be pleased

and pained by the same things, and even if they live under the same roof, they cannot share what matters most to them (1165b26–31).

Limit cases can reveal other cases for what they are, and in looking at the dissolution of friendships, we can better understand the extent to which friendship as such is the thing that most satisfies us or is the greatest good for us. Low-level friendships are subordinate to the goods and pleasures that they produce, whereas for the serious human beings who break with friends who become evil or who fail to become wise and good, virtue and understanding prove more important than affection, and more important than any individual friend. It seems that no one, even and especially among the most serious human beings, is content merely with giving and receiving affection or with opportunities to do good. Serious people can have deep affection only where they find a kindred soul, and they crave friends who are able to share the activities that they themselves most treasure. Without such a partnership, every act of assistance to others is ultimately a λειτουργία, a tax or drudgery, which calls out for honor, and which, even when honored, leaves the doer with a lingering sense of entitlement to something more.

In a way, it is the more easygoing and thoughtless people who, being less willing to scrutinize their friends' characters, often seem to have the most unconditional loyalties. The value they place upon loyalty reflects, in part, the longing we all have to love and be loved for who we are, not for anything extrinsic; but their unwillingness to demand virtue in themselves and in one another shows that the real basis of their friendship is not character, and their love rests largely on illusions or unreflecting habit. At a deeper level, they reveal the incoherent human longing for a love that not only is rooted in the particular qualities of the individual friends but also is more absolute and permanent than any qualities.[19] Aristotle acknowledges the presence of the human longing for unconditional love when he says that one should show special consideration to former intimates for the sake of the old friendship, but he clearly believes that this longing can never be met and must be overcome. The traditional family claims and attempts to provide permanent, unconditional ties, but in fact it rests upon utility, pleasure, and the love of one's own, more than upon virtue, and it tends to founder when these are not sufficiently strong. It aims at and promises unqualified affection and respect, and often it does keep people together who otherwise would drift apart; but just as often, all it really can command is the outward signs of love and respect, and it accomplishes even this much only by holding out the most serious promises and threats. The deep and lasting bonds that the family tries to provide, Aristotle teaches, are provided more successfully by the more openly conditional, but not for that reason temporary, bonds that unite men of virtue and understanding.

The most thoroughgoing rejection of Aristotle's teaching about the necessary conditionality of human love is found in the Christian injunction to "love thy neighbor," which is explicated with admirable intransigence

by Søren Kierkegaard in his book *Works of Love*. The Christian commandment to love anyone and everyone would seem on Aristotelian principles
to be utterly misguided, but Kierkegaard argues that it is only the lower
forms of love that cannot be commanded. Kierkegaard identifies both eros
and friendship with the pagan "spirit of the poet," which he opposes to the
"spirit of Christianity," refusing even to welcome eros and friendship as starting points that may ultimately direct the soul toward pure Christian charity,
or "love of the neighbor."

Here, as in much of his philosophy, Kierkegaard seems to be taking aim
especially at the Hegelian attempt to combine what is best in Christianity
and in pagan philosophy into one grand synthesis, and he insists instead on
the need for individuals to make radical choices between incompatible and
even incommensurable ways of life:

Confusion and bewilderment (which paganism and the poet are opposed to just as
much as Christianity is) develop when the defense amounts to this – that Christianity
certainly teaches a higher love but *in addition* praises friendship and erotic love. To
talk thus is a double betrayal – inasmuch as the speaker has neither the spirit of the
poet nor the spirit of Christianity.[20]

Eros and friendship both find their highest expression in the love of one and
only one, which is dramatically opposed to the Christian goal of learning
to love all. Kierkegaard rightly sees that if the friend is, as Aristotle will
argue, loved as "another self," then love of the friend is still tainted with
self-love. Genuine love, Kierkegaard argues, must escape all the invidious
distinctions that separate the beloved from others and that say, in effect,
"I love you because you are like me," for in loving the one we must not
reject the others.

Kierkegaard's boldness is certainly impressive, but Aristotle might well
insist in response that the way in which the Bible presents Christian love as
both necessary and possible shows that it is not after all so radically different
from friendship as Kierkegaard supposes. In 9.4 Aristotle says that the love
one has for the neighbor is based on and grows out of the regard that
one has for oneself (1166a1–2). But the Bible, too, takes a man's concern
for himself as the model and standard of love when it commands him to
"love thy neighbor as thyself" (Matt. 22:39). This standard remains relevant
even when the Bible demands, as a further and still more difficult step, that
self-love itself be crucified: "Greater love hath no man than this, that he
lay down his life for his friends" (John 15:13). For what more can one do
for one's friends than precisely that which one would desire to have done
for oneself? There seems on the surface to be the greatest difference in
kind between the universality and unconditionality of Christian love and
Aristotelian love, which is presented as good only where the loved one is
worthy, and possible in the fullest sense only where he is similar or akin. Yet
the Bible, too, implicitly concedes the importance of both worthiness and

similarity for all human love when it teaches that in the eyes of God all men are equally worthy, being created in his image, and equally sinful and in need of redemption. Christianity itself concedes to Aristotle the essential point that, did we not all have within us the same spark of the divine, we could not and indeed should not love one another. Christianity makes a further concession to Aristotle's argument that affection cannot be commanded when it emphasizes the active, practical, benevolent aspect of love: It is far easier to feed one's neighbor on command than to delight in his presence on command.[21] Perhaps Christianity grants most of all to Aristotle when it implicitly concedes that a life of charity, spent tending to the needs of those who are crippled in body and broken in spirit, a life lived in imitation of the life that ended on the cross, is not in itself a blessed life but is choiceworthy only in the light of extraordinary promises of something more to come.

Aristotle would say in response to Kierkegaard, then, that Christian charity does not reveal a new principle of human love but follows from Aristotle's own principles when applied to different assumptions about human nature. Having gently but relentlessly made clear his reasons for believing that human love can never be unconditional, Aristotle begins in the following chapters to lay bare what he understands to be the most powerful roots of human affection, in his deepest exploration of the connection between friendship and self-love.

7

Friends as Other Selves

In his long discussion of friendship and equality in 8.7 to 9.3, Aristotle has uncovered much self-interest at work in even the most virtuous friendships. But even if each man does love his own good "most of all" (1159a12), Aristotle has nowhere retracted his insistence that true friends also love one another for their own sakes. How are these two different concerns connected in one soul? Aristotle will suggest now that the love for the friend for his own sake is an extension or expansion of self-love.[1]

The Elements of Friendship

Aristotle begins afresh in 9.4 with a new and fuller definition of friendship, specifying the elements that are universally acknowledged to constitute friendship. Ordinary opinion tends to think of true friendship and self-regard as altogether different, the one springing from noble generosity and the other involving qualities that are base or at best morally neutral. By taking common opinion as his starting point, however, Aristotle shows that the same elements that are agreed to be essential to friendship are found primarily and most completely in a good man's relation to himself: "The features of friendship that are found in friendship toward one's neighbors, in accordance with which the various friendships are defined, seem to come out of those that one has toward oneself" (1166a1–2).[2] In the process, he proves again that the virtuous man is the one most capable of being a good friend to others. But he simultaneously raises the question of why, since the best man is best able to be a perfect friend to himself, he would ever be passionately desirous of the friendship of others.

A friend, Aristotle says, is considered in the first place to be one who wishes for and does what is good or seems good for his friend for the friend's own sake. In the second place, a friend is one who wishes the being and life of the friend for his own sake. Whereas benefiting another is an active exercise of friendship, cherishing or being cherished for what one is may be a deeper strain in friendship, not aimed at anything further but simply good in itself. The desire for the continued existence of the loved one is seen most powerfully in mothers, but it is present in every friendship. Even an estranged friend who expects and desires nothing from his former companion nevertheless wishes him to continue to be, and may feel real sorrow at the news of his death. Although this well-wishing is very cool, it does testify to an element of true disinterestedness in friendship. Third, a friend is someone who enjoys spending time with a person, and fourth, someone who chooses the same things. Fifth and finally, a friend is one who shares the sorrows and joys of his friend (1166a2–10).

These five elements characterize a good man's disposition toward himself, Aristotle says, and are also present in everyone else, to the extent that each person considers himself to be good or is satisfied with himself (1166a10–11, 29–30, 66b2–6). This last observation, although it accords with appearances and common opinion, will not turn out to be Aristotle's last word on the subject. It does indeed seem, on casual observation, that people's liking for themselves depends much more on their degree of self-satisfaction than on their real merit. At a deeper level, however, Aristotle will argue that only virtuous people can have the inner harmony and wholeness that allow one to be most truly a friend to oneself. All others, even the seemingly most self-satisfied, are torn by inner dissentions, even if these rarely meet the eye. At the deepest level of all, however, the concern with one's own good that is mirrored in the concern for the friend's good depends on neither the opinion nor the reality of goodness in oneself but is absolutely universal in human beings. These observations, taken together, will have important ramifications for our understanding of virtue.

Having enumerated five basic characteristics or elements of friendship, Aristotle takes up the same elements at 1166a10–29 and again at 1166b6–25, ostensibly seeking to prove that they are all found in the good man's disposition toward himself and are all absent from that of the wicked. In both discussions he considers the elements in almost the same order as at 1166a1–10, but each time he begins with the fourth, unanimity of choice. It is here that Aristotle draws the sharpest contrast between the virtuous man and others, and here that the virtuous man is most unquestionably at an advantage in his positive self-regard. A good man is of one mind with himself and desires the same things with his whole soul, whereas everyone else is more or less divided, desiring one thing and wishing another, perceiving what seems good to oneself but failing to do it, defeating oneself and spoiling one's own happiness in all sorts of ways.[3] Inner harmony is one of virtue's greatest rewards and inner dissension or self-hatred perhaps the worst consequence of bad character.

The full force of this contrast between the virtuous and the base becomes clearer when considered in conjunction with the fifth element that characterizes the good man's relation to himself and to a friend, the unity and consistency of pleasures and pains. The good man "shares sorrows and joys most of all with himself, for the same things are always painful and pleasant for him, and not different things at different times. He is, so to speak, a man without regrets," unlike the wicked, who "are full of regrets" (1166a27–29, b24–25).[4] By setting up freedom from regrets as the standard of true virtue and inner harmony, Aristotle suggests how rare such virtue is, for even most very decent people have regrets. To escape them entirely, one would have to have a degree of self-understanding that is hard for most of us even to imagine. All potential inner conflicts must be resolved with such clarity about one's true concerns that there is no room for the wavering that comes with uncertain priorities, and every decision must be made with such wisdom that it is beyond reproach. If one might in retrospect have chosen otherwise in some instance, one would still have the peace of knowing that one chose the best course in light of everything one knew or could reasonably have been expected to know at the time. Virtue and inner peace require, in short, complete practical wisdom:[5]

> A good man is of one mind with himself and desires the same thing with all his soul; and he wants what is and appears good for himself and does it, for it is the mark of a good man to work hard for what is good, and he does so for his own sake, for the sake of his intellect, which each person seems to be. (1166a13–17)

In particular, then, a good man will avoid that species of inner division that consists in choosing what seems best for oneself and then regretting that one did not sacrifice one's own good for a higher cause, or alternatively, making difficult sacrifices, and then envying and being angry toward those who benefit from such sacrifices while pursuing their own pleasure and comfort. The wise man will not be torn between the seemingly noble and the seemingly good, for he grasps with all his soul the truth that the truly noble and the truly good are one and the same.

By portraying everyone who is not wise and good as plagued with inner discord and regrets, Aristotle offers an important corrective to his earlier teaching about vice and moral weakness.[6] In Book 7 he distinguishes vice from moral weakness on the grounds that the vicious do from deliberate choice what the morally weak do against their better judgment. It seems there that only the morally weak would be full of vacillations and regrets, whereas the wicked would deliberately and consistently follow the wrong principles (1146b22–24, 50a19–22; cf. 50b29–31). In Book 7 Aristotle examines and gives qualified assent to the Socratic thesis that virtue is knowledge. He concludes that true knowledge of good and bad, or true practical wisdom, is always effective or sovereign within the soul that possesses it, and that the morally weak man never possesses true knowledge when he does wrong, although he may recite moral maxims in the same way that a drunken man may recite verses of poetry, by rote and without understanding (1147b9–17). But in Book 7 Aristotle never takes the final step and concedes that *all* vice is the result of ignorance. He leaves largely intact, then, the common belief that although the morally weak may be confused and pitiable in their weakness, the truly wicked are strong, deliberate, and morally blameworthy: They know what they are doing, and what they are doing is choosing evil over good. Now in Book 9, however, Aristotle shows that there is little difference between the morally weak and the wicked. Being wicked is not, as we tend to think, either a pursuit of evil instead of good or an immoral shortcut to one's own good but, rather, the mistaken pursuit of an apparent good, based on a failure to grasp clearly what one's true good is. Yet no one is so warped in his ends as not to have a glimmering of the true good, or so shallow as to be wholly satisfied by a life of indolent disregard for everything noble and important. All who fall short of virtue live lives marred by discord and confusion.

When we take the virtues and vices one by one and examine them closely, through a magnifying glass as it were, vice looks very different from moral weakness, because the vicious seem to have no hesitations and no regrets. This is only true in the short run and on the small scale, however. Particular vices, and above all immoderation, Aristotle's example in Book 7, can seem to be pursued wholeheartedly and without regrets, because, as the Epicureans divined, pleasure and happiness really are closely linked, and the happy life really does turn upon certain sublime pleasures. It would be harder to imagine that anyone could pursue a life of cowardice and injustice wholeheartedly and with unwavering good cheer – as even the charming Falstaff ultimately fails to do. Still less is it possible to live a life of folly in such a spirit. People can be entirely whole and united in their souls, Aristotle says, only when they are pleased with themselves *and believe themselves to be decent* (1166b3–4). The most consistent and unrepentant hedonist can only be united in his soul to the extent that he thinks well of himself and understands himself to be wisely and courageously defying conventional opinion in pursuit of his true, natural good. But to the extent that he sees his good as consisting in the pleasures of the body, pursued in disregard for the happiness of everyone around him, a thoroughly good opinion of himself is impossible to sustain. Even if he commits many acts of immoderation without regrets, sooner or later he must regret having such disorderly passions, and have moments, at least, of despising or desperately avoiding facing what his soul has become. Only a life of complete virtue, resting on genuine wisdom, is proof against the worst misery of all, self-hatred.[7]

At the same time, we may wonder whether there is not some exaggeration in Aristotle's portrayal of the degree of unity that is possible even in the best man's soul. To be wholly and continually "of one mind with oneself," desiring the same thing "with one's whole soul" (1166a13–14), would seem to be completely attainable only in the case of a simple being who had only one interest and one activity, such as the Aristotelian divinity that has no body and that finds its happiness solely in contemplation (1154b20–31). For composite beings such as we are, with an inability always to take pleasure in the same thing and with a variety of serious concerns, it is impossible to avoid moments of feeling torn. Even if a wise person can resolve every ambivalence promptly and appropriately, he will remain subject to them as long as he allows himself to pursue a variety of things, including the good of his friends, as ends. The very best soul would, however, enjoy inner unity of feeling to the extent that he would shift only the immediate focus of his desires, and not his judgments of good and bad or the ranking of his ends. Having such inner unity or harmony, he would certainly be able to be a better friend than one whose soul is torn by civil war and self-hatred. But perhaps Aristotle's comments on the unity of the best souls are meant to suggest something more. If *perfect* unity requires having only *one* serious concern, then the most perfectly unified human soul might be one with a steeper hierarchy of ends that others have, a soul more single-mindedly focused upon the activity that it considers best.[8]

By bringing to the fore that element of friendship that consists in unanimity of choice and desire, Aristotle points to the limits of friendship. For even if we insist, with common sense, that the best man will have and be devoted to friends, we must concede that he can never be as united in choice and desire with them as he can be within himself, since "each wants the good for himself most of all" (1159a12). But in another way, this fourth element or criterion of friendship points to the plane on which friendship can be most complete. When the focus is on the other elements of friendship – on benevolent action of the one friend to secure the advantage of the other, or on the question of survival, or on the sharing of joys and sorrows, or even on the question of how much time to spend together – the good of each friend is separate and distinct, and at times the benefit of the one requires the sacrifice of the other. In the sharing of pleasures and especially of sorrows, the feelings of two can never quite converge: Losing a father and watching a friend lose a father are two very different things, and even the loss of a mutual friend is really different for each, because it is two different friendships that have been lost. But when friends choose together to pursue a single activity, and, for example, are both absorbed in trying to understand a single question, the unanimity of two can be the most complete possible.

Aristotle turns next to the first and second characteristics of friendship, the wish for and promotion of the good and the existence of the friend. He argues that these are both found above all in a good man's relation to himself (1166a14–23). But the difference between the best man and the rest of us is on these counts less dramatic: If Aristotle is able to argue that only the man of perfect virtue has true harmony in his soul, he cannot likewise argue that he alone wishes for his own good and his own preservation. Aristotle does claim that "those who have done many terrible deeds and who are hated for their wickedness flee life and do away with themselves" (1166b11–13), but this is surely an edifying exaggeration, based on a few exceptional instances, offered to bolster the case for virtue for those too blind to see virtue's beauty for themselves. Aristotle's comment on the first criterion of friendship, the wish for and pursuit of the good of the one who is loved, puts such suicides in their proper context. Aristotle says without qualification that "everyone wants the good for himself" (1166a19–20), implying that even those who kill themselves seek a death that has come to seem best for them, either because life has become unbearable or because, like Judas Iscariot, they hope that by punishing their own iniquity they may in some measure redeem themselves.

To say that everyone seeks the good for himself, for his own sake, is to deny that anyone can be diabolically devoted to evil, choosing it for its own sake even if it is in the long run bad for oneself; it is to assert, on the contrary, that evil is only chosen, however mistakenly and however disastrously, in attempted efforts to secure the good. At the same time, Aristotle's argument in this passage makes clear his understanding that no one is simply devoted to the good itself either. What we seek is the good for ourselves and for the particular human beings that we love: "No one would choose to become a different being and for that being that has arisen to have everything good (for as it is, the god has the good already) but only being whatever he is, and it seems to be the thinking part that each is or is most of all" (1166a20–23).[9] That is to say, we do not simply, in a disinterested way, wish for the existence of the good, for it exists already, in other beings, but that does not make *us* happy.[10] Nor can we, if we are thinking straight, wish to become gods and enjoy everything good as those gods, for that would mean wishing that the beings we are would vanish and completely different beings would take their places: This would make for the happiness of someone, but not of us. As Montaigne nicely points out, the incoherent wish to become immortal and divine is really a wish that *we*, with *our* thoughts, pleasures, judgments, desires, and memories, might take on new attributes, and we wish this without sufficient reflection upon the ways in which all of our present attributes are dependent upon the corporeality, the limitedness, and the mortality that we perceive as burdens.[11]

As Stewart and Burnet both observe, this passage recalls the argument at 1159a5–12 that we would not wish our friends to become gods, but would only wish them the greatest goods (or almost the greatest) as human beings.[12] What these commentators fail to note, however, is that the reasons we do not wish divinity for ourselves and do not wish it for our friends are different, in Aristotle's account. We would not wish our friends to become gods, even assuming this to be the greatest of goods, because then we would lose them – not because they would lose their own existence – but we would not wish to become gods ourselves because becoming divine is not, after all, the greatest of goods for us, but is either the evil of annihilation or, better understood, is a logical impossibility.

But what, precisely, is the core of "ourselves" that must remain the same if "we" are to continue to be? Somewhat surprisingly, Aristotle identifies this core not as our whole souls but only as our thinking minds. Now surely he is right not to treat a man's body as his deepest core. Everyone can easily and with pleasure contemplate exchanging his body for a better, stronger, more beautiful body, for the body is more one's possession than it is oneself. Yet perhaps it would be an error to consider the body as merely a possession, which we simply use or operate from. Even if one can imagine oneself waking up in a horse's body (as one could not really imagine being a horse in one's own body), one would certainly not feel quite "oneself" if this happened. Even less would we be ourselves if we had inhabited a different sort of body from birth: Our possession of hands and tongues, our mode of reproducing, and our physical susceptibility to wounds, decay, and death are all central elements shaping the character of our souls. Our bodies are, then, something in between mere possessions and the deepest core of us. And indeed, Aristotle's comment on the impossibility of coherently wishing to become a god at 1166a20–23 suggests that our corporeality and mortality may in fact be quite fundamental in defining who we are.[13]

But on the surface, at least, Aristotle denies not only to the body but also to the passions a pivotal role in determining what each man is: What he says explicitly is that "it seems to be the thinking part (τὸ νοοῦν) that each person is or is most of all" (1166a22–23). He does not give reasons here to support the assertion, but an argument for the mind's centrality may certainly be constructed along Aristotelian lines. Aristotle often argues that it is the capacity for rational thought and judgment that makes us human and sets us apart from the animals.[14] The mind, with its faculties of judgment and deliberation, shapes all human experience, including the experience we have of ourselves. It is the mind that transforms sensory data into the recognition of objects as objects and of the world as a world. These functions of the mind are so central to us that while we can with difficulty imagine being creatures who are devoid of emotion and are mere dispassionate observers, it is impossible for us even to imagine being beings that cannot perceive and think. Moreover, it is the mind's continuity of awareness through time that provides us with the sense of a self that persists through changing experience. Without the mind's memories, we would literally not know who we are.

To be sure, much of what the mind registers, remembers, and considers as important is the individual's own passions. The imagined passionless "self" is not a self that anyone would ever care about, for the self that each person is concerned with is at bottom a being that loves and seeks the good. But the passions are themselves inextricably entwined with and dependent upon thought and, in particular, upon opinions about good and bad. Without these opinions, one may feel an inchoate sense of well-being or uneasiness, but no developed or powerful emotions. And even strong, recurring passions are not necessarily perceived by the one who experiences them as belonging to his true self. In this, the passions are very different from thoughts, and especially from considered judgments. It is possible for a man to say that "I" was overcome by anger or desire, but not by thought; it is possible to wish to be less fearful or, like Cephalus quoting Sophocles, to view one's erotic passions as "many mad masters" from whom one is glad finally to break free.[15] But if we could wish to have different minds, it could only be in the sense of having precisely their present capacities to an even greater degree; above all, we cannot wish our considered judgments of good and bad to be anything other than what they are. An indication that these judgments are the bedrock of our being is the fact that only those passions that accord with them are perceived as belonging to our true selves, rather than as erupting as more or less unwelcome intruders. If we had only a multiplicity of shifting passions with no unifying judgment to arbitrate between them and to choose and pursue a consistent course, there would be no self at all. And hence it is that, as Aristotle says, the actions that appear to us as wholly our own actions, and truly expressive of our deepest selves, are those that follow from settled, reasoned judgments (1168b28–69a3).

But if the passions and actions that we consider to be most truly ours are those that accord with reasoned judgment, it is also the case that reasoned judgment must itself accord with or take into account the deep, settled concerns and desires of the heart if it is to constitute the stable core of an integrated self. Where there is no inner unity of reason and passion, the judgments of the mind lack authority; they are easily disregarded and frequently changed, with the result that the individual may castigate himself for his irrationality or, as has become common in our time, castigate reason itself for being a poor guide to life. When people say that one should "follow the heart" and disregard reason, they fall into incoherence, for the conclusion that this is the best policy is itself an attempt at reasoned judgment, an attempt to use past experience as wisely as possible to guide future action. But those who insist on the importance of the heart have glimpsed an important truth. They see that if practical reasoning begins not with the deepest concerns and longings of the soul as they actually are but, instead, with an artificial construct of what one imagines a rational human being to be and to care about, this reasoning is unlikely to lead to a happy life.

Thus, if it is the mind that ultimately unifies and defines and thereby constitutes a whole, integrated human being, the mind must find its motive force and ultimate guidance in the needs and desires that nature gives, and the wise mind must do so searchingly and systematically. For, as Aristotle says in a famous formulation, "thought alone moves nothing" (1139a35–36; cf. *De Anima* 433a15–24). Choice, he goes on to explain, is "intelligence motivated by desire or desire operating through thought" (1139b4–5). It seems, then, that Aristotle exaggerates when he suggests that the true core of the individual is thought alone, rather than thought motivated by passion.

This exaggeration is in tension with other passages in the *Nicomachean Ethics* and especially the passage in *De Anima* just cited, in which Aristotle gives far greater weight to passion.[16]

But this is an exaggeration and a tension that to some extent pervade the whole *Ethics*. In the opening books, Aristotle presents the life of virtue as ruled by "right reason," and the correct harmony of thought and passion as the harmony between a sovereign mind, which directly apprehends what is noble, and passions that have been habituated, like good draft animals, to listen to and obey and conform themselves to their rational masters (see esp. 1102b13–3a3). But what does reason look to in determining the proper mean in each case, the mean that is not simply halfway between the ends, which is often difficult to find, and which constitutes the true perfection of each virtue? In Book 6 it becomes evident that somehow, practical reason looks to the virtues themselves for ultimate guidance, but the virtues are defined by practical reason.[17] Behind this circularity lies the truth, which Aristotle does not broadcast to his noble-minded readers, that it is not a self-subsisting nobility, higher than human beings with their human, all-too-human wants and needs that gives substance to the best life; it is those natural wants and needs themselves that give us all the direction we will ever find in living well. Precisely the opposite set of prejudices to those that make anti-intellectualism charming in our egalitarian, easygoing age made an exaggerated intellectualism of a certain sort appealing to the serious citizens who constituted Aristotle's primary audience. They liked to believe that their rational judgment was more autonomous and more fully in control than it really was.

Without openly disabusing his readers of this view, Aristotle indicates by the end of the *Ethics* that the primacy of reason means something different to the philosopher himself. In Book 10, he argues that true happiness turns upon thinking, and that true virtue lies in wisdom, so that the philosopher will treasure as his central core certain intellectual capacities that the political-minded citizen will consider less important. In particular, the practical judgment that the latter views as the source and control center of his virtuous activity may be, for the philosopher, less central than the activity of contemplation to which his own practical judgment simply points him. Aristotle does not make a point of this difference here, but by reiterating his claim about the centrality of the intellect three times in close succession, and by using a different expression for it each time (διανοητικοῦ, τοῦτο ᾧ φρονεῖ, and τὸ νοοῦν, at 1166a17, 18–19, and 22), he suggests that he is for now leaving unresolved the question of precisely which intellectual capacities are most central and in precisely what way.[18]

Aristotle proceeds next to the third criterion of friendship, the inclination of friends to spend time together. A good man, he says, enjoys his own company, since his memories of the past are pleasant, his hopes for the future are good, and his mind is well supplied with objects of contemplation

(1166a23–27). It is the wicked whom Aristotle presents as craving the company of others and seeking to flee solitude, because "when they are alone they remember many things that make them uneasy, and anticipate more such things in the future, but in the company of others they can forget" (1166b13–17). Do these comments, taken together, mean that our sociability is after all a direct result of our defects, and that in seeking out friends, we are above all fleeing the poverty and chaos of our own souls? Or does Aristotle simply mean to say that the best man will be best suited for solitude as well as for friendship, and that he will not bring to his friendships the same unhealthy neediness that, in one degree or another, impels most of us into society?

Stewart, in his notes, evinces great uneasiness at Aristotle's suggestion here that the best human beings will be in some fundamental way self-sufficient and inclined to solitude:

That Reason which gives the good man his unity of life, and in virtue of which he is his own constant "friend," is realised not in an isolated individual but in a citizen.... The "self" which the good man loves so constantly is not the isolated self of sense which seeks its own good at the cost of others, but the rational self which consists in the happy consciousness of being joined together with others in a beautiful social order.[19]

Thus, Stewart suggests that the best man will take pleasure in solitude as a kind of recreation from his serious moral and social activities, enjoying relaxing with his own reflections at the end of the day, just as the confident Churchill enjoyed a good night's rest after taking on his shoulders the fate of England and the free world in 1940. But if, as Stewart argues, the best man enjoys his own company only secondarily, and his truest self is a social one, then the good man's relationship to himself will not, on this count, stand as a model or standard for friendship as it does on the other four counts. The structure of this chapter instead suggests that we take in a more serious and radical way Aristotle's claim about the best man's love of his own company and the self-sufficiency Aristotle is beginning to attribute to him.

In our discussion of the *Lysis* in Chapter 1, we suggested that the pleasure of human company and the affection and concern people feel for kindred souls are simply irreducible. Now, with Aristotle's contrast between the uneasy sociability of the worst men and the relative self-sufficiency of the best ones, he suggests that what we think of as an irreducible sociability may, in fact, take much of its force from human deficiencies or limits, even for the best human beings. For here again, we find a certain thought-provoking exaggeration. Although the wisest men have minds well stocked with material for reflection, no one seems to be so wise as never to benefit from intimately observing and conversing with others. Although the best man has good hopes for the future, these can never be simply good: The certain approach of death, and the unavoidable disappointment of not being able to see and experience and accomplish everything that one would wish, make everyone's future something less than a simply bright prospect. This finitude, Aristotle will hint again at 9.8, is no small part of what makes it so pleasant to forget oneself in the company of others, to lose oneself for a time in their concerns, and to enjoy oneself in living their experiences vicariously. Still, if our limitations make us especially desirous of forgetting ourselves in the company of friends, this company could have no such charming power were we not already predisposed to like and take pleasure in the presence of others. To this extent, our sociability *is* irreducible.

Other Selves

The five elements Aristotle enumerates are considered the components of friendship, he says, because the good man is disposed in these ways toward himself, and he has the same attitude toward his friend as toward himself, for a friend is, in Aristotle's famous formulation, "another self" (1166a31–32).[20] Men know of no better way to treat one another than the way they wish to be treated and seek to treat themselves: Friendship is derivative from, because it is somehow a reflection of, each man's concern with himself, and an extension of that concern to others. But how satisfactory is this image of the friend as another self? The juxtaposition of "other" and "self" is at the very least paradoxical, since each man's identity and consciousness is unique.[21] Perhaps Aristotle intends this formulation to represent a kind of limit case, the never fully attained perfection at which friendship aims. But the phrase is also deeply ambiguous, as ambiguous as friendship itself is. As *another* self, is the friend loved mainly as a reflection or extension of oneself, or as a *separate* being with *different* qualities? Again, as another *self,* is he loved as belonging to oneself, or as a true, independent end?

A clue to the real meaning of this enigmatic expression is found in its other appearances in the *Nicomachean Ethics*. In each case, Aristotle shows how the friend who is loved as another self is, in some important way, cherished as an extension of oneself, an extension that can tempt one into the delusion that this other really is still oneself, and as such able to help overcome one's limitedness and mortality. He first uses the expression at 1161b27–29, where he says that children are like "other selves for the parents from whom they have sprung." Children are loved not only as separate and distinct beings but as beings who, it is hoped, will carry on one's memory and even somehow continue one's existence after death. It has now become clear that for Aristotle, the truest kin are the kindred in soul, who, if they are related by blood, are so only accidentally. But among such friends also, and perhaps especially between teachers and students, the longing to leave something of oneself behind can be a powerful source of affection.

Aristotle uses a similar expression again at 1169b5–7, where he says that according to common opinion, "no one who is self-sufficient needs anything further, but the friend, being another self [or a different self – ἕτερον αὐτὸν] provides what one cannot provide for oneself: Hence the saying, 'when providence gives in abundance, what need is there of friends?'" Aristotle criticizes as vulgar such an exclusively utilitarian view of friendship. Yet even in the most calculating friendships of utility, there can be illusions about where oneself ends and the friend begins, for people who are powerful and surrounded with allies and supporters tend to attribute more of their power to themselves and less to externals and fortune than is justified.

Finally, Aristotle uses the expression "other self" at 1170b6–7, where he explains that even the happiest and most self-sufficient of men want friends, because life and the awareness of life are good and pleasant, and the life of the friend, being another self, is cherished in the same way as one's own. Our lives seem fuller and richer and more extensive and significant when we care about and live with – and so, in a sense, live through – our friends, than when we concern ourselves only with our own narrow selves. But when one lives through another, there is a danger of obscuring from oneself, at least for a time, one's own ultimate separateness, if not also one's mortality.

In loving a friend as another self, one loves him both as other and as same. It is by having different talents and perspectives to offer that friends are able to benefit and engage one another; but true friends must be similar also, for then they can best share their aims and pleasures and pains; and it is by both friends' being good, which is to say, fundamentally alike, that they can delight in each other's being. It is in such delight that the other group of meanings suggested by the phrase "other self" come most of all into play, for in loving another for his goodness, one is indeed loving him as an end – not an end that has nothing to do with oneself, but a distinct and separate end nonetheless. If this did not happen, then friendship really would not exist. However much we wish to extend our own lives in duration, power, and fullness of experience, and however much our friendships take strength from these wishes, friendship would be neither possible nor satisfying if it did not have a deeper root in the capacity for genuine goodwill – the capacity to care for others as others and as independent ends. Aristotle's characterization of the friend as another self seems correct, then, in highlighting the importance for friendship of both similarity and distinctness.[22] Yet no degree of similarity can erase the ultimate separateness of two individuals. The paradox of the phrase "another self" points to the fact that even if a friend were identical, he would never be interchangeable with oneself, since it would never cancel the pain of personal catastrophe to know that there is someone else, just like oneself, who is still faring well.

If in friendship we love others, at best, only as second selves, is the truest friendship that which a man has with himself? Aristotle seems reluctant at this point to take up the question of whether friendship with oneself is really possible, perhaps for the reasons that he gives in the *Eudemian Ethics,* and for reasons similar to those that make him say, in Book 5 of the *Nicomachean Ethics,* that justice toward oneself is possible only in a loose or analogous sense. Still, Aristotle does observe in passing that friendship with oneself seems possible "to the extent that man consists of two or more parts, as has been said, and because extreme friendship resembles self-love" (1166a33–b2).[23] A man can be friends with himself because he is a composite being, unlike the divinity, which Aristotle portrays as a seamless, simple whole, so perfect and so self-contained as to be presumably incapable of friendship with itself or with others. Perhaps more importantly, it makes sense to speak of a man's being friends with himself because it is possible for him to be at odds with himself. A bird that flies well is not a friend to itself, though it has parts. But because man consists of parts that do not fit in any simple and easy way together, because he can suffer civil war inside and defeat his own best efforts, it makes a certain sense to think of the good man as his own best friend.

The Bible, in its commandment "Thou shalt love thy neighbor as thyself" (Matt. 22:39), sets up self-love as an unproblematic standard by which the love of others may be measured. We all pursue our own good, and the wicked do so most of all, it seems to say, and the challenge is to do the same for others. Aristotle, by contrast, teaches that being able to know and to secure one's own good effectively and with inner harmony is no easy thing. He ends the chapter with a rare direct exhortation to practice virtue in order to escape the miserable inner dissentions and self-hatred that go with vice. In Book 1 he claimed that the noble and just things were by their natures most pleasant, but in Books 3 to 5 the characteristic acts of virtue, taken in themselves, did not appear as unambiguously pleasant. Here, then, is the moral man's still-needed reward for virtue, for by cultivating it, "one can be disposed in a friendly way to oneself and can become a friend to another" (1166b28–29). Virtue, Aristotle suggests, provides the self-sufficiency that minimizes the needy, unhealthy, and utilitarian motives to friendship, while allowing true and virtuous friendship to flourish.

But what will the friendships of the healthiest, most whole, most self-sufficient human beings be like? What will draw them out of themselves and impel them to care deeply for other human beings? Similarity or kinship, a natural sympathy with kindred souls, and a natural pleasure in shared activity with them are of utmost importance. In Chapters 5–7 of Book 9, Aristotle will explore three other solid sources of friendship that are available to all of us, and that are effective in strengthening the friendships of the very best and most self-sufficient.

8

Goodwill, Concord, and the Love of Benefactors

In the remaining chapters of Book 9, Aristotle will spell out in detail the implications of his concept of friendship as extended self-love that he introduces in 9.4. In 9.5, he will analyze the elements of friendship that consist in wishing for the friend's life and well-being, or goodwill, and discuss how this crucial root of friendship comes into being. In 9.6, he will turn to friends' agreement in practical choices, or concord, and the resulting common activity and sense of solidarity that promote goodwill and that form the core of political friendship. In 9.7, he will explore the roots of benevolent activity and the ways in which it strengthens goodwill and affection. After taking up again the question of self-love in 9.8, Aristotle then in 9.9, 9.10, and 9.12 discusses the desirability and best conditions for friends' spending their days together, and in 9.11, he gives his final reflections on the possibilities of friends' sharing their sorrows and joys.

Goodwill

Aristotle makes a fresh beginning in 9.5 with the theme of goodwill, the utterly indispensable basis of friendship, the necessary beginning that is barely a beginning, the critical impulse of selflessness that remains, when left to itself, passive, idle, and weak, but without which none of the beauty and none of the joy of friendship could ever exist. The phenomenon of goodwill demonstrates the existence of an unselfish core to all friendship, as Laelius is so eager to prove,[1] but Aristotle insists against Laelius that by itself, it falls short not only of friendship but even of affection. Goodwill lacks the "intensity and desire" that belong to all love; people "merely wish for the good of those toward whom they feel goodwill, without actively assisting them (or joining with them in activity) or troubling themselves on their behalves" (1166b32–34, 67a8–10).[2] And these two elements of friendship that are missing from pure goodwill are clearly related. To be loved, the other must be desired as part of one's own happiness, the presence of whom is

155

necessary to make one's own life complete, and only when he is perceived as one's own friend, one's own other self, does one reliably exert oneself on his behalf.

Aristotle first introduced the concept of goodwill in 8.3, as part of his fundamental definition of friendship, and we have seen that it is a key to understanding the three types of friendship and their interrelation. But by postponing his main treatment of goodwill until Book 9, after he has shown the incoherence of the benefactor's demand for a reward and after he has introduced philosophy as a theme, Aristotle underscores the fact that the generous sentiment of goodwill toward those who are good survives the most rigorous analysis of moral virtue's claims for a reward. Goodwill is the natural and unconfused source of the wish to see virtue rewarded; it wishes this not because virtue needs a reward but because our sympathies are naturally with those we admire. At the same time, Aristotle says that goodwill is the natural and just response to benefits given out of kindness:

> One who has been the recipient of a good deed, in return for what he has received, gives goodwill, and so does what is just. But the one who wants to do someone good in hopes of getting assistance from another does not seem to have goodwill toward that person, but rather toward himself, just as he is not a friend if he serves him in order to make use of him. (1167a14–18)

Aristotle thus makes it clearer than ever that good deeds done out of expectation of reward do not deserve any return or reward, and that ones done generously deserve only gratitude and kind regard. The benefactor has no just claim upon a return, because his act of giving, if not mercenary, was complete in itself. But goodwill is owed in the sense that it is the natural, healthy, appropriate response to kindness. And this natural response, if less than a sense of binding obligation, is perhaps something more than the passive goodwill one has for an admirable stranger; for in becoming a benefactor, he has begun to entwine his life with one's own and has taken the first step toward becoming, and having the claims upon one's heart of, a friend.

Concord

If goodwill is a disinterested but passive seed of friendship, concord (ὁμόνοια) is an active agreement of purpose and effort that at least resembles full-fledged friendship, although it is not at first clear whether it goes beyond prudent self-interest to include genuine goodwill as well. Concord is agreement in mind or opinion, Aristotle says, but not just any such agreement: It must be mutually known, and must pertain to matters of action in which both or all parties may attain their ends. Hence, for example, agreement about the heavenly bodies is not yet concord (1167a24–26). If admiration for a fellow astronomer produces only cool and passive goodwill, agreeing with him about theoretical matters by itself adds nothing to affection and friendship. It would seem to be only in response to some problem or need – when the astronomers rally together under attack from the religious authorities, for example, or when they choose to study together, presumably because each studying alone cannot progress as far – that the crucial element of friendship, sharing in choices, comes into play.

But although friendly agreement can exist in any realm of human action, Aristotle uses the special term "concord" to denominate agreement in great matters, such as those with which political communities are concerned. Thus concord means especially political friendship (1167b2–3), and it is used in Greek as the opposite of στάσις, discord or civil war.[3] As the Paraphrist Heliodorus puts it, concord relates primarily to matters of weighty consequence, to justice and the freedom and security of whole cities and nations, and not to such matters as whether to sit at home or go for a walk.[4] The significant difference between agreement in weighty matters of action and other kinds of agreement would seem to be that only the former have the power to create mutual concern and even goodwill. Aristotle observes in the *Eudemian Ethics* that concord and goodwill "seem to some to be the same, and to others not to exist without each other" (1241a1–3). His own examples show the possibility of goodwill without concord, but never concord without goodwill, and experience confirms that cooperation in important matters tends to produce goodwill even where it has not existed before. To be sure, two people who are fundamentally hostile to each other may, if they find themselves in the same predicament, wish each other well incidentally, in the limited sense of wishing for a result that depends upon or necessarily entails the success of the other. But the deeper concord of those who must work together and who have no reason for enmity results in something more: Each comes truly to hope for the prosperity and success of the other as an extended part and not merely an incidental concomitant to the good he seeks as an end. It is simply human nature that we feel such sympathetic goodwill in these situations so long as nothing arises to thwart it.

Concord, understood as unanimity in upholding good laws and in defending the homeland, is a harmony that is attainable between ordinary people in their common life. Concord and patriotism, although different, are mutually supporting: Affection for the homeland leads men to identify their good with its good and join in its support, and common projects for the common good, by strengthening bonds among citizens, strengthen their dedication to the whole. Concord is the type of friendship that legislators seek to promote (1155a22–24), and although it helps greatly to remedy the defects of an imperfect devotion to justice, it also depends on a degree of virtue. For when people are out for themselves, each seeking to get a larger share of the community's goods and a smaller share of its burdens, Aristotle says, they must continually be on their guard against one another (1167b9–14).

Although concord is possible among ordinary people, then, it will be a fortuitous and shifting thing where virtue is weak; it will be solid and complete only among the most morally serious citizens like Laelius and Scipio. Yet Aristotle stresses that concord is *aimed* not at virtue as such but at the common advantage: It is utilitarian friendship at its most comprehensive.[5] The virtuous friendships of the most dedicated fellow statesmen, although infused with a patriotism that goes beyond a simple concern for utility, nevertheless take their bearings from a shared concern with the common advantage. To the extent that serious men make such political friendship their focus, we see another reason why Aristotle has been reluctant to deny that utilitarian friendship is real friendship.

Because the momentous issues upon which concord or political friendship turn are of concern to everyone, they provide a potential basis of friendship for everyone, including those whose central interests lie outside the political realm. Not being immune to the misery of civil strife, even the most independent and theoretical men have a stake in the stability and good government of their homelands. Yet the very fact that concord or political friendship brings so many different human types under the same tent is a reminder that ultimately its bonds are thin and distant, compared with the most intimate friendships, since these bonds must stretch to include people whose characters and deepest concerns are radically different. The elements of friendship that consist in the intimate sharing of pleasures and pains, joys and sorrows, and important activities are possible in civic friendship only to a very limited extent, even in the smallest, most fraternal polis.

These considerations point to the limitations of concord as it exists within the political community as a whole. Aristotle indicates these limitations with beautiful succinctness as he illustrates the conditions that concord requires:

Concord is found in regard to matters of action, and of those, in regard to matters of importance and ones in which it is possible for both or all to attain their goals. For example, it is found in cities in which all decide that the offices should be elective, or that an alliance should be formed with the Lacedaemonians, or that Pittacus should rule when he himself was willing to. But when each wishes himself to be ruler, as in the *Phoenician Women,* there is faction. For concord does not exist when each has the same thoughts about just anything, but the same thoughts in regard to the same persons, such as when both the people and the decent [ἐπιεικεῖς] agree that the best [ἄριστοι] should rule. In this way all get what they aim at. (1167a28–b2)

In actual political communities, concord about the most important things is at best imperfect, and all too often unattainable: The people are unwilling to be ruled by those who do not share their character, tastes, and outlook; the leading citizens are likely to agree that the best should rule; but each interprets this to mean that he should rule. Even if, in the very best case, the common people and the decent gentlemen agree that the best should rule, and even agree as to who the best are, it is not clear that they will ever agree with one another or with the best as to what the real goal of their rule should be – whether, for example, it should be peaceful security, glorious empire, prosperity, education in moral virtue, promotion of faith, or making a place within the community for philosophy. And finally, the truly best are likely to be reluctant to rule, or to rule for as long as their services might be beneficial. Political life, therefore, tends to be characterized less by friendship between superior leaders and their beneficiaries as by more or less muted struggles between more or less unworthy men.

In this chapter, then, we see Aristotle's hints about the stance toward political life that would be adopted by the very wisest man, who has digested all the lessons Aristotle has offered in 8.7–8.13 about the rational and irrational motives for seeking rule, the craving for honor, and the claims people make to deserve a reward for having acted without thought of reward. Such a wise person will wish earnestly for concord with and among his fellow citizens; hence he will, like Pittacus, be "willing" to serve in office when his services are needed for the good of all; but he will not be hungry for office or for honor. Aristotle, in discussing the thoroughly rational political affection that is concord, is silent on the love of honor. But political life will hold such a man only by one corner; his deepest loves and desires will lie elsewhere.

Commentators have expressed some puzzlement as to the function of this chapter.[6] But taken in the context of the surrounding sections, this discussion is clearly an important part of the argument Aristotle is developing about the roots of friendship. Whereas bare goodwill arises from our perception of goodness in another, mutual assistance in important matters produces true affection, and the next chapter will show that, paradoxically, this affection is rooted less in what others do for us than in what we do for them.

The Love of Benefactors for Beneficiaries

If in 9.5 we see the solid root of the desire for virtue to be rewarded, and in 9.6 we see the solid grounds for the wisest man's concern with public affairs, in 9.7 we find the deepest and most sensible reasons for the desire to benefit others. Aristotle begins the chapter with the somewhat puzzling fact that benefactors seem more attached to their beneficiaries than the reverse (1167b17–19). He rejects the common explanation that the benefactors take an interest in their beneficiaries as creditors do in their debtors, out of a desire to get something back from them. He concedes that some such concern may often contribute to their interest, since most people prefer to have good done to them than to do it. But this fact does not account for the genuine affection that benefactors feel. The true cause of this affection lies deep in human nature, he says, in our love of life itself. The affection of benefactors is like the love of craftsmen for their work, poets for their poems, moneymakers for their money, and mothers for their children. Each loves what he or she produces, because "existence is for everyone an object of choice and of love, and we exist in activity, in living and acting, and in his activity the maker is, in a sense, the work produced" (1168a5–7).[7] Or, as Aristotle goes on to say, "the work reveals in actuality what the maker is in potentiality" (1168a8–9). In these two sentences, Aristotle indicates the paradoxical character of all productive labor. In one sense, the product we love, especially if it is an inanimate product like a pot, is one step removed from the being or living that we love most of all. We exist fully in activity and only secondarily or by extension in the product that remains when our work is done. But in another sense, the finished work is the realization of what its maker was only potentially before he made it: The finished work is not just a relic of his activity but the final cause or defining purpose or true meaning of his activity.

Because ordinary productive activity is so clearly aimed at a goal, it is impossible to think of it as simply or chiefly an end in itself: However much our democratic sensibilities rankle at the Greeks' aristocratic disdain for manual labor, Aristotle seems right when he says that activity done for the sake of a product is subordinate to that product (1094a5–6). But Aristotle also seems right to point out that activity is the very stuff of life, and that work expands our existence and fulfills capacities that would otherwise be bare, dormant potentialities. The result is that in all productive work, even the most serious, there is a certain tension or absurdity, inasmuch as what is done only for a goal seems in a very real way more valuable than the goal. Let us leave aside the making of stockpots and oilcans; even the arts at the very highest face the same problem. In painting a beautiful scene, the artist draws all sorts of capacities into play and sharpens them through use. To this extent, his activity truly enhances his life and is truly good, which is why artists often find it satisfying to paint even when it does not pay. But in another sense, every brush stroke is itself incomplete and looks only to the finished work: It is with good reason that no one chooses to paint upon water, for the goal is a work that will last and be seen. When the goal is reached, however, the activity is over, and the artist has now only a relic or reminder of his activity. He, the maker, does not really exist in the painting but "is" in only a somewhat loose and paradoxical sense "the work produced" (1168a7).

As a result, it is in one sense natural and in another sense ridiculous for painters or poets to love their works as one might love a living child. It is natural to the extent that the work of a great artist or writer *can* somehow capture and preserve the essence of his spirit and insights – even more than a child does who resembles him only in form. Yet taken strictly in itself, this work is nothing more than marks upon canvas or bundles of printed paper; it has no life and joy of its own as a child does; it is not an end in itself. For the maker, it exists only as a pleasant memento of past activity or a useful epitome of past thoughts. But if we take seriously Aristotle's statements that we exist in activity and that it is the activity of the present that really counts (1168a6,14–15), then to be choiceworthy in the highest degree, the productive activity must be good taken simply in itself.

The test of whether an activity is wholly good in itself lies in how one would feel if it entailed no outward result: no effect on anyone else, no honor, no salary, no lasting product of any kind. A writer might well find his writing satisfying in this way, if he wrote not chiefly for the sake of the books produced but because he found it the best way to think: He would realize that his product or "goal" was in reality a means to the true end, a test that assisted him by challenging him to understand as well as possible the subject before him. The writing of books is in this sense a spur that the best minds have perhaps not needed, although, of course, they might well choose to produce books as the by-product and not the goal of thought, as a gift to others.

But is the work of most artists, including poets, so intrinsically satisfying as this? Could they consider the years they devote to the creation of a masterpiece to have been well spent even if the work were destroyed the day after it was finished? Curiously enough, this attitude would seem even harder to sustain than the outlook that would consider the labor worthwhile even if the *artist* were destroyed as soon as his masterpiece was finished, as happened to the seventeenth-century painter Giovanni Fumiani. After spending twenty years painting the magnificent ceiling of San Pantaleone in Venice, Fumiani put on the last brushstrokes, stepped back to admire his work, fell off the scaffolding, and died. His case seems sad but not tragic, for he accomplished what he set out to do. But if, at the moment of completion, he had been forced to choose either death or the destruction of his work, it would not have been sensible, from his own point of view, to choose the former: It would be the choice of an "immortality" that he could not himself enjoy for a single day over continued life and activity. The artist's deep need for his work to be seen and honored is evidence that if his activity is more satisfying than is the work of the widget maker, it is still not as wholly satisfying in itself as is the thinker's.

But of course, we must hasten to add, the wish to have one's work seen goes beyond the wish for honor: Every such work is also an act of generosity, a gift to the world, and this is the level on which it is often most meaningful to the artist. In such generosity, in the natural human desire to be a source of good to others, we can see the limited but real way in which it is possible to live in one's inanimate products. If to be is to be engaged with the world, then by producing things of value that enhance the lives of others even in our absence, we really are more extensively engaged and alive: Our products give us longer arms and more hands. But as lifeless objects, they are still only the instruments of the friendly or philanthropic activity that they promote, an activity that itself is the means to, and hence subordinate to, the happiness of particular other human beings. Thus the ultimate way in which we naturally seek engagement with the world is through intercourse with others, through having a positive effect upon them. We may initially seek to do this for interested reasons, out of hopes of honor or a return. But the more of our thought and energy and trouble we invest in others, the more the beneficiaries seem to be an extension of or a realization of our own life. And so, loving our own existence, we come to find their existence increasingly precious to us also.

This is a major reason why time and familiarity build affection, especially between good people: Each person's efforts on the other's behalf increase his affection, and greater affection makes him care more and trouble himself still more for the other. Thus Aristotle shows that the love of one's own, a source of so much prejudice, skewed judgment, and resistance to serious inquiry, has a thoroughly natural and even sensible root. If what we truly, deeply love is life, and if we are more alive the more we have in hand and the more we love and accomplish, then as Aristotle stresses, it is natural that we should especially love our own actions and friends and beneficiaries as part of our own fully realized existence.[8]

Aristotle does not claim that this analysis provides an exhaustive account of why people wish to be benefactors. Although he shows that the love of one's own existence can indeed be a reason in itself for benevolent activity, he never denies that acts of kindness may also be done simply out of the desire for the happiness of a loved one. But the discussion of how benevolent activity contributes to love, taken together with Aristotle's discussions of goodwill and concord in 9.5–9.6 and his account of the reasons for love in 8.3, sharpen the question of whether the ultimate roots of love itself, in contrast to goodwill, may not always be self-regarding. One may spend an hour searching for a friend's lost glasses out of love and not for one's own sake; if it is one's own full activity that one seeks, there are other and more pleasant ways to be active. But why does one love the friend in the first place? Recognition of a certain goodness and a certain similarity naturally engender goodwill, but love arises when another comes to seem good to us for ourselves, and Aristotle suggests that it is *our* need for assistance, for allies, for companionship, for diversion, and not least for a satisfying field of activity that causes us actively to love.

The Concern with the Noble

To the extent that we wish to be involved in activity that is significant and satisfying, and to the extent that we naturally are inclined to care about fellow human beings, the concerns fueling our philanthropic activity are thoroughly sensible. But inevitably, the activity of the present and the prospect of more such activity for a finite span of years does not provide all that we yearn for. We seek something more, something to compensate us for our mortality, something lasting and meaningful and noble to make sense of our suffering. And this concern for what is noble both reinforces and distorts the natural love of our work and of its objects or beneficiaries.

Aristotle says that one reason for the benefactor's feeling greater affection than the recipient is that the former is more pleased by the act that has brought them together, because "for the benefactor there is nobility in his action, so that he rejoices in the one for whom it was done, but for the recipient there is nothing noble in the doing, but at most only something beneficial" (1168a10–12). Aristotle is not, as some translators and commentators seem to assume, denying that the nobility of a generous act is *visible* to its recipient – for surely it is – or even that the recipient may admire it for what it is.[9] He is, however, suggesting that a noble act takes on very different colors depending on the angle from which it is viewed. It is not obtuseness but precisely sensitivity to nobility that makes the most high-minded souls even more inclined than others to forget good deeds of which they were the mere recipients, in which everything admirable accrues to someone else. Thus Aristotle says that the great-souled man is ashamed to be the passive beneficiary of good, seeks always to requite benefits with greater benefits, and is disinclined to remember the good deeds of others toward him, preferring to dwell instead upon those that he has done himself (1124b9–15). Despite the fact that people tend to think of a benevolent act as noble because it looks selflessly to the good of the recipient, it seems that what is loved most in the act is not given away or even shared, but accrues only to the doer. The love of the noble thus appears on inspection to be no more disinterested or impersonal than is the love of the pleasant or the good. Just as loving the pleasant and the good does not mean wishing that pleasant and good things may exist in general but wanting to have them for ourselves and those that we love, so loving the noble means above all wanting to possess it.

Aristotle hints at a further problem with benevolent activity when he says that what is cherished by the doer as noble is welcomed by the recipient merely as beneficial or useful, and what is useful is less pleasant and lovable than what is noble (1168a12). If in most benevolent activity what is noble to the giver is only of passing utility to the receiver, then Aristotle indicates that such benevolence is problematic in putting the high in the service of the low. We may say, in seeking to escape this problem, that the low-level need that the benefactor meets is not really the goal but only the occasion for a noble activity that is intrinsically good. But does this really make sense of the phenomena? The visit of a friend from out of town may provide the occasion for a dinner party, but a request from a neighbor to help rebuild a house that has been damaged in a fire is not an opportunity or occasion in the same way. Such actions would never be undertaken were they not needed. Of course, much of the help friends give each other takes place on a higher level than house repairs, and it may involve conversations that are interesting and even pleasant if the problem is not terribly serious and be conducive to a stronger friendship. But we would never engage in these particular discussions except in hopes of solving the problem. Nor could we sensibly wish the friend to face more problems or perplexities so that we might help to resolve them. This does not mean that our benevolent activity is merely a means to an end: It may be valuable for the qualities of heart and mind that it exhibits and strengthens through exercise, for the friendship it expresses and deepens, and for the example it sets. Still, when we look at an act such as a brave rescue attempt, it is clear that it is only worthwhile to direct human energies and virtues and to risk a human life in *this* way if one has a substantial chance of securing a good result. And that is what makes such acts decisively different from those that we choose simply as ends in themselves.

Benevolent activity is less constrained by necessity and less defined by utility when its goal is an education in virtue. Yet even here, we must ask what the ultimate end is. Does one help educate a young friend in virtue so that he may go on to do the same for others, and they for others still, ad infinitum? Or is education not for the sake of activity? But what activity? Noble service to others, or something else? It might be said, of course, that *all* of life's serious activities involve the difficulty we have sketched. The best, most truly satisfying thing in life is not lying on a beach or even playing tennis but meaningful work, meeting great challenges, testing our spirits, and honing our virtues; and in all of this we need important goals to strive for. If our goals were all instantly met as soon as we conceived them, life might seem to lose its meaning. But if this is so, there is a serious problem with our lives. If we work only in order to reach goals that would make our lives dull and insipid if we ever should reach them all, then we are rats addicted to a treadmill, and life is absurd (cf. 1094a18–22).

This characterization of life is partly true and to that extent a reflection of our unhealthiness, but only partly so. Most of us do tend to work in order to rest and rest in order to work, but Aristotle says that neither of these is the proper goal of life. The proper goal is not work or recreation but the activity of serious leisure (1177b4–6). Most of us do not spend much time cultivating activities that are good in themselves and not frivolous, but we do recognize them: music, good conversation, gazing into a lover's eyes, learning and contemplating what we know, a quiet, deep enjoyment of what is beautiful. Most of us are both too restless and too lazy to spend much time in such pursuits. We are ourselves not talented or accomplished in the arts, and being a spectator is less satisfying than being actively engaged in them. We find thinking difficult and unpleasant, and we are too agitated to contemplate anything for long. We need problems to tackle and common enemies to fight to give depth to our friendships, exams to take and performances to give to keep us learning and practicing, courses to teach and publication deadlines to keep us thinking. But all of these things are ultimately crutches and should be frankly regarded as such.

Returning, then, to the two different perspectives of giver and recipient, we may say that if there is something deficient and ungracious in the attitude of the recipient who is only too ready to forget a deed that was useful to him, there is perhaps also a certain lack of proportion on the other side, an inclination to exaggerate the importance of an act that really was, at core, just a means to a practical end.

Aristotle also continues in the most delicate and gentle way to probe the intrinsic importance and lovableness of the noble through his comments on its permanence:

Pleasant is only the activity of the present, the hope of the future, and the memory of the past; and what activity gives us is the pleasantest and the most lovable too. For the one who has done it, the work endures (for the noble lasts a long time), but for the recipient the utility is transitory. And while the memory of noble acts is pleasant, the memory of useful things is not altogether pleasant, or is so to a lesser degree, though the reverse seems to be true of anticipation. (1168a13–19)[10]

Why is this? The utility is transitory, it seems, even when the benefit remains – as, for example, the benefit of a repaired house – because when the work is completed one simply has one's house back, which is certainly good, but the useful assistance is over. But does the nobility of the assistance not cease together with its usefulness? Apparently not, because the *benefactor* continues to cherish his noble act as both pleasant and lovable, whereas the useful is "less pleasant and lovable" than the noble (1168a12). But if the noble is so very pleasant and not just austerely choiceworthy to the most elevated souls, we would expect everyone to prefer and compete to be a benefactor, whereas Aristotle has just said that the majority of men, in fact, prefer to receive than to do good deeds (1167b27–28).

The explanation seems to be that what is noble is more pleasing and lovable for everyone *in retrospect* than what is useful. Hence even vulgar people will love their beneficiaries and feel pleased with the good that they themselves have done, and they will prefer the memory of their own good deeds to the memory of useful ones whose profits have long since been spent. The memories of good deeds, like the memories of great difficulties one has overcome, are pleasant because they demonstrate and remind us of our virtues and strengths: Such victories are loved for the same reason that honor is loved, but are more solid. Aristotle ties the love of the noble to a love of what is "lasting" and to the pleasure of remembering, but he gently reminds us that what matters most for our happiness is not memories but present action. Thus noble action cannot be counted as altogether good if it is not best and most choiceworthy at the moment of acting as well as afterward. Good people will indeed choose noble actions over all others, but perhaps they do not always love them most in the moment of doing them. A good man is very glad afterward to have stopped in a freezing rain to help a stranger whose car has skidded off the road, but he does not think, as he is pushing the car out of a ditch, "This is what I live for." He will do such things because he is good, but doing them will not be what he aims at most. Hence they will not be the core of his virtue.

Therefore, when life's sweetness is elusive or insufficient and one hungers for something splendid and lasting, when one's focus is on sacrificing for others because it is noble, when one throws oneself into charitable or political work not out of love for others or for the activity itself but out of a cold sense of duty or a hope for fame or reward, one tends to live for one's memories or one's hopes. And these two are closely connected: In the final analysis, the memories of difficult and noble deeds are so lasting because they carry with them hopes, not only the perfectly reasonable hope that in future trials one may perform just as well as before, not just the kind, sensible hope that those one has benefited may continue to prosper, but vaguer and vaster hopes for oneself as well. One's attention drifts away from the present that matters most, away from joyful, active life, to settle instead on thoughts of permanence. If one does not consciously or half-consciously hope for everlasting life as a reward for virtue, one hopes at least that one's memory will live on. And this thought is likely self-deceiving, for one is tempted to imagine that one can live on in one's work after death much more than one actually can. It is true that, to some extent, Shakespeare is still alive in his plays and Lincoln in his speeches. Their spirits and thoughts persist enough that we can come to know them and love them. They are alive for us, then, but they are not alive for themselves. Therefore, if Shakespeare, in writing his plays, took pleasure in the present imagination of the pleasure he would give to us, and even took pleasure in loving thoughtful readers he would never meet, this was a solid pleasure that enhanced his inherently happy activity of writing.[11] But if he imagined that fame would somehow give him a happiness that would go on after his death, he was deceived. If the most important thing is living and being in the activity of the present, not hopes or memories, then to be the best thing in life and the core of happiness, virtuous action must not be a sacrifice for the sake of something else beyond the action itself.

Benefaction at Its Best

Taking activity for its own sake as the goal, we can see now a hierarchy of activities that involve helping others. Lowest is that which is directed to the needs of the body, and which simply seeks to remove obstacles, such as poverty and illness. Higher is that which educates the soul, especially when it is directed to the activities that are most choiceworthy for their own sakes. If the benevolence is ultimately absurd that seeks to instill virtue so that the beneficiary may in turn instill virtue, and so on without end, there is nothing absurd at all in the life that seeks satisfying activity, and in finding it, seeks also to share it with others. Best of all, then, is the activity that is helpful and delightful to both partners – the engaging discussions of teacher and student that educate the student while pushing the teacher to greater clarity, or the trip to a skating pond of mother and child, in which the mother takes pleasure in seeing a child awaken to the discovery of something new and wonderful, and each enjoys both the company of the other and the activity itself. But every such apprenticeship ultimately makes sense only as aiming beyond itself to a mature partnership in excellent, joyful activity.

Indeed, in the very finest educational activity, we may see a resolution to many of the problems and pitfalls of virtuous benevolence and the affection surrounding it that Aristotle has been quietly indicating throughout this chapter. If benefactors are inclined to make too much of their beneficence, and to rely on vague hopes of happiness in the future to compensate them for their pains, the benefaction that involves helping another's soul to blossom is surely the most pleasant and the least likely to need any distorted and distorting hopes. The clear-sighted teacher knows that his position is more choiceworthy than that of his student because he is the wiser of the two. He may love more than he is loved, but he will find that actively loving, when it involves sharing what gives one joy, really is more satisfying than merely being loved. He may benefit more than he is benefited, but here, too, he will feel no deprivation, since his teaching allows him a fuller and richer array of activity than solitary thought alone is likely to do. If indeed the benefactor loves more than the beneficiary, he will not find his friendship equalized by greater affection from the inferior in the way that Aristotle proposed in 8.8, then, but neither will he feel a need for such equalization. In sum, being a benefactor is a solid good when kept in perspective, and keeping it in perspective means knowing that one has chosen it as rewarding in itself, and fully accepting the fact that, as Aristotle says in 9.5, one is owed no more than goodwill in return for one's efforts.

But such a friendship is likely to be the most satisfactory of all unequal friendships for the beneficiary as well. The problems, the discomfort, the dishonor of being the beneficiary of noble generosity are really the problems of being a passive recipient, whose helplessness and lack of resources are highlighted by the power and activity, not to speak of the moral superiority, of the benefactor. But one who is undergoing a true education is by no means the passive receptacle of knowledge, let alone the unwilling captive of his teacher. Indeed, in a true education the student must be, eventually if not initially, at least as active in seeking out the teacher as the teacher is active in seeking him; the student must study long hours and undergo long hours of soul-searching; and if the efforts of both are fruitful, it would not be surprising if the student's affection in fact equaled or even surpassed that of his mentor. When the superior's help is not merely useful but reaches and changes the heart; when the beneficiary can say of him, "He made a man of me," or "He gave me my life"; when he can take pride in the qualities that made the superior choose him, and in the efforts of his own that made the benefactor's investment bear fruit, then it is perhaps impossible not to love him deeply in return.

In the light of these considerations, we must wonder whether there are not, in fact, many cases in which the beneficiary loves more than the benefactor does. We may leave aside the needy, devoted, and sometimes embarrassing hangers-on, the Apollodoruses and Aristodemuses, who ride in the wake and cling to the fringes of every great teacher's life. These unpromising students' love is characterized more by hopefulness and self-flattery than by gratitude for anything solid that they have gained. There would seem to be many counterexamples to Aristotle's thesis found among the genuinely beneficial relations of teachers to students and mentors of all kinds to their protégés. Although, as Aristotle says, children usually do not love their parents as much as the parents love them, it may be that this seemingly paradigmatic example of benefactors' relations to beneficiaries, precisely because it is so comprehensive, unchosen, and unconditional, has special problems that other relationships that turn upon benefiting the soul do not have. Because the child depends on the parents for sustenance as well as for guidance, and because he receives from them so much guidance and attempted guidance that he never asked for, their influence tends to be felt as too stifling, and hence there is a natural need to diminish its importance and break free. This sometimes happens with teachers and other mentors as well, but more rarely.

Aristotle does not directly discuss the healthy relations of teachers and students, which seem to stand as an important counterexample to his thesis; his main focus is on prompting the reader to think through the problems of less satisfactory forms of benefaction. Yet his analysis in no way rules out and indeed indirectly points to the possibility that the best benevolent relations may embody a solution to the problems he highlights. Especially when the teacher is clear-sighted about his activity; especially when, profiting from it and enjoying it himself, he feels no need to make a point of his generosity; and especially if he does not teach that the best of all things is to possess the unshareable position of one who nobly sacrifices for another but, instead, turns his own and his student's attention to shared pursuits, then the inferior will not feel that his benefactor is gaining moral superiority at his expense, and will not wish to forget a benefit that has cast his own moral inferiority into sharp relief. Thus the truest benefactor will, among other gifts, remove the excessive pride and prickliness to which moralism is prone, and will show the way in which inferiors and superiors may gain the best possible friendship. The great paradox is that here, in friendships such as that of Plato and Socrates, or Goethe and Eckermann, where the superior feels no need for an equalizing return of greater affection, he is most likely of all to find it.

9

Self-Love and Noble Sacrifice

In Chapter 8, Aristotle provides the capstone of the argument he has been building that the best friend is not another but oneself. He thereby demonstrates that the most important thing for happiness is not to have a good friend in another but to have the right stance toward oneself and the capacity to secure what is good for oneself, especially for one's soul or mind. Aristotle does not bend his efforts to making the case that all men in fact love themselves most of all, although he clearly indicates that they do. For showing that all the actual men that we know love themselves most would not prove that the rarest and best man, leading the best possible life, might not love others more. Instead, he makes the more radical claim that the greatest self-love is characteristic of the very best people, even or especially in their moments of seemingly greatest self-sacrifice; and what is more, that the truest form of self-love, in the best individuals, does in fact take precedence over everything and everyone else.[1] In the process, Aristotle illuminates the difference between the self-love of ordinary people and that of the most moral citizens, while prompting some reflections upon the self-love of a third group, the philosophic souls who possess complete self-understanding.

The Goodness of Self-Love

Aristotle begins from the obvious truth that self-love is almost universally an object of reproach. Giving this disapproval its due, he nevertheless contends that the "facts" do not agree with the speeches or arguments that the best men put others first and neglect their own good for the good of their friends (1168a35–b1). But curiously, the facts he adduces on the other side are not, for the most part, human beings' actual behavior but, rather, more speeches or arguments. To prove that loving oneself most is right and good, Aristotle must show not only that good men in fact love themselves most, but also that people and especially serious people reveal in their speeches and beliefs a recognition of the supreme goodness and nobility of a certain kind of self-love, and even a certain kind of putting-oneself-first. And he must further show that this somewhat obscure recognition, when brought to light and clarified, leads to a more comprehensive and satisfying understanding of the phenomenon of self-love than the blanket condemnation that is usually expressed. Nowhere does Aristotle exhibit more beautifully his careful manner of writing and his capacity to answer simultaneously the needs of different groups of readers than in the dialectics of this chapter.

The relevant facts are, then, the common beliefs that one should love one's best friend above all, that the best friend is one who truly wishes a person's good for his own sake and displays the other marks of friendship, and that these marks or attributes of friendship are to be found most of all in a man's regard for himself (1168b1–5). It is, after all, only natural that, loving life and activity, each should love most the life and actions that he is able to live and experience directly. It is only natural that each individual, experiencing directly his own needs, desires, sufferings, hopes, and fears, should feel them more fully and vividly than anyone else can who merely looks on sympathetically, and that he should care most deeply about responding to them. And once one is grown, there is normally no one else so capable of providing for each person's happiness, and especially for his own virtue and wisdom, as he himself is. Even the best of parents and teachers can do no more than set one's feet on the right course and offer advice and encouragement from the sidelines: It is each man who must take for himself every step toward understanding and perform for himself every virtuous action that is the substance of happiness. And thus, after all, the greatest benefactor is perhaps neither the good king, nor the father, nor the parents together, nor even the wise teacher, but one's own self.

Aristotle appeals to many common proverbs to support his contention that the friendship one has with another is an extension, an imitation, and as such never more than a fragmented reflection of the complete unanimity and depth of solicitude that each naturally feels within and for himself. The love of self and the love of another are not different in kind, one basely seeking to acquire the good and the other nobly indifferent to it. Both aim at the good and take their bearings by what promotes human happiness. If it is good to seek the good of another, how can it be bad to seek the good of oneself? If it is right to love the benefactor that one has in another, how is it wrong to love the even greater benefactor that one has in oneself? Aristotle argues that it is not merely natural but good and just that one should do so, and wholly in accord with his contention that we should love not just anything but what is good, and good for us. By these criteria, the very best man, being his own greatest benefactor and most truly lovable for his own sake, should have not the least but the greatest love for himself.

But this proof of the goodness of self-love, though ingenious, is only a beginning, for clearly it is sometimes and in some ways wrong to promote one's own good. Aristotle's next step, then, is to argue that if we think carefully about the way in which self-love is used as a term of reproach, we will see the kernel of truth in this reproach, and see at the same time that its validity does not extend to every form of self-love. "Those who blame self-love," Aristotle says, "call men lovers of self who assign to themselves a larger share of money and honor and bodily pleasures: for these are the things which the many set their hearts upon and zealously pursue as the greatest goods, and thus they are objects of contention" (1168b15–19). It is not really rational to blame people for desiring these things and pursuing them in a just and moderate way, for even those who nobly seek to secure them for others consider them good, and it is only fair that each should have his proper share of them. But even those who condemn the unjust pursuit of these goods often have precisely the same inclinations as those they censure. "I, too, would like to get rich without ever having to work, and to be waited on hand and foot," they think, "but I restrain myself; I take nothing that is not mine, I do my share of the work, and bear my share of the dangers, and so should you." Here, as in all indignation, there is an element of envy.[2] It follows that where there is indignation, there is not yet perfect virtue, for the virtuous man does with pleasure what the merely self-controlled man does with difficulty and against his inclination.

The most virtuous man, feeling no envy toward the disorderly souls who would put self-aggrandizement ahead of justice, sees clearly with Aristotle that the deepest problem with ordinary self-love is not that it seeks too much but that it seeks too little. What the majority blame in others largely because they want to do the same themselves, Aristotle blames because it is bad to set one's heart on a lesser good, rather than on the greatest good. Those who zealously pursue money, bodily pleasures, and even honor, Aristotle says, are gratifying their desires and passions and, in general, the irrational parts of their souls. These are the many, and their self-love is bad both in leading them into conflict and injustice and in keeping them from what is truly best.

By contrast, Aristotle says, the man who is characterized by the higher form of self-love gratifies and obeys the dominant part of himself, his mind, in everything. Aristotle reiterates his arguments that the mind is the true core of each human being, and that those who act irrationally, out of moral weakness, are not really acting voluntarily in the true sense (cf. 1178a2–3). But if the mind that a virtuous man gratifies most is most truly himself, more truly than are the pleasures and passions that drive the vulgar, then the virtuous man loves himself in the deepest sense, and his is the greatest self-love. Obeying and gratifying one's true self means doing what one should, choosing virtue, because "intelligence always chooses what is best for itself" (1169a17).

Now the force of this argument is not at first glance fully apparent. Let us grant that acting virtuously means doing what is truly good for oneself; why must it mean preferring one's own good to that of others? Even if each, by natural inclination, cares most for himself, does virtue not seek precisely to overcome this innate bias and put others on a par with oneself, or even, in great acts of heroism, to choose for oneself what is right and good, but to give the greatest benefit to others? After all, Aristotle says in this very context that the morally serious man will do many things for others, including giving up his life for them, and that if everyone bent all his efforts to performing noble acts of virtue, the result would be good for everyone individually and for the community as a whole (1169a8–11 and 18–20). Aristotle thus provides reassurance that choosing the best for oneself or one's mind need not by any means entail neglecting the good of others. But if noble action is in fact good for others, why can it not be reasonably understood as chosen because it is good for them, and not because it is best for oneself?[3]

Noble Sacrifice and Thinking Bees

The answer to this question comes in Aristotle's vivid account of the spirit in which a noble-minded man chooses his actions. He is consistently prepared to give up all the ordinary goods that ordinary men fight over, but always as one who is setting aside a lesser good for the sake of a greater:

> The morally serious man . . . will do many things for the sake of his friends and his fatherland, and if necessary he will give up his life for them. He will give money and honors and all the contested goods, seeking above all the noble for himself. He would prefer to feel pleasure intensely for a short time than mildly for a long time, and to live nobly for one year than indifferently for many; he would rather perform one great noble act than many small ones. Those who give up their lives perhaps achieve this, and they choose great nobility for themselves. The morally serious man will give away money so that his friends may have more, for they thus get money, but he gets the noble: He assigns the greatest good to himself. (1169a18–29)[4]

The noble-minded man, like Achilles, longs for a great, splendid action to crown his life, even if the cost is an early death. He does wish to benefit others, but he seeks above all to gain nobility for himself, and nobility means performing fine actions of his own volition, rationally and deliberately. If one's overwhelming concern were really the welfare of one's fellows and not one's own character or nobility, it would make little difference whether one served them through deliberately chosen action or otherwise, so long as their good was secured. But in fact, for human beings, the difference between serving others voluntarily and doing so involuntarily is the greatest difference in the world. The same man who would consider it supremely honorable to lay down his life for his country would be outraged if his fellows simply seized him and sacrificed him as a passive victim to appease the enemy. The noble-minded man will give up wealth, honor, and everything that men fight over, including life itself, but he will not give up what he loves more than mere existence: his own rational judgment and moral integrity, his autonomous power of choice and action. It is not the good of others as such but his own nobility that the virtuous man prizes most.

Now if the nobility that human beings sought were merely the nobility of *possessing* virtue and following reason, then this nobility, although indeed treasured more than the welfare of others, would rarely in practice come into direct conflict with others' welfare. But the noblest souls, as Aristotle's penetrating portrayal brings out, inevitably want more than the unwavering possession of virtue and reason. They want to exercise their virtue, and in the greatest of actions; they want to be the cause of the greatest goods, and the worthy recipients of the greatest honor; and all these things, unlike bare virtue, are scarce and subject to keen competition. As Aristotle says in Book 1, "If the good is the same for the individual and the city, still it is greater and more perfect to obtain and secure that of the city, for the good of the individual is desirable, but the good of a people or a city is nobler and more divine" (1094b7–10).[5] But as Machiavelli says, in any given country at any given time, no more than forty or fifty men can have any significant hand in shaping great events, and competition for the supreme command is even keener.[6]

True, Aristotle implies at 1169a20–22 that the nobility that a noble man seeks is not a contested good, but he also says at 1169a8–9 that such a man competes to perform great deeds and win great honors.[7] To be sure, Aristotle explicitly says that the noble man will freely give away honor together with other lesser, generally contested goods, but honor immediately creeps back in as a concern: Even when the noble man gives away honors, he gets for himself what is noble and praised (1169a30–31, 35). True, the noblest man may give away the opportunity to perform virtuous actions, standing aside to let a friend do them in his stead, as Achilles stood aside and allowed Patroclus to fight in his armor. But he will gladly relinquish opportunities to another only in special cases. If, through his own careless blunders, he provides a friend with the occasion for a brilliant, daring rescue, he will not be pleased. If, by never putting himself forward, never proving his capabilities, a gifted man makes it easier for his equally gifted friend to win the highest honors, this is a kind of self-denial that would satisfy no one.[8] Rather, the noble man enjoys stepping aside when doing so is glorious, after he has conferred great benefits on his country and won great honors, as the final, crowning generosity of a great career, in the spirit of a Cincinnatus or a Washington.[9] As Achilles shows, the heroic soul cannot bear to relinquish the greatest glory to another. In the case of this most famous friendship, the yearning of the one for nobility and glory results in disregard for the welfare of the other, destroying in the end both friendship and friend.

Noble souls more thoughtful than Achilles will find better resolutions to the conflicts that arise between friends. Being more thoughtful, they will be more gentle and just, like Laelius and Scipio, and having some respect at least for the contemplative life, they will be less fiercely desirous of victory. Aristotle's point is not that such conflicts between devotion to virtue and devotion to a friend are irresolvable but, rather, that the self-contradictions into which people fall in noble acts of self-sacrifice cannot be resolved on the plane of the heroic mentality: Such a life is almost necessarily tragic.[10]

It is possible to conceive of a being that would pursue the good of something else, above or beyond itself, as its highest end, but that being would be utterly different from us. There is, for example, nothing logically inconsistent in the possibility that there should be a kind of thinking, self-conscious bee, whose overwhelming concern was the good of its hive, who rejoiced in nothing but the hive's prospering and was distressed by nothing but its threatened destruction, and who could conceive of no possible joy apart from it. If we were to say to such a being, "You, too, are selfish: You do what gives you the most joy," it might reply, "Certainly I do so, but I scarcely think of that. *My* joy is a shadow that must follow the good of the hive, so long as I exist, but it is never my purpose, any more than it is your purpose when you walk to bring along your shadow." Such a bee, unlike a man, really would not care whether it served the community through long, obscure labor or a heroic death, through deliberately chosen action or the action of others, so long as the good of the hive was secured. A serpent-like human being might, of course, attempt to corrupt this bee, by pressing on it the question of whether a hive, a mere organized collection of bees, itself able neither to think nor to rejoice, can really enjoy a good as great as that enjoyed by conscious individuals, and whether it might not be better to think more about its own faint pains and pleasures, as worthy of greater attention, and as possibly secured through other channels than service to the hive. But the bee, if indeed its overwhelming concern were for the hive, might well reply, "This is how I am made; different beings have different ends; my conscious mind is certainly a useful thing for the hive, but otherwise is nothing great, and my happiness apart from it is unthinkable."[11]

In a similar vein, there might be an intelligent race created to serve the happiness of another race, each individual being devoted far more to that other race than to its own good, or a race created only to love its maker and uninterested in anything else. There might even, without any self-contradiction, be a strange race whose chief desire and concern was not for the welfare of any being at all but simply for symmetry, or for the number three, or for some such thing; its members would ceaselessly strive to create as much symmetry or as many groups of three as possible wherever they could. Each individual might naturally begin by seeking to rearrange its own life in this way, but it would gladly give up symmetry or threeness in its own life, or life itself, if that were to make possible a greater increase of it in the universe as a whole.

In all of these cases, it would seem necessary that the individuals should not perceive any possibility of a substantial, independent happiness for themselves as individuals; if they did, they would be deeply divided beings, and incapable of wholehearted devotion. By the same token, they could not be, like us, beings with a great horror at the prospect of death, for then, too, they would be divided. But why should this not be possible, even among the most self-conscious beings? Why might they not be as thoroughly reconciled to being limited in time as we are to being limited in space, and, dwelling chiefly in the present, as little distressed by the fact that their life must have an end as we are by the fact that ours had a beginning?

But it is abundantly obvious that all of these imaginary beings that love something other than themselves most of all are very far from being human. In particular, the virtuous man, at the moment of making a sacrifice, is different from all of them in two key respects. First, it is crucial that it be *his* sacrifice, deliberately chosen; and second, he must be able to understand this sacrifice as ultimately best for the best part of himself, his rational soul, or at least consistent with its good. He would be horrified at the thought of sacrificing his highest good, or at the thought of anyone he loves sacrificing their highest good, and becoming base, vile, foolish, or weak-willed for the sake of someone else. The legendary gymnastics coach Bela Karolyi could say with sincerity that he would gladly have given up his leg for his star gymnast who was injured at a critical moment, but he would not have given up his mind for her. A hero on the battlefield may face death believing that his soul is about to be extinguished, but if he chooses this death for its nobility, he will do so with the judgment that a brief moment of great glory is *better* for him than a lifetime of mediocrity, or of shame at his cowardice in the crucial test. In these most glorious moments, it is the nobility of a great sacrifice that seems to the hero so choiceworthy. Thus, Aristotle indicates, moral nobility is not something that accrues to the moral man incidentally as he goes about seeking to help his fellows; it is precisely the prize that he keeps his sights fixed upon.

But Aristotle has now deftly pulled away the curtain and shown that acts of apparent noble sacrifice, made by those who understand such nobility as the highest good, really are not acts of sacrifice at all. What at first seemed to be a sacrifice is in fact, or at least is judged by the one choosing it, an exchange of lesser goods for greater goods.[12] And sacrifice of the greatest goods – one's mind and integrity – would be morally repugnant. The question is whether, when noble acts of sacrifice are so clearly seen for what they are, they can still make sense as the epitome of virtue and the highest purpose of a virtuous life. Is there not something absurd about trying to get the better of everyone else by giving up the most for them?[13] But if so, we must reassess what makes a generous or apparently selfless act noble. If nobility is a great good that the most virtuous men are eager to secure for themselves, its sensible core cannot lie in sacrifice, or in the magnitude of what is given up. Rather, a generous deed must be noble because it is the rationally chosen act of a strong soul, able to see clearly what is good, to love friends who are good, to marshal great capacities to benefit those one cares about, and to pursue one's highest concerns with enlightened, unwavering self-command. And if the essence of nobility does not lie in sacrifice, then the most clear-sightedly virtuous person will not compete for the opportunity to make sacrifices, although he will still willingly make them if there are compelling reasons to do so.[14]

The Preference for Self and the Exclusive Love of Self

What is the character of virtuous self-love and the virtuous dedication to friends, then, once they have been purged of the confused thought that the best thing is to monopolize the position of noble benefactor who sacrifices his good for others? Does loving one's true and best self as much as possible still imply loving oneself in preference to others? Yes, inasmuch as it is simply a fact of our nature that the happiness that matters most to us is our own. The desire to be just may qualify one's pursuit of one's own good, but it does not alter the priority of one's innate concerns. Clear-sighted self-love will be less competitive than either the vulgar form, which seeks wealth and bodily pleasures, or the more noble-minded form, which also seeks a fundamentally unshareable good, but no one can avoid making choices between one's own good and the good of others. The self-love of the wisest men, who need so little of the goods men fight over, would seem to be among the least problematic. Yet to the extent that even the leisure to acquire wisdom is scarce, and the time devoted to thought cannot be devoted to helping others, these men's self-love must still entail some active preference for themselves.

However, all of this is still very far from saying that the wise love only themselves, or that they will never do anything for their friends that is not also best for them. Aristotle presents the noble-minded gentleman as acting to secure the noble for himself but also to save his friends and fatherland (1169a18–20). He thereby suggests that once freed from his noble confusion, such a man may still retain a love of others for their own sakes as an independent concern and reason for acting.[15] But if, as we would like to think, the best and most clear-sighted life is not simply self-regarding, what are we to make of Aristotle's bold statement that "intelligence always chooses what is best for itself" (1169a17)? Does Aristotle mean, after all, that the truly intelligent mind will pursue its own wisdom as its exclusive end? Does he mean that it will always choose whatever is best for *oneself*, as a being with a number of ends, but all of them properly understood as components of one's own happiness? Or does Aristotle mean something more limited and open-ended – that intelligence always chooses what is good for it in the sense of according with its virtue and rationality, choosing, in other words, to pursue the deepest wishes of the individual in a virtuous and rational manner, but without any restriction that these wishes be only wishes for the individual's own happiness?

The first reading, that the mind cares only about its own wisdom, is not impossible, but it requires treating as merely provisional or exoteric many things that seem both seriously meant and true to experience, including everything Aristotle says about goodwill. If it is correct, the intelligent mind would consider everything and everyone as either a means to knowledge, an obstacle to knowledge, or absolutely of no concern to it.[16] It would regard not only such things as food and sleep, but all the pleasures of fine autumn days, coffee with friends, good jokes, music and painting, wine and eros to be nothing more than distractions, or grist for the mind's mill, or a needed recharging of its batteries. Such a mind would regard the compassion or fellow feeling that arises toward strangers as a natural, harmless human emotion, but would always object to acting on that feeling (say, to give directions to a traveler) as a waste of time if one could possibly spend the same time thinking. It would never, except in a mercenary spirit, welcome the opportunity to be a benefactor, even to one's closest associates, even to very promising followers, and it goes without saying that such a mind would and could never love a friend for his own sake. If such is the outlook of intelligence, then it would be hard to maintain that even Socrates, who spent so much time with friends and students, or Aristotle himself, who wrote works for students he would never meet, was governed wholly by intelligence.

Moreover, as Cooper observes,[17] such a reading is at odds with the context of this chapter, in which Aristotle is speaking of the mind that constitutes the essence of each man not as theoretical intelligence but primarily as practical intelligence: It is the mind as judging, directing practical choices, choosing noble and virtuous actions, and in general ruling over the whole man that Aristotle is here considering. Although Aristotle uses the word νοῦς, which can refer narrowly to theoretical intelligence, he is here evidently applying the term in its broader meaning of designating intelligence generally. Indeed, in the line immediately following the statement in question, Aristotle cites the outlook of the man greedy for nobility as if in confirmation of his claim that intelligence always chooses what is best for itself. Aristotle is not specifying which aspects of his own mind the wisest man will consider most precious and seek most to gratify. As Cooper puts it, "it is . . . not the content of the action but its form that is essential here: when Aristotle says that the good man 'gratifies his mind,' he means only that, whatever he does, he does it because he has decided upon it by reasoning."[18] In the context in which it is made, the statement that *every* intelligence chooses what is best for itself suggests that the gratification of intelligence that Aristotle has in mind applies in some way to all intelligent, deliberate action.

The second possible interpretation of the statement that intelligence always chooses what is best for itself is, on its face, more plausible. If intelligence always chooses what is best for *oneself*, this leaves room for the mind to pursue many different pleasures and satisfactions as ends, including not only knowledge and the pleasures of the senses but also presumably the satisfactions of helping others and seeing loved ones prospering. Yet all of these ends would be ultimately sought merely as components of one's own happiness or greatest good.[19] One might find one's life so intertwined with the lives of others that their happiness would become in some measure essential for one's own: One would therefore wish to benefit them, but ultimately only for one's own sake. This interpretation, like the first, allows for the feeling of compassion toward friends and even strangers, and in contrast to the first, allows for one's compassionate feelings to become the basis of rational action, but this still would be action chosen only upon a calculation of one's own pleasures and pains. Intelligence would presumably seek to make the soul as little vulnerable as possible to the misfortunes of others, and would never sanction even the smallest sacrifice of one's true good for that of another. If one chose an apparent sacrifice, it would always be because, circumstances being what they were, one would see one's own best prospects for happiness to lie in giving up one thing to gain something greater, if only a relief from the pain of watching another suffer. This reading of Aristotle, in sum, leaves room for compassion, but not for goodwill or genuine friendship.[20]

As Charles Kahn points out, the argument that a rational friend always acts with a view to his own good is hard to refute conclusively because wherever there is friendship, there *is* a good for oneself that accompanies every good enjoyed by the friend: the good that consists in the pleasure of perceiving the friend's happiness, especially when one has contributed to it, and the pleasant hope for the continued company and affection of a good man who is doing well.[21] The difficulty in ascertaining one's true motives in helping a friend is that every time one troubles oneself on his behalf, one gains for *oneself* the satisfaction of doing a good deed and of seeing the happy result, and it is hard to say with certainty which the real motive is.

But the difference between wanting a friend to *be* happy and wanting the pleasure of *seeing* him happy, a difference so narrow as to seem almost semantic, can perhaps be pried open and examined by means of a thought experiment, which may help us to see which reading of Aristotle is more true to human nature. What would happen if a clear-sighted mind could be offered pleasing illusions about a friend, and could be wholly assured that those illusions would remain completely convincing and would never cause him harm? What if he were confronted with a choice between such pleasing illusions for himself and the genuine but for him unperceived happiness of his friend?

Let us suppose that such a man has a daimonion who often appears to him and tells him things that will happen in the future, which invariably come true. Now he and his son have been arrested by an evil tyrant and falsely charged with plotting the tyrant's overthrow. He is condemned to spend the rest of his life in prison but has not learned what has become of his son. The trusty daimonion appears to him and says that, indeed, he will never get out of prison, but he has a choice. Either his son, a promising young man, will be freed and will spend a long and happy life, using his talents to the fullest, as a great scholar and a teacher of many others, or he will be hanged tomorrow. If he is freed, he will write the father many letters, relating all his thoughts and adventures, and expressing great affection, esteem, and gratitude to him – but none of these letters will ever reach him. Indeed, the tyrant will persuade him that his son is dead. If the son is hanged, on the other hand, the tyrant (a clever man with a perverse sense of humor) will, for his own amusement, persuade the father that his pleas have won freedom for his son, and the tyrant will successfully forge just such letters as the son would have written had he lived. Thus, for the rest of his life, he will have the satisfaction of *thinking* that his son prospers and loves and honors him, but in this he will be utterly deceived. "You have three minutes to decide whether your son lives or dies," says the daimonion, "and the instant you decide, all memory of this conversation and of your decision will be immediately and permanently erased from your brain." How would a wise mind choose?

It seems evident that anyone sensible who was not hopelessly soft and who had a natural love for his son would choose the true happiness of the son, because that choice, although worse for himself, would be in accord with his own truest wishes and concerns. These concerns include not only the desire for pleasures and satisfactions for oneself but also a love for others. And just as we desire not to live in a fool's paradise ourselves, so our concern is for the true and not merely the apparent good of those we love.

On the deepest level, the second alternative is unpersuasive because it fails to account for the pleasures and pains that it posits as our real motives in apparently selfless actions. Without goodwill, there could be no intrinsic pleasure in benefaction, no pain in beholding a friend's suffering, except a kind of animal instinct and a fear of suffering the like oneself, and no real pleasure in human company, except the pleasures of triumph, power, and diversion, which Hobbes so chillingly describes as the roots of human sociability. It is true that to please a friend is also to please ourselves, but pleasing him is only pleasing to us at all because we love him.[22] And if nature inclines us to love, to care for the welfare of others for their own sakes, why should intelligence, which takes its guidance from our true concerns, not choose to pursue their good as well as our own?[23]

It is, therefore, the third possible reading of Aristotle's statement on intelligence that seems truer to experience, and at least equally true to Aristotle: The intelligent mind always chooses what is best for itself as a rational mind, and this means acting intelligently, consistently, with self-command, and guided by a full understanding of its own deepest concerns, concerns which begin but do not end with the concern for the personal happiness of the being whose mind it is. The true mind will never, even for a friend, give up acting rationally, but the requirements of rationality do not exhaustively account for its every choice. The rational mind will choose means suited to its ends, just as the good doctor will choose the remedy that is best for his patient, but it is the needs of the patient and not autonomous reason that give content to his choice. Reason discovers our wants and concerns, and frequently trims and shapes them to fit one another, but it does not create them from whole cloth. The mind, in choosing what is best for itself, may still choose to give as well as to take.[24]

This conclusion is supported also by Aristotle's arguments against simple hedonism in Book 10. In his discussion of pleasure in Book 7, he has gone quite far in the direction of hedonism, and has stated, I believe somewhat provisionally, that there is no reason why the highest good may not prove to be some kind of pleasure (1153b7–8). But in Book 10, although he shows that the true good and the highest and best pleasures are intimately related and even inseparable, he indicates that simply maximizing pleasure is not our core concern. A healthy soul does not regard pleasure as a greedy soul regards money, seeking to heap up as much of it as possible, in any form and from any source, and treating its learning, its practical activity, and its associations with others as so many means to the accumulation of a single, undifferentiated substance. Rather, Aristotle argues, pleasures differ in kind, and not all pleasures are equally desirable or even desirable at all: We would not choose to live out our lives with the minds of children, even if we could have everything a child desires (1174a1–11). We want pleasure, to be sure, but more fundamentally, we want the *good*: we want life, health, wisdom, and the unimpaired activities that constitute happiness. Pleasure accompanies and completes these activities, Aristotle says (1174b20–23), but he silently corrects the apparent error of Book 7 (1153a12–15): Pleasure is not itself an activity. It is, therefore, not the very substance of life, but is the sweet bloom that accompanies full life or choiceworthy activity, like the bloom of youth (1174b31–35). And if our core concern is not for pleasure as such but for our true good that answers our natural wants and is therefore pleasant, so it seems right that friendship involves a parallel concern for the true good of the other self, and Aristotle reminds us of this concern at 1173b32–74a1.

Indeed, we may even say that it is the phenomenon of friendship that shows most clearly the inadequacy of the hedonistic outlook. Even if our choices for ourselves can always be described in terms of a calculus of pleasures, our wishes for our friends, circumscribed though they are by our more powerful self-concerns, still have a kernel that cannot be reduced to the desire for enjoyment.[25] We thus see another function of the entire discussion of friendship, and the reason for Aristotle's enfolding it between two discussions of pleasure. The treatment of moral strength and weakness in Book 7 made clear that virtue, if it is to be sovereign in the soul, cannot be at odds with the true desires and pleasures of the soul; but that conclusion opened up the possibility of seeing happiness as nothing more or less than a life of maximal pleasure for those endowed with a good nature. The final three books show at once that the happy life is indeed supremely pleasant, and that its concerns run deeper than pleasure.

If this is correct, then it seems that one can clear-sightedly pursue the good of others in two possible ways. First, one may find one's own action inherently rewarding as a contribution to a common good that one shares in, as an interesting challenge, as a source of pleasant interaction with those one cares about, or as an opportunity to learn and to improve one's own abilities. Here there is no sacrifice of personal good, and no felt need for honor or reward. Second, one may choose the act out of love, seeing with perfect clarity that it is a sacrifice of one's personal good, but preferring it anyway because of one's affection for another. Now if, as Aristotle says, everyone loves his own good most of all, a clear-sighted person will not set aside his own good to secure a good of equal magnitude for his friend, but he may well do it to secure a greater good for his friend. He will prefer having a good day to knowing that his friend has had a good day, or hearing Itzhak Perlman to knowing that his friend has heard Itzhak Perlman, but he will gladly give a concert ticket to his friend if he knows it will mean more to him than it would to himself.[26] Such a clear-sighted friend will not compete for the opportunity to die for the other, but he may nonetheless choose to do so, just as Socrates did, who preferred to give up a few uncertain years in exile and in decline so that philosophy might win renown, and so that his young friends like Plato, who had as yet written almost nothing, might prosper.

We asked earlier whether, out of love, one can truly sacrifice one's own good for that of another, and truly be content to do so without expecting a reward. Our answer now can be a qualified yes. Such a thing can only be done by one with thorough self-knowledge so that confused expectations do not muddy his motives. He will not rush to embrace the sacrifice, but if the reasons are compelling enough, he will make it. It will not be in every respect a sacrifice, for indeed it will be precisely the thing that, at that moment, he most wants to do, yet it will be a sacrifice to the extent that it will not be the thing most calculated to produce the greatest happiness in the long run for himself: He only wants to do it because it will give another, whom he loves as an end, more happiness than he himself will lose. He will not be free of disappointment if his friend shows no gratitude because friendship matters to him, the virtue of his friend matters to him, and a good man does feel affection and gratitude to his benefactor as a matter of course. He will feel disappointment, then, at ingratitude, but no sense of betrayal or outrage, since his choice was not premised upon the expectation of a return. Thus it turns out that the wisest man is the one most capable of both the truest self-love and the truest friendship, for only he has a mind that is perfectly good and lovable, only he can love what he is without inner conflicts, and only he can love another without illusions, without competition over the noble, and without surreptitious expectations of repayment or reward.

But if the very best friends will not see their sacrifices for one another as either the peak of nobility or the core of their friendship, what will the focus of the friendship be? Precisely at the same point at which Aristotle shows the self-contradiction of competing for the noble, he introduces the concern that can lead to the truest common good: the love of reason (1169a2–6). In wisdom there is a nobility that is rare but not scarce. Thoughts can be truly shared, unlike money and honors and power and all the bodily goods, which can only be divided. From this point on, then, Aristotle will bring philosophy increasingly to the fore as a focus for the best friendships and the best life.

10

Friendship in the Happy Life

In Chapter 9 of Book 9, Aristotle gives his deepest reflections on the relationship of friendship to human neediness. As he does so, he brings his discussion of friendship onto a new plane. He mentions happiness for the first time in Books 8 and 9, and mentions it repeatedly. In connection with the new focus on happiness, several other themes now come prominently to the fore, including those of nature, pleasure, human self-sufficiency, and the philosophic life. Gently but persistently, Aristotle presses the question of why a truly happy man will need friends, clearly implying that if he feels no such need, he will not love. This need may not be a need for anything separable that arises out of friendship; it may be a simple need to love, an inclination to concern oneself with and contribute to the happiness of others. We have hitherto regarded this inclination or need as an irreducible part of human nature. But Aristotle now asks how such a need can be explained, and how its satisfaction fits together with the satisfactions of the other wants and needs that collectively constitute human happiness.

The question becomes important at this point because of Aristotle's argument in 9.4 that good men can be their own best friends and especially because of what he has shown in 9.8 about the self-love of noble souls.[1] It has long been evident that, in the lesser friendships of utility and pleasure, people love one another chiefly because of what they seek for themselves, but it had seemed that the most virtuous were given to loving and benefiting one another for their own sakes. Now that we have seen the way in which friendship only approximates the unity that is possible in one soul, and now that we have seen the largely self-regarding and even competitive nature of the concerns that fuel most noble-minded beneficence, we must wonder again whether the wisest, happiest, and most self-sufficient human beings will have sufficient reason to love deeply. Thus we return to the question of the *Lysis*: Why would one who is self-sufficient treasure another enough to love him? Until this question is fully examined, our conclusions in the previous chapter about the possibility of the wisest human beings' making true sacrifices for their friends must remain provisional.

Aristotle, speaking as a champion of friendship, puts the question of why a happy man needs friends in the mouths of those with the most vulgar outlook. Friends are good for getting us what we need, these people think, and so if someone already has everything good, what use are friends? To this question, Aristotle replies first of all that it would be strange to assign all good things to a happy man and not friends, which are considered the greatest of external goods (1169b8–10). In calling friends "external goods," Aristotle refers to his division of good things into external goods, goods of the soul, and goods of the body at 1098b12–14. Elsewhere, he includes wealth, political power, noble birth, good children, and especially honor among external goods.[2] Goods such as honor are truly external and dependent on the whims of chance; they can come and go like fortunes in a casino. Who are the people who think of friends as such external goods? Ordinary people who are not so crude as to think of friends as tools may still consider them as possessions. They imagine a happy man to be one blessed by fortune with money, good looks, a splendid sports car, beautiful women, a stable full of polo ponies, and rich, famous, glamorous friends.

But a true friend, if he is another self, would seem not to be simply external to oneself but, in a deep sense, intertwined with one's own soul; a true friend is far more secure than goods that depend chiefly on fortune or public opinion; and most importantly, having a friend means at bottom not having a possession but engaging in an activity of the soul. As the Greek commentator Michael Ephesius says in discussing 1169b29, friendship and the other components of happiness are not static objects that one possesses, as houses and cloaks are, but rather consist in activity, as sight does.[3] People who wish to pile up friends as they do possessions seem more interested in providing the equipment for life, or making a display of their lives, or perhaps building up walls to protect themselves against evils that are really inescapable, rather than bending their efforts to being active in the best possible way during the time that they have.

On the other hand, there is perhaps a serious kernel to Aristotle's characterization of friends as the greatest of external goods. For if the capacity to be a good friend is inherent in the soul of a good man, the discovery of a kindred soul capable of becoming another self is a matter of good fortune.[4] This seems to be what Socrates has in mind when he says in the *Lysis* that a good friend is the possession he has always ardently longed for:

Now it happens that since I was a boy I've desired a certain possession, just as others desire other things. For one desires to acquire horses, another dogs, another gold, and another honors. Now me, I'm of a gentle disposition regarding these things, but when it comes to the acquisition of friends I'm quite passionately in love; and I would like to have a good friend rather than the best quail or cock to be found among humans, and indeed, by Zeus, for my part, rather than a horse or dog. And I suppose, by the Dog, that I would much rather acquire a companion than the gold of Darius, and rather than Darius himself – that's the kind of lover of companions I am. (211d5–e8)

Socrates expresses his wish to possess a friend in comical terms and in paradoxical contrast to the action of the dialogue, in which he befriends and quickly wins the admiring affection of the boys Lysis and Menexenus, whose friendship with each other he pretends to envy.[5] With his hyperbolic language Socrates gives the impression that he has always wanted a friend more than anything, but as we are reminded by a similar list of objects of men's affections at 212d6–7 (horses, quail, dogs, wine, gymnastics, and wisdom), Socrates is silent in this earlier passage about his greatest love, the love of wisdom. It is his love of wisdom that makes Socrates fundamentally self-sufficient, fundamentally happy in his own, self-generated if not absolutely autonomous activity, and at the same time, quite incapable of finding in such fundamentally vulgar men as Darius a proper soul mate. Socrates, who has yet to find a perfect soul mate, is nonetheless very happy, and capable of increasing his happiness by helping and enjoying the company of such gifted and promising young people as are easily found; but perhaps a true second self, a Plato encountered in Socrates' youth and not merely at the end of his life, would have made his splendid life even better. May it be that Socrates, with this playful comment, and Aristotle, by first calling honor the greatest of external goods (1123b18–20), then indicating that honor is of no intrinsic value from the highest perspective (1159a17–27), and finally naming friendship as the greatest external good, signal their agreement that the most supremely delightful of all external goods would be that rarest of finds, a perfectly suited friend?

Aristotle's second argument for the desirability of friendship in the happy life is directed to a more serious and moral questioner than the first: "If it is more characteristic of a friend to benefit than to be benefited, and it is characteristic of the good and virtuous man to do good deeds, and it is nobler to benefit friends than strangers, then the serious man will be in need of people he can benefit" (1169b10–13). The conclusion to this sentence is a little surprising; we would have expected Aristotle to say that the serious man will need friends. But Aristotle's analysis of noble-minded benevolence in 9.8 shows why it does make a certain sense to say that the most determined benefactor needs beneficiaries more than friends. As much as he might wish to direct his benevolence chiefly to friends, two friends cannot both, in their mutual relations, benefit more than they are benefited. People who grasp the problem at least partially will abstain from unseemly contests with their friends over the moral high ground, and will perhaps turn more attention to finding truly needy inferiors – beneficiaries more than friends – to whom they may do good. Friends who see this problem with perfect clarity will not seek out and cherish one another as potential beneficiaries of noble sacrifice, but as partners in intrinsically satisfying activity. They will of course be pleased to help when help is needed, yet the pleasure of giving benefits is not the chief reason for friendship's intrinsic desirability in the good life, as Aristotle will show as he proceeds.

After mentioning noble deeds, Aristotle continues his ascent to the highest constellation of reasons why the happy man will need friends, and he mentions nature for the first of many times in this chapter. The arguments that follow will be based less than the first two upon conventional opinion. The third argument Aristotle gives is that "it would perhaps be strange to make the blessed man live in isolation, for no one would choose to have all the good things all alone. For man is by nature a political being and lives together with others" (1169b16–19; cf. 1097b11, *Politics* 1253a2–3). But immediately Aristotle returns to his pesky, ungentlemanly questioners. What good is it, they persist, to have the company of others if one's own inner life is truly full? And to these Aristotle now makes a considerable concession: The happy man not only has no need of useful friends, since his moderate wants do not exceed his means, but he also does not need pleasant friends, at least not much, and not those of the usual sort, for if his life is truly blessed and full, he will need no "imported" pleasure to brighten it up (1169b24–27; cf. 1099a15–16). That is, he will never feel the need that the rest of us so often feel for distracting amusements to help us relax from our labors and forget our troubles, for his own habitual activity will be so satisfying as to make such amusements appear, by contrast, like extraneous noise. With a few brushstrokes, Aristotle portrays a man who, in outward simplicity and even asceticism, enjoys in fact the greatest pleasures in sublime self-sufficiency. But he leaves open a window for friendship to enter such a life: If it has no need of extraneous pleasures, still it may find its own proper pleasures enhanced by sharing its activity with a friend.

In response to his questioners, Aristotle now makes his fourth, fifth, and sixth arguments, which are his most serious. The fourth is that if happiness consists in living and acting, if the activity of the good man is good and pleasant in itself, and if what is one's own is pleasant, then observing the activity of good men who are one's own friends will be choiceworthy, too. For a good man naturally "rejoices in actions that conform to virtue" (1170a8–9), and especially so when the actions are somehow "one's own," inasmuch as they belong to one's own friends (1169b30–70a4). After much discussion of the ways in which friends help one another and provide opportunities for one another, Aristotle now gives full due to that essential marrow of friendship of the good, the cherishing of the other for what he is, altogether apart from any benefit that he gives oneself. Such cherishing is naturally pleasant because it is pleasant to contemplate good men, and naturally good because it constitutes one of life's finest pleasures, a pleasure of the soul that is not the replenishment of a deficiency but simply sweet.

But Aristotle introduces a curious qualification into this argument, tying the choiceworthiness of observing a good friend to the proposition that "one is more able to observe his neighbor than himself" (1169b33–34). If the pleasure of observing and contemplating good activities really were invariably greater in the case of those around us than in our own case, and most of all in the case of others who are felt to be one's own, then indeed friendship would be central to happiness. But in what sense is this true? Certainly young people who are learning to know themselves and understand human nature can recognize many things in others before they recognize them in themselves, and can learn more from observing as well as discussing and reading about others than they ever could learn from solitary self-reflection.[6] Certainly, also, one can never understand human nature until one turns outward beyond oneself and one's narrow circle to reflect on the political community – which alone shows the implications of our natural sociability fully unfolded and developed – and upon humanity as a whole.[7]

But surely the mature, wise, truly happy man, who sees his neighbors with perfect clarity, has no inexplicable failure of understanding when it comes to himself.[8] The most that it seems sensible to say is that his own pleasures of acting and contemplating himself may be supplemented by a similar pleasure of contemplating others who are good, a pleasure that will be especially great if they are his friends, and greatest of all if he has himself helped to form them. But is the pleasure of watching good activity ever as great as the pleasure of engaging in it, and can the actions of one's friends ever be one's own actions in any but a weak and derivative sense? Is there not, finally, a tension between saying that one can see a friend's activity better than one's own (which is true in the case of the immature), and saying that it *is* one's own, which is surely always an exaggeration?[9] With this paradox, Aristotle points to the fact that people are often more inclined to claim others as their own, or to rest upon the laurels of others, or to try to live through others, than is reasonably justified. It follows that the most blessed, being wisest, would have a somewhat cooler, more sensible recognition of their own separateness and of the mere vicariousness of the pleasure they take in observing the good activities of others. We see again the problem that first arose in the discussion of 8.3, the problem that cherishing seems at once to be the core of what it means to love a friend for himself, and yet too passive to capture what is best in friendship; and soon we shall have the resolution to this problem.

Aristotle now shifts his sights slightly to take up the fifth argument (1170a4–13), which helps to put in perspective and explain the previous ones. What is supremely good for us is not, after all, our friend's activity but our own activity. However good and pleasant good activity is, "by oneself it is not easy to be continually active, but with others and toward others it is easier" (1170a5–6). In the face of the unfortunate human tendency to flag easily even in the activities we care most about, it is most helpful to have the spur that an excellent companion in the activity can provide, whose energy and enthusiasm can reinforce our own, whose accomplishments can inspire a desire to rival them,[10] and whose approval can confirm for us the validity of our own thoughts and accomplishments: "The morally serious man, insofar as he is morally serious, rejoices in actions that conform to virtue and is pained by actions done out of wickedness, just as the musical man takes pleasure in beautiful melodies and is pained by bad ones. Thus a certain training in virtue comes from living together with good men, just as Theognis says" (1170a8–13; cf. 1172a8–14).

In the case of musicians and aspiring musicians, this training consists in the training of ear and taste that comes from the example of good music, as well as the crucial inspiration that comes when a student watches a virtuoso play, with fluid, graceful, seemingly effortless brilliance, the music that he himself can produce only haltingly after difficult labor. The case is similar, especially at the outset, with moral virtue. Great deeds of valor or self-denying justice have an outward splendor that is pleasing and inspiring to one for whom the performance is still difficult and painful. Where there is love, the power of example is correspondingly greater, for one wishes especially to share in the activities and acquire the fine qualities of those whom one both admires and loves.[11] And the inspiring example and fellowship of others is perhaps even more necessary throughout life in the case of moral virtue than in the case of music, for although an accomplished musician will more easily retain his excellence if he has the encouragement and example of fellow musicians to keep him at his peak, even without them, he will not be in danger of becoming unmusical again and preferring bad music to good. But moral virtue is perhaps always, even to heroes, more impressive and splendid to see than pleasant to experience, so that being able to admire oneself, to see this admiration reflected in the eyes and honor of others, and to feel solidarity with others who are similarly virtuous is really crucial. If it is conceivable to live as the only musician in one's circle and still be happy, it is inconceivable that one could live a life of moral virtue in the midst of scoundrels without becoming disillusioned and bitter.[12]

Beginners in every kind of endeavor, even philosophy, are greatly helped by the inspiring example of others, but once one becomes fully philosophic, the example and support of others would seem to be less necessary than in any other field of activity. Company in this, as in all activity, makes the activity even more pleasant, but in Book 10 Aristotle will argue that the wisest souls do not need company in order to remain active in philosophy, which for this among many reasons he calls the best activity (1177a28–b1). The advantages of friendship in helping us see ourselves indirectly and in helping us stay active seem to apply especially to the friendships of young or imperfect individuals, and the fact that Aristotle includes such factors in his final statement on the goodness of friendship is further evidence that, in his view, the very most important friendships will be found on the ascent to the best life, and that friendships at the summit itself will be more tranquil and less intense.[13]

Sixth and finally, Aristotle turns to his profoundest account of the necessity of friendship in the happy life, an account based most emphatically on nature and stressing most explicitly the importance of thinking for happiness (1170a13–b19). To summarize his complex argument very briefly, Aristotle says that friendship is good to the good man because life is good to him, and human life is defined above all by the capacity for sense perception and thought, and realized in their exercise. A good man's life is good and pleasant in itself, being one of the things that are finite or determinate (ὡρισμένος). But if life is in itself good and pleasant, and life consists in sensation and thought, in activity, and especially in the awareness of that activity, and if awareness of our own activity is awareness of life or being, then it is precisely through awareness of ourselves in action that we enjoy the good thing we call life. Since, finally, such awareness of ourselves is good, and since we are disposed toward our friends as toward ourselves, the friend being another self, it follows that "just as each person's own being is choiceworthy to him, so also, or nearly so, is that of his friend" (1170b7–8).

As Cooper has observed, Aristotle spells out the first steps of this argument in elaborate detail, with great logical precision, giving what seems to be an overabundance of proof for the proposition that life is good, but after this long windup, he rather suddenly introduces the theme of friendship and concludes that the friend's life will be cherished just as one's own is.[14] Granted that *if* one is disposed toward a friend as toward oneself, one will also love the friend's existence as one does one's own, how does this amount to a proof that friendship itself is a good thing? Or, as Cooper puts it, how does it help to explain why the good man will love anyone in the first place?

The answer, it seems, is in the details, and especially what Aristotle is showing here about the nature of life's goodness. In this passage Aristotle does not, indeed, explain why we are initially drawn to others, and especially to others who seem to us good and akin; this is simply due to our natural sociability, of which he has spoken at 1169b17–19. But the present argument does explain why the friendships that nature prompts us to form are so sweet and satisfying, and why, once having experienced them, even the best and most self-sufficient human beings will consider a life without them to be incomplete. Now we all think we know without any need for argument, as surely as we know anything, that life is good and death is bad, but Aristotle makes an argument for life's goodness that calls the common understanding into question. He argues that life is not, as we think, good absolutely. It is good because it is among those things that are by nature determinate or defined (ὡρισμένος).

In Aristotelian usage, what is determinate has a definite purpose and perfection (e.g., 1106b28–35), which in the case of human life is to realize fully in action what is best and most distinctive about us, our capacity for perception and thought. Life seems good to all of us because we all have an inkling that it can be good, but in fact, only the life of a virtuous man, spent in naturally good activity, truly is good. By contrast, lives given over to vice or spoiled by extreme suffering are "indeterminate," or swamped by disorder, imbalance, or decay. Human life, like everything truly good, has an optimal state of harmonious, balanced perfection and an indefinite number of ways that it can go wrong and fall apart, death being the complete loss of life's ordering principles. Because death is inevitable, life is also ὡρισμένος in the sense of being finite: Life is a determinate, ordered thing the nature of which is to be potentially good, and often to realize the good, but not to remain good. The preciousness of happiness, when it is attained, is heightened and made poignant by the preciousness of our prime years, and the knowledge that with each day they grow closer to their close, and we to a state of dissolution, of slow decay if not great pain, a state of growing indeterminacy. In the face of this recognition (however dim), friendship becomes precious as a way of augmenting and intensifying the goodness – the full, active aliveness – that we love and cannot keep.[15]

To this extent, friendship gains its deepest justification from its capacity to enhance the awareness of activity and pleasure. Animals act without self-consciousness, but human beings, in whatever they do, are aware of themselves doing it. Aristotle uses both the words αἰσθάνεσθαι (1170a29, 31–b3) and συναισθάνεσθαι (1170b4–5) to describe this second-order perception, but he also uses συναισθάνεσθαι to describe the analogous meta-perception one has of a friend's being and activity (1170b10), which is a further extension of self-awareness or consciousness into what Alexander Grant aptly calls "sympathetic consciousness."[16] This sympathetic consciousness has a great power to reflect, confirm, and expand the awareness we have of our own activity. Hence, as Aristotle says, in seeing, hearing, walking, and thinking, we are aware of ourselves doing so, but this awareness is even greater when we act in concert with a friend. Hiking and watching for birds, one delights in discovery and delights doubly in sharing it. Looking to the friend to see his response, one is no longer seeing the bird, and yet, curiously, the experience of bird watching is heightened. Were it not for an underlying liking and sympathy for one's companion, one would not care what he saw, but feeling this, we simultaneously are pleased by his activity and being, and find that it augments *our* perception of *our* activity and being and so is good for us – as Aristotle's change to the first person at 1170a31 helps make clear. In such shared perception and shared thought, the experiences of two people can most closely approach a perfect unity, by converging upon a single object.[17]

How solid a good is this good of enhanced aliveness, charged as it is by our awareness of life's brevity and the desire to find a compensation for it, if not to escape it altogether? Is it a good necessarily laced with self-deception? It seems that in its healthy form, this good can be perfectly solid and perfectly clear-sighted, but that such clear-sightedness is hard indeed to attain and to keep. There is nothing necessarily illusory about friendship's power to magnify and enrich life, just as there is nothing necessarily illusory about the pleasure of being a source of good to friends; both shared activity and benefaction can provide a similar, genuine amplification of being. Nor is there anything necessarily self-deceiving in the refreshing change of scene and pace that comes with immersing ourselves, for a time, in the absorbing affairs of others. But here a danger can arise. For there is a darker and more enchanting aspect of the power of life's determinacy or limitedness to make friendship sweet. Life's finitude, when faced squarely, provides an impetus to enjoy it to the utmost, and seeking out friends can be a sensible way of doing just this; but this same mortality, when glimpsed but not quite accepted, tempts us to try to escape its grip by escaping ourselves altogether, as Montaigne perhaps sought to do in his friendship with La Boétie. If it is wise to cultivate friendships to heighten the intensity of life, this is wise only so long as we remember who we are, and that it is only as mortal and ultimately separate individuals that we are capable of happiness.[18]

On the other hand, it is by keeping the truth of one's situation in perspective that one can be the most valuable friend to another, by helping him attain the most solid happiness possible. Through the shared activity of thinking and helping each other to think as clearly as possible, two people can each in a real sense become and take pleasure in becoming the helpful mirror, the other self, and a great benefactor of each other, and this pleasure too is solid, so long as it is not distorted by the thought that one can truly live on in the other when one's own life has ended.

In sum, while observing and admiring the life of another who is good and akin is very pleasant, taking part in that life is even better, and it is above all in shared thought and conversation that two people truly can partake in and enjoy each other's activity: The life that Aristotle calls the best life is also the life most capable of being shared. Thus the vital sap of friendship is found in living together, and as Aristotle says, living together for human beings means above all conversing together, not feeding in the same place, as it does in the case of cattle (1170b10–14). In posing the two extremes of rational conversation and feeding together as the possible meanings of living together, Aristotle is silent about noble acts of benefaction. These are still necessary in misfortune, as Aristotle will reiterate in chapter 11, but they are not what we live for, not what friendship truly turns upon.[19] And everyone somehow sees this: The truest, most characteristic activity of friendship is conversation.[20]

The Right Number of Friends

For such friendship, it is now abundantly clear that a few friends or even one good friend will suffice: Both the deepest pleasure and the most important benefits of friendship can be found with only a few, Aristotle argues in 9.10 (1170b24–28). But if pleasure and utility do not require large circles of friends, is there not a sense in which the most virtuous man *should* have as many virtuous friends as possible? Does it not, indeed, seem appropriate that the virtuous should be the friends of all virtuous people everywhere, without arbitrary, restrictive, invidious preferences? In voicing this thought, Aristotle gives expression to a powerful objection to friendship as it is in fact practiced, an objection carried even further by Christianity's call for universal charity and by Derrida's more recent contention that we should befriend everyone everywhere without restricting ourselves to those whose characters we happen to approve.[21] Aristotle's response would be to say that this objection, in all its forms, confuses friendship with goodwill or with the virtue of friendliness. It is possible for a good person to feel respect and goodwill toward all other good men, and to behave in a gracious way toward everyone he meets; it is perhaps possible to feel a very weak goodwill toward everyone whatsoever. But the genuine, meaningful friendship that consists in living together and choosing and sharing in the same activities is possible only on a very small scale, just as the polis is.[22] Aristotle calls obsequious those who try to be friends with everyone: They pretend to give more affection than they in fact have to give and pretend to approve and love those who are neither admirable nor lovable.[23]

In a political sense, indeed, Aristotle says that it is possible for a good man to be a friend or ally or champion of many (1171a17–19), although the proximity of such friendship to obsequiousness makes it necessary to tread a fine line, so as to avoid both displeasing coldness and ignoble pandering. More seriously telling with respect to political friendship is what Aristotle says about all utilitarian friendship, of which political friendship is one species: "To be obliged to return favors to many people is burdensome ... and having more friends than are sufficient for one's own life is superfluous and an impediment to living nobly" (1170b24–27). It would be another matter if in political friendship one could simply dispense an endless stream of benefits to whoever seemed worthy, but in fact, the power to do good must always be bought and kept by striking deals and paying favors to many who are merely useful. Since Aristotle argues that such activity is ultimately an obstacle to living well, it seems that the best course would be to be a friend to one's country in the sense of giving good counsel when counsel is invited and being prepared to give one's all in times of crisis, but otherwise to keep utilitarian friendships to a minimum and focus upon sharing the best activities with a very few.

Indeed, Aristotle says that the best number of friends is a circle so small that all can spend their days together and each can be a true friend to every other. He raises the question of whether, for the most perfect mutual knowledge, shared activity, and unity of feeling, a friendship of two may not be best of all, as Montaigne argues. Certainly Aristotle concedes that the friendships most celebrated in stories have all been friendships of pairs. But if one's primary desire is to live and especially to think well, the company and conversation of four or five may well be even better than the company of a single companion. It is only when one thinks of the unqualified mutual devotion of the friends as the highest thing that one cannot tolerate the thought of a third. Since the exclusivity of clear-sighted friendship depends not on the demand for complete devotion but on the rareness of virtue and the limits of human time and energy, this exclusivity is never in principle confined to just two. Aristotle does indeed say that those who have many friends have no true friends, but his analysis of friendship in the *Ethics* gives no ground for attributing to him, as Diogenes Laertius does, the saying that "he for whom there are friends has no friend."[24] Instead, Aristotle's last word on the proper number of friends is that we should be content with only a few.

Friendship in Good and Bad Fortune

A small circle of friends is also best with a view to the most complete possible sharing of joys and sorrows. Aristotle begins his final analysis of this aspect of friendship in 9.11 with the question of whether there is more need of friendship in good fortune or in bad. Friendship is more necessary in bad fortune, he answers, but nobler in good fortune, when one can do good to others. Aristotle agrees with common opinion that the potential of friendship to alleviate suffering and magnify joy is very great. But in the course of inquiring whether friendship is more necessary in good or bad fortune, he reminds us that people's feelings are not actually the same unless their experiences are the same, and that what they think of as sharing joys and sorrows is, in fact, something more complicated.

When misfortune strikes, Aristotle says, pain is alleviated if friends share the sorrow (1171a29–30). But does a friend really share it in the sense of taking on some of the precise sorrow that the sufferer feels? Does this even make sense? Or is pain not rather alleviated by a compensating pleasure, the pleasure of seeing that one is not alone in one's sorrows, and that they are felt also by another who wishes for one's happiness almost as much as one does oneself? But why, the noble soul may ask, should I take pleasure rather than pain in the thought that another whom I care for is suffering, too? A desire not to cause pain to his friends as well as a reluctance to give in to lamentation – to say nothing of pride, about which Aristotle is tactfully silent here – will thus cause the virtuous man to remain rather reserved in misfortune. Such a man's virtuous friends, on the other hand, will hasten to his side without being asked, Aristotle says, for this is noble. And perhaps being with a friend in misfortune is less painful than the high-minded sufferer tends to think – and less so than Aristotle paints it as being in this passage. For, as he stresses elsewhere, there is pleasure in being able to be a benefactor (and as such a superior) as well as in the reminder that one's own circumstances are relatively happy.

Indeed, the opportunity to be of service to a friend in need would seem to be precisely the circumstance that the most noble-minded man will most welcome, *if* being a benefactor is the finest thing in life and *if* benefiting a worthy friend is noblest of all. But this means that the sufferer's reluctance to trouble his friend is self-deceiving.[25] Of course his friend, truly caring about him as well as about his own performance of noble deeds, will also experience pain on his behalf, but what the noble sufferer cannot bear to face fully is the fact that his suffering that is painful to the friend as friend is in some sense welcome to the friend as morally virtuous and noble-minded. The sufferer, in other words, deceives himself in thinking that the friend responds to him only as a friend, who has no separate concerns and perspective.

In good fortune, there is a similar, subtle divergence of experiences. The noble man who is blessed by fortune will gladly invite his friends to share in his joy. He will take pleasure in their company, in being able to benefit them, and in the thought that they are pleased by the good he is enjoying – as indeed they will be, if they are true friends. But again, perhaps they are not quite so pleased as he is, or as he in his high-mindedness imagines them to be.[26] Aristotle is silent on the pain of envy, but not on the decent man's reluctance to appear eager to enjoy the fruits of his friends' good fortune, for this is ignoble. The high-minded stance is to try or imagine oneself to feel for the friend precisely what the friend feels for himself, and in turn, to believe in such perfect sympathy on the part of the other, but in all of this there is a mixture of truth and fiction. In revealing these fissures that lie beneath the surface of ordinary friendship, Aristotle indicates that it is not in the sharing either of fortune's blows or of fortune's smiles that friendship is in fact at its best, and that lives that turn upon the attempt to secure the goods of fortune are not the lives that can be best shared.

A rather different way of sharing a friend's burden when he is in need and sharing one's own abundance is seen in Xenophon's *Memorabilia*. When Socrates finds his companion Aristarchus looking miserable, he urges him to share his burden with his friends so that they might try to lighten it for him. But what Socrates offers is not commiseration or charity but good advice, advice that turns on the idea that one should not be prouder than one can afford to be. In the life that is lived according to Socratic wisdom, there would seem to be little mourning of misfortune, whether one's own or another's, and indeed little rejoicing at good fortune, since so little is required of fortune, but on the other hand, much common pleasure in the shared pursuit of knowledge, which is open to all who are keen and capable.[27]

Friendship and Philosophy

In his final remarks on friendship in 9.12, Aristotle brings to the fore this element of friendship that consists in sharing one's days and most cherished pursuits with friends. Here indeed, is the nub of the matter:

And whatever being consists in for each person, or whatever it is for the sake of which he chooses to live, in this he wants to spend time together with his friends. Therefore some drink together, others play dice together, others engage together in gymnastics and hunting, or philosophize together: Each group of friends passes its days together in that which it loves most in life. For wanting to live together with their friends, they do and share in those things by which they suppose that they live together. (1172a1–8)

Aristotle, having so often denigrated pleasure-friendship, now gives surprising weight to the sharing of simple, even frivolous pleasure, acknowledging that the highest friendships are, in fact, remarkably like the lowest in revolving around pleasant activities with those whose desires are akin to our own.[28] For after all, these are the activities of leisure, the ones that are chosen for themselves when all the chores are done and the problems are cleared away. Philosophy certainly stands out among them as different from the rest, but perhaps in the end not so much because it is grave and the others light-hearted, as because it is a deeper, more satisfying, more unmixed, and more lasting pleasure. With this conclusion to his discussion of friendship, Aristotle moves to his final themes of pleasure and the philosophic life.

We began this study wondering whether friendship might not be the peak of noble virtue and of the human good, able to make us both happy and worthy of happiness. Can we be so nobly devoted to others that we love them more than ourselves? Can such devotion give meaning to empty and unhappy lives, making us whole and somehow saving us from the abyss of our mortality? Aristotle has shown that friendship is neither so lofty nor so powerful. Can we truly love and care for others, pursuing their good for their own sakes and not as a mere means to our happiness? Absolutely, and such love is indeed noble, though not quite in the sense that we all at first imagined it to be. Is friendship an important and integral part of the happy life? Certainly it is, although we now see the full extent to which its intrinsic goodness is augmented by its goodness as a means, as a bulwark against evil, a source of inspiration and assistance in reaching the good, a confirmation of one's worth, an object of confused efforts at self-overcoming, and, not least, a distraction from sorrows and disappointments and death.

Now that we have unearthed all these extraneous props that turn out to undergird most friendship in Aristotle's analysis, it is clear that there is less of a divide than initially appeared between his teaching on friendship and those of the seminal modern philosophers who argue that man is fundamentally solitary and selfish. Indeed, precisely by taking human benevolence as seriously as he does, Aristotle is able to find a certain self-interest at work even in it (albeit self-interest of a high and splendid sort) that such modern philosophers as Hobbes, Locke, and Rousseau did not fully recognize. True benevolence is possible, according to Aristotle, because true goodwill is possible, but benevolence is able to be as strong and active as it is only because those who do good find their own lives expanding and growing richer in the process. Not only friendship when it is sordid, but precisely friendship when it is more generous and kind than a Hobbesian will ever concede the human heart can be, is shot through with the concern for one's own existence and well-being.

Yet the difference that remains on this point between Aristotle and most of modern political philosophy, if narrower than we may have thought, is nonetheless profound. For Aristotle's insistence on the irreducible goodness of friendship follows from his insistence on the naturally social and political character of man, as a being distinguished above all by speech and reason, and possessed of a natural insight that only together with others in a life ordered by reason can we be what we were meant to be.[29] It is precisely because we exist above all in our capacity for awareness and thought that the marrow of friendship, the shared awareness that comes through shared activity, becomes so important to us, making beautiful things more beautiful, laughter more delightful, insights more satisfying, and our very beings more fully alive. Friendship is important for Aristotle for much the same reason that virtue and philosophy are: Each in a different way is a perfection of man's potential as a rational being. In contrast, because most modern philosophers reject the idea that human beings are naturally directed to any specific fulfillment, they regard friendship, like philosophy, as a matter of individual taste, rather than as an essential part of the naturally best life.

On final reflection, Aristotle's disagreement with Plato about friendship seems to be even smaller, and to consist chiefly in a difference of emphasis. In the *Lysis* and *Symposium,* Plato emphasizes the ways in which human love points either downward to the most basic needs or upward to an object so high it is no longer human; Aristotle, in his splendid sobriety, takes the phenomenon of friendship on its own terms and does full justice to the ordinary experience of human affection. Socrates, in the *Lysis,* cuts the ground out from under his two young interlocutors at every turn so as to pulls them up short and make them think; Aristotle, addressing himself especially to statesmen and educators, focuses on the things of solid worth in friendship that readers should cultivate and build upon, and allows the problems with conventional friendship to remain largely in the shadows. Plato in the *Lysis* dwells relentlessly on the question of what drives us to friendship and so says little about goodwill; Aristotle explores in detail the ways in which respect for the virtue of another can inspire goodwill and enormously enrich friendship, even when it is not the cause of it. Finally, while Plato speaks cryptically of the love of the kindred at the end of the *Lysis,* Aristotle shows why the sharing of satisfying activity with kindred souls is the lifeblood of true friendship and an indispensable part of the happy life.

But if friendship is in Aristotle's view essential for happiness, it is still not quite the core of the happiest life. Friendship is fundamentally good because it magnifies life, expanding our concerns and intensifying our joys: Friendship makes even better "whatever it is that people love most in life" (1172a5–6). What matters most for happiness, then, is not the companionship that friendship brings but the pleasures and good activities that it augments, and even its goodness as an enhancer of life would not be so very good if it were not for the inevitability of death. Still, the recognition of our mortality only adds fire to the desire for a fullness of activity and joy and engagement with the world and especially with other people that is visible already in the smallest children, still innocent of the knowledge of death.

However much there is in Aristotle's account of friendship to satisfy the heart, this implicit relegation of friendship to the second rank of good things is bound to strike many of his readers as disagreeable, especially in light of the fact that it is philosophy that he ultimately puts first, and because the philosophic life seems to so few of us to provide the answer to our deepest longings. Particularly today, in a world in which piety has receded and the cultivation of virtue seems like an old-fashioned pursuit, what seems to matter most in life is the depth and quality of our connections with the people we love. However preoccupied people are with accumulating money and prestige and power, it is spending time with loved ones that always appears most important when the prospect of death forces them to take stock. If we are correct that Aristotle refuses to put friendship at the very center of the best life, is he reasonable in doing this?

Aristotle, of course, agrees that friendship is one of the most important ingredients in the happy life, and that the affection and especially the companionship that constitute the intrinsic goodness of friendship are solid goods indeed. But he shows, especially in his extended analysis of the necessity of equality for friendship from 8.7 to 9.3, that affection and companionship are not absolutely central even in most ordinary lives. Friendship needs, in most cases, a rough equality of benefits, inasmuch as it must be good for each party; friendship understood as a sacrificing or overcoming or utter forgetting of one's own good does not accord with the phenomena, as the sacrificing superior's expectations of reward make clear. Even in the connections in which benefits are never repaid, especially those of parents with children, it turns out that there is and must be a rough equalizing of satisfactions, through the experience of having one's *own* life expanded and deepened by being a benefactor. The closeness that can accompany such benevolent activity is very sweet, but secondary: Every serious parent cares more about rearing and educating well than about being loved. In a similar way, the need for approximate equality of merit in every mature friendship points to the fact that serious human beings seek above all not souls that will be devoted to them but souls that are akin and at least potentially equal, so that they may share as partners in their most important activities.

Aristotle does not explore in detail what it would look like to reverse these priorities and make simple companionship the focus of a life, but Montaigne does. One of the requisites of such an inversion is the denial of what we all somehow know to be true: that when we love we love for reasons, reasons that ultimately must stand as a measure of every friend and friendship, reasons that require a withdrawal from any friend who becomes irreparably evil. Loyalty is indeed a virtue, but it is one that must be qualified by higher virtues; it is not the defining mark of the best human beings.

Aristotle shows his recognition of the displeasure that this ranking of ends will give in his very first use of the word φίλος in the *Nicomachean Ethics,* as he gently takes issue with his teachers:

But perhaps it is necessary to examine the universal good and look into the problem of what is meant by it, although such an inquiry is irksome, because those who introduced the theory of forms are friends. But for the sake of securing the truth it would perhaps seem better and necessary, especially for philosophers, to give up even one's own. Both are beloved, but it is our duty to prefer the truth. (1096a11–17)

It is fortunate that such hard choices are rare indeed in the lives of men like Aristotle and Plato, and seldom cause for more than polite disagreements at the periphery of powerful friendships. It is not that Aristotle means to force us to choose between friendship and virtue, or friendship and philosophy; all are needed in the best life, and all are compatible when one chooses one's friends well. But perhaps he does mean to force us to decide how we should choose, should a choice be necessary. And on the proper choice he is quite clear: A good life does not shape its standards, its judgments, and its central activities to fit the people one happens to love, the people who are, for accidental and unreflective reasons, "one's own," but instead, it gathers around it, in the most thoughtful way, people to *make* one's own, because and to the extent that they are suitable companions in life's most important activities. And this preference for excellence over mere belonging and affection is confirmed at least in part even by the intuitive understanding of those who insist that it is love that matters most for happiness: It is not quite companionship as such that seems to them the core of a life well lived, but treating people well and kindly and justly and leaving them better and happier than they were before.

Such activity for the benefit of those whom one loves, especially when done together with others whom one loves, can bring moral virtue and friendship together into a deeply satisfying whole.[30] But Aristotle, who is normally so gentle and genteel, is disconcertingly dogged in his insistence on ranking activities and lives, and in his books on friendship he shows some of his reasons for judging even this finest of active lives to be not quite the best simply. Even when the grave confusions surrounding self-sacrifice are cleared away, Aristotle insists that practical, political activity (under which he subsumes the work of moral education) is too much driven and constrained by necessities to be simply choiceworthy in itself (1176b2–9, 77b1–26). To be sure, it can be both choiceworthy and satisfying when it is needed, and doing it can make us better in ways that are good in themselves, and it is best of all when the beneficiaries have good natures and the goal is the cultivation of virtue. But all such activity has ultimately the character of removing obstacles or of laying groundwork, and therefore seems to point beyond itself to activities that are simply good in themselves. Thus philosophy comes to sight as doubly valuable. It is both the source of the clarity we need to be truly good, without any of the wavering that results from confusion and self-contradiction; and it is in itself a delightful activity quite unconstrained by problems and pressing necessities. As such it is an eligible focus not only for the happiest of lives but also for the happiest of friendships, as partnerships in which the capacity to see and enjoy and think and reflect is given the fullest possible scope.

Yet if friendship is always precious, in the movement to philosophy with which Aristotle concludes his *Ethics,* he presses us to think hard about the possibility that the best life, in its mature form, may be much more self-sufficient than most. In Book 1, Aristotle posited self-sufficiency as an attribute of the best life, but he did not even attempt to persuade his readers that the happy life could be a solitary one. Self-sufficiency, he said there, meant being able to provide for oneself and others in a life furnished with family, friends, and fellow citizens (1097b8–11). But now, having shown us how much the impetus to friendship lies in weakness, deficiency, and confusion, he prepares us for the possibility that the best life, involving the most engrossing and self-sustainable of activities, may likewise involve a less fervent need for friendship. For in Book 10, it is the self-sufficiency of the philosophic life, rather than the goodness of friendship within it, that Aristotle emphasizes. Perhaps, then, just as the theme of friendship is in the *Ethics* a bridge to the theme of philosophy, so friendship and the longing for it may be, in the very best lives, most important as a bridge to philosophy, giving fire to one's desire to understand virtue and justice and the human heart, and giving inspiration and help and companionship along the way, but less critical and hence less fervent, though still delightful, on the other side of the divide.

If this is so, it is nothing to be mourned. Whatever such friendship loses in intensity, it must surely gain in clarity and purity. For only in perfect clear-sightedness can two people love without all of the freight of lies, self-deception, flattery, self-flattery, subtle struggles for moral superiority, unattainable hopes, unreasonable demands, anger, ruptures, and disappointments with which ordinary friendships are burdened. Only with the clarity that comes with well-examined lives can the joys of shared conversation be unalloyed. And if, in the final analysis, friendship is in large measure precious as a bridge to philosophy, then the friendships between mature philosophers and those who are not yet philosophic are ample proof of the continuing interest in friendship, the continuing generosity of soul, of those on the other side, a generosity with astounding power and reach. For after all, the *Nicomachean Ethics* itself and the discussion of friendship within it are, like other classical introductions to the philosophic life, nothing but bridges created by friends for friends, most of whom they would never meet, bridges across which splendid souls sometimes manage to cross quite alone, but most do so only with the inspiring presence and generous help of a good friend.

Notes

Introduction

1. Herodotus 6.123; Thucydides 1.20.2, 6.53.3–59.4; Aristotle *Constitution of Athens* 18–19; see also Paul Rahe, *Republics Ancient and Modern: Classical Republicanism and the American Revolution,* 131–33.

2. Cicero *Tusculan Disputations* 5.63. For other versions of the story, see David Konstan, *Friendship in the Classical World,* 114 n. 33.

3. Diogenes Laertius reports the existence of treatises on friendship among the works of Simmias of Thebes; Speusippus and Xenocrates, Plato's two immediate successors as directors of the Academy; Theophrastus, Aristotle's student and successor in the Lyceum; and the early Stoic Cleanthes (*Lives of Eminent Philosophers* 2.124, 4.4, 4.12, 5.45, and 7.175). Clearchus, a later Peripatetic, is reported to have written a similar work in F. Wehrli, *Die Schule des Aristoteles,* vol. 3, fragments 17–18 (Athenaeus 8.349f and 12.535e). Plutarch records another by Chrysippus in *On Stoic Self-Contradiction* 1039b. In addition to fragments of a lost treatise on friendship by Seneca, several short ones by Plutarch have also come down to us: "How to Tell a Flatterer from a Friend," "On Having Many Friends," and "On Brotherly Love." See also J. G. F. Powell, ed. and trans., *Cicero: Laelius, On Friendship and the Dream of Scipio,* 2–3 and 23–24.

4. For this reason, I have as a rule translated φιλία and its cognates with "friendship" and its cognates, while using the broader term "love" wherever it seems better to capture the authors' meaning. For further discussions of the range of meaning of φίλος, φιλεῖν, and φιλία, see Arthur W. H. Adkins, "'Friendship' and 'Self-Sufficiency' in Homer and Aristotle," 30–45; A. W. Price, *Love and Friendship in Plato and Aristotle,* 11; Martha Nussbaum, *The Fragility of Goodness: Luck and Ethics in Greek Tragedy and Philosophy,* 354–55; David Robinson, "Plato's *Lysis*: The Structural Problem," 65–68; and Gregory Vlastos, *Platonic Studies,* 3–4.

5. On the eclipse of friendship in the Christian world, see especially the comments of Shaftesbury and Bishop Taylor in Shaftesbury, *Characteristics of Men, Manners, Opinions, Times,* 66–69 and 67–68 n. 1.

6. For a good anthology, including selections from most of these authors, see Michael Pakaluk, ed., *Other Selves: Philosophers on Friendship.* For Nietzsche, see esp. *Thus Spoke Zarathustra,* Part 1, chap. 14, "On the Friend."

7. *Nicomachean Ethics* (*NE*) 1129b28–30, 1130a3–4. All translations from the *Ethics* are my own, based upon the Oxford text of Ingram Bywater.

8. On the whole, the introduction to the theme of friendship in the *Eudemian Ethics* (*EE*) at 1234b18–35a4 brings out even more clearly than the parallel passage in the *NE* the possibility that friendship is simply the summit of the moral-political life.

9. The apparent abruptness of Aristotle's elevation of the contemplative life over the practical in *NE* 10.7–8 has been noted, among others, by Sarah Broadie, who is inclined to take it as an exaggeration: *Ethics with Aristotle*, 372, 391.

10. See, e.g., Henry Sidgwick, *Outlines of the History of Ethics for English Readers*, 70: "On the whole, there is probably no treatise so masterly as Aristotle's *Ethics*, and containing so much close and valid thought, that yet leaves on the reader's mind so strong an impression of dispersive and incomplete work."

11. J. L. Ackrill, "Aristotle on *Eudaimonia*," 15–33.

12. R.-A. Gauthier also charges Aristotle with self-contradiction in ultimately making moral virtue, which should be an end in itself, a means to philosophy, and questions how it even conduces to philosophy; he offers as a partial explanation the fact that for Aristotle, moral virtue in a sense perfects the intellect: "On the Nature of Aristotle's *Ethics*," 19–20.

13. Ackrill, "Aristotle on *Eudaimonia*," 33.

14. Susemihl, review of *The Ethics of Aristotle*, by John Burnet, 1508–9; Bodéüs, *The Political Dimensions of Aristotle's Ethics*, chap. 4. Even Werner Jaeger's assumption that the book is Aristotle's own lecture notes, unrevised for publication, does injustice to the care of composition (*Aristotle: Fundamentals of the History of His Development*, 230).

15. See esp. Helen Lang, *The Order of Nature in Aristotle's Physics*, 11–27.

16. *NE* 1094b11–27, 98a26–b8, 1103b34–1104a11; Plutarch *Alexander* 7.3–5; Aulus Gellius *Attic Nights* 20.5.

17. *NE* 1102a26–27, 40a2–3; cf. 1096a3–4. See Jaeger, *Aristotle*, 246–58; Ostwald, trans. and ed., *The Nicomachean Ethics*, 9 n. 17; Bodéüs, *Political Dimensions*, chap. 4. But cf. Alexander Grant, *The Ethics of Aristotle, Illustrated with Essays and Notes*, 1: 398–409, and Eduard Zeller, *Aristotle and the Earlier Peripatetics*, 1: 105–23, who argue that the expression ἐξοτερικοὶ λόγοι was a term loosely applied by Aristotle both to his own more popular works and to oral arguments in general circulation in educated circles.

18. Plutarch *Alexander* 7.4–5.

19. For a further critique of the thesis that Aristotle wrote esoterically, see George Boas, "Ancient Testimony to Secret Doctrines," 79–92; and Ingemar Düring, *Aristotle in the Ancient Biographical Tradition*, 426–43. For other perspectives on this question, see Plato *Seventh Letter* 332d6–7, 341c4–42a1, and 344d3–e2; Isocrates *Panegyricus* 11–12; the ancient and medieval commentators collected in Düring, esp. 201 and 426–43; Alfarabi, *Alfarabi's Philosophische Abhandlungen, Aus dem Arabischen Übersetzt*, 11; *The Complete Essays of Montaigne*, 379–80; Francis Bacon, *The Advancement of Learning*, 2.17.5, in *The Works of Francis Bacon*, 6: 290–91; Thomas Hobbes, *Leviathan*, chap. 46; Leo Strauss, *Persecution and the Art of Writing*, chap. 2; *What Is Political Philosophy?* Chap. 9; and *The Rebirth of Classical Political Rationalism*, chap. 5; Miriam Galston, *Politics and Excellence:*

The Political Philosophy of Alfarabi, 22–43; David Bolotin, *An Approach to Aristotle's Physics: With Particular Attention to the Role of His Manner of Writing*, esp. 5–7; Kathy Eden, "Hermeneutics and the Ancient Rhetorical Tradition," 127–50.

20. Bodéüs, *Political Dimensions*, esp. chap. 1. This view has been adopted by Michael Pakaluk in *Aristotle: Nicomachean Ethics Books VIII and IX*, 45–46. See also Strauss, *The City and Man*, 21, 28–29; *NE* 1094a18–b11, 1102a5–26, 1109b30–35. For a thoughtful critique of Bodéüs's book, stressing the ways in which the *NE* stands also as an autonomous study of individual human excellence, which ultimately surpasses the excellence that is possible for the city, see Paul. A. Vander Waerdt, "The Political Intention of Aristotle's Moral Philosophy," 77–89.

21. See esp. Bodéüs, *Political Dimensions*, 54–57, 63–66.

22. Ibid., 5. On the independence of Aristotle's ethical principles from those of his natural science, see also Strauss, *City and Man*, 25–27; for an opposing view, see Terence Irwin, *Aristotle's First Principles*, esp. 9–10, 23–25, and Chapters 16–21; and Stephen Salkever, "Women, Soldiers, Citizens: Plato and Aristotle on the Politics of Virility," 172.

23. On the relation of the *NE* to the *EE*, see esp. Anthony Kenney, *The Aristotelian Ethics: A Study of the Relationship between the* Eudemian *and* Nicomachean Ethics *of Aristotle*. Kenney makes an impressive case that *NE* 5, 6, and 7 belonged originally to the *EE*, and a more tentative argument that the *NE* is an earlier work, superseded by the *EE*. I believe the evidence for the original provenance of the disputed books actually supports better the idea that the *NE* is a quite late and unfinished rewriting of the *EE*, which perhaps developed out of an appendix to the *EE*. But I do not put much weight on this or any other conjecture about the temporal order of Aristotle's writings; my reason for focusing on the *NE* is simply that this is the richer study of friendship (a difference which Kenney, incidentally, never explains).

    The developmental approach to Aristotelian interpretation, given its main impetus by Jaeger's 1935 *Aristotle*, has enjoyed something of a resurgence of late: See esp. Daniel Graham, *Aristotle's Two Systems*; John Rist, *The Mind of Aristotle: A Study in Philosophical Growth*; and Terence Irwin, *Aristotle's First Principles*, 13. For a good analysis of the pitfalls of making this the basis for an interpretation, see Lang, *Order of Nature*, 12–16.

24. On the dialectical character of the *NE*, see John Burnet, *The Ethics of Aristotle*, xxxix–xlii; James J. Walsh and Henry L. Shapiro, *Aristotle's Ethics: Issues and Interpretations*, 4; John M. Cooper, *Reason and Human Good in Aristotle*, 69–71; Aristide Tessitore, *Reading Aristotle's Ethics*, 9–23.

25. Ibid., 18.

26. The extent of this achievement is often overlooked today, since we live in a world in which the "philosopher," with his tweedy idiosyncrasies, is routinely accepted as perfectly harmless. For evidence of a different view in antiquity, see Anton-Hermann Chroust, *Aristotle: New Light on His Life and on Some of His Lost Works*, 1: 145–54; Rahe, *Republics Ancient and Modern*, 208–18; and Peter Ahrensdorf, "The Question of Historical Context and the Study of Plato," 113–35. Consider also the well-attested story that, late in life, Aristotle himself was forced to flee Athens to avoid prosecution for impiety, remarking that he left in order to prevent Athens from "offending a second time against philosophy,"

a clear reference to the death of Socrates: See Diogenes Laertius *Aristotle* 5.5; and Düring, *Aristotle in the Ancient Biographical Tradition,* 341–42.

27. Bodéüs, *Political Dimensions,* 125, 43–45.
28. On the difficulties involved in this ascent, see esp. Strauss, *The Rebirth of Classical Political Rationalism,* 67–69.
29. Tessitore, *Reading Aristotle's* Ethics, 9–23; cf. Carnes Lord, Introduction to *Essays on the Foundations of Aristotelian Political Science,* 2–3.
30. See Strauss, *City and Man,* 23.
31. Xenophon *Memorabilia* 1.2.40–46.
32. For different versions of the argument that the books on friendship provide a transition to philosophy, see Pakaluk, *Aristotle,* 162–65 and 226–27, who stresses the way in which shared philosophizing provides best for the equality that friendship needs; and Amélie Rorty, "The Place of Contemplation in Aristotle's *Nicomachean Ethics,*" 378, 388–91, who emphasizes the power of friendship to deepen self-awareness. What I hope to add to these good observations is an examination of how *NE* 8 and 9 reveal not only the incompleteness but also the inner incoherence of conventional moral opinions and conventional friendships in lives that have not been subjected to rigorous self-examination.
33. Cf. 1124b31–25a1; Pakaluk, *Aristotle,* 47.
34. Our natural sociability does not take us very far in the direction of loving all mankind, however. According to Aristotle, this sociability is above all a capacity for reason and speech, which points to the polis as its best fulfillment: Human sociability expresses itself not chiefly in affection for the whole species but in conversing and sharing in life and rule together with a small number of others (*Politics* 1252b27–53a18).
35. See especially *Politics* 1280a31–b12 on the ways in which a polis goes beyond a mere alliance or compact, and also John A. Stewart, *Notes on the Nicomachean Ethics of Aristotle,* 2: 263, 267.
36. Franz Dirlmeier notes the frequency throughout the opening chapters of Book 8 of words such as δοκεῖ, ἔοικε, and οἴονται, signifying his reliance on common opinion to provide the starting points for discussion: *Aristoteles Nikomachische Ethik, Übersetzt und Kommentiert,* 514.
37. Homer *Odyssey* 17.218; Empedocles fragments 22, lines 4–5; 62, line 6; and 90, lines 1–2 Diels-Kranz.
38. Hesiod *Works and Days* 25–26.
39. Euripides fragment 898.7–10 Nauck; Heraclitus fragments 8 and 80 Diels-Kranz.
40. In a parallel passage, *EE* 1235a33–b3, Aristotle mentions what seem to be a fourth and a fifth possibility: that love of one's own and utility are really at the root of all friendship. But these two are ultimately the same as, or refinements of, the first two, and so Aristotle's account in the *NE* brings out more clearly the fact that if all friendship can be attributed to one fundamental root, it must be either similarity, need, or virtue.
41. As Dirlmeier points out (*Aristoteles,* 511), "Der Ausdruck [ἀνώτερον] enthält an sich keine Kritik." To say that this group of arguments belongs to the "higher" study of nature is *not* to criticize them as extraneous to the current work, for the study of man is part of the study of nature.
42. Cf. also Aristotle's comments at 1159b19–24.

43. According to Price, Aristotle, in treating friendship, "effectively takes the *Lysis* as his starting point; with no other Platonic dialogue does he show such detailed, yet implicit, familiarity": *Love and Friendship*, 1; see also 9–10.

1. The Challenge of Plato's *Lysis*

1. *Lysis* 215a6–b2, trans. David Bolotin, in *Plato's Dialogue on Friendship: An Interpretation of the* Lysis, *with a New Translation*. Further quotations from the *Lysis* will be from this translation.

2. Vlastos, *Platonic Studies*, 6–11; Versenyi, "Plato's *Lysis*," 185–98; Bolotin, *Plato's Dialogue on Friendship*, esp. 176–77; Gadamer, *Dialogue and Dialectic: Eight Hermeneutical Studies on Plato*, esp. 17–18. This more recent disagreement was foreshadowed by the great debate between Max Pohlenz and Hans von Arnim early in the twentieth century, as we shall see.

3. Donald N. Levin, "Some Observations concerning Plato's *Lysis*," 246. For similar views, see also George Grote, *Plato and the Other Companions of Sokrates*, 1: 515–16; W. R. M. Lamb, Introduction to the *Lysis*, in *Plato III: Lysis, Symposium, Gorgias*, 3; Paul Shorey, *What Plato Said*, 115; and Ronald Levinson, *In Defense of Plato*, 61–62.

4. Gadamer, *Dialogue and Dialectic*, 6; Bolotin, *Plato's Dialogue on Friendship*, esp. 12–13; Versenyi, "Plato's *Lysis*," 186. Price likewise identifies elements of the argument that are in fact never refuted, either in this work or elsewhere in Plato: *Love and Friendship*, 12. If I myself am relatively silent on the dramatic context of the dialogue, it is because I have little to add in this regard to the excellent analysis of Bolotin.

5. Instead of the question "what is friendship?" – a question susceptible of the deceptively easy answer that it is a relationship between two people who like each other – Socrates asks the more treacherous question "who or what is a friend?" or "what is it that we truly love?" For discussions of just what the basic question of the *Lysis* is, compare Levin, "Some Observations," 239–40, and W. K. C. Guthrie, *A History of Greek Philosophy*, 4: 144, with David Sedley, "Is the *Lysis* a Dialogue of Definition?" 107–8.

6. See, e.g., Grote, *Plato*, 1: 519; Julia Annas, "Plato and Aristotle on Friendship and Altruism," 532–33, and David K. Glidden, who calls Socrates' refutations in this section "cheap victories" in "The *Lysis* on Loving One's Own," 41. Paul Friedländer, in contrast, sees in this analysis a clarification of "substantial problems that are concealed by the ambiguities of language" (*Plato*, 2: 95); and Price agrees that Socrates' initial failure to identify the root causes of friendship in 212a8–13c9 is "a stumbling upon real obstacles" (*Love and Friendship*, 5).

7. For a paradoxical argument that the best friend may indeed be also an enemy, see Nietzsche, *Thus Spoke Zarathustra*, Part 1, chap. 14, "On the Friend."

8. Socrates will return to the idea of similarity or kinship as a separate source of love at the end of the dialogue, but even sooner, at 219b6–8, he hints that implicit in love of the good that we lack and that is therefore *unlike* us, there is an element precisely of similarity or affinity: the affinity between that which needs and that which naturally fulfills the need and therefore naturally "belongs" to it. This remark points forward to Socrates' remark at 222c4 that "the good is akin to everyone."

9. On the meaning of Socrates' charge of boastfulness, see Bolotin, *Plato's Dialogue on Friendship,* 160, 167–69. Vlastos argues, along similar lines, that according to Socrates, it is just as much an error to think we love other human beings for their own sakes as it is to think that we love money for its own sake: *Platonic Studies,* 10 n. 25.

10. There has been much speculation as to just what the real good is that Socrates says we desire and seek, but most of it shows an amazing disregard for what Socrates says about the good at 220c–d. Setting aside Socrates' description of the good as a "remedy" for evil, which would be "useless" were we not suffering, and importing into the dialogue ideas taken out of context from other ones, many scholars have assumed that the good we really love is nothing other than the self-subsisting "idea of the good" of Plato's *Republic* or the "beautiful in itself" of the *Symposium:* See F. Horn, *Platonstudien,* 115; Hans von Arnim, *Platos Jugenddialoge und die Entstehungszeit des Phaidros,* 53–54, and "Platos Lysis," 381–82; Jaeger, *Paideia: The Ideals of Greek Culture,* 2: 175; Friedländer, *Plato,* 2: 98–99, 314; Levin, "Some Observations," 246–48. Versenyi, much more sensibly, observes that the good that men love, according to the *Lysis,* being something "beneficial, fulfilling, belonging to their nature but not yet possessed," is necessarily *relative,* "relative to the nature of the lover . . . and in particular to the evils or deficiencies that each lover is characterized by" ("Plato's Lysis," 189; cf. 195). He goes on to equate the good that is the true φίλον with the positive concept of εὐδαιμονία (194). Price concurs, but observes that "Plato tends to count as truly 'good' not εὐδαιμονία itself but what reliably yields or produces it" (*Love and Friendship,* 8 n. 9). Bolotin rightly goes further: In the *Lysis,* at least, Plato tends to identify as "good" only what produces release from evil or *unhappiness* (*Plato's Dialogue on Friendship,* 171–73). Versenyi, recognizing the relational quality of the good, does not quite see that Socrates is presenting evil as more fundamental. He does observe that if the good is merely remedial, happiness is itself not good, but he never acknowledges how strange a result this is ("Plato's Lysis," 195).

11. Bolotin, *Plato's Dialogue on Friendship,* 176–77.

12. In a different context, Suzanne Stern-Gillet also stresses the possibility of loving what one needs and is *not* deprived of, in "Epicurus and Friendship," 280.

13. The same exaggeration or distortion that is implicit in this discussion of fathers and sons appears more vividly in Socrates' opening conversation with Lysis at 207d5–10d8, where Socrates draws the absurd conclusion that fathers love their sons only insofar as the sons are useful to them. This exaggeration is remarked upon by Robinson, among others: "Plato's Lysis," 69 n. 15.

14. Bolotin, *Plato's Dialogue on Friendship,* 173–76. Shorey thinks that this use of ἕνεκα, in violation of the distinction between ἕνεκα and δία that he has just carefully made at 218d6–19b4, is meant to emphasize 1) the opposition between the useful "friend," who or which is loved for the sake of a further good and because of an evil, and the first friend, "which can only be φίλον because of evil and not for the sake of anything," and 2) the fact that even the "good itself" is good only in contrast or opposition to a real or potential evil: "The Alleged Fallacy in Plato Lysis 220E," 380–83. One may well concede this last point, that the concept of "good" entails or requires a correlative concept of "evil" in order to have any meaning, and yet not concede at all Socrates' controversial suggestion that the

good is only a remedy for evil; but Shorey seems to confuse these two lines of reasoning. Nor does either of the reasons he gives show why διά would not be the more appropriate preposition. Von Arnim, in contrast, thinks Socrates uses ἕνεκα precisely to ridicule the idea that the good is loved only because of any evil: *Platos Jugenddialoge,* 54–55.

15. Or perhaps, as L. A. Kosman interprets these lines, but without any explanation of the words ἐχθροῦ ἕνεκα at 220e4, the true object of love is "our own true but fugitive nature," with the wholeness that is proper to us: "Platonic Love," 60.

16. Bolotin, *Plato's Dialogue on Friendship,* 175–76.

17. Bolotin, "Response" to review by Stewart Umphrey, 423–29. In this essay, Bolotin offers the alternative suggestion that the self for whose sake we act is an enemy insofar as it distracts us from our true good by pursuing a "supposedly selfless love for a spurious good that we imagine as existing (and as being good) independently of any evils" (428). I believe the dialogue as a whole does call into serious question the existence of any such good and indicates the folly of imagining ourselves to be selflessly devoted to it. But there seems insufficient textual evidence for thinking that this is what Socrates has in mind at 220e. For after saying that "that friend to us into which all the others terminate" is "a friend to us for the sake of an enemy," Socrates adds that "if that which is an enemy would go away, it is no longer, as it seems, a friend to us." But if the enemy were our self-deceptions about the good, surely the disappearance of this enemy would not remove our concern with the good altogether.

18. What I take to be an exaggerated account of the fundamental truth that the good is relative to need, von Arnim takes even more ironically, and interprets as nothing but a parody of the views of other thinkers: *Platos Jugenddialoge,* 50.

19. Cf. ibid., 62.

20. Cf. Aristotle *NE* 1154b20–31, 1175a3–10.

21. Cf. Plato *Republic* 357b4–d2.

22. *NE* 1152b33–53a6, 1154b15–20, and 1173b13–20; cf. Plato *Gorgias* 492e–95a.

23. Max Pohlenz justly stresses this point in "Nochmals Plato's *Lysis,*" 572.

24. As Robinson points out, Socrates' claim at 222a5–6 that *any* two people who are akin in spirit will necessarily be friends is unrealistic and depends upon a certain confusion of οἰκεῖον as that which is congenial or appropriate to oneself, which one may lack and will naturally love when one seeks and finds it, with οἰκεῖον as that which is merely similar in some way ("Plato's *Lysis,*" 76). We feel no need to befriend everyone who resembles us in *any* respect, and as Robert G. Hoerber suggests, Lysis and Hippothales may only be similar in both being bashful: "Plato's *Lysis,*" 24.

25. Cf. Cicero *Republic* 1.28; Montaigne, *Essays,* 115 and 185–86. Socrates may well have had this pleasure even though he did not write, since he knew that he was being written about.

26. I thus disagree with the claim of Max Pohlenz that friendship between perfectly good men would be impossible according to the *Lysis* on the grounds that they would need nothing from one another: *Aus Platos Werdezeit,* 367; followed by Friedländer (*Plato,* 2: 98). But neither would I go as far as von Arnim goes (followed by Gadamer) in arguing that good men would love one another without any need or desire whatsoever: *Platos Jugenddialoge,* 62; cf. 58; Gadamer, *Dialogue and Dialectic,* 17–18. For a good account of the debate between Pohlenz

and von Arnim on this question, see Bolotin, *Plato's Dialogue on Friendship*, 201–25. Bolotin claims that in arguing for a true friendship of the good for the good as the most serious teaching of the *Lysis*, von Arnim ignores what Plato also teaches about the nature of our love for the good as being "for the sake of a further good and because of...an evil" (213). As I have argued, I think that this whole analysis only applies to our love of instrumental goods, and those friends we love out of a need for assistance. Thus I think the *Lysis* does leave room for a friendship of the good for the good, involving desire but not defectiveness, as the perfect friendship.

27. Bolotin, *Plato's Dialogue on Friendship*, 191–95; quotation is from 194.
28. Ibid., 181.
29. Ibid., 180.
30. This point is well made by Versenyi, "Plato's *Lysis*," 196.
31. Von Arnim, *Plato's Jugenddialoge*, 62. I continue to disagree, however, with his understanding of the good we want as an end as something wholly "good in itself" and not merely good for us.
32. On this point, see esp. Bolotin, *Plato's Dialogue on Friendship*, 222. Hoerber is thus wide of the mark in insisting that friendships of kinship are simply higher than those of utility according to the *Lysis*: "Plato's *Lysis*," 23–24.
33. See Bolotin, *Plato's Dialogue on Friendship*, 164.

2. The Three Kinds of Friendship

1. St. Thomas Aquinas, indeed, interprets the "good" in this passage as equivalent to "the honorable": *Commentary on the Nicomachean Ethics*, 2: 708. Pakaluk, in contrast, is troubled by the lack of specificity about the "good" and its unclear relation to the noble: *Aristotle*, 55. In general, of those who have commented on *NE* 8 and 9, Pakaluk is the most perceptive of the real problems in the text and is consistently unwilling to gloss over them with simplistic solutions; his commentary is well worth consulting throughout. My disagreements with him are invariably disagreements not about where the problems are but about how they should be approached in the light of the whole. Whereas Pakaluk seeks on each point a single consistent teaching, I seek explanations for otherwise insoluble difficulties in terms of Aristotle's dual audience, his dialectical ascent from common opinion, and his movement in 8 and 9 from the life of moral virtue to the life of philosophy.
2. See also 1099a13, 1166a12–13, 1170a13–16, 1176a15–19, 1176b24–26.
3. Pakaluk expresses with admirable clarity this understanding of the simply good and the simply pleasant in Aristotelian usage: *Aristotle*, 58. A failure to grasp what Aristotle means by the good that virtuous men love has led other commentators, most seriously Troels Engberg-Pedersen, to conceive of the Aristotelian good in strangely abstract and impersonal terms, resulting in a serious misunderstanding of the relationship between friendship, self-love, and self-sacrifice: *Aristotle's Theory of Moral Insight*, esp. 46. Stern-Gillet wavers between the clear understanding of Pakaluk and the clear misunderstanding of Engberg-Pedersen, whose approach she sees as anachronistic but still attractive. Grasping somehow that the "intrinsically good" for Aristotle is nothing other than what the virtuous,

healthy man wants and pursues, she insists in the same breath that this good is not "relational" and that "no reference to individual preferences, needs, and wants is required to justify its goodness": *Aristotle's Philosophy of Friendship*, 69; see also 103–22. Indeed, a wavering between genuine insight into the unique character of Aristotle's moral analysis and the importation of alien moral concepts that cause her to lose sight of those very insights pervades her entire book.

4. Pakaluk (*Aristotle*, 60–61) misses the strong claim inherent in these lines, which is that it *is* possible to wish the good of wine (or of a slave, or of one's own foot) in the sense of wishing it to be in an optimal condition for the sake of or as a part of one's own good – and this is *not* what we mean by goodwill or genuine friendship.

5. Cf. *Rhetoric* 1381a1–3, a similar definition of friendship that also stresses the centrality of goodwill, but cf. also *EE* 1236a14–15, where Aristotle gives a definition of friendship that does not involve goodwill.

6. This tension in Aristotle's basic definition of friendship has been observed by several commentators. See Stewart, *Notes*, 2: 274; Burnet, *Ethics*, 355; Terence Irwin, trans. and ed., *The Nicomachean Ethics*, 359. Burnet tries to resolve the problem by saying that goodwill is not really essential to friendship but is included only as a bow to popular belief, but in succeeding chapters he reverts to the idea that goodwill is crucial.

7. See, e.g., Homer *Iliad* 6.215–31; Pat Easterling, "Friendship and the Greeks," 13–15.

8. Commentators overwhelmingly assume that friendships of utility are concerned only with what H. H. Joachim calls "tangible advantage or profit": *Aristotle: The Nicomachean Ethics, A Commentary*, 247. Aristotle seems indeed to wish to give this impression in 8.2–8.6; it is only in 8.8 that he mentions friendships of the ignorant and learned as instances of useful friendships.

9. Stern-Gillet, in pointing out that perfect friendship has more of the character of an activity chosen for its own sake than have the lesser friendships, which she says resemble processes with an external goal (cf. *Metaphysics* 1048b18ff.), does insufficient justice to the way in which pleasure-friendship *is* an end in itself: *Aristotle's Philosophy of Friendship*, 42–43.

10. Moreover, as Pakaluk points out, it is when two people have the same interests and are encouraging and helping each other to grow in the same direction that they are likely to remain good partners for the longest time: *Aristotle*, 78–80.

11. Montaigne seems to allude to this in "Of Friendship," in *Essays*, 137: "During the reign of this perfect friendship those fleeting [erotic] affections once found a place in me, not to speak of my friend, who confesses only too many of them in these verses." This statement is somewhat ambiguous and has been taken to refer to one or more love affairs of La Boétie with women. But Montaigne goes on to say that the passions of friendship and eros "thus . . . came to be known to each other" within him, as if they did converge in his friendship with La Boétie. Indeed, one important function of the essay "Of Friendship" seems to be quietly to show the superiority of the right kind of homosexual friendship over heterosexual marriage.

Socrates, in Xenophon's *Symposium,* gives a spirited attack on the idea that the most famous friendships were sexual, but he does portray them as embodying a higher form of eros, rather than as unerotic. See esp. 8.16, 31. See also Easterling, "Friendship and the Greeks," 18–20.

12. Cf. Plato *Laws* 837a.

13. This is the interpretation taken by Adkins in "'Friendship' and 'Self-Sufficiency,'" 30–45, an argument whose historical basis is critiqued by Konstan in *Friendship in the Classical World,* chap. 1. Adkins understands Aristotle to mean that in a friendship of virtue, one loves the other because he is good for oneself, and one really loves him "for his own sake" (ἐκείνων ἕνεκα), only to the extent of loving him for capacities that are integral and not incidental to his character (39). Adkins accuses Aristotle of a "linguistic trick" in thus shifting from the ordinary Greek meaning of ἐκείνου ἕνεκα "as an end in himself" at 1155b31 to the new meaning "because of what he is in himself" or "because of his character" at 1156b10. This is indeed an interesting shift that Adkins points out, but I think Aristotle adopts it not in order to negate the force of loving the other as an end in himself, hence denying the possibility of any true goodwill, but rather, in order to strengthen the impression he wishes to give that true goodwill can arise *only* in response to virtue. As Vlastos argues, in *Platonic Studies,* 33 n. 100, Aristotle's implicit equation of loving another as an end and loving him for his virtue is not self-evident and is never adequately demonstrated, but as I will argue, this equation is not ultimately Aristotle's position. Vlastos indeed makes the unlikely supposition that Aristotle has never even "noticed" the ambiguity of the expression "loving another for his own sake."

14. Cf. 1156a10, 12, 14, 31–32 with 1156b7, 57a20. I thus do not quite agree with W. W. Fortenbaugh, who argues, in "Aristotle's Analysis of Friendship: Function and Analogy, Resemblance, and Focal Meaning," 52–54, that friendships of pleasure and utility are "analogous" to perfect friendship insofar as they stand in exactly the same relation to the ends they seek as perfect friendship stands to the goal it seeks. To some extent this is true, since all friends seek some good from their friendships, but what the goal of the friendship is, and to what extent it exists for the sake of attaining a specific goal at all, is much less clear in the case of perfect friendship. See also A. D. M. Walker's critique of Fortenbaugh in "Aristotle's Account of Friendship in the *Nicomachean Ethics,*" 180–84.

    The analogy is also made tighter if we follow Cooper's interesting suggestion that the διά in δι' ἡδονὴν and διὰ τὸ χρήσιμον should be translated not as "for the sake of" but as "on the basis of," or "in response to," in other words, as referring not prospectively to the friendship's goal but retrospectively to its causal condition: "Aristotle on the Forms of Friendship," 632–34. But even if every friendship is based partly on hopes and partly on an affection growing out of what the other is or has been, the balance is different: Aristotle stresses the priority of expectations in the lesser friendships and not in character friendships.

15. Price gives a helpful account of why loving another for who he is means, in Aristotle's philosophy, loving him especially for the moral qualities he possesses, in *Love and Friendship,* 108–10.

16. Pakaluk recognized the problem: *Aristotle,* 75–76.

17. On this point, see also *EE* 1236b27–37a2. In this admittedly obscure passage, Aristotle suggests that another who is "absolutely good" may or may not be good for oneself, and says that "a thing not good for oneself is of no concern to oneself" (1236b39). But he seems to say, both here and at 1237a18–b8, that if loving is in itself pleasant, this pleasure can be the key element that makes another who is good for himself also good to the one who loves him.

18. Of course the best men seek only a few friends, but they will so seldom find their true equals that they might well befriend each one that they meet. Cf. Plato *Lysis* 211d6–12a7.

19. Hermann Rassow, in *Forschungen über die Nikomachische Ethik des Aristoteles,* 82–83, accepts this as the whole reason for Aristotle's inclusion of the two lesser types in the category of friendship. See also Fortenbaugh, "Aristotle's Analysis of Friendship," 53.

20. A number of scholars have discussed the aptness of Aristotle's argument at *EE* 1236a16–23 that the three forms of friendship are related not as members of a common species but focally, as surgical gloves and surgical operations are related to a surgeon, the definition of the primary element, the surgeon, being implicit in the definitions of each of the others. This analysis has the virtue of bringing out the fact that the two lesser forms are related to each other by means of the primary, each resembling a different aspect of it. But as Fortenbaugh has argued, the relation between Aristotle's three forms of friendship is ultimately not a focal one in the sense of the surgical illustration he gives, since the lesser forms do not share a single function with the primary form and do not depend for their existence or for their definitions on the form and definition of primary friendship. Fortenbaugh argues that because focal analysis is not really appropriate to friendship, the *EE* fails to follow through and show how it applies to friendship, and the *NE*, being a more mature work, uses other means to show the connection of the three. In particular, he says, the *NE* brings out the ways in which the lesser forms resemble perfect friendship and share certain elements with it, such as goodwill, reciprocal affection, and awareness of one another's affection: "Aristotle's Analysis of Friendship," 57–62. As Price observes, it is difficult to evaluate the applicability of a focal analysis to friendship because Aristotle never defines sufficient conditions for cases of focal connection: *Love and Friendship,* 137. I believe, however, that a kind of complicated focal analysis may be appropriate to friendship, once we give due weight to the fact that primary friendship is a composite thing with disparate goals that are not all reducible to a single goal. Just as a court jester, a throne, and a council of ministers are all focally related to a king, though they are not all accounted for by any single goal that the king may have, so the lesser forms of friendship are focally related to primary friendship in each pursuing, in incomplete and imperfect ways, a goal pursued most wisely and effectively in primary friendship.

The more important reason for Aristotle's applying focal analysis to friendship in the *EE* but not in the *NE* is, I think, rather different. In the former, in contrast to the latter, he conspicuously leaves goodwill out of his definition of friendship (1236a14–15) and says unequivocally that goodwill is not present in the two lesser types (1241a2–5). But a class of "friendships," two members of which lack the element of goodwill that everyone recognizes as the very essence of friendship, cannot properly be treated as a single genus; the lesser friendships must then be related to one another only through their relationships to the true one. If, in the *NE*, Aristotle does seriously mean to attribute a degree of genuine goodwill to all forms of friendship, he must drop the use of focal analysis to describe the relationship of the three kinds, and this is precisely what he in fact does.

21. Burnet, *Ethics*, 356. Stewart (*Notes*, 2: 275), Price (*Love and Friendship*, 148–54), and Pakaluk (*Aristotle*, 64–65) adopt the same line of interpretation, which also finds support in *EE* 1241a1–10.

22. Recognizing this phenomenon, and taking quite seriously Aristotle's definition of friendship at *NE* 1156a2–5, Cooper makes a strong argument that Aristotle is attributing true goodwill to all forms of friendship, and he suggests that this goodwill arises out of a natural warmth that we feel for those who please or benefit us: "Aristotle on the Forms of Friendship," 623–45. Stern-Gillet (*Aristotle's Philosophy of Friendship*, 38) and Walker ("Aristotle's Account of Friendship," 184–92) also see goodwill in the lesser forms of friendship, but in a qualified way and in response to something that is peripheral to the friend's true character.

23. On the textual difficulties of these lines as we have them, see M. van Straaten and G. J. de Vries, "Notes on the VIIIth and IXth Books of Aristotle's *Nicomachean Ethics*," 198–99.

24. These qualifications are well brought out by Cooper in "Aristotle on the Forms of Friendship," 636, and by Nussbaum in *The Fragility of Goodness*, 356.

25. Cicero's Laelius expresses the same thought even more forcefully when he argues that without goodwill between men, "no house or city could stand, nor would even the tillage of the fields abide": *Laelius On Friendship* 23.

26. These include Stahr (cited by Stewart, *Notes*, 2: 280) and Gottfried Ramsauer, *Aristotelis Ethica Nicomachea*, 518. Rassow (*Forschungen*, 24) also treats them as a mere repetition.

27. Thus at b20 Burnet translates "either for pleasure simply or for pleasure to the lover, i.e., pleasure depending on a similarity," giving as an example of "pleasure simply" the pleasure a king takes at witty men, and as an example of "pleasure depending on a similarity" the pleasure a bad man may take at another bad man's vice: *Ethics*, 361. But this reading is unpersuasive, for what is truly and absolutely pleasant – what gives "pleasure simply" – is the pleasure a good man takes in complete virtue, not in mere diversion (see 1099a11–16, 1169b30–70a2, 1176a26–29, 1177a1–11); and as Aristotle has just said (1156b14–17), the former is precisely a pleasure in his own virtue or a similar virtue in one who is similar to himself. On the other hand, the pleasure that is such not absolutely but only for oneself is not necessarily based on a similarity. It may be, for example, the pleasure of dominating a weak person. Thus Burnet's two categories of that which is pleasant simply and that which is pleasant on the basis of similarity are neither mutually exclusive nor, when taken together, a comprehensive account of the sources of pleasure-friendships. On the problems of Burnet's reading, see also Geoffrey Percival, "Notes on Three Passages from the *Nicomachean Ethics*, Bk. VIII," 174; Dirlmeier, *Aristoteles*, 515; cf. 517; and van Straaten and de Vries, "Notes," 202–3, who with Dirlmeier consider similarity to be a crucial ground of friendship in Aristotle's analysis.

Following Aspasius, *Aspasii in Ethica Nicomachea Quae Supersunt Commentaria,* 19: 167, Grant (*Ethics,* 2: 257) offers a different and more interesting reading. Omitting the comma after φιλοῦντι at b20, and taking ὁμοιότητα to mean "metaphorically" or "by analogy," Grant translates, "Every friendship is for good or for pleasure, either absolute, or else relative to him who feels the friendship, and only bearing a certain resemblance to the absolutely good or pleasurable." This reading suggests a new division of friendship into true friendship and friendship by extension or analogy, as if both the true and the shadow-friendships could be found among friendships of virtue and among friendships of pleasure. Perhaps the true friendships are those based on what is simply good or simply pleasant (since these amount to the same thing), so that true friendships are as much friendships of pleasure as they are friendships of virtue. At the same time, perhaps not all friendships based on character are true friendships; those that rest on shared, mistaken notions of virtue and of what is noble (including many friendships of high-minded gentlemen) would in fact be friendships only by analogy and not friendships of the truest kind. But no doubt such an important extension of Aristotle's classification should not be based on a single phrase.

In line 22 the overwhelming weight of MS authority favors the reading of Kb and Γ – a reading that is followed by Fritzsche, Rassow, Susemihl, and Burnet – that virtuous friends are similar (ὅμοιοι) to one another. The variant reading noted by Aspasius and followed by Bywater and Grant, that to these friendships the rest are similar (ὅμοια), fits with the suggestion of a new classification of true friendships and friendships by analogy. To my mind, however, no one has made a convincing case for emending the text and rejecting the reading of the best manuscripts.

28. Francis Sparshott finds it particularly troubling that Aristotle equates friendship based on character with friendship based on virtue, and that he neglects the large class of friendships that are based on similarity of temperament and interest: *Taking Life Seriously: A Study of the Argument of the Nicomachean Ethics,* 277–78. Charles H. Kahn observes the presence of kinship (if only the literal kinship of birth) as a fourth root of friendship in Aristotle's discussion, and suggests as reason for his relative silence on this root of friendship the fact that "his theoretical concern with *philia* was oriented towards problems that involve *prohairesis* or deliberate choice: an affection based upon family connection or childhood experience is not *chosen*": "Aristotle and Altruism," 22 n. 1. I believe this fourth root is already in evidence here in Aristotle's observations about similarity.

29. In the *EE,* indeed, Aristotle writes as if the recognition of virtue is the only source of goodwill. If it were, the fact that we seem to see goodwill in most actual friendships might be explained by the fact that, as Aristotle says at *EE* 1238a35–39 and b12–14, there is some good in everyone. Hence most actual friendships are some mixture of the forms that Aristotle isolates for the sake of analysis – forms which, as John Muirhead argues, tend to be elements of most friendships, rather than truly distinct kinds: *Chapters from Aristotle's Ethics,* 179. It is possible to interpret the *NE* account along similar lines and view the goodwill actually found in virtually all friendships as due to an element of virtue and virtue-friendship

there, as Price does: *Love and Friendship,* 159. But I am inclined to think that the *NE* account represents a deeper, more subtle rethinking of the question, or at least a deliberately more probing exploration, which acknowledges more fully both the element of generosity in all friendship and the ways in which even the noblest generosity is shot through with self-concern, as we shall see in *NE* 9.8 – a chapter that is in many ways the apex of the analysis of friendship and that has no parallel in the *EE*.

30. Price is helpful in pointing out the ways in which, for Aristotle, the deepest and fullest similarity is possible only between the virtuous: *Love and Friendship,* 127–29.

31. Francis Bacon, "Of Friendship," in *Works,* 12: 165–74; cf. Cicero *Laelius* 57. This beneficial aspect of friendship, while not spelled out in such detail by Aristotle, is captured by Aristotle's term ὠφέλιμος, which Dirlmeier identifies with ἀγαθός (*Aristoteles,* 515) and van Straaten and de Vries equate with the "useful" ("Notes," 200–1), but which in fact, like the English "beneficial," nicely spans both of these meanings.

32. Bacon, "Of Friendship," in *Works,* 12: 172.

33. Ibid., 166.

34. The goodness of affection itself is the clearest instance of why Stewart (*Notes,* 2: 295) is right to criticize Rassow (*Forschungen,* 83) for simply identifying the good for oneself (αὐτοῖς ἀγαθός) with the useful (χρήσιμος): The good is what we need, and the useful merely provides the means to it.

35. For much of what follows, I am indebted to Paul Rahe's excellent discussion of Bacon in *Republics Ancient and Modern,* esp. 277–78 and 288.

36. Bacon, *Works,* 12: 249.

37. As Dirlmeier observes, Aristotle's use of friendships between witty people, turning upon the pleasures of conversation, as an example of pleasure-friendship (e.g., at 1157a3–7), helps to narrow the gap between pleasure-friendships and the highest kind: *Aristoteles,* 515.

38. For a fuller account of the differences between the characters of the young and the old, showing especially the vices of the latter, see *Rhetoric* 1389a3–90a27.

39. Cf. Montaigne's vivid indictment of the unsociability of old age (spoken from the midst of it): "Besides a silly and decrepit pride, a tedious prattle, prickly and unsociable humors, superstition, and a ridiculous concern for riches when we have lost the use of them, I find there more envy, injustice, and malice. Old age puts more wrinkles in our minds than on our faces; and we never, or rarely, see a soul that in growing old does not come to smell sour and musty" (*Essays,* 620).

40. Cf. *Magna Moralia* 1210a2–6.

41. See 1124a1–2, 29b27–30a1, 20a21–23, 26b28–31, 27a2–3, 27b33–28a4, 58a1–4.

42. Moreover, friendship involves virtue in the sense of requiring virtue for its full exercise. See Geoffrey Percival, *Aristotle on Friendship: Being an Expanded Translation of the Nicomachean Ethics Books VIII & IX,* 30. But we should go further: Friendship is in some sense a peak of the moral life, and a most revealing one. This, I think, is the answer to Dirlmeier's question at 1155a3–4: "Warum sagt er dann nicht gleich: Freundshaft ist etwas Ähnliches wie Tugend, und erspart sich das 'oder'?" (*Aristoteles Nikomachische Ethik,* 509). Aristotle does not initially rule out the possibility that friendship is a virtue because he wants us to ponder the

ways in which it represents, in fact, the pinnacle of virtue, or the best solution
to the problem of virtue.

43. Just as we cannot simply choose whom to like, so being liked in return is not
"up to us" in the way that the exercise of the moral virtues is. Aristotle does
not stress this more vulnerable side of friendship, but as Nussbaum observes,
a certain vulnerability is intrinsic to friendship understood as reciprocity: *The
Fragility of Goodness*, 354.

44. Muirhead observes that the absence of any discussion of friendship as a mean
between two extremes is the clearest sign that Aristotle does not seriously intend
for it to be understood as a virtue: *Chapters*, 169. Behind this difference is perhaps
the fact that the proper mean in such virtues as generosity, moderation, and
courage is defined by some end beyond the virtue that the virtue serves, whereas
friendship and wisdom, whose most fundamental aims are simply their own
exercise or enjoyment, are good in a more immediate and irreducible way.

45. This rendering of 1158a26 (δεῖ δ' ἴσως καὶ ἀγαθοὺς τοιούτους ὄντας, καὶ ἔτι
αὐτοῖς) follows Rassow (*Forschungen*, 83–84) and Stewart (*Notes*, 2: 295) and
most modern translators; Rassow's arguments for it are especially persuasive.
But Fritzsche (cited by Stewart, ibid.) and Grant have an interesting alternative
interpretation: "And perhaps (in seeking friends) one ought (to require) that
even good men should have this qualification (*i.e.* pleasantness), and moreover
not in a merely universal way, but relatively to oneself": Grant, *Ethics*, 2: 263.
This would allow us to take μακάριοι not as the merely rich, but in its more primary sense as the truly and completely happy – who as such cannot be lacking
wisdom.

3. Aristotle and Montaigne on Friendship as the Greatest Good

1. Jefferson to John Adams, 28 October 1813, *The Adams-Jefferson Letters*, 2: 388.
Cf., however, *NE* 1132b31–33a5, where Aristotle indicates that even in politics,
distributive justice is not in fact primary, or most essential, although according
to strict justice perhaps it should be. For whereas strict justice, as Pakaluk says,
tends to "magnify differences" in the merit of different people (*Aristotle*, 96),
what Aristotle says in fact holds the polis together is not giving to each precisely
what he deserves by merit, but commutative justice or reciprocity, which consists
of fairness in exchange, favors voluntarily given and returned, but also the
repayment of evil with evil, so that no one feels himself to be "a slave," at the
mercy of anyone else. This passage in Book 5 suggests that many of the most
important and solid elements of justice are found most fully in friendship,
whereas the present discussion of friendship and justice in Book 8 suggests that
the only friendships that work well are those that include justice, rather than
attempting to dispense with the need for it. Therefore Burnet goes too far when
he says that in justice proportion is everything, and it does not matter how great
the superiority or excess is: *Ethics*, 376.

2. As Irwin and Pierre Aubenque both point out, the transformation of one's
friend into a god would spell the end of the friendship, not merely because we,
with our particular limitations, would cease to be of interest to him, but because
he would lose interest in friendship altogether: Irwin, *Nicomachean Ethics*, 361;

Aubenque, "On Friendship in Aristotle," 24–27. See also *EE* 1245b14–15: "From the fact that god is such as to have no need of friends, one might postulate that a godlike man has no need either"; cf. *Magna Moralia* 1212b34–13a7. According to Aubenque, "It is the tragic fate of friendship that the purer it is the greater the desire for the friend's good, yet, if it is to flourish, the friends must remain as they are: neither godlike nor even wise, but simply human. Friendship tends to consume itself in the very transcendence it desires; ultimately, *the perfect friendship destroys itself*" (24). There is more than a grain of truth in this. However, as Aristotle goes on to say in the *EE* passage just quoted and also in 9.4, and as Aubenque himself points out, godlike perfection is not the perfection we seek as human beings.

3. This passage is so bold in its assertion of the primacy of self-love that it has made many commentators uneasy, and several have attempted to reinterpret it so as to soften its impact. Aspasius and Fritzsche take the statement to refer only to friends of pleasure and utility, and Aspasius seeks support for this unstated limitation in the fact that, at the start of the next chapter, Aristotle clearly is describing the common run of people: *Aspasii in Eth. Nic.*, 19: 179; see also Stewart, *Notes*, 2: 300. Burnet (*Ethics*, 377) and Irwin (*Nicomachean Ethics*, 221 and 361) go further, and interpret Aristotle to mean that the reason we do not wish our friends the happiness of becoming divine is that then they would lose the happiness of having us as friends (or of having any friends at all) – a reading justly criticized by Kahn in "Aristotle and Altruism," 21 n. 2; by Cooper in "Aristotle on Friendship," 337 n. 15; and by Pakaluk in *Aristotle*, 98. Percival goes to the opposite extreme, and interprets Aristotle to imply that we cannot wish for anything except our own good: *Aristotle on Friendship*, 43.

Jens Timmermann, in "Why We Cannot Want Our Friends to Be Gods," 209–15, following Heliodorus, *Heliodori in Ethica Nicomachea Paraphrasis*, 19: 174, makes an ingenious effort to bridge the more obvious, selfish interpretation of the passage and Burnet's more generous but less plausible one, but in the end he only muddies the waters. He translates 1159a5–8 as "This is the origin of the difficulty of whether friends really wish their friends the greatest of goods, as that of being a god; for then friends will no longer be friends to each other, and therefore no goods either; for friends are goods" (212). This much seems very good, and helps to bring out the fact that each friend desires not only the good of the other's affection but the opportunity to be a source of good to him. But Timmermann asserts without argument that friends, qua friends, must be dedicated above all to preserving the shared good that is their friendship: "They must not be so unreasonable as to destroy friendship, no matter how great the advantage for one party would be" (213). This claim disregards Aristotle's advice about the dissolution of friendships in 9.3, and leaves unanswered the question of why any sensible person *would* prefer the continuation of one friendship to wisdom, for instance, or why, if not out of self-interest, he would make such a choice for his friend.

Cooper more plausibly explains our not wishing for our friends to become gods on the grounds that we love them and wish them well as the human beings that they essentially are, and that, as Aristotle will argue in 9.4, the idea of becoming a god while remaining oneself is fundamentally incoherent: "Aristotle on the Forms of Friendship," 636–38. This seems right, but we also do not wish for our friends any other great elevation of status, even as human beings, that would end our friendship, as St. Thomas (*Commentary* 2: 738) and the context of 8.7 make clear.

4. Plutarch, who has a higher estimation of the love of honor than Aristotle, likewise shows more sympathy for the victims of flatterers, who he says are among the most honorable and decent human beings: "How to Tell a Flatterer from a Friend," 49b. This little essay provides a charming illustration of why, as Aristotle says, time and testing are so essential in finding a true friend. But it is also interesting for a different reason: It illustrates the ancients' "preoccupation with the topic of flattery and insincerity," noted by Powell (*Cicero*, 94), and the ways in which the art of flattery was carried to rather a higher degree of perfection in ancient times than nowadays, resulting in an even greater difficulty in distinguishing true from cleverly counterfeited friends. Since friendship counted for more in the ancient world, it was more fraught with pretense.

5. Pakaluk observes that the demotion of honor in 8.8 implies also a demotion of the political life: *Aristotle,* 101–2.

6. *Rhetoric* 1371a17–24 seems to suggest that being admired and honored are intrinsically pleasant.

7. Burnet brings out well the inferiority of unequal friendships as Aristotle sketches them: *Ethics,* 377.

8. See also *NE* 9.7 and esp. *EE* 1241a35–37, where Aristotle acknowledges that the balance of affection that is just, according to the schema of 8.7, is not what is in fact normally found. Pakaluk observes the problem: *Aristotle,* 103, 129.

9. In demanding such devotion from their leaders (and in so often being disappointed in this demand), the people who rule in a democracy are somewhat like the ruler Aristotle speaks of at 1158a34–36, whose demands for affection or honor make it difficult for the virtuous man to befriend him unless he is in fact the virtuous man's superior in merit as well as in power, for only then can the virtuous man freely give the affection that is demanded and thereby establish proportional equality.

10. Montaigne, "Of Friendship," in *Essays,* 136. Further quotations from Montaigne's *Essays* will be cited in the text by page number of the Frame translation.

11. J. M. E. Moravcsik explores the tension between loving for a reason and loving with the loyalty that friendship seems to demand in "The Perils of Friendship and Conceptions of the Self," 133–51.

12. On the political and philosophical context of Montaigne's and La Boétie's friendship, see Floyd Gray, "Montaigne's Friends," 203–4; Allan Bloom, *Love and Friendship,* 410–28, who emphasizes and perhaps exaggerates the thoroughly rational and philosophical character of this friendship; and Michael Platt, "Montaigne, Of Friendship, and On Tyranny," who stresses the opposition of friendship as such to tyranny as such. In contrast, David Lewis Schaefer brings out the interesting problem that if indeed the "Memoir on the Edict of January 1562" that is presumed to be La Boétie's really is his, Montaigne and La Boétie must have had an important disagreement of opinion on the question of religious toleration, which Montaigne favored and which the memoir as we have it opposes: "Montaigne and La Boétie," 3, 3 n. 5, 27–28 n. 73.

13. Price gives a trenchant criticism of Montaigne's refusal to give grounds for his friendship in *Love and Friendship*, 13.
14. Cicero *Laelius* 37.
15. Bloom, *Love and Friendship*, 414–18.
16. Ibid., 419.
17. Bloom and Platt both see in this account of a friendship echoes of Abraham's encounter with God. Bloom finds in Montaigne's comments about his daughter an assertion that "he would never participate in a sacrifice of Isaac," and a reminder that "God is not a friend, partly because he cannot be known": Ibid., 417. Platt hears in Montaigne's line "because it was he, because it was I" an echo of God's words to Abraham, "I am that I am": "Montaigne, Of Friendship, and On Tyranny," 57.
18. See Platt's argument that the main tyrant depicted in "On Voluntary Servitude" is really the biblical God, in ibid., 61–65.
19. This oft-quoted ancient saying was attributed to Chilo, one of the proverbial seven sages, by Gellius (*Attic Nights* 1.3.30) and to Bias, another of the seven sages, by Aristotle (*Rhetoric* 1389b24), Diogenes Laertius (*Bias* 1.87), and Cicero (*Laelius* 59).
20. Immanuel Kant, "Friendship," in *Lectures on Ethics*, 206, 208; but cf. *The Metaphysical Principles of Virtue*, 138–39.
21. Montaigne, following Diogenes Laertius *Aristotle* 5.20, attributes this saying to Aristotle, but Aristotle himself cites it only as a common proverb: *NE* 1168b7. ·
22. Paul Rahe argues that the chief purpose of the essay on friendship is also to stress the rarity of perfect friendship, so as to encourage us to be self-sufficient and to involve ourselves with others only cautiously: "Don Corleone, Multiculturalist," 144–47.
23. There is some dispute as to the true authorship of the essay. Schaefer and Daniel Martin argue that it was probably or likely written by Montaigne himself: Schaefer, "Montaigne and La Boétie," 4–30; Martin, "Montaigne, Author of *On Voluntary Servitude*, 127–88.
24. Or is his account of this friendship an exaggeration and idealization of the truth, as has been argued by Floyd Gray in "Montaigne's Friends," 204–8, or indeed wholly fictitious, as Schaefer hints in *The Political Philosophy of Montaigne*, 342?
25. Montaigne's interspersing of claims about the inconclusiveness of all philosophy with arguments that philosophers have invariably used rhetorical covers to protect themselves certainly suggests the possibility that he himself may have chosen skepticism as a cover for views even more likely to bring down the wrath of the Catholic Church: See esp. "Apology for Raymond Sebond," in *Essays*, 370–80. But it is also quite possible that, as Schaefer argues in *The Political Philosophy of Montaigne*, 114–52, 203, and 243–44, Montaigne was a genuine skeptic on questions of metaphysics, even while he envisioned a new role for philosophy in governing human conduct. See also Montaigne, *Essays*, 707–8.
26. Montaigne's rejection of Socratic dialectic shows, at the least, that he did not resolve the question in the way that Socrates did: See *Essays*, 79; Schaefer, *The Political Philosophy of Montaigne*, 121, 247–48.

27. Cf. 139 with 309–10, where Montaigne repeatedly uses such expressions as "I know not what," "I know not how," and "this cannot be expressed."

4. Friendships in Politics and the Family

1. See, e.g., Euripides *Orestes* 735.
2. Sparshott, unwilling to face the implications of this statement for all friendships, tries to maintain that it does not apply to virtue-friendship, where he insists no justice is needed at all: *Taking Life Seriously*, 280–81.
3. President Bill Clinton expressed this notion of universal human obligations when he said that "the world has a responsibility to see to it that children in Cambodia can get to school in safety" (PBS *News Hour*, May 15, 1996).
4. See esp. *Politics* 1265a1–b16, 1276a24–30, and 1325b33–26b25. See also Bernard Yack, *The Problems of a Political Animal: Community, Justice, and Conflict in Aristotelian Political Thought*, chap. 4, which emphasizes the limits of political friendship even for fellow citizens in a small polis.
5. For a full examination of passages in both the *NE* and the *EE* that might seem to leave open the possibility of friendship between men and gods, see Dirlmeier, *Aristoteles*, 521.
6. Compare, for example, the account of the army's goals at 1160a16–18 with the statement at 1115b10–13 that the overriding aim of the courageous soldier should be to do what is noble. Stewart (*Notes*, 2: 303–4), following Zell and Fritzsche, and Burnet (*Ethics*, 382) are clearly uneasy at the omission of the noble from the account of the city's aims in 8.9, and seek to rectify this account by introducing Aristotle's statement at *Politics* 1278b21–24 that the city aims at living nobly.
7. Susemihl, *Aristotelis Ethica Nicomachea*, 186; Bywater, ed., *Aristotelis Ethica Nicomachea*, 169.
8. This perspective is adopted by Grant, *Ethics*, 2: 275.
9. Wayne Ambler, "Aristotle's Understanding of the Naturalness of the City," 163–85.
10. Cf. *EE* 1245b27–32. Vlastos, struck by this powerful acknowledgment of such a powerful form of love, doubts that Aristotle ever reconciles his recognition of such selfless and undemanding love with his portrait of the *highest* form of love as friendship between equals that is pursued as good for both: *Platonic Studies*, 6. I think the answer is that Aristotle sees both the sacrifice *and* the self-love inherent in the maternal love he describes, and at the same time, taking εὐδαιμονία as his standard, rightly refuses to take such impressive but unfortunate cases as paradigms of human excellence.
11. Kahn brings out well the paradoxical connection between maternal selflessness and mothers' strong sense of the children as their own: "Aristotle and Altruism," 22.
12. Stewart, *Notes*, 2: 308.
13. On the connection between the celebration of manliness and the subordination of women and even the family in classical Greece, see esp. Hannah Arendt, *The Human Condition*, 30–31, 48 n. 38, 72–73; and Rahe, *Republics Ancient and Modern*, 31–37.

14. See, e.g., *Politics* 1334a11–b5, 1338b9–16. Salkever helpfully brings out the extent of Aristotle's critique of this ranking of the virtues in "Women, Soldiers, Citizens," 165–90.

15. For an excellent discussion of this justification of slavery, see Ambler, "Aristotle on Nature and Politics: The Case of Slavery," 390–410.

16. St. Thomas, who reproduces perfectly so many of the ambiguities in Aristotle's text, says both: *Commentary* 2: 754, 759.

17. This is, for example, the view taken by Fortenbaugh in "Aristotle on Slaves and Women," 138, but opposed by Arlene Saxonhouse in "Family, Polity, and Unity: Aristotle on Socrates' Community of Wives," 208.

18. Saxonhouse observes both of these ambiguities in ibid., 208–9.

19. Of course Aristotle may have been just thoughtlessly using a common saying, as most commentators assume. But if the hypothesis that he wrote carefully leads us to interesting insights that make us more thoughtful ourselves, is that not good reason for suspecting him of thoughtful writing?

20. See esp. lines 552–56. Mary Whitlock Blundell brings out well Ajax's problematic view of reason in *Helping Friends and Harming Enemies: A Study in Sophocles and Greek Ethics*, 68–69.

21. On the similarity between Tecmessa and Odysseus, see ibid., 103.

22. Only the prospect of insanity is unbearable to him, at least initially: At the opening of the play, he recoils in horror from the sight of even an enemy gone mad. Although he seems to have come to terms with his vulnerability to every external misfortune and even death, he perhaps still feels an unjustified pride and confidence in the soundness of his own mind. He does relent when Athena insists that he face this prospect as well. Yet his reasons are not her reasons. The issue for him is facing every truth; the issue for her is triumphing over an enemy.

23. Nussbaum, in exasperation at what she takes to be Aristotle's lack of seriousness about the question of women's nature, charges that, "had he devoted to the psychology of women, or even to their physiology (about which he makes many ludicrous and easily corrigible errors) even a fraction of the sustained care that he devoted to the lives and bodies of shellfish, the method [of working from common opinion] would have been better served": *The Fragility of Goodness*, 371. Perhaps, however, this very anomaly in a thinker usually so omnivorously curious is a sign of something else at work.

24. On the extent of the husband's authority in classical times, see esp. Fustel de Coulanges, *The Ancient City*, 85–94. As Rahe brings out in *Republics Ancient and Modern*, 31, women's subordination and domestic confinement was even more complete in the classical period than it was before or afterward.

25. Ramsauer, Percival, and H. Rackham, uneasy with this frank admission that the superior partner claims greater benefits for himself, bracket the word ἀγαθόν, although it appears in all the manuscripts, Rackham arguing that it is only "a larger share of affection" and not greater benefits that superiors justly claim and receive (*Nicomachean Ethics*, 494 note b). But Aristotle's statement here is really only a more direct acknowledgment of what he has already indicated at 1160b13: that even or especially the most noble-minded rulers insist that the best should receive the greatest rewards in accordance with their merits.

26. As Judith Swanson observes, the opportunity to exercise one's own reason as much as one is able is absolutely central to the concept of happiness developed in Book 1 (1097b22–98a12): *The Public and the Private in Aristotle's Political Philosophy,* 53.

27. On the father's claim to be the sole source of good, see also Fustel de Coulanges, *The Ancient City,* 39 and 57. Aristotle generally seems to assume that fathers provide the form and mothers only the matter in generation (*NE* 1161a17; *Generation of Animals* 727b31–33), but cf. *Politics* 1262a14–18.

28. Saxonhouse indeed suggests that the prerogatives of husbands were seen by Aristotle as chiefly or entirely ceremonial, and perhaps based on no greater capacities at all, in "Family, Polity, and Unity," 206.

29. Salkever argues that Aristotle did seek to elevate the status of women, as part of his project of strengthening a private realm that could counterbalance, soften, and civilize the tendencies of an excessively warlike and politically charged public life; he understands Aristotle's promotion of philosophy as part of the same project: "Women, Soldiers, Citizens," 183–87. If Aristotle's chief goal were to cultivate better-rounded human beings, and to move gentlemen in the direction of the cultivated, balanced self-sufficiency that we see, for example, in the heroes of Jane Austen's novels, then it certainly would be reasonable to seek to elevate the dignity of women and the family. I believe that Salkever errs, however, in understanding Aristotle's promotion of philosophy to have been a *means* to social improvement, rather than his constant and overriding *end* that informed all of his practical proposals, even at the political or sub-philosophic level. Indeed, it may have been Aristotle's paramount concern with philosophy that stopped him from advocating radical reform of the practice of keeping women confined, uneducated, and dull. This practice had the effect of liberating men's erotic longings from women, and Plato's *Symposium* gives an intriguing look at the range of objects, from boys' bodies to battlefield heroism to philosophy, upon which this eros came ultimately to land.

30. It is this tension that Swanson fails sufficiently to consider in arguing that, for Aristotle, the quiet, private life of women may in fact make them better suited than men for philosophy: *Public and Private,* 61–65.

31. In the *Politics* Aristotle argues that societies dominated by a large number of citizens of a middling condition, as would be found in a timocracy, are the most stable and the least prone to civil discord: 1296a7–9, 1318b6–17; see also Salkever, *Finding the Mean: Theory and Practice in Aristotelian Political Philosophy,* 87–88.

32. Indeed, the friendless state of tyrants puts to the test and reveals the true meaning of Aristotle's statement that no one would choose to live without friends, even if he had everything else good (1155a5–6). The tyrant-interlocutor of Xenophon's *Hiero* paints a vivid picture of the miseries of his friendless state (3.1–4.2; 5.1–2); yet still he chooses to live without friends, rather than not to live.

33. Bacon, "Of Friendship," *Works* 12: 167–68.

34. Ostwald, *Nicomachean Ethics,* 226 n. 18; H. Rackham, trans. and ed., *The Nicomachean Ethics,* 474 note a.

35. Cf., however, 1179a24–32, where Aristotle does leave open the possibility that the gods care for and benefit in some way men who are like themselves. But the fact that this statement contradicts Aristotle's other statements about the gods, and that it comes at the very end of his book, in a passage so clearly intended to make one last recommendation for the life of virtue to men who are not yet wholeheartedly convinced that it is good on its own terms, suggests that this statement is to be taken less seriously than the others.

5. Cicero's *Laelius*: Political Friendship at Its Best

1. Montaigne, *Essays,* 139–40; Cicero *Laelius* 36–37. Unless otherwise indicated, all further references to Cicero are to the *Laelius,* and will be cited in the text by section number, with quotations taken from the Falconer translation.
2. For more historical background on Laelius's life, see Powell, *Cicero,* 8–12. For a discussion of Tiberius Gracchus and his political program, see ibid. 97–98 and the references cited there.
3. This speech has been variously read as a source of practical advice and a compendium of late republican commonplaces, handed down from various philosophical schools (esp. by Powell, in *Cicero*) or as a source of historical knowledge about actual Roman social practices: see, e.g., P. A. Brunt, "Amicitia in the Roman Republic"; Konstan, *Friendship in the Classical World,* 130–37. But rarely if ever have scholars taken it seriously as an original and carefully written work of philosophy. Their failure to do so is related to their tendency to regard the dialogue form and framing stories as nothing more than elegant literary devices (e.g. Powell, ibid., 75), and to view Laelius as merely Cicero's mouthpiece (e.g., Thomas H. Habinek, "Towards a History of Friendly Advice: The Politics of Candor in Cicero's *de Amicitia,*" 167; A. E. Astin, *Scipio Aemilianus,* 9). Once we consider that the conventional and sometimes contradictory opinions of Laelius are not necessarily all Cicero's own, and indeed that the most important character in the dialogue may be the thoughtful young Cicero who listens silently, the possibilities for interpretation grow much richer.
4. To the extent that he does speak of friendship's utility, Laelius gives a more gentlemanly version of Socrates' earthy praise of friendship in Xenophon's *Memorabilia* 2.4.5–7.
5. Cicero *On Duties* 1.50–58; 1.157–58.
6. See Plutarch *Sulla* 8; Powell, *Cicero,* 77.
7. As Astin points out, the portrait we have here of Laelius is not intended to be strictly historical in its presentation either of Laelius's character or of his views, any more than Plato's presentation of Socrates is meant to be. But Astin's skepticism gives way to a common naïveté when he assumes that the views that are not necessarily the historical Laelius's *are* necessarily Cicero's: *Scipio Aemilianus,* 9.
8. What is more, after attributing to Laelius's son-in law Scaevola the augur the opinion that Laelius was wise, Cicero immediately casts a shadow over the augur's judgment by giving first place for acumen and judgment not to him but to another mentor of Cicero's, Scaevola the pontiff (1).
9. Cf. 20.71. On the need to fabricate equality where it does not exist, see also Habinek, "Towards a History of Friendly Advice," esp. 180, and Eleanor Leach, "Absence and Desire in Cicero's *De Amicitia,* 14–15. The problem raised by

Habinek of the delicacy of full mutual frankness when two friends are true equals and rivals for the same offices and honors helps explain why a friendship such as Laelius's with Scipio was so rare, in contrast to those of clients and patrons. On the other hand, friendships of public men with private ones, such as Cicero's with Atticus, would likely have functioned more smoothly. But Habinek seriously misunderstands Cicero when he fails to take seriously the latter's claim that the fundamental criterion for determining the relative worth of two friends is not political power but virtue and wisdom.

10. See esp. Cicero *Republic* 1.30–33; cf. Montaigne's remarkably similar assessment of theoretical studies in "Of Pedantry" and "Of the Education of Children," in *Essays*, 97–131.

11. Powell observes the tension: Laelius's argument that friendship is not rooted in neediness, and that the best and most self-sufficient men make the best friends, "squares rather badly with sections 44, 52-55, and 88, where he says that life without friends is hardly tolerable" (*Cicero*, 94).

12. This passage paraphrases Euripides' *Hippolytus* 253ff. It is spoken there by the nurse, who seems to approve these strictures and yet follows none of them. See also Powell, *Cicero*, 102.

13. Epicurus, Letter to Menoeceus 128; Principal Doctrines 3 and 18; fragment B60, in *Epicurus: The Extant Remains*, ed. Cyril Bailey. Unless otherwise noted, all fragments from Epicurus are my translations based on the text of this edition.

14. Vatican Saying 33; Principal Doctrine 21; fragment B59; Vatican Saying 58. See also fragment 523 in *Epicurea*, ed. Hermann Usener, 318–19, where Epicurus is quoted as saying that no form of community is natural to human beings at all.

15. Fragment B11; cf. Letter to Menoeceus, 128; Cicero *Tusculan Disputations* 3.41.

16. Letter to Pythocles 85; Principal Doctrines 5, 11, 17, 28, and 33; cf. Seneca *Moral Epistles* 9.8.

17. Letter to Herodotus 76–77; see also Principal Doctrine 1.

18. Cicero *On The Ends of the Good and Bad Things* 2.79; Seneca epistle 9.8.

19. Plutarch *That Epicurus Actually Makes a Pleasant Life Impossible* 1097a.

20. See esp. David O'Connor, "The Invulnerable Pleasures of Epicurean Friendship," 175.

21. Fragment B74; Vatican Saying 78.

22. Vatican Sayings 27, 10 (quoting Homer *Iliad* 1.70).

23. Principal Doctrine 27; Vatican Saying 52; Diogenes Laertius *Epicurus* 10.9–10. See also Vatican Saying 78; A. A. Long, *Hellenistic Philosophy: Stoics, Epicureans, Sceptics*, 15, 72.

24. Plutarch *That Epicurus Actually Makes a Pleasant Life Impossible*, 1101a; Vatican Saying 28; Plutarch *Reply to Colotes* 1111b; Diogenes Laertius *Epicurus* 10.120.

25. Phillip Mitsis, "Epicurus on Friendship and Altruism," 127–53. Bernard Williams, in the title essay of *Moral Luck: Philosophical Papers 1973–80*, and Nussbaum, in *The Fragility of Goodness*, have made a similar case for the tension between the ideals of self-sufficiency and friendship in the ancient philosophers altogether.

26. O'Connor, "Invulnerable Pleasures," esp. 175. On the other hand, if, as John M. Rist reports, Epicurus advocated the rather free enjoyment of sexual pleasures, and himself had sexual relations with the wives of several of his friends, it

seems that Epicurean principles would have introduced new sources of conflict as well as removing old ones: "Epicurus on Friendship," 126–27; Plutarch *Live Unknown* 1129b; *That Epicurus Actually Makes a Pleasant Life Impossible* 1098b; Diogenes Laertius *Epicurus* 10.5–7 and 23.

27. O'Connor, "Invulnerable Pleasures," 170–73.

28. Ibid., 174; see also Cicero *On Ends* 1.65.

29. Plutarch *That Epicurus Actually Makes a Pleasant Life Impossible* 1090e; see also Diskin Clay, "Sailing to Lampsacus: Diogenes of Oenoanda, New Fragment 7," 49–59.

30. At *On Ends* 1: 53, for example, the Epicurean spokesman says that friends' affection makes life safer *and* more pleasant; cf. Plutarch *That Epicurus Actually Makes a Pleasant Life Impossible* 1097a and Vatican Saying 32. A. J. Festugière, seeing keenly the problem here, argues that friendship for Epicurus is "fully an end in itself" and even more important than quiet and peace of mind (ἀταραξία) for attaining the blessed life, ἀταραξία being merely the "indispensable condition of happiness," but positive joy being its central constituent: *Epicurus and His Gods*, 30–37.

31. Vatican Saying 23, following Usener's generally accepted emendation of this line, which reads αἱρετή for the ms. ἀρετή. As Mitsis says, the problem with the MS reading is that it is hard to see what it would mean for friendship to be a virtue for its own sake: "Epicurus on Friendship and Altruism," 129.

32. See A. A. Long and D. N. Sedley, *The Hellenistic Philosophers*, 1: 138 for the latter view. Rist makes a rather confused attempt to say that friendship is "choiceworthy for its own sake" as an immediate *means* to the acquisition of pleasure, which is the only true end: *Epicurus: An Introduction*, 132. I see no problem, however, in a hedonist's classifying as ends not only pleasure conceived abstractly but all pleasant activities: Listening to music is not a means to some separable end of pleasure but is choiceworthy as inherently pleasant.

33. Some such calculus of pleasures is suggested by Bigone's conjectural editing of Vatican Sayings 56 and 57, followed by Brad Inwood and L. P. Gerson, who translate, "The wise man feels no more pain when he is tortured [than when his friend is tortured, and will die on his behalf; for if he betrays] his friend, his entire life will be confounded and utterly upset because of a lack of confidence" (*The Epicurus Reader: Selected Writings and Testimonia*, 39). These sayings are found in the MS as a single but not intact sentence: See Bailey's note on this in *Epicurus: The Extant Remains*, 384. Mitsis argues that, especially since Epicurus believed that death was not an evil, dying for a friend in order to avoid the pain and insecurity of a friendless state might well be a sensible thing to do. But he acknowledges that Epicurus nowhere makes this justification for self-sacrifice explicit: "Epicurus on Friendship and Altruism," 128–29.

34. Vatican Saying 56.

35. Cf. Mitsis, "Epicurus on Friendship and Altruism," 135–36.

36. Rist, conflating valuing friendship for its own sake with valuing a friend for his own sake, seems not to see this: "Epicurus on Friendship," 124.

37. For an Epicurean account of how friendship may have arisen historically among human beings who at first had no need or inclination for it, see Lucretius *On the Nature of Things* 5.925–1027; cf. Konstan, *Friendship in the Classical World*, 110–11.

38. *On Ends* 2.78–81.

39. Powell, however, thinks Laelius means only that the feelings of the virtuous man should be more elastic, in that he should allow his heart to expand with joy and contract with pain at his friends' joys and sorrows, rather than remaining stonily impassive: *Cicero*, 103–4. But see Cicero *Laelius* 61, where Laelius says virtue itself should bend for a friend.

40. For a fair but uninquiring summary of Seneca's opinions about friendship, see Anna Motto and John Clark, "Seneca on Friendship," 91–99. For a synopsis of views on friendship in Stoic philosophy more generally, see Glen Lesses, "Austere Friends: The Stoics and Friendship," 57–75.

41. Seneca *Moral Epistles* 9.5; see also 6.7, 7.8, 9.10, 48.4 and Gummere's note to 48.4 on 316. Unless otherwise noted, further quotations from Seneca are taken from Gummere's translation of the epistles and cited in the text by letter and section number.

42. This he certainly advocates and seeks to do, and in particular to cultivate a "friendship" with sages of former times, perhaps especially because such a friendship is immune to the vicissitudes of fortune: *On the Shortness of Life* 14–15, in *Moral Essays*.

43. See also *On Benefits* 2.22 in *Moral Essays*: "as it is a legitimate source of happiness to see a friend happy, it is a more legitimate one to have made him so."

44. Lesses brings out well the extreme coolness of friendship that is strictly compatible with stoic self-sufficiency: It consists only in impersonal justice, a universal benevolence, and admiration for virtue: "Austere Friends," 69–75.

45. Cf. epistle 52.2; Aristotle *NE* 1170a5–8, and Chapter 10 in this volume.

46. Gellius, in *Attic Nights* 17.5, reports an ancient criticism that this passage is illogical in assuming the disputed possibility of disinterestedness in generous deeds in order to prove it in friendship. But Laelius seems with both examples to be merely appealing to his listener's intuitive understanding of human nature.

47. Leach observes the importance of politics in giving weight to Ciceronian friendship, and also the fact that the pressures of political life create an especially keen desire for a constant, loyal friend. Yet she expresses surprise that Cicero presents the greatest ambition as crowding out the concern for friendship: "Absence and Desire," 10–11; see also Cicero *Letters to Atticus* 1.18.1.

48. Perhaps seeing the tension between these different statements, Powell (*Cicero*, 85) argues that the injunction to "put friendship before all things human" merely means that one should rank friendship higher than other *external* or physical goods. But this qualification is not in the text.

49. Cf. Bacon, "On Friendship," in *Works* 12: 174.

50. Cf. 42, 89. See also *On Duties* 2.51, where Cicero insists that a judge should never be partial to his friends, but makes the surprising concession that, when called upon to plead for friends who are in trouble, "we need not have scruples against undertaking on occasion the defense of a guilty person, provided he be not infamously depraved and wicked. For people expect it; custom sanctions it; humanity also accepts it. It is always the business of the judge in a trial to find out the truth; it is sometimes the business of the advocate to maintain what is plausible, even if it be not strictly true."

   Powell, who finds this argument "muddled," thinks Cicero at *Laelius* 61 is excusing somewhat those who join friends in schemes of wrongdoing, against what he says at 42 and 89: *Cicero*, 107–8. But probably Laelius means only to excuse what Cicero excuses in *On Duties*: a bending of principles for the sake of saving a friend's life or reputation when the friend is in dire straits. Still, I agree with Powell that Laelius seems unclear on just where to draw the line in bending the demands of justice.

51. Cf. Xenophon *Memorabilia* 2.4.

52. The depth of Laelius's concern with honor is indicated, I think, by his tendency to exaggerate the extent to which Scipio, and he as Scipio's friend, are likely to remain prominent in the minds of Romans and of all posterity. As Powell observes, Laelius seems to overstate both the glory of Scipio's youthful exploits and the esteem in which he was held at the time of his death, and also exaggerates the passions, whether for good or for ill, that Roman benefactors and traitors living three centuries before Laelius were still capable of arousing in Romans of his own time: Powell, *Cicero*, 81, 83. Of course, as Leach observes, Laelius's efforts to preserve and burnish Scipio's reputation would also serve to make his own lasting fame more likely: "Absence and Desire," 16.

6. Quarrels, Conflicting Claims, and Dissolutions

1. For a good treatment of the technical problems involved in 8.13–8.14, see Pakaluk, *Aristotle*, 133–48.

2. Cf. 1124b9–15, *Rhetoric* 1398a24–26.

3. Pakaluk is almost the only commentator to recognize a genuine source of conflict for character-friendships in this competition, and he also observes that other possible sources are outlined in 9.1–9.3. But he thinks that the problem of competition over the noble is sufficiently resolved by Aristotle's teaching, in 9.8, that everyone ought to prefer himself to others (*Aristotle*, 133–37), whereas I do not think that this teaching wholly solves the problem of moral competition either in theory or in practice.

4. Cooper, "Aristotle on the Forms of Friendship," 626.

5. As Bernard Yack observes, this passage has seldom-recognized implications for civic friendships, which, being one type of utilitarian friendships, also range from the relatively "contractual" to the relatively "ethical," and are prone to the problems of ethical friendships. Political communities that are more frankly utilitarian and that rest on relatively explicit agreements about what everyone owes one another are often more stable and less prone to disagreements than are the friendships among citizens who expect a higher level of self-sacrifice from one another, whereas republics that are the most serious about virtue are often more turbulent: *Problems of a Political Animal*, 114–18.

6. See also Grant, *Ethics*, 2: 276.

7. If we understand such a reevaluation of conventional morality to be pointed to by the *NE*, although clearly not explicitly carried out there, this may provide the key to the problem of disunity in the book so perceptively described by Ackrill in "Aristotle on *Eudaimonia*," esp. 32–33.

8. Commentators have observed the artificiality of the book division here (which Rassow attributes to a later editor), and have tried to account for it by such things as the desire to make all the books of the *Nicomachean Ethics* similar in length: Rassow, *Forschungen*, 25 n. 2; Grant, *Ethics*, 2: 280; cf. Stewart, *Notes*, 2: 334–35.

9. Pierre Aubenque calls the early chapters of Book 9 a "casuistry" of friendship ("On Friendship in Aristotle," 23), and W. F. R. Hardie accuses Aristotle of falling into "platitude" in these chapters (*Aristotle's Ethical Theory*, 322).

10. There is some disagreement as to what passage this phrase refers to – Dirlmeier, for example, cites 1165a5–12 (*Aristoteles*, 541) – but the only suggestion that fits is 1162b23–25, as Ramsauer argues (*Aristotelis*, 589–90). Hardie also considers these five chapters to constitute a single section: *Aristotle's Ethical Theory*, 322.

11. Stewart, *Notes*, 2: 340; see also Plato *Protagoras* 328b1–c2.

12. It is worth noting that as Aristotle sketches different possible conflicts of obligation, he does not include any obligation to act utterly without regard to persons, or in a way that is motivated only by pure duty and not by such sentiments as gratitude and affection, as Nancy Sherman observes in a helpful summary of the difference between Aristotelian and Kantian views of obligation in *The Fabric of Character: Aristotle's Theory of Virtue*, 119–24.

13. Tolstoy gives a wry account of this phenomenon in his description of Vronsky's gentlemanly code of conduct, according to which Vronsky makes magnificent gifts and displays his freedom from pettiness in gambling freely and paying debts of honor promptly, but lets his debt to his tailor go unpaid month after month: *Anna Karenina*, Part 3, Chapters 19–20.

14. Pakaluk, *Aristotle*, 157.

15. Cf. *Politics* 3.12.

16. There are considerable disputes as to the correct text of this line, but none of the proposed emendations would change the basic meaning – or the ambiguity – of the passage. See Stewart, *Notes*, 2: 349–50.

17. The possibility of friendship on the basis of similarity between bad people is acknowledged more openly at *EE* 1238a32–35, 39b17–23, and *Magna Moralia* 1209b34–36.

18. Cf. Cicero *Laelius* 76–78.

19. Kosman makes the interesting observation that not only Platonic and Aristotelian love, in which one loves for a reason, but even Christian "agape," or "unconditional love," fails to live up to "our pre-reflective paradoxical demands that love be charitable and unconditional, yet not independent of features of the beloved that the lover recognizes and values": "Platonic Love," 56–57.

20. Søren Kierkegaard, *Works of Love: Some Christian Reflections in the Form of Discourses*, 59.

21. On the difficulties of loving another on command, see Immanuel Kant's *Groundwork of the Metaphysic of Morals*, 67, where he interprets the biblical command as requiring only charitable action and not feeling; Oswald Hanfling, "Loving My Neighbor, Loving Myself," 148–51; and Stern-Gillet, *Aristotle's Philosophy of Friendship*, 39–40.

7. Friends as Other Selves

1. In discussing both this chapter and 9.8, modern commentators tend overwhelmingly to frame the issues in terms of the concepts of "egoism" and "altruism," and to ask whether and in what way Aristotle's treatment of friendship acknowledges the possibility of altruism. But even Thomas Nagel, who gives the classic contemporary treatment of the concept of altruism, observes that the question of the

possibility of altruism, as a "general, passionless motivation" that regards oneself as "merely one individual among many," is "not clearly posed" by Aristotle: *The Possibility of Altruism,* 1, 11, 82. Or as John Benson says, in one of the few arguments made for the inappropriateness of this concept for interpreting Aristotle, "the aim of isolating a moral attitude to others that is quite free of any taint of the dear self is not his, and it is not clear why this is the appropriate standard by which to judge it" ("Making Friends: Aristotle's Doctrine of the Friend as Another Self," 61). But Benson goes too far in the other direction when he suggests that in Aristotle's view, one never exerts oneself for another until the other becomes somehow "one's own" and one has "expanded the boundaries" of one's self to include his good (62–63). If this were the case, it would be impossible to account for the acts of kindness that precede and generate friendship. Granting Benson's very important proviso regarding the alien concepts with which the idea of altruism is freighted, I think that the "altruism" question *is* relevant to *NE* 8–9 to this extent: It is an important question whether Aristotle thinks human beings can and should act for the sake of another's good when doing so is contrary to their own good – and, *pace* Benson, Aristotle does acknowledge the possibility of such conflicts throughout his discussion, especially in 8.13–8.14 and 9.8.

2. The words τῶν πρὸς ἑαυτὸν in 1166a2, which I have translated "those that one has toward oneself," have been variously interpreted to refer to the dispositions (Burnet, *Ethics,* 409), the relations (Ostwald, *Nicomachean Ethics,* 252), or the features of friendship that one has toward oneself (Irwin, *Nicomachean Ethics,* 245). Although Burnet is reluctant at this point to interpret Aristotle as referring to affection for oneself when he has not yet discussed the possibility of friendship with oneself, van Straaten and de Vries argue, I think rightly, that the existence of affection or love for oneself has nowhere been called into question; the only question will be whether such self-love can appropriately be characterized as friendship: "Notes," 223.

I think Kahn and Dennis McKerlie are right that this claim is not or not chiefly a claim about the psychological origins of friendship as growing out of a temporally prior self-love, but is essentially a claim about the close parallelism between men's concern for others and their deeper but fundamentally similar self-concern. Or as Richard Kraut says, "friendship towards others 'comes from' self-love in the sense that the latter provides the paradigm case of the attitudes characteristic of the former": Kahn, "Aristotle and Altruism," 22–23; McKerlie, "Friendship, Self-love, and Concern for Others in Aristotle's Ethics," 90–91; Kraut, *Aristotle on the Human Good,* 132; cf. Pakaluk, *Aristotle,* 165–67.

3. Cf. Plato *Lysis* 214c6–d1.

4. As Hardie points out, the analogy between the single soul and friendship regarding the sharing of pleasures and pains is only a loose one. We can never precisely feel another's pain, or "sympathize" with our own: *Aristotle's Ethical Theory,* 324–25.

5. It is a failure to understand the absolute centrality of wisdom for all of virtue that leads Alasdair MacIntyre to assume that Aristotle's claims about the unity of the virtues must have been just an exaggeration: *After Virtue,* 147.

6. Grant (*Ethics,* 290–91) and Irwin (*Nicomachean Ethics,* 367–68) see the tension between 7.8 and 9.4 on this point, but cf. Stewart, *Notes,* 2: 364.

7. C. F. J. Martin, in a very interesting article, tries to give a much less morally freighted reading of the μεταμέλεια (regret or remorse) with which the wicked are said to suffer: "On an Alleged Inconsistency in the *Nicomachean Ethics* (IX,4)," 188–91. Unlike most commentators, Martin sees how much is at stake. If Aristotle really means to say that all the wicked suffer remorse and "civil war" within their souls (1166b19), then Aristotle is indeed agreeing with the Platonic dictum that virtue is happiness – and that in some important way, all vice is involuntary. Martin seeks to save Aristotle from this allegedly un-Aristotelian conclusion. But unlike Stewart, who tries to preserve Aristotle's consistency by taking 1166b2–29 to refer only to the morally weak and not the truly wicked (*Notes*, 2: 364), Martin argues that Aristotle is discussing precisely the wicked in this passage, and implicitly dividing them into the "run of the mill" wicked and the "thoroughly bad." He suggests that at b7–11 Aristotle is drawing an analogy between the "run of the mill" wicked and the incontinent. Just as the latter chooses the pleasant but harmful, instead of what seems good for himself, so the former, through a lack of energy and daring, fails to pursue with consistency the *immoral* projects – such as bold seductions and thefts – that he believes would be good for him. This suggestion is intriguing and persuasive, but Martin fails to spell out the full consequences: Such a man is likely not only to regret the failure of his schemes but also to have a certain moral regret or self-reproach for his deficiency in the virtues that he in fact respects.

Martin goes on to argue that the man of unbridled, ruthless energy and cleverness will be free of such unsteadiness of purpose. He, too, will have regrets, but only regrets for the fact that he is hated by others, especially since he has a special need of companionship. This seems to me inadequate. Why would such a man have any special need for company if he did not wish to flee the haunting sense that he is despicable even in his own eyes?

In sum, I think Aristotle is not inconsistent in his own thought but is revealing progressively deeper layers of his own thinking. Hardie seems much closer to the mark when he says that "even the man who is relatively single-minded in pursuing bad or inadequate ends is likely to despise himself at times, at least if he sees that others despise him": *Aristotle's Ethical Theory*, 325. I should only add that no one – at least no one who is "all there" – is wholly single-minded in pursuing bad or utterly selfish ends.

8. Joachim cites this discussion of the inner wholeness (and, by implication, the relative self-sufficiency) of the wise man as one instance of the way in which "the life of action contains in itself . . . features which point onwards to their own more perfect fulfillment in the life of thought, . . . [and] the life of thought admits of being exhibited as the extension and fuller realization of some leading characteristic or characteristics in the life of action," a development which he says Aristotle's treatment of friendship especially reveals: *Commentary*, 242.

9. γενόμενος δ᾿ ἄλλος αἱρεῖται οὐδεὶς πάντ᾿ ἔχειν ἐκεῖνο τὸ γενόμενον (ἔχει γὰρ καὶ νῦν ὁ θεὸς τἀγαθόν) ἀλλ᾿ ὢν ὅ τι ποτ᾿ ἐστίν· δόξειε δ᾿ ἂν τὸ νοοῦν ἕκαστος εἶναι ἢ μάλιστα. Susemihl, following a tendency among editors to reject as spurious or emptily redundant the lines that contain so many of Aristotle's most striking thoughts, brackets this whole sentence (*Aristotelis Ethica Nicomachea*, 203–4); and Ramsauer (*Aristotelis*, 596–97) brackets most of it, although all the manuscripts contain it. Vermehren and Bywater, much less drastically, bracket ἐκεῖνο

τὸ γενόμενον, but still without clear justification: Bywater, *Aristotelis Ethica Nicomachea*, 185. As Burnet nicely brings out (*Ethics*, 411), the slight awkwardness of this phrase reflects the difficulty of speaking about *oneself* becoming another being and that *other being* enjoying the good. The phrase ἀλλ' ὢν ὅ τι ποτ' ἐστίν has also caused controversy. My translation follows the punctuation suggested by Grant (*Ethics*, 2: 289) and followed by Bywater, Burnet, and such modern translators as Ross and Irwin, but most earlier commentators read the phrase as referring to god: "for as it is, the god has the good, but only as the being that he is." Stahr, for example, then goes on to interpret the whole sentence to mean almost the opposite of what most more recent scholars and I have taken it to mean. He translates, "Ein Jeder wünscht sich aber das, was für ihn ein Gut ist; wird er aber ein Anderer, so wird kein Mensch wünschen, dass das neue, so entstandene Wesen noch Alles das fortbehalte, was es in seinem früheren Zustande besass. Freilich hat die Gottheit auch heute noch das absolut Gute in sich, aber eben nur darum, weil sie ewig ist, was sie ihrem Wesen nach ist" (quoted by Stewart, *Notes*, 2: 358). In other words, Stahr understands Aristotle to mean that one *would* wish to become a different sort of being, but in that case, one would not wish that being to possess one's present goods but, rather, good things appropriate to it. This reading cannot be absolutely ruled out, but it contains no such original and profound thought as the sentence does when taken as Grant suggests.

10. This crucial qualification on our love of the good seems to me to be the real reason for Aristotle's bringing up the divinity at this point, which Pakaluk argues is unnecessary for establishing the thesis that we wish for our own existence and preservation: *Aristotle*, 171–72.

11. Montaigne, *Essays*, 254, 385.

12. Stewart, *Notes*, 2: 359–60; Burnet, *Ethics*, 411.

13. Bernard Williams makes perhaps the best case that can be made for the centrality of body to personal identity (although this is still not to show that it is the true core of the self) in chap. 1 of *Problems of the Self: Philosophical Papers 1956–1972*.

14. See esp. *Politics* 1253a7–18.

15. Plato *Republic* 329c3–4.

16. On the other hand, the discussion of thought and passion in *De Anima* may also contain a distortion, in failing to account for the independent desire for knowledge.

17. On the problem that moral virtue and prudence both look to the other to provide specific content and direction for action, see especially 1106b36–7a2, 1109a24–30, 1144a6–9, 1144b21–24, 1145a4–7, and Tessitore, *Reading Aristotle's Ethics*, 42–47. Gauthier and Ackrill also recognize a problem and argue that Aristotle failed adequately to explain why the principles that practical wisdom recognizes as right really are the right principles: Gauthier, "On the Nature of Aristotle's *Ethics*," 28; Ackrill, "Aristotle on *Eudaimonia*, 29–31.

18. Sir David Ross (*Aristotle*, 232), Dirlmeier (*Aristoteles*, 542) and Kahn ("Aristotle and Altruism," 29–30) view both the presentation of the mind as the true self in 9.4 and the discussion of self-love in 9.8 as deliberate preparation for the discussion of philosophy as self-sufficient happiness in Book 10. The *EE*, which does not close with such a discussion, has no such emphasis upon mind as the

true self, as Kahn observes (28). But in contrast to Kahn, who argues that it is the mind taken as a whole that Aristotle identifies as the true self in every case, and Rist, who argues that it is theoretical wisdom that he consistently has in mind (*Human Value: A Study in Ancient Philosophical Ethics*, 47–49), Cooper makes a good case that there is a tension between the treatment of theoretical intelligence as our core in Book 10 and the suggestion in the earlier books that it is practical wisdom or the mind broadly understood that is each man's real self (*Reason and Human Good in Aristotle*, 168–80). Indeed, Aristotle in Book 10 depicts the mind as so pure and godlike that we must wonder why such a mind would even engage in political philosophy, let alone stoop to ruling the passions and solving practical problems. Here again, we have perhaps a rhetorical exaggeration, and Aristotle leaves it to us to think through just what mix and balance of concerns the wisest practical mind, embedded in a mortal human being, would have.

19. Stewart, *Notes*, 2: 353.

20. This description of the friend as another self could be understood as applying only or chiefly to the friendships of good men, since it is these that Aristotle is discussing in the immediate context. But Pakaluk (*Aristotle*, 173) takes the description as applying to all friendships, and even providing the common thread between the different types of friendship explored in Book 8. If Pakaluk is right that every friend is in some sense another self, this would lend further support to the idea that goodwill is a feature of every friendship.

21. Irwin tries to show that another person can be fully another self inasmuch as he can be loved just as one loves oneself and for just the same reasons: "If Al loves himself, he does not value simply his spatio-temporal uniqueness.... If he is a virtuous person Al does not love his character for its idiosyncrasies.... Al loves himself since he loves his character as a particular correct way of realizing human capacities in rational agency.... [His virtuous friend] Ann is another Al in so far as she has what Al loves about himself." Irwin begins by denying (correctly) that we love *simply* our spatio-temporal uniqueness, and he ends by implicitly denying (absurdly) that we have any special concern for ourselves as particular, unique beings at all: *Aristotle's First Principles*, 396. Aristotle's suggestion in 9.4 that we love ourselves only insofar as we find ourselves virtuous does lend some color of plausibility to Irwin's position, but it is a position that flies in the face of all the rest of Books 8 and 9, especially 1155b24–25, 1159a12–13, and all of 9.7–9.8.

22. The essential element of separateness in the image of the friend as "another self" is lost sight of by many commentators. Seeking a perfect harmony between self-concern and concern for a friend, they characterize friendship as a blurring or obliteration of boundaries between two people. Thus Ross (*Aristotle*, 230–32) characterizes Aristotle's theory of friendship as "an attempt to break down the antithesis between egoism and altruism by showing that the egoism of a good man has just the same characteristics as altruism" (231); he says that the good man loves an expanded self that has extended its concerns to include the well-being of another (cf. also Muirhead, *Chapters*, 183). Ross does not really make clear, however, whether the good man pursues the friend's good as an independent end – in which case, his "altruism" will qualify and not simply constitute

a part of his "egoism" – or whether he pursues his friend's good merely as a part of his own – in which case, there is really no friendship for the other as another. Benson and Elijah Millgram are clearer. Both view the friend merely as an extension of self, or even, as Millgram says, a part of oneself – thus making of friendship, as Stern-Gillet aptly puts it, merely an "enlarged narcissism": Benson, "Making Friends," 58–61, 63; Millgram, "Aristotle on Making Other Selves," 361–76, esp. 375; Stern-Gillet, *Aristotle's Philosophy of Friendship*, 44. As Nussbaum argues, loving another as part of an expanded self, a part whose good is wholly comprehended in one's own, is not friendship; this is the relation of master to slave, but a friend must be loved as an independent end: *The Fragility of Goodness*, 355. Loving another as an independent end, for his own sake, means neither expanding one's personal boundaries to include the other as part of oneself, nor simply expanding one's happiness to encompass another's happiness (although this does happen and is important), but more precisely, extending one's *concerns* and *wishes* to encompass the happiness of the other, or in other words, extending them to an object other than one's own personal happiness. The happiness of the other that one thus comes to care about often contributes substantially to one's own happiness, but it also has the potential to conflict with one's own.

23. Grant (*Ethics*, 2: 290) and Stewart (*Notes*, 2: 362) read ἢ ἐστὶ δύο ἢ πλείω ἐκ τῶν εἰρημένων (1166a35–b1) as meaning "insofar as two or more of the above-mentioned criteria are present." The alternate reading that I follow, "insofar as man consists of two or more parts, as has been said," is supported by parallel passages in the *EE* (1240a8–22) and *Magna Moralia* (1211a33–34), and accepted by Bywater: *Contributions to the Textual Criticism of Aristotle's Nicomachean Ethics*, 63. It is rejected by Grant and Stewart on the sole grounds that the words τὰ εἰρημένα are used in a different sense in 1166b2. This consideration hardly seems decisive. Burnet (*Ethics*, 413) raises the obvious objection to their reading: Why *two* or more of the criteria?

8. Goodwill, Concord, and the Love of Benefactors

1. Cicero *Laelius* 26–28.
2. That the reciprocal, mutually known goodwill that seemed to constitute friendship in 8.2 now turns out to fall short of friendship should occasion no surprise: see Pakaluk, *Aristotle*, 178. For Aristotle has increasingly revealed the absolute centrality of activity to friendship.
3. See, for example, Aristotle *Politics* 1306a6–10; Thucydides 8.93.
4. *Heliodori in Ethica Nicomachea Paraphrasis*, 19: 196.
5. Even political friendships of virtuous men are not, as such, virtue-friendships, as Yack reminds us, since their central aim is not to foster the virtuous flourishing of the friends but to secure, in the community at large, such things as life and prosperity, and, at most, the useful preconditions that help others attain a virtuous flourishing: *Problems of a Political Animal*, 110–14.
6. Pakaluk especially questions the relevance of concord for Aristotle's treatment of friendship as a whole: *Aristotle*, 180–81. But cf. 162–65, where he gives a good account of how this and the surrounding chapters may fit together.

7. The proper understanding of this sentence in the Greek has in fact been a source of some dispute, but as van Straaten and de Vries argue ("Notes," 226), the reading I have followed is the most straightforward and the only one that works in the context.

8. Benson and Millgram both argue that this dynamic is the explanation of why friends love one another as "other selves." According to Millgram, "Aristotle believes that one makes one's friends in the most literal sense" – that people make friends with one another only by forming one another, and come to love one another as the products of their own benevolent action: "Aristotle on Making Other Selves," 361; cf. Benson, "Making Friends," 50–68. Some such dynamic is doubtless at work in the deepest and most enduring friendships, especially those that begin in youth. But Millgram gives short shrift to the importance of gratitude in engendering love, and more seriously, to the presence of another as a like-minded companion (and hence another self) in activity that is chosen for its own sake, activity that is more choiceworthy than productive activity, and as Aristotle will show in 9.9, is more truly of the essence of friendship.

9. See, e.g., Stewart, *Notes,* 2: 273, and Ostwald, *Nicomachean Ethics,* 259, who translates τῷ δὲ παθόντι οὐδὲν καλὸν ἐν τῷ δράσαντι as "but the recipient finds nothing noble in the giver." The irrationality of this statement persuades me that the first τῷ here in 1168a11 and the one in the line before must be taken as datives of advantage and the participle τῷ δράσαντι as referring to the action. See also Price, *Love and Friendship,* 115–16.

10. St. Thomas, seeing the troubling shadow it casts over noble action to concede that it is not as pleasant in anticipation as in retrospect, struggles to avoid the natural implications of this last sentence: *Commentary,* 2: 820.

11. I cannot help thinking that Shakespeare, because he was so wise, would have enjoyed his writing even if his work had never been read: His plays must have been for him, as they are for us, fascinating explorations of human problems and types, executed with such a spirit of lightness that they can only have been a pleasure to write.

9. Self-Love and Noble Sacrifice

1. I am indebted to Vasilis Politis, "The Primacy of Self-Love in the *Nicomachean Ethics,*" 153–74, for so clearly distinguishing the two separate arguments Aristotle is making here: first, that one ought to love one's true self as much as possible, and second, that one ought to love oneself in preference to all others. Politis seeks but fails to find a compelling path from the first to the second. I agree, at least, that Aristotle does not demonstrate the second proposition as fully as he does the first. He shows that loving oneself as much as possible is good because it is characteristic of the noblest men and clearly conducive to their happiness, and he also shows that the opposite view – that one should not love oneself – is based on a misunderstanding. With the second proposition, Aristotle shows that preference for self is in fact characteristic of the noblest souls and, as Pakaluk argues (*Aristotle,* 189–90), is not unreasonable, but Aristotle does not and perhaps cannot show that preference for self is essential to virtue in the same way that seriousness about one's true good is essential.

He does not try to argue that a being that preferred others to itself would not be noble, but he does help us see why it would not be human. By deliberately blurring these two arguments, Aristotle is able to emphasize the ways in which self-love is morally good, and leave in the background the less pleasing but perhaps ultimately more significant consideration that preference for self is simply an inescapable fact of human life.

2. Consider 1108b1–7, where, at the end of his first catalogue of the virtues, Aristotle defines righteous indignation as a mean between envy and spite. Having thus indicated the dubiousness of such a passion, he silently drops it from his canon of virtues in Books 3–5. On this interesting "mean" that is not a virtue, see Ronna Burger, "Ethical Reflection and Righteous Indignation: *Nemesis* in the *Nicomachean Ethics*," 127–39.

3. Stern-Gillet argues that the man who makes a noble sacrifice is not in any sense acting with a view to getting the best for himself, and that the best thing, moral nobility, accrues to him only incidentally, as a kind of unintended by-product of action that is done for the friend's sake: *Aristotle's Philosophy of Friendship*, 70–71. Pakaluk (*Aristotle*, 201) follows the same line. Stern-Gillet immediately goes further, however: Seeking to avoid the idea that the real motivation for a virtuous act is any personal concern at all, she argues that the virtuous friend "desires *the* good rather than *his own* good"; the real motivating force becomes a kind of Kantian dedication to the "impersonal requirements of morality." This is a possible way of understanding virtuous action, but it is, as we shall presently see in detail, certainly not Aristotle's.

4. Hardie is right to observe that an early death may not, in fact, be the best thing for one's own happiness, especially if happiness requires a complete life (1098a16–20) and turns out to consist chiefly in contemplation: *Aristotle's Ethical Theory*, 329–34. Similarly, McKerlie argues that while the nobility of any virtuous act contributes something to happiness, Aristotle fails to prove that this increase in happiness will outweigh any and all harm the act may do to the one who performs it, but that he "refuses to admit" the contrary: "Friendship, Self-Love, and Concern for Others," 92. Arthur Madigan is also troubled by the absence of a full explanation of why and how *every* noble action can be seen as the very best for the one doing it: "*Eth. Nic.* 9.8: Beyond Egoism and Altruism?" 77–80. I think a stronger case can be made for this position than these commentators acknowledge. According to Aristotle's view of moral virtue, it is not open to a virtuous man to pick and choose when to be virtuous. Being virtuous (in contrast to merely performing some virtuous acts) means being consistently virtuous and acting out of a settled, deeply ingrained disposition that habitually chooses what is noble just because it is noble. If this is so, yet virtue is the indispensable core of happiness, then it is best for oneself always to act virtuously, even if this leads to an early death. Stern-Gillet gives a Spinozistic version of this argument in *Aristotle's Philosophy of Friendship*, 107–15.

But Pakaluk provides the basis for an interesting objection to this argument. The nobility in question in 9.4 is the nobility of voluntarily giving up something *for a friend,* and acts demanded by justice, being obligatory, are not really done for another individual's sake; thus true acts of generous self-sacrifice must be those rare acts of supererogatory beneficence that justice does not demand and that the virtuous man is free not to do if they are bad for him: *Aristotle*, 196–97. This seems sensible, but in fact, Aristotle makes no such distinction between obligatory and supererogatory noble acts. Nor does it seem reasonable that he should, if noble activity is not an unfortunate necessity, like taxes, but is the chief substance of happiness.

I believe Hardie is right that in the final analysis, Aristotle himself does not equate happiness with a life of heroic risks and sacrifices. While he honors the active moral life, it is the tranquil life of philosophy he ranks highest. But the moral hero, as Aristotle presents him, does make this equation. Aristotle's crucial point in 9.8 is that somehow, in the moment of choosing, the *hero* must believe that his action is best for himself – even if he simultaneously believes it to be a sacrifice.

5. Cf. *Politics* 1277b25–30, where Aristotle says that it is only in ruling and not in being ruled that the virtue of practical wisdom is exercised, and 1325a16–b32, where he argues that the desire to be as active as possible naturally leads to the desire to rule over others – unless, in fact, contemplation is more truly active than ruling is.

6. Machiavelli, *Discourses on Livy*, 1.16.

7. Irwin, clearly uncomfortable with this language of competition, suggests that perhaps in this sentence, ἁμιλλάομαι should be taken in its less common meaning of "to strive": *Nicomachean Ethics*, 370. St. Thomas likewise softens the language: *Commentary*, 2: 830.

8. St. Thomas, in one of his few explicit additions to his explanatory restatement of Aristotle's argument, says that the noble man will give away opportunities for noble action "particularly... when the opportunity remains for him to do the same or greater deeds at another time": Ibid., 831.

9. Modern commentators such as Politis and Stern-Gillet are, I think, insufficiently attuned to the essentially competitive quality of moral nobility because they think of moral virtue in terms of following certain rules, rather than in terms of a desire to be as active as possible in the most splendid and sovereign way. Kraut, who has a better sense than most commentators of the way in which moral seriousness naturally seeks *political* expression and influence, sees more clearly the competitiveness of moral virtue: *Aristotle on the Human Good*, 83, 90–99; but cf. 115–23. See esp. 98 n. 27, where Kraut cites, in addition to *NE* 1094b7–10, 1099a32–b2, 1177b16–17, and 1178b1–3 as evidence that moral virtue, at its fullest, requires the greatest equipment and power. Interestingly, it is in Book 10, where Aristotle discusses the limitations of the life of moral action, that he makes its dependence on power and equipment most explicit.

10. Aristotle expresses this criticism of the heroic outlook with great delicacy, and he leaves it to us to put it together with what he shows in 8.13–8.14 about the deep incoherence of all such angry demands as Achilles' for gratitude and honor. A more explicit attack on Achilles would not have been constructive. Since the life of virtue must ultimately take its sights either by self-sacrificing heroes or by sober philosophers, and since few if any of us can be sufficiently inspired to make the most of ourselves by the cool example of the philosopher alone, Aristotle is loath to broadcast too loudly his critique of the heroes who combine so many genuine virtues with such ignorance of their own hearts. This is a good

illustration of the way in which Aristotle was an eminently political and politically responsible writer. While all of his ideas are there for anyone to see and ponder, he says some things emphatically and others more softly, the relative volume of his arguments being in direct proportion not to their philosophic significance but to their practical value, to their likelihood of making the world a better place in which to live for everyone, including philosophers.

11. Engberg-Pedersen, with certain well-founded reservations as to whether this is really Aristotle's position, argues that the "reason" Aristotle is or should be thinking of in 9.8 is a reason that teaches us to consider things as our thinking bee does. Reason, in his view, "does not ordain acts with a view to the good of any particular person," but is bent merely on furthering the good of "the community of humans involved as a whole": *Aristotle's Theory of Moral Insight*, 46. Madigan rightly stresses, in criticizing Engberg-Pedersen's "anachronistic" interpretation, that Aristotle's view of both mind and the noble is eminently personal, something belonging to the individual and satisfying him as an individual: "Beyond Egoism and Altruism," 87. Stern-Gillet, seeing the force of this criticism, nevertheless tries to justify dying for the sake of a friend in terms of a "universalizability" within the restricted community of a circle of virtuous friends: *Aristotle's Philosophy of Friendship*, 109. She never explains, however, why only a friend and not a virtuous stranger has a moral claim to be treated as equally important as oneself, or why, if he is only "equally" important, "the preventable loss of a primary friend should be avoided at all costs," including the loss of oneself (113), or finally, why his being more valuable to the community at large should give him a greater claim to live than one has oneself (112), if the community as a whole has no such direct claim upon one's life. Thus she imports a modern concept of duty to explain what is, in Aristotle, not a duty at all but a freely chosen sacrifice.

12. Price gives a clear account of the contradictions involved in noble self-sacrifice according to Aristotle, but he places the blame on Aristotle for having "stumbled" into self-contradiction: *Love and Friendship*, 110. Unfortunately, he never offers an alternative account of the moral self-understanding that avoids this contradiction. Politis argues more persuasively that Aristotle is indeed denying the possibility of moral self-sacrifice and doing so with perfect consistency: "Primacy of Self-Love," 170. Politis, however, perhaps gives insufficient weight to the importance of sacrifice in the common understanding of what makes virtuous action noble, as is seen in the way the very noblest actions tend to evoke tears, a sense of tragedy, and a sense that they deserve the greatest honors or recompense. Although the discussion of the moral virtues in the early books of the *Ethics* stresses this side of nobility less than the tragic poets do, it is still present in crucial ways. Thus Politis fails to see the extent to which 9.8 offers a major reinterpretation of the character of nobility, even as it has hitherto been presented in the *Ethics*.

13. Kraut spells out how such competitions could be adjudicated so that everyone, keenly desiring as much nobility as possible but also being committed to justice, would take only his fair share of the noble and help his fellows to get their fair share of opportunities for noble action too: *Aristotle on the Human Good*, 126–27. The question is whether the kind of friendly, fair rivalry he describes would not

utterly change its character once everyone involved in it acknowledged that 1) every act of virtuous "sacrifice" is really a gain from the highest perspective; 2) acts of virtuous "sacrifice," being best for the one doing them, deserve no reward or praise; and 3) when friends allow one to benefit them, they are really doing one a favor.

14. Madigan sees a deep tension between the image in 9.8 of the mind as enjoining a self-sacrificing nobility and the mind in Book 10 as seeking pure contemplation. So troubled is he by this tension, and by the unanswered question of how exactly self-sacrificing nobility is good for oneself, that he wonders whether Aristotle might be simply reiterating a view of nobility that he takes from the Greek heroic tradition in 9.8, and in Book 10 developing a wholly unrelated view of nous that comes from the pre-Socratics and Plato: "Beyond Egoism and Altruism," 84. The problem Madigan raises is an important one. But if, as I suggest, the chapters culminating in 9.8 are meant to provide a dialectical path leading from the heroic Greek ethos to a better understanding of virtue, then there need be no conflict between the true teaching of 9.8 and that of Book 10.

15. It is interesting that Aristotle here uses the word "fatherland" (the most characteristic object for which men give up their lives) for the first time in the *NE*. In his entire discussion of courage in Book 3, Aristotle conspicuously avoided using the word or otherwise acknowledging the obvious fact that citizen courage is most fundamentally good as a means to the country's freedom and survival: To acknowledge this would be to acknowledge that the most impressive moral virtue is not, as the noble mind has to view it, an end in itself (cf. 1177b2–26). It is only in the spirit of friendship, and not in the spirit of nobility as such, that one can truly make the good of others one's end.

16. Fragments of possible support for this view may be found at 1145a6–9, 77b1–78a8, and *EE* 1249b17–23.

17. Cooper, *Reason and Human Good in Aristotle*, 172–73.

18. Ibid., 172.

19. D. J. Allan reads Aristotle in this way: "Every point confirms the impression that Aristotle does not think it psychologically possible for a man to choose otherwise than in his own interest, and is seeking . . . to say what really happens when men *appear* to subordinate their interest to that of another. . . . Self-interest, more or less enlightened, is assumed to be the motive of all conduct and choice": *The Philosophy of Aristotle*, 187 and 89. Millgram concurs: "Aristotle's explanations of friendship are uniformly self-oriented" ("Aristotle on Making Other Selves," 376).

20. McKerlie, who tries to reconcile this position with true friendship, falls into incoherence as he tries even to describe as a possible position the "egoistic eudaimonism" that would include loving another as an end. The man who was determined to act only for his own good, and who wanted a happiness that turned out to include friendship, or acting for the sake of others, would be required to forget and indeed directly violate his purpose and principles in order to achieve them: "Friendship, Self-Love, and Concern for Others," 85–86.

21. Kahn, "Aristotle and Altruism," 26.

22. Hardie considers this argument a decisive refutation of what he calls "psychological hedonism": *Aristotle's Ethical Theory*, 326.

23. A full appreciation of the importance of truly spontaneous concern for others seems to be what is missing from Kahn's otherwise good account of the motivations of friendly actions in the first half of "Aristotle and Altruism." Kahn sees that in the best cases, friends both act for *one another's* sakes and pursue friendship because friendship is a component of *their own* happiness, but he gets into trouble when he tries to make each man's need for friendship the *reason* for his loving the other for his own sake. It is a contradiction in terms to love another as an end for the sake of happiness or of anything else, as Kraut observes in *Aristotle on the Human Good,* 136–37. The only way out of this contradiction is to say that while we pursue friendships in order to be happy, these friendships merely strengthen or call into play our natural, preexisting disposition to feel goodwill and affection for others. It may be for our sakes that we choose to cultivate rather than uproot such goodwill and affection, but in themselves, the goodwill and affection are not for the sake of anything. Thus the reasons Aristotle will give for the importance of friendship in 9.9 will not, as Kahn says, provide "a reason for wanting the welfare of others for their own sake" ("Aristotle and Altruism," 30–31), but merely a reason for encouraging, rather than opposing, such a want.

24. This seems to be the view that J. O. Urmson is groping toward in *Aristotle's Ethics,* 115–16. As he puts it, one may sacrifice one's life for a friend on the grounds that "one would despise oneself for ever after if one did not," but it is only "because one values him for his own sake that it would be sordid not to make the sacrifice." Urmson does not do justice to Aristotle's argument that the noble man loves himself most of all, but he is right to stress that an uncalculating love of the other for his own sake must underlie any rationally chosen sacrifice.

25. Bernard Williams makes this argument very effectively in *Problems of the Self,* chap. 15.

26. Aristotle's student Theophrastus expresses a similar thought in his lost treatise *On Friendship:* "When the interests of a friend are put into the balance with our own honor in matters of equal importance, or nearly so, our own honor unquestionably turns the scale; but when the advantage of a friend is far greater, but our sacrifice of reputation in a matter of no great moment is insignificant, then what is advantageous to a friend gains in importance in comparison with what is honorable for us, exactly as a great weight of bronze is more valuable than a tiny shred of gold": quoted or paraphrased by Gellius in *Attic Nights* 1.3.25.

10. Friendship in the Happy Life

1. Benson recognizes the problem. He remarks that in taking the unity of the virtuous soul as a standard in 9.4, Aristotle "leaves the unfortunate impression that what is good about friendship is nothing different from what is good about the virtuous life of the individual," and concludes that the arguments of 9.4 and 9.8 are somewhat at cross-purposes with what he takes to be Aristotle's true teaching about the centrality of friendship in the best life: "Making Friends," 65.

2. See 1099b1–3, 1123b18–20, *Rhetoric* 1360.

3. Michael Ephesius, Commentary on the Ethics, 20: 511.

4. On the various ways in which good friendship depends on good fortune, see especially Nussbaum, *The Fragility of Goodness*, 359–60.

5. The irony of Socrates' claim to envy the boys' friendship is observed by Gadamer: *Dialogue and Dialectic*, 9.

6. This benefit of learning about oneself from others is, however, not dependent on the other's being a friend or even a personal acquaintance, as Irwin observes: *Aristotle's First Principles*, 614 n. 6.

7. Thus Stewart says that it is only by thinking in universal terms that we can fully understand ourselves – only by considering his actions as the actions of "all good men" can the virtuous man see them for what they are: *Notes*, 2: 386.

8. The parallel discussion in the *Magna Moralia* at 1213a7–27 makes clear that the value of friendship for self-knowledge depends on the presence of bias, passion, and poor judgment – limitations that St. Thomas considers universal (*Commentary*, 2: 836) but that Aristotle does not.

9. Hardie, with some justification, charges that Aristotle does not bring out with sufficient clarity the difference between the ways in which a friend can be aware of his own activities and thoughts, and the ways in which he can be aware of those of a friend, and that he thus obscures the distinction between direct and vicarious experience: *Aristotle's Ethical Theory*, 331–32.

10. See also *Rhetoric* 1381b23–5, where Aristotle suggests that an honorable rivalry is a grounds for friendship in itself.

11. On the educational power of affection, see esp. Nussbaum, *Fragility of Goodness*, 362–63.

12. This need for support in the moral life is perhaps the reason why, as Benson complains, Aristotle's remarks in this passage "introduce a rather heavy didacticism into a relationship that should be a source of pleasure": "Making Friends," 59. The sense of lightness and joy that we sense should characterize friendship at the peak is perhaps not wholly available so long as friendship is subordinated to moral concerns.

13. Cf. *EE* 1244b1–21; Stern-Gillet, *Aristotle's Philosophy of Friendship*, 133–37 and 141–42; Cooper, "Friendship and the Good in Aristotle," 310–15; and Rist, *Human Value*, 56–57. Stern-Gillet struggles somewhat unsuccessfully to resist the conclusion that friendship will be more important for the less fully developed than for the most self-sufficient. Cooper notes that Aristotle's arguments for the necessity of friendship all point to human weakness, but he doubts that such weakness is ever overcome, even by the best men. Rist goes further, and does see friendship as being especially characteristic of the "second-best" human type, the man of practical rather than theoretical wisdom.

14. Cooper, "Friendship and the Good in Aristotle," 290–302. Burnet, *Ethics*, 428–30, provides a good account of the logical progression of this complex argument, dividing it into two prosyllogisms and three syllogisms.

15. I am indebted to Christopher Bruell for pointing out the importance of the concept of determinacy or limitedness in this argument.

16. Grant, *Ethics*, 2: 305; see also Burnet, *Ethics*, 430.

17. McKerlie argues that in bringing out the centrality for our own happiness of perception of ourselves and our own activities, and the centrality for friendship of perception of the friend and his activities, Aristotle is giving further credence

to the idea that the friend is another self, and is naturally loved in much the same way and for much the same reason that one loves oneself: "Friendship, Self-Love, and Concern for Others," 95–98. This is substantially true, but McKerlie goes much too far when he claims that for Aristotle, "friendship is an equal to self-concern" (97). It is because self-love is so predominant that its extension to others must be justified in terms of it, and not merely shown to be similar to it.

18. Kahn attributes to Aristotle just such an illusion when he interprets him to believe that the friendship of wise men is a perfect unity because both are infused with a single, eternal mind. He is quite right to concede that such a reading requires the importation of ideas not present in the text: "Aristotle and Altruism," 34–40. For a good critique of this argument, see Benson, "Making Friends," 56–58.

19. Cf. *EE* 1245b4–9: "Therefore friends should contemplate together and feast together, not on food and necessary things (for such a partnership does not seem to be real community but mere enjoyment), but each wishes to share the end that he is capable of attaining, or failing this, people choose most of all to benefit and be benefited by their friends."

20. If what is the very best and also most shareable in our common life with others turns out to be conversation or shared thinking, this is further support for Joachim's suggestion that what is best in the life of action points forward to the life of philosophy: *Commentary*, 242. Or, as Burnet says, *pace* Hardie, it is "φιλία and φιλία alone that can bridge the gulf between φρόνησις and σοφία, the practical and the theoretical life": Burnet, *Ethics*, 345; Hardie, *Aristotle's Ethical Theory*, 332–33.

21. Jacques Derrida, *The Politics of Friendship*.

22. In considering the exclusiveness of true friendship, Irwin makes the interesting observation that it is *only* in the discussion of friendship that Aristotle gives a reason for caring about the good of another (which justice requires) for the other's sake; the other-regarding aspects of justice and all of the virtues are grounded, insofar as they are grounded at all, only in friendship, yet true friendship seems to be exclusive: *Aristotle's First Principles*, 397–406. The problem is a real one and suggests that a reconsideration of Book 5 in the light of Books 8 to 10 would be necessary to uncover Aristotle's final teaching on justice.

23. 1171a15–17; cf. 1108a27–30, 1126b11–27a12.

24. ᾧ φίλοι, οὐδεὶς φίλος (Diogenes Laertius *Aristotle* 5.21), evidently a corruption of *NE* 1171a15–16. Much less is there warrant for attributing to Aristotle, as Montaigne and Derrida do, the saying that must be a corruption, in turn, of this one, "O my friends, there is no friend": Montaigne, *Essays*, 140; Derrida, "The Politics of Friendship," 632. This last corruption involves merely the substitution of ὦ for ᾧ.

25. Irwin observes the problem. Puzzled by Aristotle's suggestion that the noble man will *not* embrace the opportunity to confer upon his friend the opportunity to help him, Irwin says, "Aristotle does not seem to pursue the full implications of his own views here": *Nicomachean Ethics*, 373.

26. Isocrates remarks, indeed, that many even of those who are kind to their friends in misfortune are unable truly to rejoice with them in their good fortune

(*To Demonicus* 26); and Xenophon observes the frequency of such envy also, though he says that those who feel it are not wise (*Memorabilia* 3.9.8).

27. Xenophon *Memorabilia* 2.7, 1.6.14.
28. Or, at least, revolving around the supposition that we are sharing pleasures and activities (οἶς οἴονται συζῆν), which is the reading of most manuscripts at 1172a8, although not that of Kb. Stewart (*Notes*, 2: 401), Ostwald (*Nicomachean Ethics*, 271), and others have tried to emend or reinterpret it, clearly troubled by its unsettling implications. But perhaps Aristotle does mean to hint that in our direct consciousness of our own activities and pleasures and our indirect perceptions of and surmises about our friends' activities and pleasures, we suppose that we share them more fully than we really do. If Aristotle is suggesting that in the final analysis all pleasures and activities exist only in and for individual and fundamentally separate souls, this line may anticipate his arguments about the superiority of the self-sufficient philosophic life in Book 10.
29. See esp. *Politics* 1253a1–18.
30. Pierre Aubenque brings out well the way in which friendship, even or especially in the best lives, is able to unite the desire for active engagement with the world and the desire for completeness or wholeness in one's own life, of which the true friend has become an integral and stable part: "On Friendship in Aristotle," 25–27.

Bibliography of Modern Works and Editions

Ackrill, J. L. 1980. "Aristotle on *Eudaimonia*." In *Essays on Aristotle's Ethics,* ed. Amélie Rorty. Berkeley: University of California Press.

Adkins, Arthur W. H. 1963. "'Friendship' and 'Self-Sufficiency' in Homer and Aristotle." *Classical Quarterly* n. s. 13: 30–45.

Ahrensdorf, Peter. 1994. "The Question of Historical Context and the Study of Plato. *Polity* 27: 113–35.

Alfarabi. 1892. *Alfarabi's Philosophische Abhandlungen, Aus dem Arabischen Übersetzt.* Edited by F. Dieterici. Leiden: E. J. Brill.

Allan, D. J. 1952. *The Philosophy of Aristotle.* Oxford: Oxford University Press.

Ambler, Wayne. 1985. "Aristotle's Understanding of the Naturalness of the City." *Review of Politics* 47: 163–85.

————. 1987. "Aristotle on Nature and Politics: The Case of Slavery." *Political Theory* 15: 390–410.

Annas, Julia. 1977. "Plato and Aristotle on Friendship and Altruism." *Mind* 86: 532–54.

Arendt, Hannah. 1958. *The Human Condition.* Chicago: University of Chicago Press.

Aspasius. 1889–93. *Aspasii in Ethica Nicomachea Quae Supersunt Commentaria.* Vol. 19 in *Commentaria in Aristotelem Graeca,* ed. Gustavus Heylbut. 24 vols. Berlin: Georgii Reimeri.

Astin, A. E. 1967. *Scipio Aemilianus.* Oxford: Clarendon Press.

Aubenque, Pierre. 1998. "On Friendship in Aristotle." *South Atlantic Quarterly* 97: 23–28.

Bacon, Francis. 1861. *The Works of Francis Bacon.* Edited by James Spedding, Robert Ellis, and Douglas Heath. 14 vols. Boston: Brown and Taggard.

Badhwar, Neera Kapur, ed. 1993. *Friendship: A Philosophical Reader.* Ithaca, N.Y.: Cornell University Press.

Barkas, Janet L. 1985. *Friendship: A Selected, Annotated Bibliography.* New York: Garland.

Benson, John. 1990. "Making Friends: Aristotle's Doctrine of the Friend as Another Self." In *Polis and Politics: Essays in Greek Moral and Political Philosophy,* ed. A. Loizou and H. Lesser. Aldershot, Eng.: Avebury.

Bloom, Allan. 1993. *Love and Friendship.* New York: Simon and Schuster.

Blosser, Philip, and Marshell Bradley, eds. 1997. *Friendship: Philosophical Reflections on a Perennial Concern.* 2d ed. Lanham, Md.: University Press of America.

Blundell, Mary Whitlock. 1989. *Helping Friends and Harming Enemies: A Study in Sophocles and Greek Ethics.* Cambridge: Cambridge University Press.

Boas, George. 1953. "Ancient Testimony to Secret Doctrines." *Philosophical Review* 62: 79–92.

Bodéüs, Richard. 1993. *The Political Dimensions of Aristotle's Ethics.* Translated by Jan Edward Garrett. Albany, N.Y.: SUNY Press.

Bolotin, David. 1979. *Plato's Dialogue on Friendship: An Interpretation of the* Lysis, *with a New Translation.* Ithaca, N.Y.: Cornell University Press.

———. 1982. "Response" to review by Stewart Umphrey. *Interpretation* 10: 423–29.

———. 1998. *An Approach to Aristotle's Physics: With Particular Attention to the Role of His Manner of Writing.* Albany, N.Y.: SUNY Press.

Broadie, Sarah. 1991. *Ethics with Aristotle.* New York: Oxford University Press.

Brunt, P. A. 1988. "Amicitia in the Roman Republic." In *The Fall of the Roman Republic and Related Essays.* Oxford: Clarendon Press.

Burger, Ronna. 1991. "Ethical Reflection and Righteous Indignation: *Nemesis* in the *Nicomachean Ethics.*" In *Essays in Ancient Greek Philosophy.* Vol. 4: *Aristotle's Ethics,* ed. John P. Anton and Anthony Preus. Albany, N.Y.: SUNY Press.

Burnet, John. 1900. *The Ethics of Aristotle.* London: Methuen and Co.

Bywater, Ingram. 1892. *Contributions to the Textual Criticism of Aristotle's Nicomachean Ethics.* Oxford: Oxford University Press. Reprint, New York: Arno Press, 1973.

———. ed. 1894. *Aristotelis Ethica Nicomachea.* Oxford: Clarendon Press.

Carpenter, Edward. 1902. *Ioläus: An Anthology of Friendship.* London: George Allen & Unwin Ltd.

Chroust, Anton-Hermann. 1973. *Aristotle: New Light on His Life and on Some of His Lost Works.* 2 vols. London: Routledge & Kegan Paul.

Cicero. 1913. *On Duties.* Translated by Walter Miller. Cambridge, Mass.: Harvard University Press, Loeb Classical Library.

———. 1923. *Laelius On Friendship.* Translated by W. A. Falconer. Cambridge, Mass.: Harvard University Press, Loeb Classical Library.

———. 1928. *Republic.* Translated by Clinton Walker Keyes. Cambridge, Mass.: Harvard University Press, Loeb Classical Library.

———. 1931. *On the Ends of the Good and Bad Things.* Translated by H. Rackham. Cambridge, Mass.: Harvard University Press, Loeb Classical Library.

———. 1945. *Tusculan Disputations.* Translated by J. E. King. Cambridge, Mass.: Harvard University Press, Loeb Classical Library.

Clay, Diskin. 1973. "Sailing to Lampsacus: Diogenes of Oenoanda, New Fragment 7." *Greek, Roman, and Byzantine Studies* 14: 49–59.

Cooper, John M. 1975. *Reason and Human Good in Aristotle.* Cambridge, Mass.: Harvard University Press. Reprint, Indianapolis: Hackett, 1986.

———. 1977. "Aristotle on the Forms of Friendship." *Review of Metaphysics* 30: 619–48.

———. 1977. "Friendship and the Good in Aristotle." *Philosophical Review* 86: 290–315.

———. 1980. "Aristotle on Friendship." In *Essays on Aristotle's Ethics,* ed. Amélie Rorty. Berkeley: University of California Press.

Coulanges, Fustel de. [1864]. *The Ancient City.* Garden City, N.Y.: Doubleday Anchor Books.

Derrida, Jacques. 1988. "The Politics of Friendship." Translated by Gabriel Motzkin. *Journal of Philosophy* 85: 632–44.

———. 1997. *The Politics of Friendship.* Translated by George Collins. London: Verso.

Diels, Hermann, ed. 1951–52. *Die Fragmente der Vorsokratiker.* 3 vols. 6th ed. revised by Walter Kranz. Berlin: Weidmann.

Dirlmeier, Franz. 1967. *Aristoteles Nikomachische Ethik, Übersetzt und Kommentiert.* Berlin: Akademie-Verlag.

Düring, Ingemar. 1957. *Aristotle in the Ancient Biographical Tradition.* Göteborg: Elanders Boktryckeri Aktiebolag.

Easterling, Pat. 1989. "Friendship and the Greeks." In *The Dialectics of Friendship,* ed. Roy Porter and Sylvana Tomaselli. London: Routledge.

Eden, Kathy. 1997. "Hermeneutics and the Ancient Rhetorical Tradition." In *The Rhetoric Canon,* ed. Brenda Schildgen. Detroit: Wayne State University Press.

Engberg-Pedersen, Troels. 1983. *Aristotle's Theory of Moral Insight.* Oxford: Clarendon Press.

Enright, D. J., and David Rawlinson. 1991. *The Oxford Book of Friendship.* Oxford: Oxford University Press.

Epicurus. 1887. *Epicurea.* Edited by Hermann Usener. Leipzig: Teubner.

———. 1926. *Epicurus: The Extant Remains.* Edited and translated by Cyril Bailey. Oxford: Clarendon Press.

———. 1994. *The Epicurus Reader: Selected Writings and Testimonia.* Edited and translated by Brad Inwood and L. P. Gerson. Indianapolis: Hackett.

Festugière, A. J. 1955. *Epicurus and His Gods.* Translated by C. W. Chilton. Oxford: Basil Blackwell.

Fortenbaugh, W. W. 1975. "Aristotle's Analysis of Friendship: Function and Analogy, Resemblance, and Focal Meaning." *Phronesis* 20: 51–62.

———. 1977. "Aristotle on Slaves and Women." In *Articles on Aristotle.* Vol. 2: *Ethics and Politics,* ed. Jonathan Barnes, Malcolm Schofield, and Richard Sorabji. London: Duckworth.

Friedländer, Paul. 1964. *Plato.* Translated by Hans Meyerhoff. 3 vols. Vol. 2: *The Dialogues: First Period.* London: Routledge & Kegan Paul.

Gadamer, Hans-Georg. 1980. *Dialogue and Dialectic: Eight Hermeneutical Studies on Plato.* Translated by P. Christopher Smith. New Haven, Conn.: Yale University Press.

Galston, Miriam. 1990. *Politics and Excellence: The Political Philosophy of Alfarabi.* Princeton, N.J.: Princeton University Press.

Gauthier, R.-A. 1967. "On the Nature of Aristotle's *Ethics.*" In *Aristotle's Ethics: Issues and Interpretations,* ed. James Walsh and Henry Shapiro. Belmont, Calif.: Wadsworth.

Glidden, David K. 1981. "The *Lysis* on Loving One's Own." *Classical Quarterly* 31: 39–59.

Goethe, Johann Wolfgang von. 1901. *Conversations with Eckermann.* Washington, D.C.: M. Walther Dunn.

Graham, Daniel. 1987. *Aristotle's Two Systems.* Oxford: Clarendon Press.

Grant, Sir Alexander. 1885. *The Ethics of Aristotle, Illustrated with Essays and Notes.* 4th ed. 2 vols. London: Longmans, Green.

Gray, Floyd. 1961. "Montaigne's Friends." *French Studies* 15: 203–12.

Grote, George. 1867. *Plato and the Other Companions of Sokrates.* 2d ed. 3 vols. London: John Murray.

Guthrie, W. K. C. 1962–81. *A History of Greek Philosophy.* 6 vols. Cambridge: Cambridge University Press.

Habinek, Thomas H. 1990. "Towards a History of Friendly Advice: The Politics of Candor in Cicero's *de Amicitia.*" *Apeiron* 23 (4): 165–85.

Haden, James. 1983. "Friendship in Plato's *Lysis.*" *Review of Metaphysics* 37: 327–56.

Hanfling, Oswald. 1993. "Loving My Neighbor, Loving Myself," *Philosophy* 68: 145–57.

Hardie, W. F. R. 1980. *Aristotle's Ethical Theory.* 2d ed. Oxford: Clarendon Press.

Heliodorus (the Paraphrist). 1889–93. *Heliodori In Ethica Nicomachea Paraphrasis.* Vol. 19 in *Commentaria in Aristotelem Graeca,* ed. Gustavus Heylbut. 24 vols. Berlin: Georgii Reimeri.

Hoerber, Robert G. 1959. "Plato's *Lysis.*" *Phronesis* 4: 15–28.

Horn, Ferdinand. 1893. *Platonstudien.* Vienna: F. Tempsky.

Irwin, Terence H. 1988. *Aristotle's First Principles.* Oxford: Clarendon Press.

———, trans. and ed. 1985. *The Nicomachean Ethics.* Indianapolis: Hackett.

Jaeger, Werner. 1939–43. *Paideia: The Ideals of Greek Culture.* Translated by Gilbert Highet. 3 vols. New York: Oxford University Press.

———. 1948. *Aristotle: Fundamentals of the History of His Development.* Translated by Richard Robinson. London: Oxford University Press.

Jefferson, Thomas, and John Adams. 1959. *The Adams–Jefferson Letters.* Edited by Lester J. Cappon. 2 vols. Chapel Hill: University of North Carolina Press.

Joachim, Harold H. 1951. *Aristotle: The Nicomachean Ethics, A Commentary.* Oxford: Clarendon Press.

Kahn, Charles H. 1981. "Aristotle and Altruism." *Mind* 90: 20–40.

Kant, Immanuel. 1963. "Friendship." In *Lectures on Ethics,* trans. Louis Infield. New York: Harper and Row, Harper Torchbooks.

———. 1964. *Groundwork of the Metaphysic of Morals.* Translated by H. J. Paton. New York: Harper and Row, Harper Torchbooks.

———. 1964. *The Metaphysical Principles of Virtue.* Translated by James Ellington. Indianapolis: Bobbs Merrill.

Kenney, Anthony. 1978. *The Aristotelian Ethics: A Study of the Relationship between the Eudemian and Nicomachean Ethics of Aristotle.* Oxford: Clarendon Press.

Kierkegaard, Søren. 1964. *Works of Love: Some Christian Reflections in the Form of Discourses.* Translated by Howard and Edna Hong. New York: Harper and Row.

Konstan, David. 1997. *Friendship in the Classical World.* Cambridge: Cambridge University Press.

Kosman, L. A. 1976. "Platonic Love." In *Facets of Plato's Philosophy,* ed. W. H. Werkmeister. Assen: van Gorcum.

Kraut, Richard. 1989. *Aristotle on the Human Good.* Princeton, N.J.: Princeton University Press.

La Boétie, Etienne. 1998. "On Voluntary Servitude." In *Freedom Over Servitude: Montaigne, La Boétie, and "On Voluntary Servitude,"* trans. and ed. David Schaefer. Westport, Conn.: Greenwood Press.

Lamb, W. R. M. 1925. Introduction to the *Lysis.* In *Plato III: Lysis, Symposium, Gorgias.* Cambridge, Mass.: Harvard University Press, Loeb Classical Library.

Lang, Helen. 1998. *The Order of Nature in Aristotle's Physics.* Cambridge: Cambridge University Press.

Leach, Eleanor. 1993. "Absence and Desire in Cicero's *De Amicitia. Classical World* 87(2): 3–20.

Leaman, Oliver, ed. 1996. *Friendship East and West.* Surrey, Eng.: Curzon.

Lesses, Glen. 1993. "Austere Friends: The Stoics and Friendship." *Apeiron* 26(1): 57–75.

Levin, Donald N. 1971. "Some Observations concerning Plato's *Lysis.*" In *Essays in Ancient Greek Philosophy,* vol. 1, ed. John P. Anton and George L. Kustas. Albany, N.Y.: SUNY Press.

Levinson, Ronald B. 1953. *In Defense of Plato.* Cambridge, Mass.: Harvard University Press.

Long, A. A. 1974. *Hellenistic Philosophy: Stoics, Epicureans, Sceptics.* London: Duckworth.

Long, A. A., and D. N. Sedley. 1987. *The Hellenistic Philosophers.* 2 vols. Cambridge: Cambridge University Press.

Lord, Carnes. 1982. *Education and Culture in the Political Thought of Aristotle.* Ithaca, N.Y.: Cornell University Press.

Lord, Carnes, and David O'Connor, eds. 1991. *Essays on the Foundations of Aristotelian Political Science.* Berkeley: University of California Press.

MacIntyre, Alasdair. 1981. *After Virtue.* Notre Dame, Ind.: University of Notre Dame Press.

Madigan, Arthur. 1991. "*Eth. Nic.* 9.8: Beyond Egoism and Altruism?" In *Essays in Ancient Greek Philosophy.* Vol. 4: *Aristotle's Ethics,* ed. John P. Anton and Anthony Preus. Albany, N.Y.: SUNY Press.

Martin, C. F. J. 1990. "On an Alleged Inconsistency in the *Nicomachean Ethics* (IX, 4)." *Journal of Hellenic Studies* 110: 188–91.

Martin, Daniel. 1998. "Montaigne, Author of *On Voluntary Servitude.*" In *Freedom Over Servitude: Montaigne, La Boétie, and* On Voluntary Servitude, ed. David Schaefer. Westport, Conn.: Greenwood Press.

McKerlie, Dennis. 1991. "Friendship, Self-Love, and Concern for Others in Aristotle's Ethics." *Ancient Philosophy* 11: 85–101.

Michael Ephesius. 1889–93. *Commentary on the Ethics.* Vol. 20 in *Commentaria in Aristotelem Graeca.,* ed. Gustavus Heylbut. 24 vols. Berlin: Georgii Reimeri.

Millgram, Elijah. 1987. "Aristotle on Making Other Selves." *Canadian Journal of Philosophy* 17: 361–76.

Mitsis, Phillip. 1987. "Epicurus on Friendship and Altruism." *Oxford Studies in Ancient Philosophy* 5: 127–53.

Montaigne, Michel de. 1976. *The Complete Essays of Montaigne.* Translated by Donald Frame. Stanford, Calif.: Stanford University Press.

Moravcsik, J. M. E. 1988. "The Perils of Friendship and Conceptions of the Self." In *Human Agency: Language, Duty, and Value: Philosophical Essays in Honor of J. O. Urmson,* ed. Jonathan Dancy, J. M. E. Moravcsik, and C. C. W. Taylor. Stanford, Calif.: Stanford University Press.

Motto, Anna, and John Clark. 1993. "Seneca on Friendship." *Atene e Roma* 38: 91–98.

Muirhead, John. 1900. *Chapters from Aristotle's Ethics.* London: Murray.

Nagel, Thomas. 1970. *The Possibility of Altruism.* Oxford: Clarendon Press.

Nauck, A., ed. 1926. *Tragicorum Graecorum Fragmenta.* 2d ed. Leipzig.

Nussbaum, Martha C. 1986. *The Fragility of Goodness: Luck and Ethics in Greek Tragedy and Philosophy*. Revised ed. Cambridge: Cambridge University Press.

O'Connor, David. 1989. "The Invulnerable Pleasures of Epicurean Friendship." *Greek, Roman, and Byzantine Studies* 30: 165–86.

Ostwald, Martin, trans. and ed. 1962. *The Nicomachean Ethics*. New York: Macmillan.

Pakaluk Michael. 1992. "Friendship and the Comparison of Goods." *Phronesis* 37: 111–30.

_____, ed. 1991. *Other Selves: Philosophers on Friendship*. Indianapolis: Hackett.

_____, trans. with commentary. 1998. *Aristotle:* Nicomachean Ethics *Books VIII and IX*. Oxford: Clarendon Press.

Percival, Geoffrey. 1935. "Notes on Three Passages from the *Nicomachean Ethics*, Book VIII." *Classical Quarterly* 29: 171–76.

_____. 1940. *Aristotle on Friendship: Being an Expanded Translation of the Nicomachean Ethics Books VIII & IX*. Cambridge: Cambridge University Press.

Platt, Michael. 1998. "Montaigne, Of Friendship, and On Tyranny." In *Freedom Over Servitude: Montaigne, La Boétie, and* On Voluntary Servitude, ed. David Schaefer. Westport, Conn.: Greenwood Press.

Pohlenz, Max. 1913. *Aus Platos Werdezeit*. Berlin: Weidmann.

_____. 1917. "Nochmals Plato's *Lysis*." *Nachrichten von der Königlichen Gesellschaft der Wissenschaften zu Göttingen, Philologisch-historische Klasse*.

Politis, Vasilis. 1993. "The Primacy of Self-Love in the *Nicomachean Ethics*." *Oxford Studies in Ancient Philosophy* 11: 153–74.

Powell, J. G. F., ed. and trans. 1990. *Cicero: Laelius, On Friendship and the Dream of Scipio*. Warminster: Aris and Phillips.

Price, A. W. 1989. *Love and Friendship in Plato and Aristotle*. Oxford: Clarendon Press.

Rackham, H., trans. and ed. 1975. *The Nicomachean Ethics*. Cambridge, Mass.: Harvard University Press, Loeb Classical Library.

Rahe, Paul A. 1992. *Republics Ancient and Modern: Classical Republicanism and the American Revolution*. Chapel Hill: University of North Carolina Press.

_____. 1997. "Don Corleone, Multiculturalist." *Business and Professional Ethics Journal* 16: 133–53.

Ramsauer, Gottfried. 1878. *Aristotelis Ethica Nicomachea*. Leipzig: Teubner.

Rassow, Hermann. 1874. *Forschungen über die Nikomachische Ethik des Aristoteles*. Weimar: Hermann Böhlau.

Rist, John M. 1972. *Epicurus: An Introduction*. Cambridge: Cambridge University Press.

_____. 1980. "Epicurus on Friendship." *Classical Philology* 75: 121–29.

_____. 1982. *Human Value: A Study in Ancient Philosophical Ethics*. Leiden: E. J. Brill.

_____. 1989. *The Mind of Aristotle: A Study in Philosophical Growth*. Toronto: University of Toronto Press.

Robinson, David B. 1986. "Plato's *Lysis*: The Structural Problem." *Illinois Classical Studies* 11: 63–83.

Rorty, Amélie, 1980. "The Place of Contemplation in Aristotle's *Nicomachean Ethics*." In *Essays on Aristotle's Ethics*, ed. Amélie Rorty. Berkeley: University of California Press.

Ross, Sir David. 1949. *Aristotle*. 5th ed. London: Methuen.

_____, trans. and ed. 1925. *The Nicomachean Ethics*. Oxford: Oxford University Press; World's Classic Paperbacks, 1980.

Salkever, Stephen. 1990. *Finding the Mean: Theory and Practice in Aristotelian Political Philosophy.* Princeton, N.J.: Princeton University Press.

———. 1991. "Women, Soldiers, Citizens: Plato and Aristotle on the Politics of Virility." In *Essays on the Foundations of Aristotelian Political Science,* ed. Carnes Lord and David O'Connor. Berkeley: University of California Press.

Saxonhouse, Arlene W. 1982. "Family, Polity, and Unity: Aristotle on Socrates' Community of Wives." *Polity* 15: 202–19.

Schaefer, David Lewis. 1990. *The Political Philosophy of Montaigne.* Ithaca, N.Y.: Cornell University Press.

———. 1998. "Montaigne and La Boétie." In *Freedom Over Servitude: Montaigne, La Boétie, and* On Voluntary Servitude, ed. David Schaefer. Westport, Conn.: Greenwood Press.

Sedley, David. 1989. "Is the *Lysis* a Dialogue of Definition?" *Phronesis* 34: 107–8.

Seneca. 1917. *Moral Epistles.* Translated by Richard M. Gummere. 3 vols. Cambridge, Mass.: Harvard University Press, Loeb Classical Library.

———. 1965. *Moral Essays.* Translated by John W. Basore. 3 vols. Cambridge, Mass.: Harvard University Press, Loeb Classical Library.

Shaftesbury, Anthony, Earl of. 1964. *Characteristics of Men, Manners, Opinions, Times.* Edited by John M. Robertson. Indianapolis: Bobbs-Merrill.

Sherman, Nancy. 1989. *The Fabric of Character: Aristotle's Theory of Virtue.* Oxford: Clarendon Press.

Shorey, Paul. 1930. "The Alleged Fallacy in Plato *Lysis* 220E." *Classical Philology* 25: 380–83.

———. 1933. *What Plato Said.* Chicago: University of Chicago Press.

Sidgwick, Henry. 1931. *Outlines of the History of Ethics for English Readers.* 6th ed. London: Macmillan.

Sparshott, Francis. 1994. *Taking Life Seriously: A Study of the Argument of the Nicomachean Ethics.* Toronto: University of Toronto Press.

Stern-Gillet, Suzanne. 1989. "Epicurus and Friendship." *Dialogue* 28: 275–88.

———. 1995. *Aristotle's Philosophy of Friendship.* Albany, N.Y.: SUNY Press.

Stewart, John A. 1892. *Notes on the Nicomachean Ethics of Aristotle.* 2 vols. Oxford: Clarendon Press.

Strauss, Leo. 1952. *Persecution and the Art of Writing.* Glencoe, Ill.: Free Press.

———. 1959. *What Is Political Philosophy?* Westport, Conn.: Greenwood Press.

———. 1964. *The City and Man.* Chicago: Rand McNally.

———. 1989. *The Rebirth of Classical Political Rationalism.* Edited by Thomas L. Pangle. Chicago: University of Chicago Press.

Susemihl, Franz. 1880. *Aristotelis Ethica Nicomachea.* Leipzig: Teubner.

———. 1900. Review of *The Ethics of Aristotle,* by John Burnet. *Berliner Philologische Wochenschrift* 20: 1505–13.

Swanson, Judith. 1992. *The Public and the Private in Aristotle's Political Philosophy.* Ithaca, N.Y.: Cornell University Press.

Tessitore, Aristide. 1996. *Reading Aristotle's* Ethics. Albany, N.Y.: SUNY Press.

Thomas Aquinas, St. 1964. *Commentary on the Nicomachean Ethics.* Translated by C. I. Litzinger. 2 vols. Chicago: Henry Regnery.

Timmermann, Jens. 1995. "Why We Cannot Want Our Friends to Be Gods. Some Notes on *NE* 1159a5–12." *Phronesis* 40: 209–15.

Urmson, J. O. 1988. *Aristotle's Ethics.* Oxford: Basil Blackwell.

Vander Waerdt, Paul A. 1985. "The Political Intention of Aristotle's Moral Philosophy." *Ancient Philosophy* 5: 77–89.

van Straaten, M., and G. J. de Vries. 1960. "Notes on the VIIIth and IXth Books of Aristotle's *Nicomachean Ethics.*" *Mnemosyne* 13: 193–228.

Versenyi, Laszlo. 1975. "Plato's *Lysis.*" *Phronesis* 20: 185–98.

Vlastos, Gregory. 1973. *Platonic Studies.* Princeton, N.J.: Princeton University Press.

von Arnim, Hans. 1914. *Platos Jugenddialoge und die Entstehungszeit des Phaidros.* Leipzig: Teubner.

———. 1916. "Platos *Lysis.*" *Rheinisches Museum für Philologie* 71: 364–87.

Walker, A. D. M. 1979. "Aristotle's Account of Friendship in the *Nicomachean Ethics.*" *Phronesis* 24: 180–96.

Walsh, James J., and Henry L. Shapiro, eds. 1967. *Aristotle's Ethics: Issues and Interpretations.* Belmont, Calif.: Wadsworth.

Wehrli, Fritz. 1944–59. *Die Schule des Aristoteles.* Basel: B. Schwabe.

Welty, Eudora, and Ronald Sharp, eds. 1991. *The Norton Book of Friendship.* New York: W. W. Norton and Co.

Williams, Bernard. 1973. *Problems of the Self: Philosophical Papers 1956–1972.* Cambridge: Cambridge University Press.

———. 1981. *Moral Luck: Philosophical Papers 1973–80.* Cambridge: Cambridge University Press.

Yack, Bernard. 1993. *The Problems of a Political Animal: Community, Justice, and Conflict in Aristotelian Political Thought.* Berkeley: University of California Press.

Zeller, Eduard. 1897. *Aristotle and the Earlier Peripatetics.* Translated by B. F. C. Costelloe and J. H. Muirhead. 2 vols. London: Longmans, Green.

Index of Names

Made in the USA
Lexington, KY
26 August 2017